Gouache

IN 4 EASY STEPS

A Beginner's Guide to
Creating Beautiful Paintings in No Time

ANNA KOLIADYCH
Author of *15-Minute Watercolor Masterpieces*

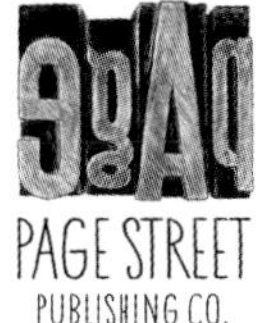

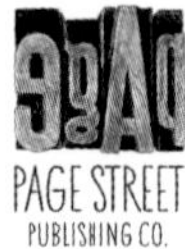

Copyright © 2021 Anna Koliadych

First published in 2021 by
Page Street Publishing Co.
27 Congress Street, Suite 105
Salem, MA 01970
www.pagestreetpublishing.com

All rights reserved. No part of this book may be reproduced or used, in any form or by any means, electronic or mechanical, without prior permission in writing from the publisher.

Distributed by Macmillan, sales in Canada by The Canadian Manda Group.

25 24 23 22 21 1 2 3 4 5

ISBN-13: 978-1-64567-233-3
ISBN-10: 1-64567-233-6

Library of Congress Control Number: 2020944073

Cover and book design by Meg Baskis for Page Street Publishing Co.
Illustrations by Anna Koliadych

Printed and bound in China

Page Street Publishing protects our planet by donating to nonprofits like The Trustees, which focuses on local land conservation.

TO MY HUSBAND AND SOUL MATE IGNAT.
THERE ARE NO WORDS TO EXPLAIN HOW
LUCKY I AM TO HAVE YOU IN MY LIFE.

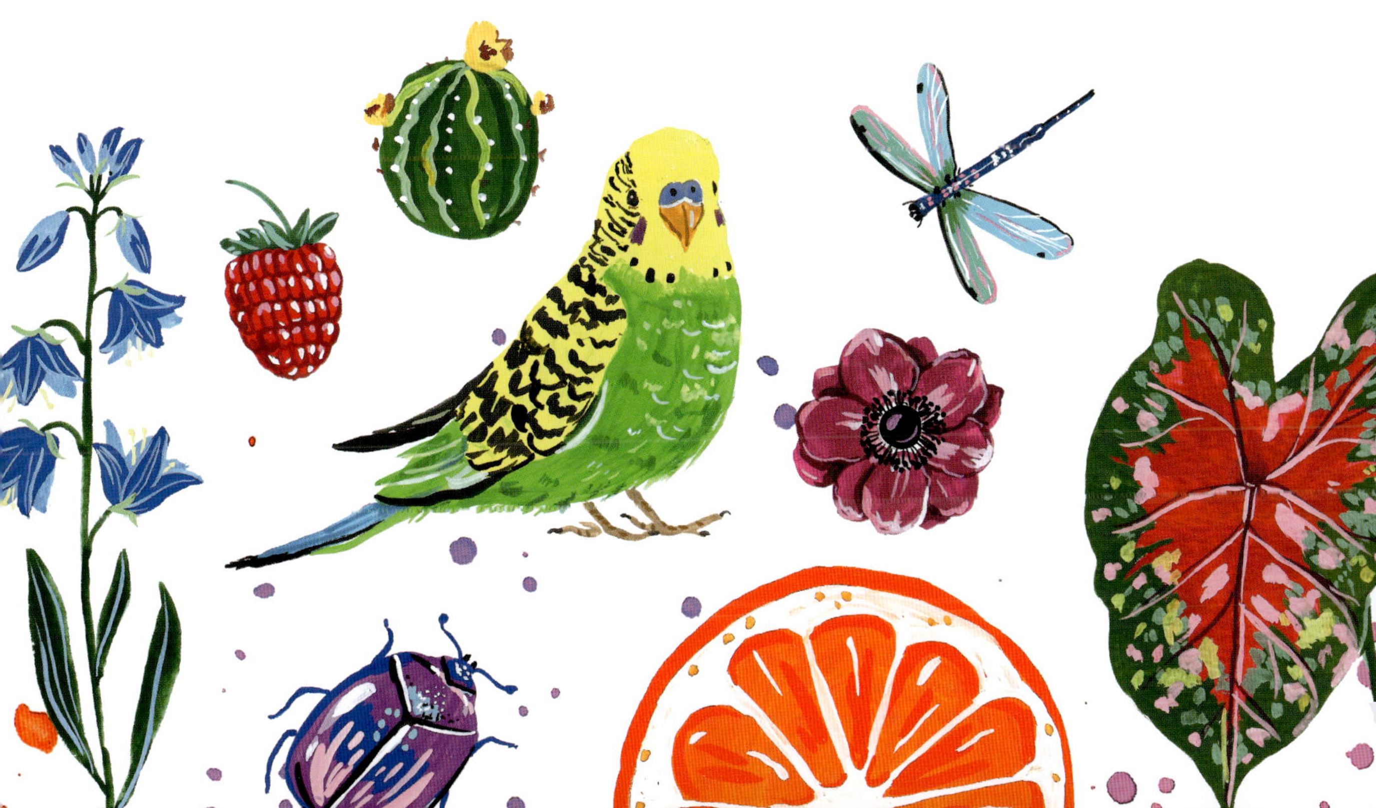

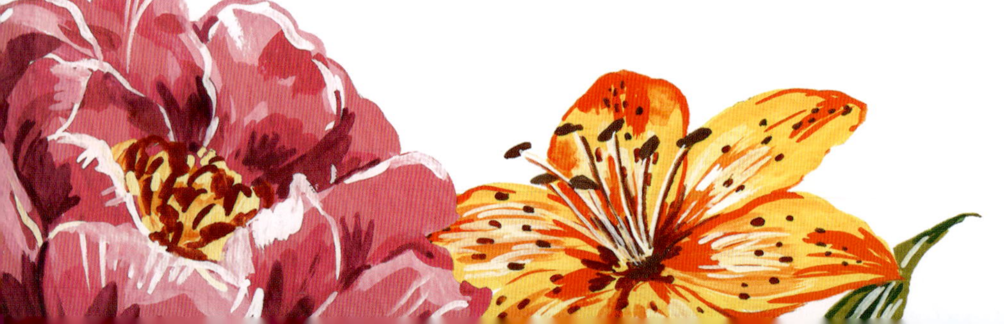

INTRODUCTION

Hello, my name is Anna. I am an illustrator, artist and art teacher. Since I began my artistic journey with watercolor about five years ago, I have enjoyed diving into this wonderful world.

Because I am a creative person and always love experimenting and trying new things, I wanted to start with a new medium that I would love just as much as I love watercolor.

Once I bought my first gouache set of just a few tubes of paint, I immediately fell in love with this medium. It was an amazing feeling. And from that time on, I never stopped painting with this magical paint.

I always say that gouache is magical because it's super vivid, unbelievably flexible and so relaxing to paint with. Gouache allows you to paint in different styles, easily fix mistakes and make the process effortless, fun and relaxing.

Gouache painting does not have as many techniques and rules as other media, such as watercolor. As a result, it is much easier to get started painting with gouache.

Inside you'll find 50 quick and easy projects for anyone who wants to start painting, try a new medium or unlock their creativity. The best way to learn a new art medium is by practicing it. With the projects from this book, you will gain confidence, boost your painting skills and discover for yourself the magic of gouache.

By practicing with this book, you will quickly learn gouache. Each project takes less than an hour. I divided each lesson in this book into steps that will help you easily and quickly create impressive and beautiful results.

HOW TO WORK WITH THIS BOOK

This book is very easy to work with. It includes the basics for a better understanding of gouache, as well as chapters featuring projects on various themes.

Make sure that you read the first chapter on gouache techniques (page 7) before jumping into your first project. It will help introduce you to gouache and learn the particulars of this medium. After that, pick any project from a chapter you like and practice. All the projects are listed in order from easy to more complicated, but I advise you to choose the lessons that most appeal to you. By following all instructions and tips, you will get an easy and quick, but beautiful, painting.

Enjoy the process and the magic of gouache! I hope you will fall in love with gouache as much as I have.

With love,

Anna

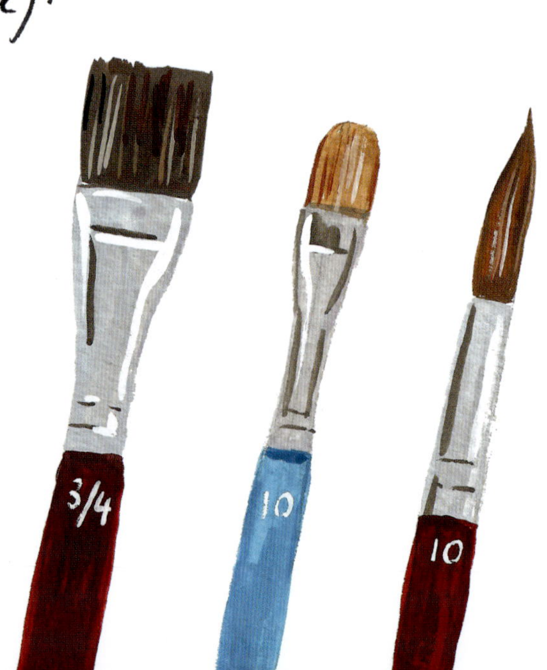

GOUACHE TECHNIQUES, TIPS & EXERCISES

WHAT IS GOUACHE?

"What is gouache?" is the most common question I have received recently via my social media. And I totally understand the interest in this medium. Gouache is becoming super trendy because it is versatile and easy to use. Here I have broken down the most important facts about gouache. This way, you will get a clear and basic understanding of what gouache is.

- Gouache is a water-soluble paint.
- Gouache combines some characteristics of both watercolors and acrylics.
- Gouache has a thick, creamy consistency and is an opaque paint.
- Gouache gives a matte finish when it dries.
- Gouache paint dries quickly.
- Gouache can be used as watercolor. If you add a large amount of water to the gouache, you will get a transparent layer.
- Gouache works from dark to light layers, as well as from light to dark layers.
- Gouache can be used on different types of paper.
- Gouache usually comes in tubes and is best when freshly squeezed from the tube.
- When gouache dries, dark colors become a bit lighter and the light colors become darker.

CONSISTENCY OF GOUACHE PAINT

If you squeeze gouache paint from the tube onto a palette, you will see that the consistency of gouache is pretty thick and creamy. However, because it's a water-based paint, it should be applied with water.

First of all, your brush should always be moistened, but not wet. The exception would be for the dry-brush technique (page 12).

You want to add a little bit of clean water to the gouache paint to get the right consistency. It will still be creamy and thick, but much more flexible, and it will apply to the paper easily and smoothly.

In this book, all the projects are intended to use this consistency of gouache. The more water you add to the gouache paint, the more transparent it will become, and it will work more like watercolor. If you're painting with gouache for the first time, I recommend practicing with a quick exercise just to get a feel for how to get the right consistency (see Figure 1).

Image No. 1: Squeeze a small amount of gouache on the palette. Moisten your brush and pick up the paint from the palette. Now paint any shape with this paint consistency. You will get the effect of the dry brush, and it's a really nice texture. While it's a nice texture, it's not the best consistency for a smooth finish.

Figure 1

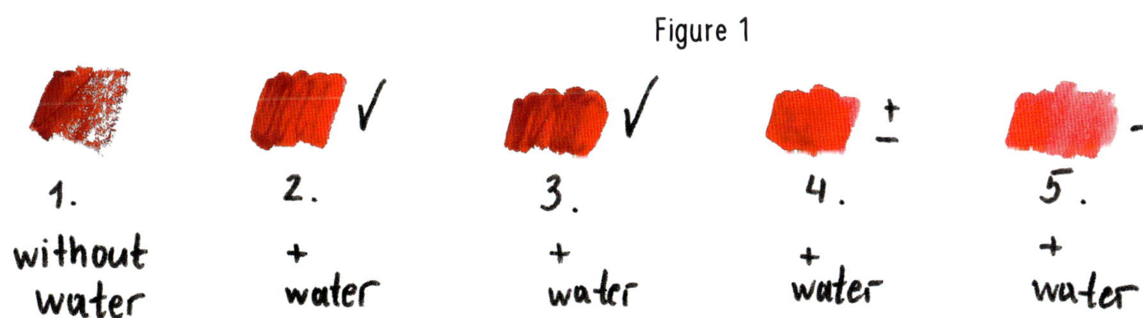

Image No. 2: Now add a little bit of water to the paint on the palette and paint any shape with this consistency. Notice how, this time, the paint laid down so well and smoothly.

Image No. 3: Then add more water to the paint on the palette. Paint another shape, next to the first two. And as in the previous example, the result is still opaque, and it feels like the right consistency.

Images No. 4 & No. 5: If you keep adding water you will see that the layers become more and more transparent. Eventually you will get a transparent layer, as with watercolor paint. Your goal is to create an opaque and creamy consistency—not too thick and not too transparent.

COLOR CONTRAST WITH GOUACHE

Contrast is a principle in art that refers to the difference in parameters such as color, size and texture. High contrast means adding intensity and bringing more attention to the elements of the piece. Without contrast, the viewer may have trouble connecting with the painting and lose interest in it.

In this section, I will show you how to add contrast in the easiest way: with color. Let's have a look at a few color contrast variations.

1. Color contrast with gouache can be achieved by adding light colors onto a dark layer (see Figure 2). The highest contrast you can get is painting with white on a dark layer.

2. Color contrast also works if you add dark colors to a light layer (see Figure 3). In this case, the highest contrast you can get is painting with black on a light layer.

3. Color contrast is created by adding white (see Figure 4). For this technique, use one color as a base. Then add white to the base color so you have two colors: base and base + white. You can swap colors and paint first with either of them. Then add the other on top. In both cases, you will get a gentle contrast.

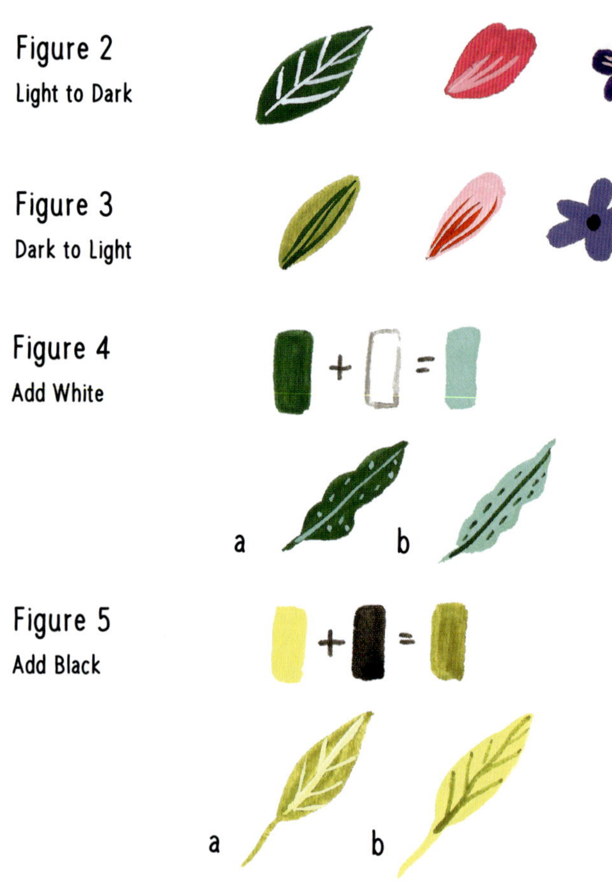

4. Alternatively, color contrast is created by adding black (see Figure 5). This rule works the same as adding white. But instead of white, add black or any other dark color.

COLOR MIXING

Mixing colors is a very important skill that can be learned with practice. While working on projects from this book, some basic principles will help you feel more confident when choosing colors and mixing them.

Color mixing is based on color theory. Let's begin with the color wheel (see Figure 6).

The color wheel is a circle containing twelve hues arranged according to their relationship with one another. It is divided into three main color groups.

The primary colors are yellow, red and blue. The group is called "primary" because no other colors can be mixed to create these colors.

The secondary colors are orange, green and purple. They're made by mixing equal amounts of two primary colors.

There are six shades that make up the tertiary colors: red-orange, red-purple, yellow-green, yellow-orange, blue-purple and blue-green. They are made by mixing a secondary color with a primary color.

In theory, you need just three primary colors to create any palette.

However, keep in mind the principle of warm and cool tones. The warm tones are reds, oranges and yellows. The cool tones are greens, blues and purples. Yellow-green and red-purple are in-between tones and can be used as both warm and cool tones. Any one color can have two tones: warm and cool. In Figure 7, you can see the two tones of yellow. The first one is "Primary Yellow" and it is a cool color. The second one is "Permanent Yellow Deep," a warm color that's almost orange. Depending on the cool or warm tones you use for mixing, you will get different results.

Mixing gouache paints has some specific rules. First of all, white gouache is, in my opinion, an essential color in gouache painting. Second, the saturation of the color depends not on the water balance, as with watercolors, but on the proportion of the colors. Mixing gouache is a matter not only of which colors to mix but also the proportions of each color and the presence of white (see Figure 8).

Figure 6

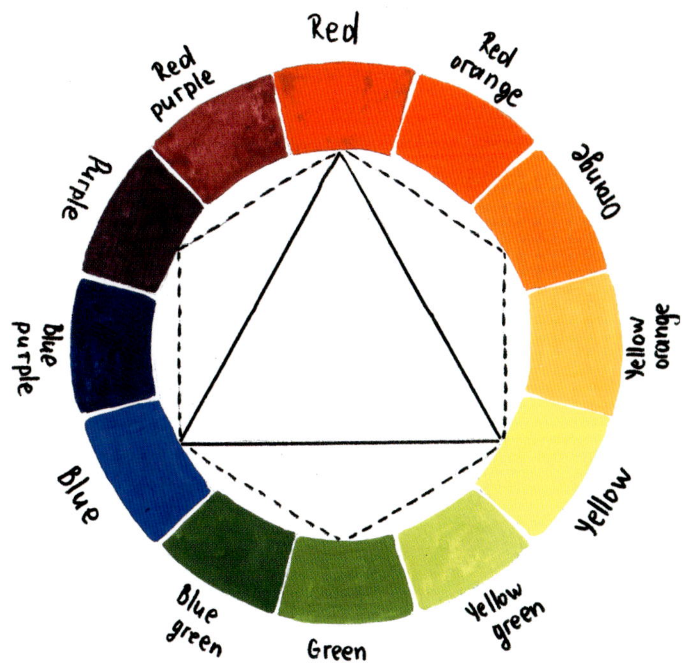

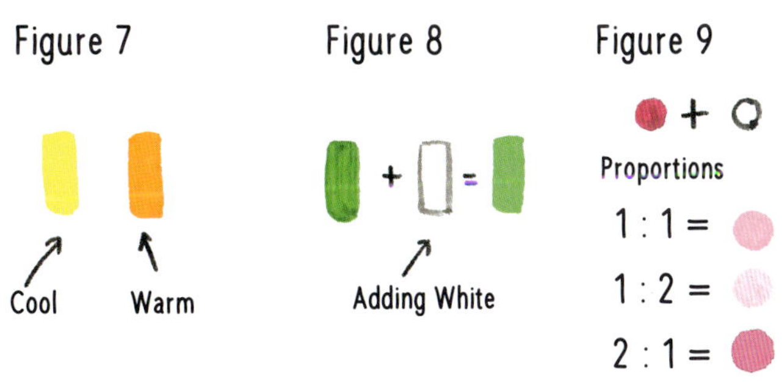

Each project in this book includes a color mixing section (see Figure 9). There you can see the visual swatches as well as a description with proportions. Of course, these proportions are very approximate because the results will depend on the brands of gouache you use (some colors may differ). But I do recommend you follow all these proportions, especially at the start of your gouache journey.

BRUSH STROKES

This section is divided into two parts. First, I will explain the various brush strokes and why it's so important to know and use them. Then you'll have a chance to practice these techniques. Let's discuss everything step by step.

Brush stroking is how you can use a particular brush more effectively (see Gouache Brushes [page 185] for more information on brush types). It's one of the basic skills in painting and makes your painting process much easier. That's why it's essential knowledge in painting with any medium.

Depending on the brush type, you can produce different brush strokes and patterns. Figure 10 shows different strokes for: the round brush, filbert brush, flat brush and detail brush. For each kind of brush, there are a few main types of stroke. Those brush strokes vary depending on how you hold the brush, how you move it on the paper and how long you maintain contact with the paper.

Figure 10

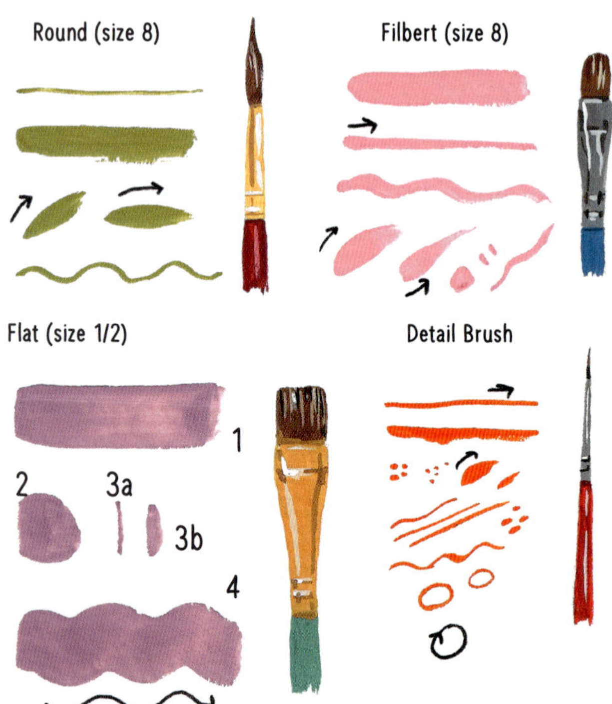

Let's consider the example of the flat brush. The very first line was made with the brush sloped to the paper and then pulled forward along the surface of the paper (1 in Figure 10). The second stroke is the same method, but instead of pulling the brush onto the paper (2 in Figure 10) you can make the next stroke by holding the brush vertically above the paper so that only the tip of the brush touches it. Gently press the brush onto the paper (3a in Figure 10). Similarly, press the brush and pull it forward a little along the surface of the paper (3b in Figure 10).

Finally, I sloped the brush horizontally to the paper and then pulled it forward a little along the surface of the paper and at the same time changed direction to achieve a wavy effect (4 in Figure 10).

At first, it may not sound easy to control the brushes and get a handle on all these strokes. Practicing them now will save you a lot of time in the future. Below I prepared some exercises that will help you master brush stroke skills. The main brush we will use is the round brush.

COLORING THE SHAPE. By using the round brush, first paint the outline of the shape and then fill it in with the same color (see Figure 11).

COLORING THE SHAPE WITH A DRY-BRUSH EFFECT. I recommend practicing this exercise with the filbert or flat brush. Just paint the rectangular area and then continue painting the edges using the dry-brush effect. To do this, paint by using the rest of the paint, or take additional paint and spread it around the edges to achieve a rough effect (see Figure 12). This exercise is a demonstration of the dry-brush technique, which is used often in the projects in this book.

Figure 11 Figure 12

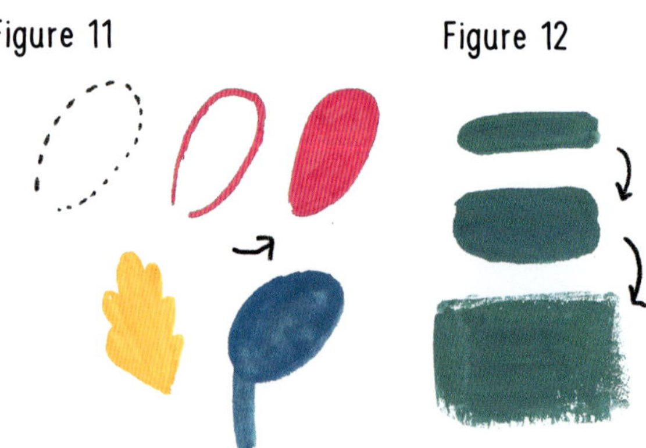

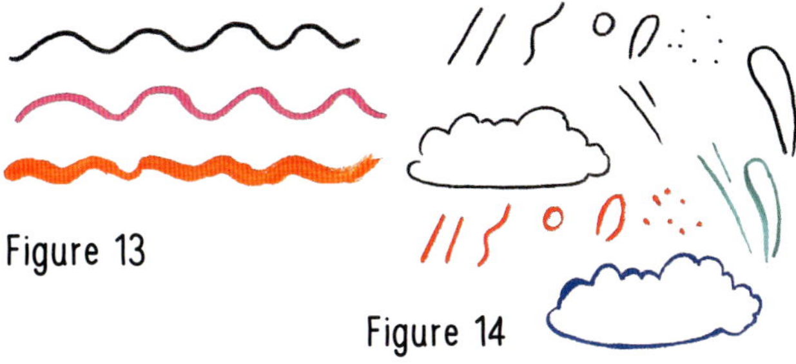

Figure 13

Figure 14

WAVY LINES. Hold the brush vertically and paint wavy lines as shown in Figure 13. Practice with round and filbert brushes.

USING THE BRUSH TIP. With the detail brush or a liner, use the examples in Figure 14 to paint lines using only the brush tip.

ONE BRUSH STROKE PAINTING. By following the example shown in Figure 15, try to repeat shapes of leaves and petals by using a single stroke. For this, press the brush, pull it along the paper and then lift it. The more you move the brush, the longer the stroke will be. Practice with round and filbert brushes in different sizes.

BRUSH STROKE ONE BY ONE. Take a small round brush or detail brush and paint the strokes one by one. In Figure 16, you can see how this looks if you paint on top of another layer.

Brush stroking is all about practicing. And practice always makes sense, even if you are an experienced artist. Experiment with your brushes and practice as often as possible.

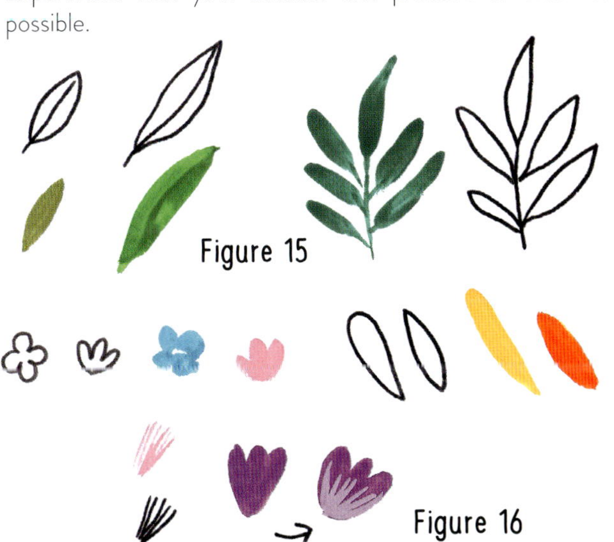

Figure 15

Figure 16

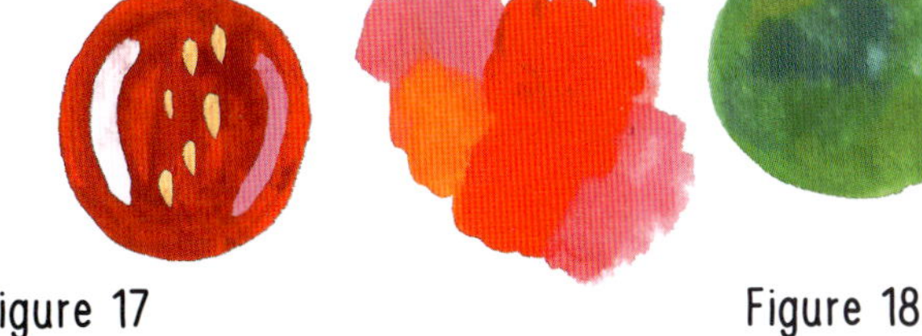

Figure 17

Figure 18

GOUACHE TECHNIQUES

In this section, I will introduce some techniques I use when painting with gouache. These methods will help you learn to paint with gouache, understand this medium from different sides and more effectively utilize the projects from this book. I recommend you learn each of these techniques before you start working on the projects in the following chapters.

The names of these techniques may differ from those used in other sources. Also, you might encounter other techniques elsewhere. If so, don't skip those methods—try them out. I always say the more skills and knowledge you have, the better.

The first technique is **layering** (see Figure 17). This basic technique is the one most often used in the book. It has just one rule: Before painting the next layer, let the previous layer dry. To use this technique it is important to use the right consistency of gouache paint. So make double sure that your gouache paint is not watery so it will not destroy the base coat.

Next is **direct blending** (see Figure 18). This is a commonly used technique in gouache painting. I personally find it very creative. So how does it work? Apply two or more colors on the paper and blend them with a brush. Take the different colors one by one from the palette, then use a moist brush to make the layer nice and smooth. This method is perfect for painting background layers as well as some separate elements.

The **gradient technique** (see Figure 19) is a variation of the direct blending technique. The name speaks for itself; it is perfect for painting a gradient. So paint on one edge of the paper with one color and then add another color from another edge, leaving some free area between them. Little by little add each color to the other, blending them closer together until they meet in the middle. This way, you will get a beautiful and flowing gradient.

The next technique is **softening** (see Figure 20). Softening involves blurring the gouache layer with a wet brush. You can apply this technique in two ways. The first is to blur the layer edges, and the second is to blur the transition between two colors. In both cases, you need to be careful to blur the edges of the paint gently. Make sure that your brush is not too wet, and don't make unnecessary movements with the brush.

The **dry-brush technique** (see Figure 21) is a great and creative technique that adds a nice texture to the painting. For this method, you should moisten the brush with water, then remove most of the moisture by wiping the brush with a paper towel. Next, take some gouache paint on the brush. Instead of the usual paint consistency (read more about the consistency of gouache paint on page 7), use the thick gouache paint directly from the tube. Or, if it's a mix of colors, use a minimal amount of water so you get the effect of the dry-brush technique. For a better understanding of how this technique works, I recommend you practice and paint several types of lines and outline some simple objects. (Read more about brush strokes on page 10).

Dry-brush forming (see Figure 22) is a variation of the dry-brush technique. It works perfectly for painting backgrounds or some base layers. However, there is a secret to applying this technique.

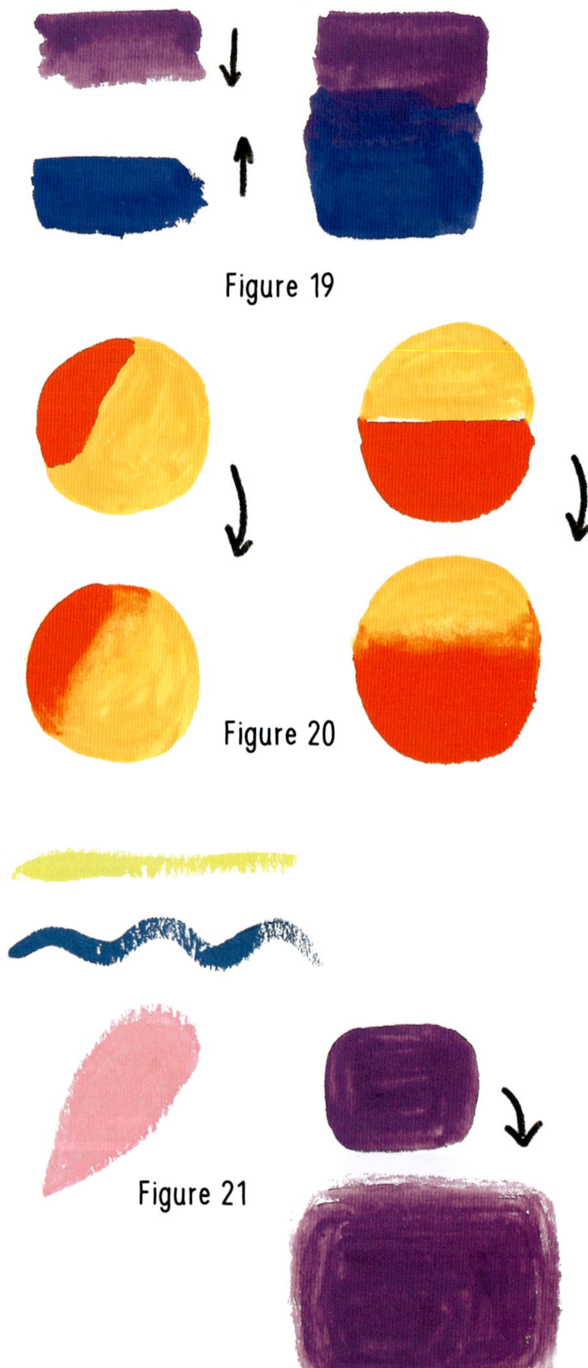

Figure 19

Figure 20

Figure 21

Figure 22

It would be difficult to paint the entire shape (especially if it's a big shape) by using the dry-brush technique. So instead, first fill the shape with a smoother consistency of paint, then add only the edges with the dry-brush technique. Filbert and flat brushes work best for this technique.

The **blending technique** (see Figure 23), unlike in watercolors, isn't used very often in gouache painting. But it is used in some of the projects in this book. Paint a layer and then add another color on the still-wet layer. Work quickly, because the gouache dries very fast.

Splattering (see Figure 24) is also used in watercolor painting and brings some freshness, freedom and ease to your work. This technique is perfect for adding stars to a dark sky with white gouache. Splattered drops can be large or small, depending on the size of the brush you use. Splattering is usually added onto a dry layer, so let the previous layer dry first, then use paper or a paper towel to cover the area where you don't want to add splattering. Take a little pigment onto the brush and flick it onto the exposed area.

And that's all you need to get started with gouache! Just remember to keep practicing and have fun.

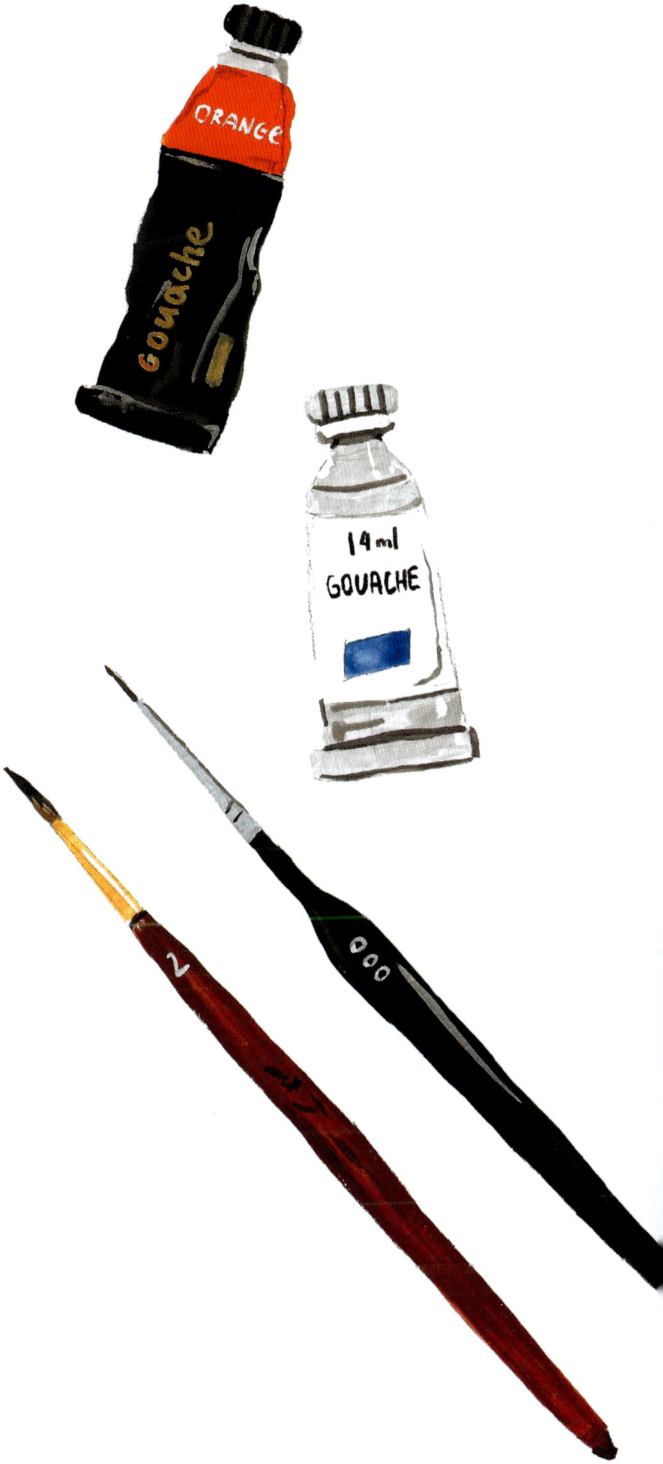

Figure 23

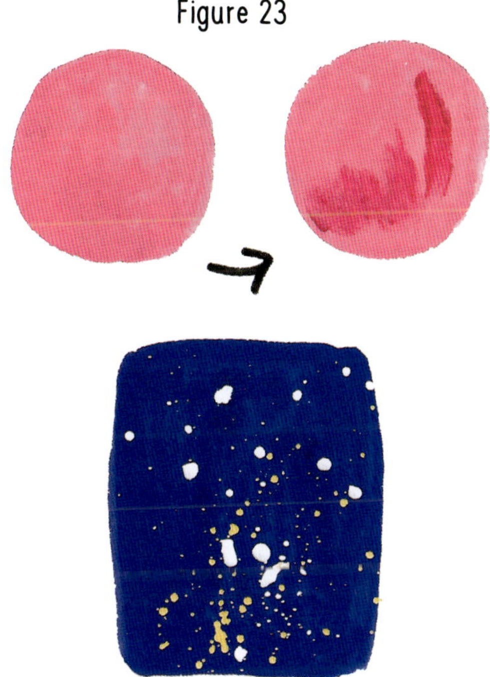

Figure 24

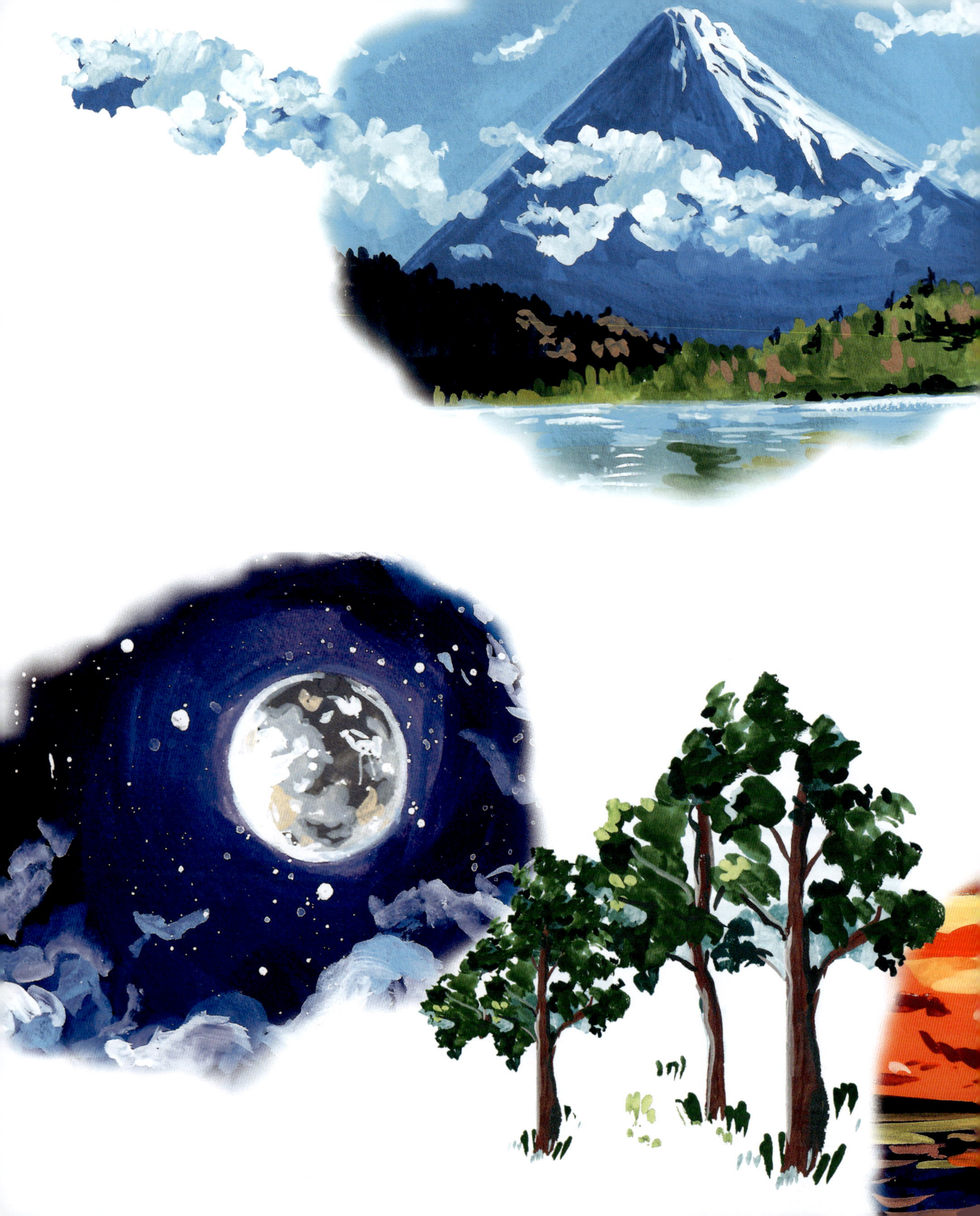

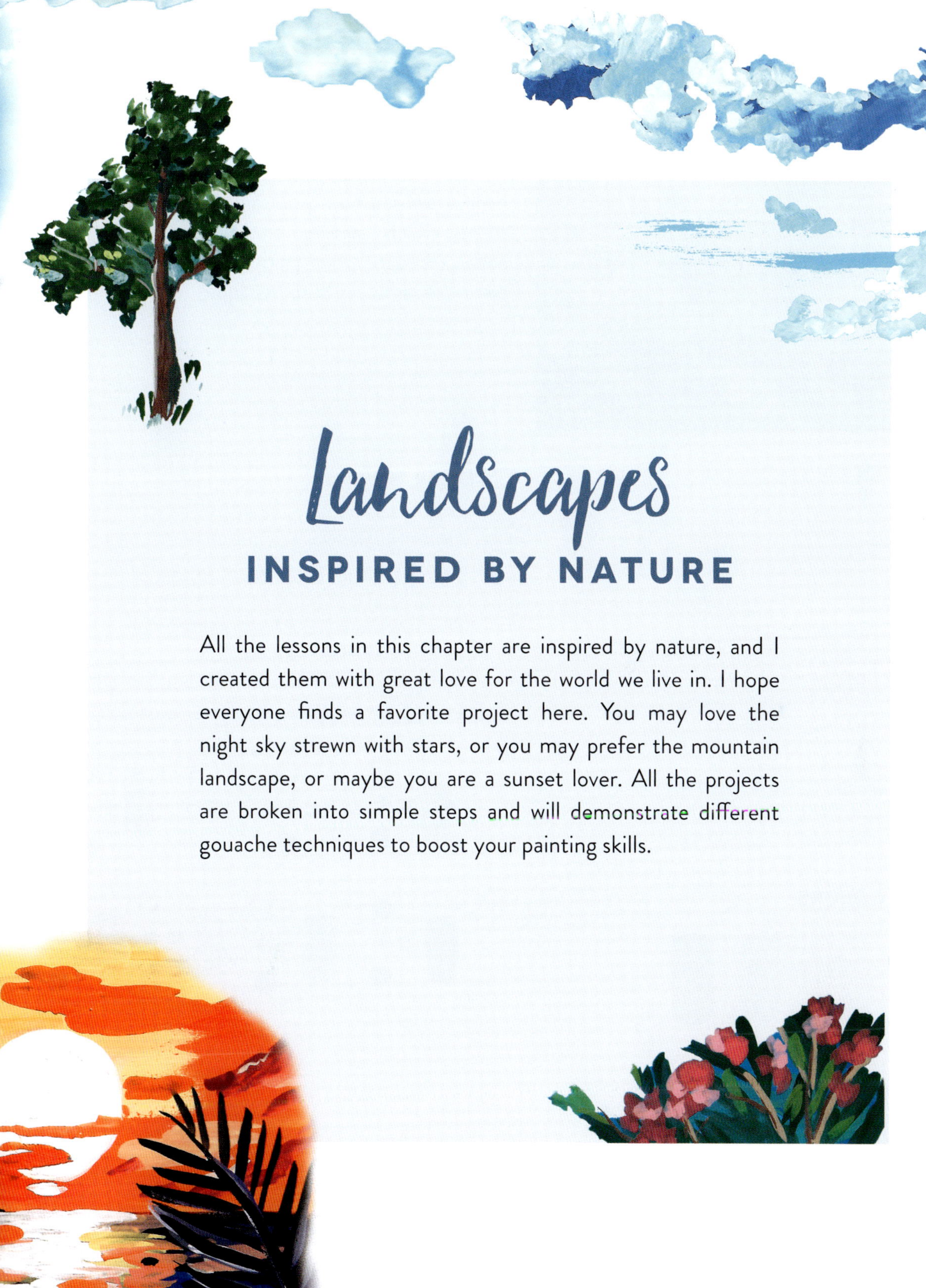

Landscapes

INSPIRED BY NATURE

All the lessons in this chapter are inspired by nature, and I created them with great love for the world we live in. I hope everyone finds a favorite project here. You may love the night sky strewn with stars, or you may prefer the mountain landscape, or maybe you are a sunset lover. All the projects are broken into simple steps and will demonstrate different gouache techniques to boost your painting skills.

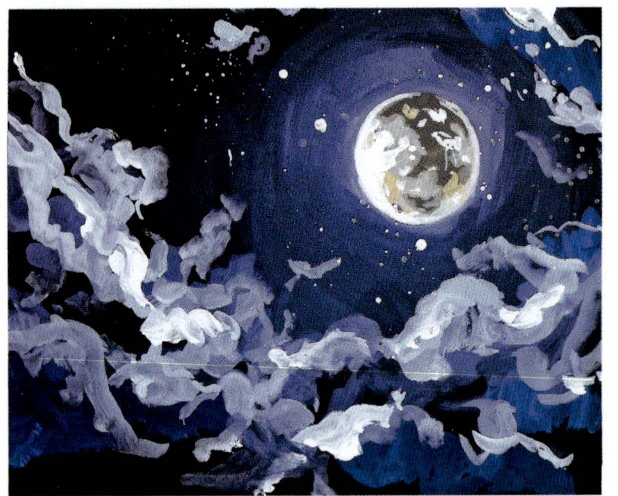

STARRY NIGHT SKY

I love starry night skies. It's so romantic watching the stars and the moon in full silence. And with gouache, I will show you how quick and easy it is to paint this scene, which captures this silence and beauty on paper. Prepare your paints and brushes, and let's paint the night sky step by step.

SUPPLIES

- White paper
- Masking tape
- Compass, or a round object with a small diameter
- Pencil
- Round brushes in different sizes
- Filbert brushes in different sizes
- Flat brush (optional)
- Detail brush
- Scrap paper or paper towels

NOTE: We'll use the compass or a small round object for drawing the moon. For this project, I'll trace inside a small washi tape roll, which is almost 1¼ inches (3 cm) in diameter.

PROJECT COLORS

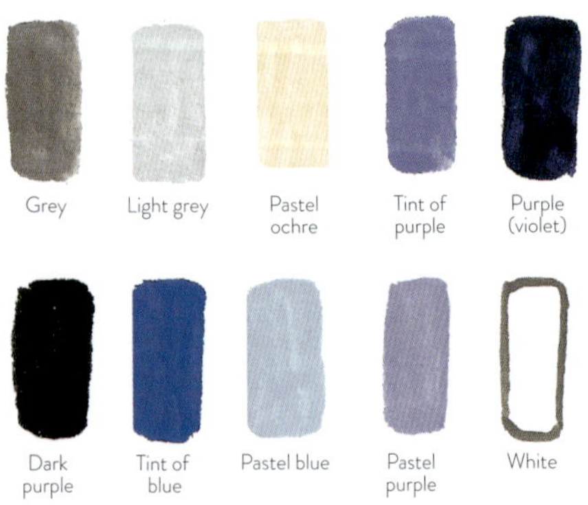

COLOR MIXING

- Grey (black + white, proportion 1:2)
- Light grey (black + white, proportion 1:6)
- Pastel ochre (yellow ochre + white, proportion 1:2)
- Tint of purple (white + violet, proportion 2:1)
- Dark purple (black + violet, proportion 1:2)
- Tint of blue (white + ultramarine blue, proportion 1:4)
- Pastel blue (white + ultramarine blue, proportion 2:1)
- Pastel purple (white + violet, proportion 4:1)

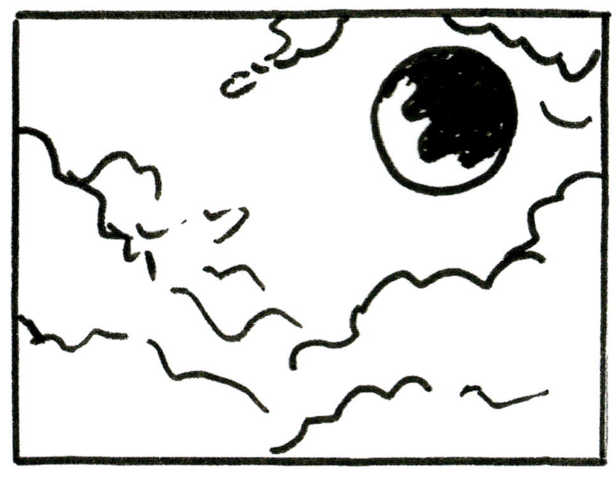

Figure 1

STEP 1

First, secure the paper to your board or table with masking tape to define the painting area. Now draw a little circle with a pencil, as shown in Figure 1. There is no need to draw the details in the sketch.

Let's start the main work by coloring the moon. Prepare the following colors: grey, light grey and pastel ochre. Take the small round brush and paint the area with grey, as shown in Figure 2. Let the paint dry and then paint the rest of the moon with light grey. To make the moon look more colorful, you can also add a few touches of pastel ochre. (Read more about layering on page 11.)

Because the illustration will be done in a sketch style, I don't advise painting additional details on the moon. However, later we'll add some highlights for better contrast.

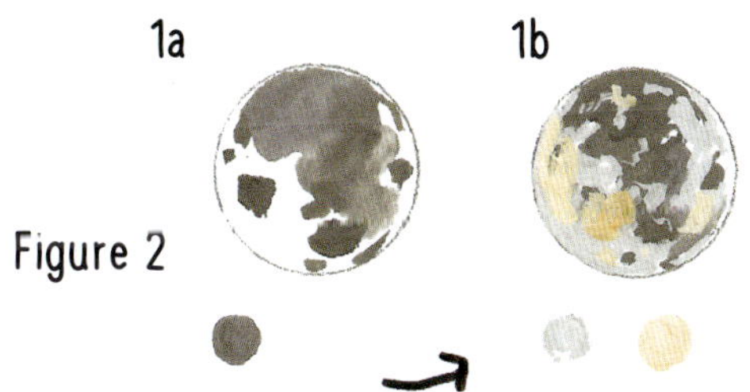

Figure 2

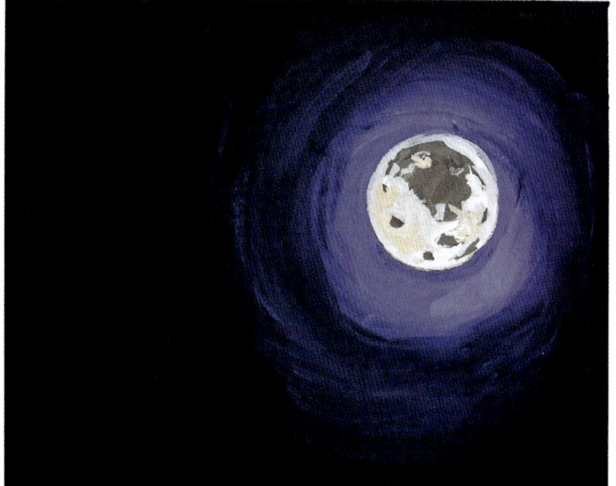

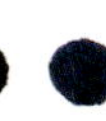

Figure 3

STEP 2

It's time to fill the working area with the background (Figure 3). There are a few ways to do this. I will show you the one I think is more interesting. We'll paint the radial gradient. It means that the color will be changing in a circular direction. In our case, the center is the moon. The gradient will start with the tint of purple, then smoothly shift to purple and finish in dark purple.

To make the gradient, we'll apply the direct blending technique (page 11).

Take a large-sized filbert brush (or flat brush) and start filling the rectangle in with dark purple, from the edges toward the moon. One-third of the way to the moon, change to painting with purple. At the last two-thirds of the distance, start painting with the tint of purple. Make circular movements around the moon, and try to blend colors directly on the paper as you go.

Paint very carefully at the edges of the moon. I advise you to switch to a thin-tipped brush or even a detail brush to make the edges accurate.

Let the painted layer dry completely.

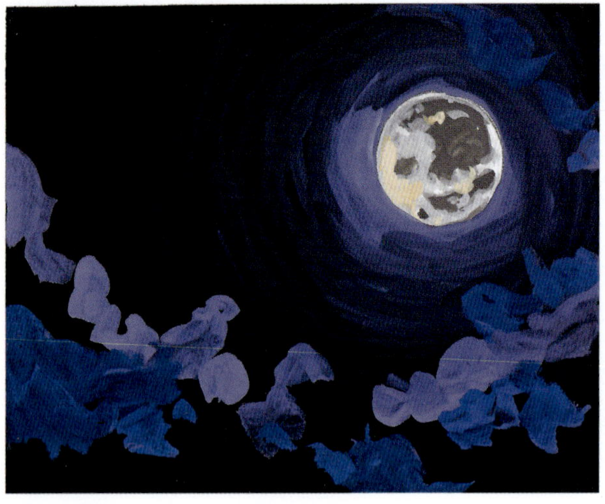

Figure 5

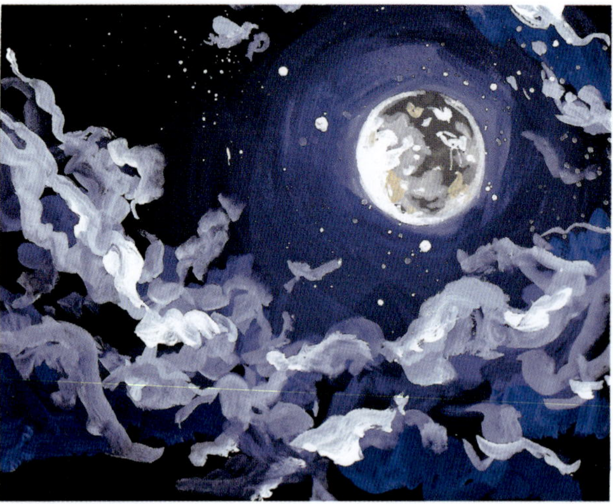

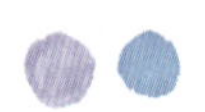

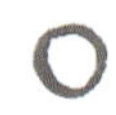

Figure 6

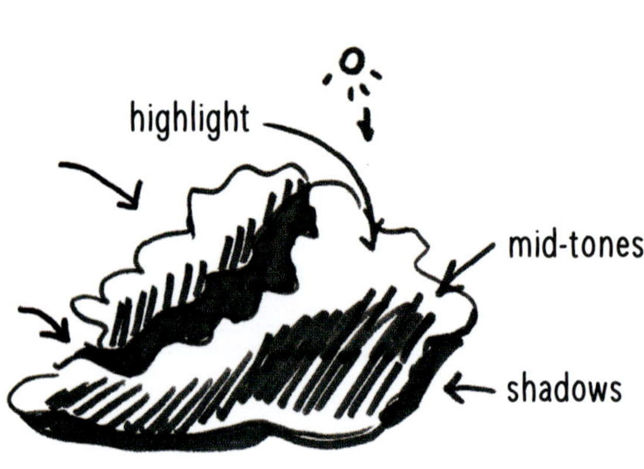

Figure 4

STEP 3

The background is done, and we can paint some clouds on top of it. To simplify the cloud painting, you can break it down into highlights, mid-tones and shadows (see Figure 4).

The background will play the role of the shadows. We need to add the mid-tones and highlights. Take the small filbert brush (or you can use a round brush) and add a layer in the tint of purple. Then paint the layer in the tint of blue, as shown in Figure 5. Don't make these elements symmetrical; they should look random and realistic. After the painting is completely dry, move on to the final step.

STEP 4

In this step, we will also use the layering technique (page 11).

We are at the last stage, and let's make it look like a proper starry night sky painting. First of all, let's finish out the clouds (Figure 6). Paint bold highlights with pastel blue and pastel purple by using the filbert brush. Let the painted layer dry completely and paint one more layer to highlight areas of the cloud in white. This time use a small round brush. Now arm yourself with the detail brush and add highlights to the moon in white, as well as some additional details. But don't add too many details; a few touches will be enough. Let the painted layer dry completely.

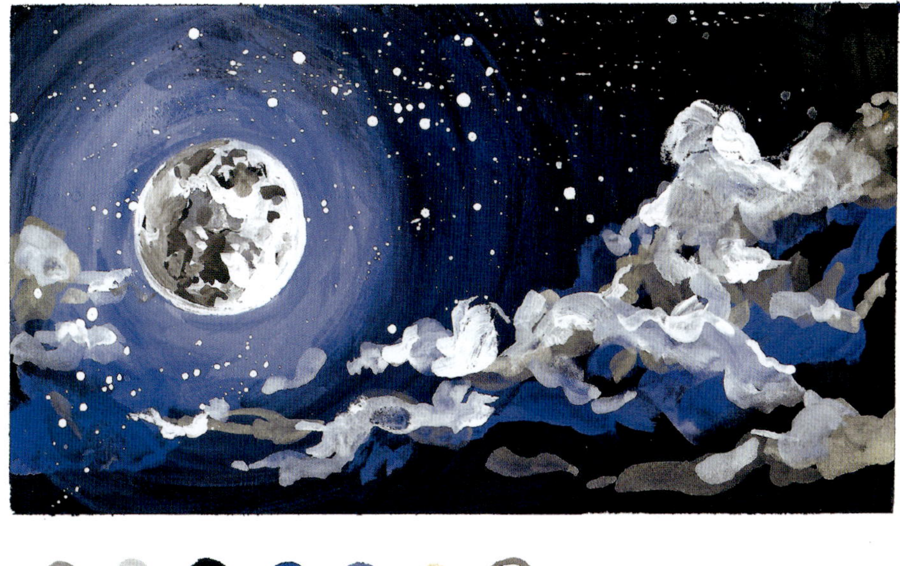

Figure 7

The final touch is adding the stars (Figure 7). We'll apply the splattering technique (page 13) for this. It brings some charm and the effect of randomness.

First, cover the areas of the clouds and the moon with some paper or paper towels to protect these areas from the splatters. Then, take a bit of white gouache on the small round brush and flick it on the painting. Don't overdo the splattering; one or two flicks will be enough.

TIP: Before adding the splattering on the painting, you can practice splattering on another sheet of paper so you know what to expect.

Our beautiful painting is ready. Once it's completely dry, take off the masking tape and . . . *voilà!*

As for practicing, you can always play with shades and composition. Choose some analogous shades and try to apply other colors for the current project. I suggest you use some references for a better understanding of how to paint the clouds. Try to keep the clouds simple. Figure 7 shows another painting I completed using the lesson. I like painting the sky and clouds so much. I always get such an impressive result, while also enjoying a great opportunity to practice with gouache. I hope you will enjoy it too.

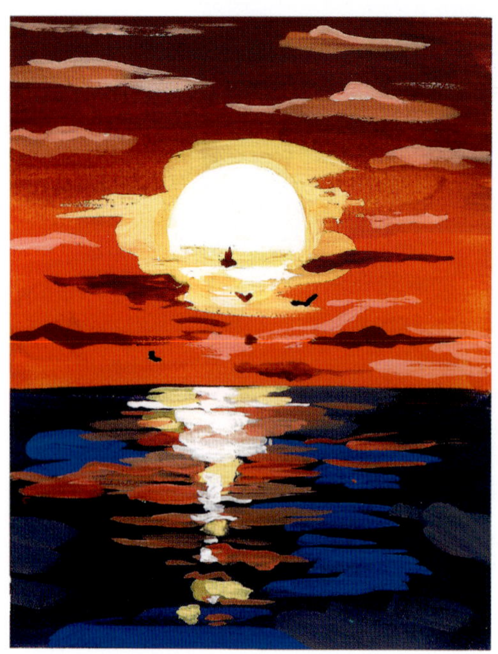

DREAMY SUNSET

The sunset is so inspiring to me. Because I am fortunate enough to live by the Baltic Sea, I see incredible sunsets over the sea almost every day. Each time it's made up of different shades: from tender pastel tints to very saturated and vivid colors. It's incredible. I couldn't pass up including the sunset in this chapter and will show you how to paint it with gouache in a very cute and a bit surreal style. But still, the instruction is broken down into easy and straightforward steps, so let's get started.

SUPPLIES

- White paper
- Masking tape
- Filbert brush
- Flat brush
- Round brushes in different sizes
- Detail brush

PROJECT COLORS

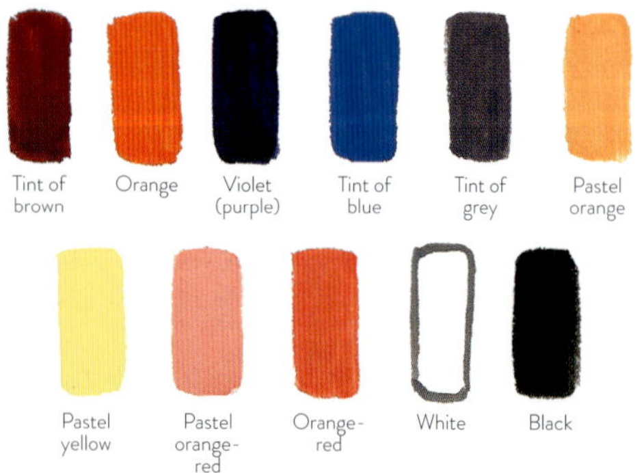

COLOR MIXING

- Tint of brown (red + burnt umber, proportion 2:1)
- Tint of blue (white + ultramarine blue, proportion 1:1)
- Tint of grey (white + violet + black, proportion 4:1:1)
- Pastel orange (white + orange, proportion 2:1)
- Pastel yellow (white + yellow, proportion 2:1)
- Pastel orange-red (white + orange + red, proportion 4:1:1)
- Orange-red (white + orange + red, proportion 2:1:1)

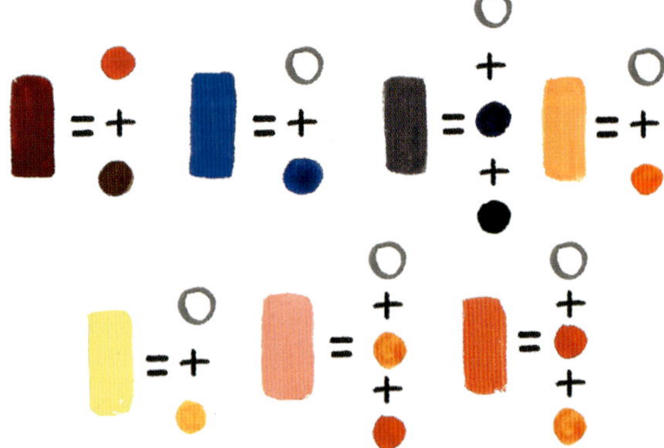

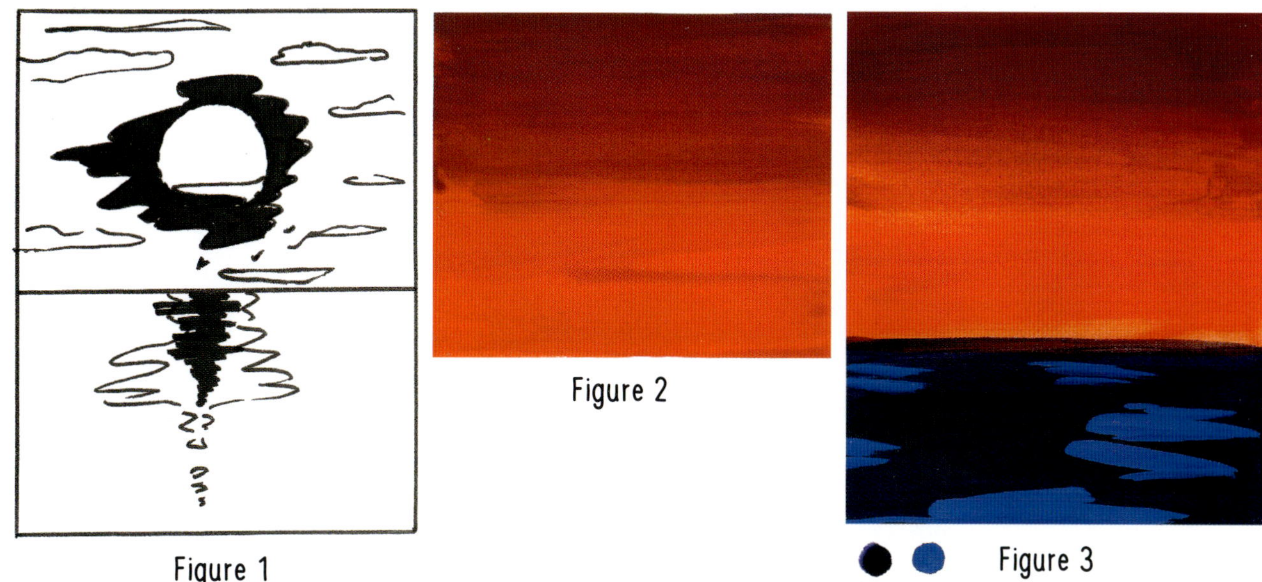

Figure 1

Figure 2

Figure 3

STEP 1

This project doesn't require a sketch. However, we need to define the working space. So, with the help of masking tape, define the vertical rectangular area you intend to paint.

To start, take a filbert brush, or a flat one, and paint the sky of the landscape. For painting the sky, we use the direct blending technique (page 11).

NOTE: The size of the brush depends on the size of the piece you are painting for this project. During this step, I use a big filbert brush in size 10.

First, paint the upper part in the tint of brown. Make smooth, horizontal strokes with the filbert brush. Then, starting from two-thirds down your paper, and moving toward the brown area, fill the rest of the sky in orange (Figure 2). You want a smooth and flowing gradient.

Let the painted layer dry completely.

TIP: To make the transition smoother, take a clean, moistened brush and rub the transition area in one direction.

STEP 2

Keep working with the same filbert or flat brush. This time, paint the water part of the landscape in the blank portion of the paper with violet. As soon as the layer dries, add on one layer of the tint of blue, as shown in Figure 3 (read more about the layering technique on page 11). Allow the painting to dry completely.

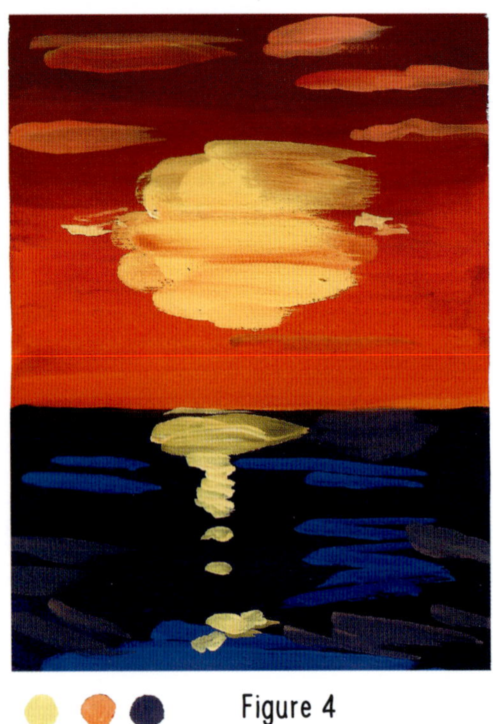

Figure 4

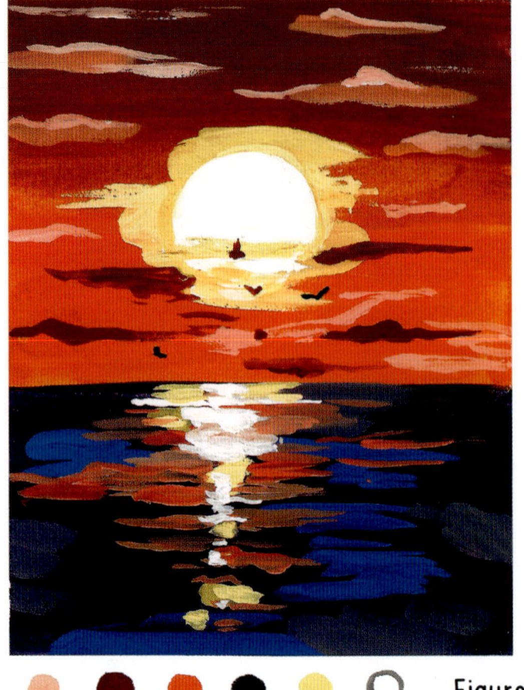

Figure 5

STEP 3

We already have the base for our sunset landscape. Let's move on. During this step, you can continue to work with the filbert brush or use round brushes in medium and small sizes.

Prepare the next colors: tint of grey, pastel orange and pastel yellow. Using the layering technique (page 11), add the details, in their corresponding colors, as shown in Figure 4. Once again, let the painting dry.

STEP 4

Although this is the last step, we still have a lot of work to do. Be patient and consistent. Let's add color to the sun. As you can see in Figure 5, it is painted in white and the circle shape is broken. So, paint the sun according to the example, or paint the round-shaped sun in white gouache.

TIP: If, after it dries, the white becomes transparent, add one more layer on the top for an opaque effect.

Because we already have a sun in the piece, add all the reflections one by one in the following shades: pastel orange-red, orange-red, white and pastel yellow. Use a detail brush for this. Allow the work to dry completely. There are a few manipulations left before we complete the illustration.

First, add clouds in the bottom part of the sky in the tint of brown and the pastel orange-red. Then add highlights to the upper clouds in pastel orange-red. Last, add birds in black and the tint of brown. The birds' silhouettes shouldn't be clearly defined; some little spots will be enough. Carefully take off the masking tape. After all your hard work, we are finally done!

Don't worry if everything doesn't work out the first time you try it. Be patient and keep practicing. I recommend you practice first with the same colors, then change the composition slightly to add interesting details and play with the placement of elements. After you have some more experience, you can also change the colors of the project. Whatever you paint, practice makes everything better.

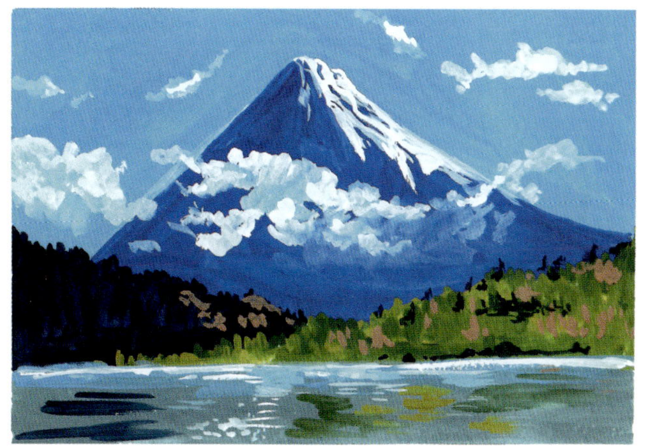

MOUNTAIN LANDSCAPE

This project is a quick and simple portrait of a mountain landscape, which will help you understand how to use gouache for more complicated scenes. Gouache allows you to paint in a simplified style or in a more detailed, realistic manner. I will guide you during this project and will demonstrate various tricks and techniques for using gouache to paint landscapes so you will be able to understand and use both styles. Let's get started!

SUPPLIES

- White paper
- Masking tape
- Pencil and eraser
- Large filbert or flat brush
- Round brushes in different sizes
- Detail brush

PROJECT COLORS

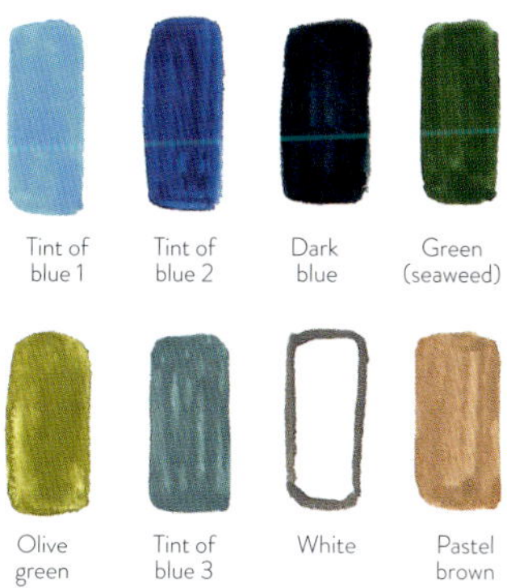

TIP: If you don't have exactly these two shades of green, use any other two you have: one lighter and one darker.

COLOR MIXING

- Tint of blue 1 (white + cerulean blue, proportion 1:3)
- Tint of blue 2 (Prussian blue + cerulean blue,
- proportion 1:1)
- Dark blue (Prussian blue + black, proportion 3:1)
- Tint of blue 3 (white + cerulean blue + black, proportion 2:6:1)
- Pastel brown (white + yellow ochre + burnt umber, proportion 1:2:1)

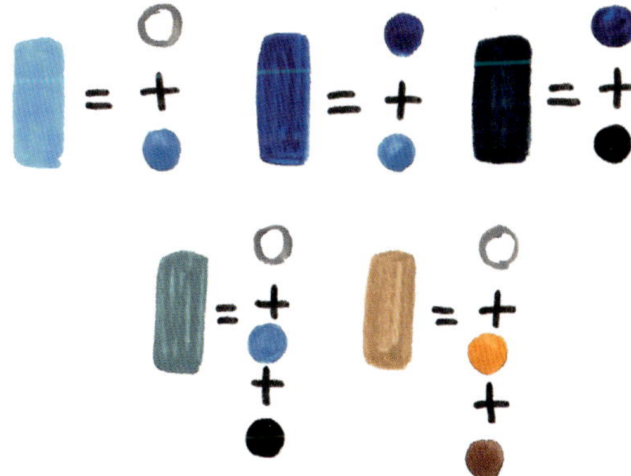

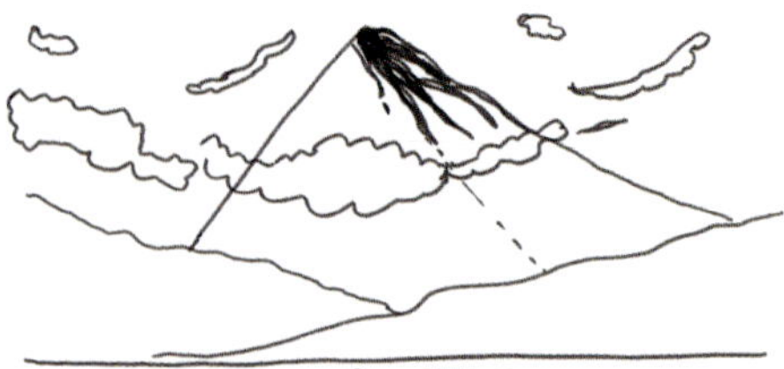

Figure 1

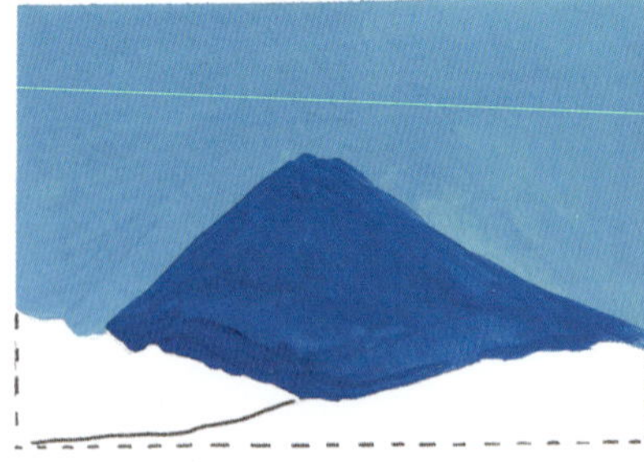

Figure 2

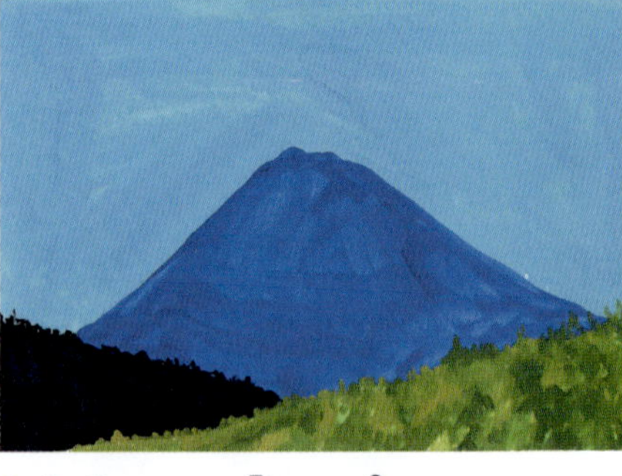

Figure 3

STEP 1

Begin by using masking tape to secure the paper to your table or board to define the working area of the landscape painting. Once that's done, proceed to the sketch of the landscape, following the outline in Figure 1. The sketch should not be detailed. Just draw a baseline of the mountain and mark forest areas and the horizon line. You don't have to draw the clouds in this sketch; we'll add them later with gouache.

With a big flat or filbert brush, first fill the sky area of the piece with the tint of blue 1 and let the layer dry. Then fill the mountain area in the tint of blue 2 (Figure 2).

Let the painting dry completely.

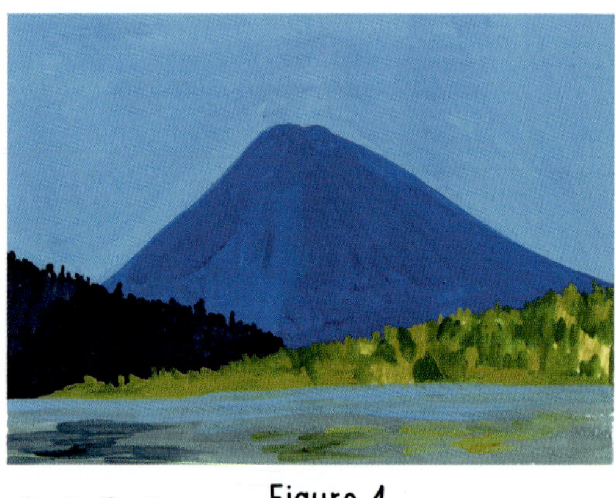

Figure 4

STEP 2

Switch to a medium round brush with a thin tip and paint the forest line at the left side in the dark blue (Figure 3). Try to make the upper part of this area imitate the peaks of the trees. It's okay if you overlap the mountain layer with the trees a bit.

Once this area is completely dry, paint the forest line at the right side in green and olive green, alternating with each other. It's best to use the direct blending technique (page 11) for a smoother color transition effect. And don't forget to make this area imitate the tree peaks, just as you did on the left side. Allow the painting to dry.

STEP 3

Finally, we are ready to paint the water portion of the landscape. For this, take a flat, filbert or even a round brush and fill in the bottom part of the painting using tint of blue 3. Don't wait until the layer is dry (see blending, page 13) and add the tint of blue 1, green and olive green, as shown in Figure 4. These are reflections on the water surface, and the more detailed you create them, the more realistic the final piece will appear. Because we are painting the sketch variation, I recommend not adding too many of the reflection's details. Allow the painting to dry.

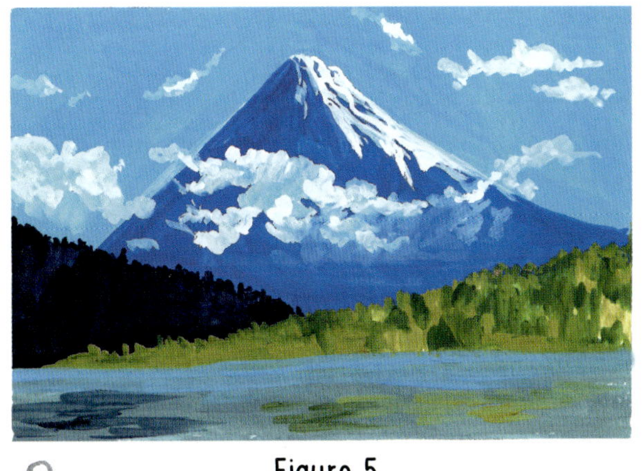

Figure 5

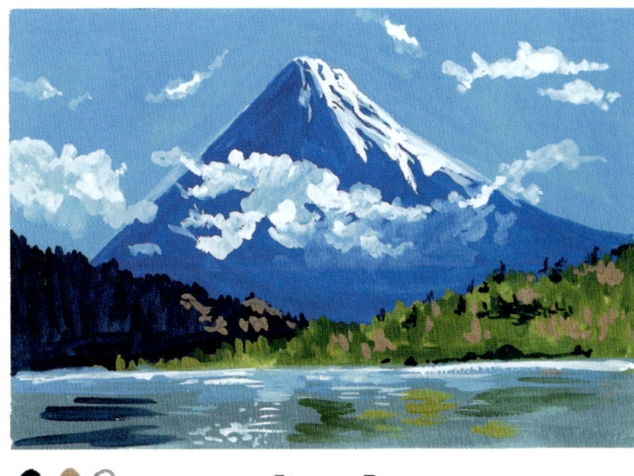

Figure 7

STEP 4

Time to add details to the painting (Figure 5). As I mentioned earlier, depending on how realistic you want your painting to be, you can add more or fewer details. I will go for a sketchier style and will add minimal details.

Arm yourself with a small round brush and paint the snowcap on the mountain peak with white gouache. Let it dry and then paint the clouds. I advise painting the clouds in two stages (Figure 6):

- Paint the base and blur it with a tiny amount of water (see softening, page 12).
- When the base is dry, add more accent with white.

If you are going for a more realistic style of painting, you can add even more layers of clouds, but at the same time try to keep them balanced and don't add too many layers.

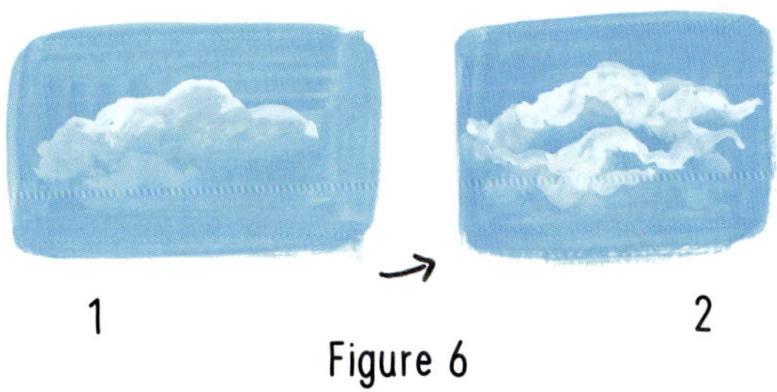

Figure 6

STEP 5

Now take a detail brush and add some shine on the water with the white. I applied the spots and some horizontal dashes for adding the highlights. Once again, you can add more details with white for a more realistic painting.

Use the same detail brush for painting the details such as trees, rocks, some highlights and so forth. Paint the details in pastel brown and dark blue, as shown in Figure 7.

I stopped myself at this point. However, if you would like, keep working with the details. Add more color on the forest lines, add some special details like a tiny house or maybe birds or whatever you want. I also recommend using different references to find some interesting ideas for accents.

You can also experiment with the colors if you would like to practice this lesson (Figure 8). At the same time, keep the composition simple and play with the details. I hope you find this lesson useful and fun. It will be a great start for painting any other mountain landscape with gouache.

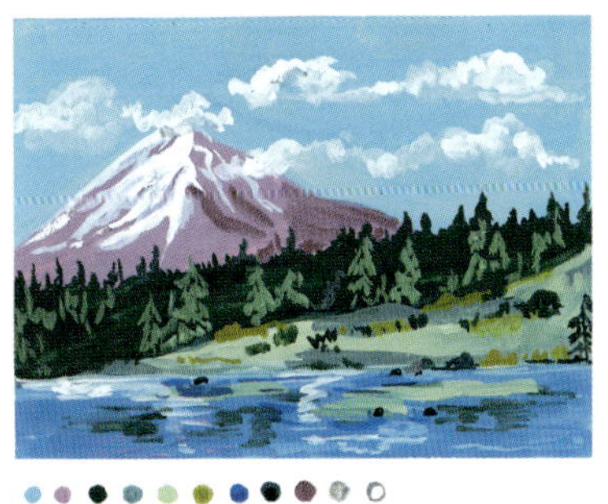

Figure 8

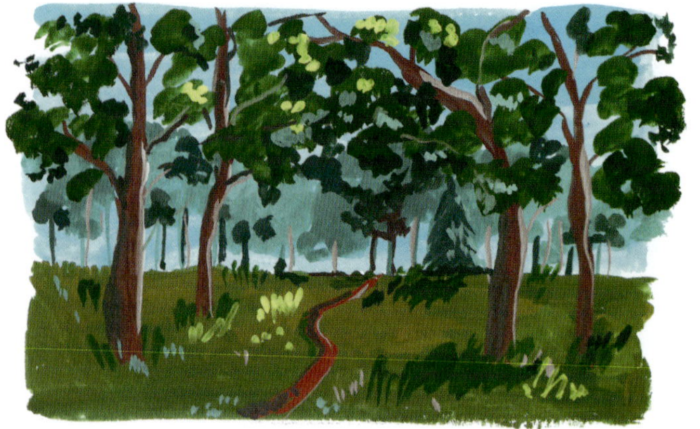

ENCHANTING FOREST

The forest is a place where we can find so much inspiration, as well as enjoy long walks and breathe fresh air. I personally love the forest.

In these next pages, you will find a project that was inspired by the beauty of the forest. This lesson is about how to paint this type of landscape with gouache. Let's begin.

SUPPLIES

- White paper
- Masking tape (optional)
- Pencil and eraser
- Filbert brushes in different sizes
- Round brushes in different sizes
- Flat brush (optional)
- Detail brush

PROJECT COLORS

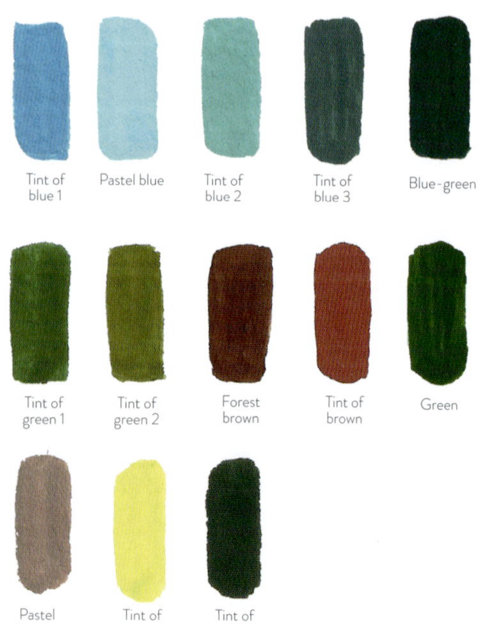

COLOR MIXING

- Tint of blue 1 (white + cerulean blue, proportion 1:1)
- Pastel blue (white + cerulean blue, proportion 2:1)
- Tint of blue 2 (white + cerulean blue + green, proportion 2:1:1)
- Tint of blue 3 (white + cerulean blue + green, proportion 2:2:1)
- Blue-green (cerulean blue + green, proportion 1:1)
- Tint of green 1 (green + yellow ochre, proportion 2:1)
- Tint of green 2 (green + yellow ochre, proportion 1:1)
- Tint of brown (white + burnt sienna, proportion 1:4)
- Pastel brown (white + burnt umber, proportion 2:1)
- Tint of green 3 (yellow + sap green, proportion 4:1)
- Tint of green 4 (green + burnt umber, proportion 2:1)

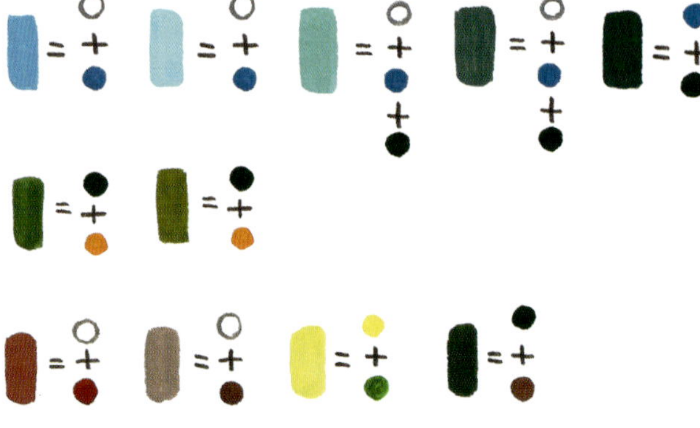

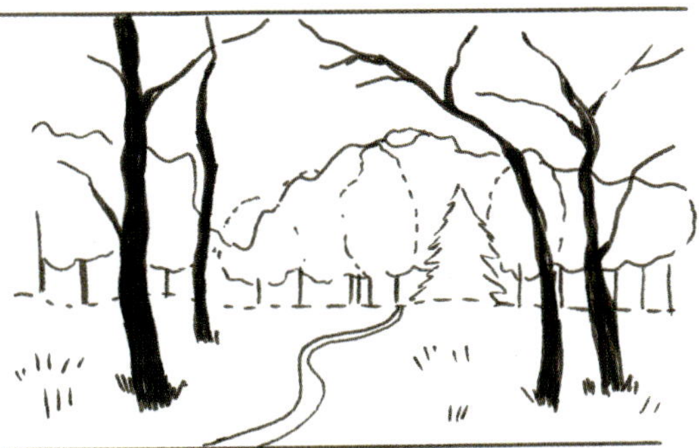

Figure 1

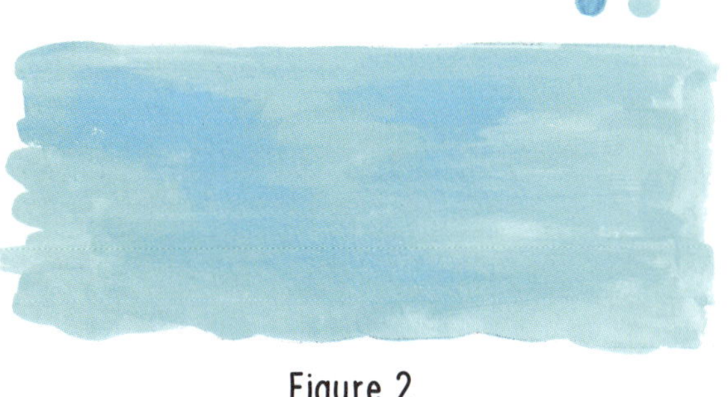

Figure 2

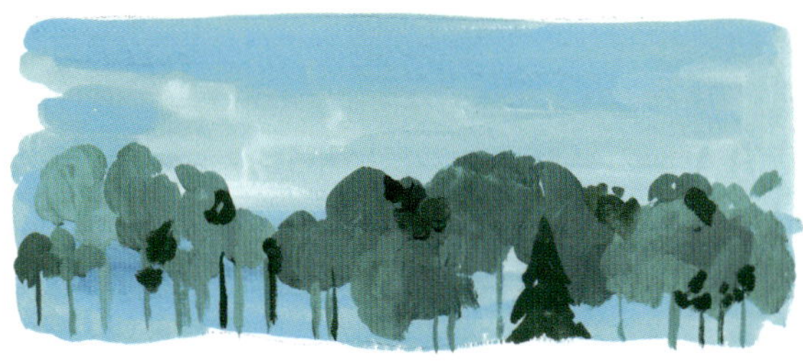

Figure 3

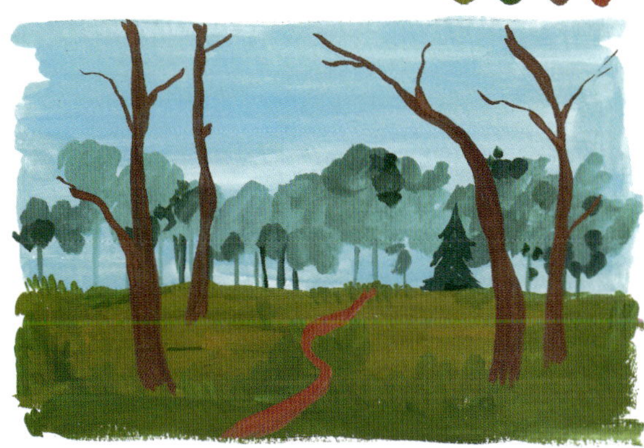

Figure 4

STEP 1

Before sketching the project, let's define a painting area. Choose one of the following options:

- Use masking tape.
- Create an abstract rectangular shape that does not require a preliminary draft; you can just mark the angles of the rectangle.
- Draw a rectangle with a pencil.

I will use the second method to show you how it works and that it's not always necessary to use masking tape.

Now let's deal with the sketch. Pay attention to Figure 1, which shows the basic outline of the forest landscape. The landscape includes the background and foreground, which are separated by the skyline. In the background scene, we can see the trees and sky. In the foreground, there are big trees, a green field and a path. You could sketch all these elements, but because the gouache will cover the pencil lines it doesn't make sense. So I recommend you add only the skyline but keep the outline image in your mind while working on the project.

Take a large filbert brush and fill the sky area in the tint of blue 1 and the pastel blue by using the direct blending technique (page 11) (Figure 2). If you don't have a filbert brush, a round one or a flat brush should work too. Allow the layer to dry completely.

STEP 2

Switch to a medium filbert brush or round brush. Using the same technique, paint the background trees in the tint of blue 2 and the tint of blue 3. Let the layer dry and then paint some details of the background trees in blue-green, as shown in Figure 3.

Try to make the background tree line asymmetrical and not perfect. This will make the painting look more realistic. Allow the painting to dry.

STEP 3

It's time to add the green field to the landscape (Figure 4). As in step 1, fill the bottom part in the tint of green 1 and the tint of green 2, by using the direct blending technique (page 11). Use a big filbert or round brush for this step. Let the layer dry completely.

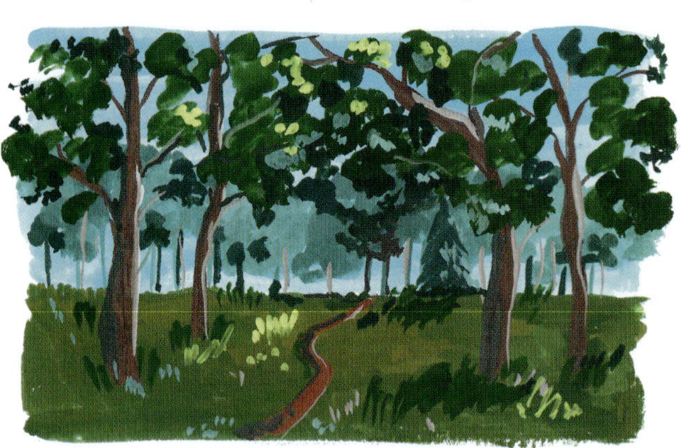

Figure 5

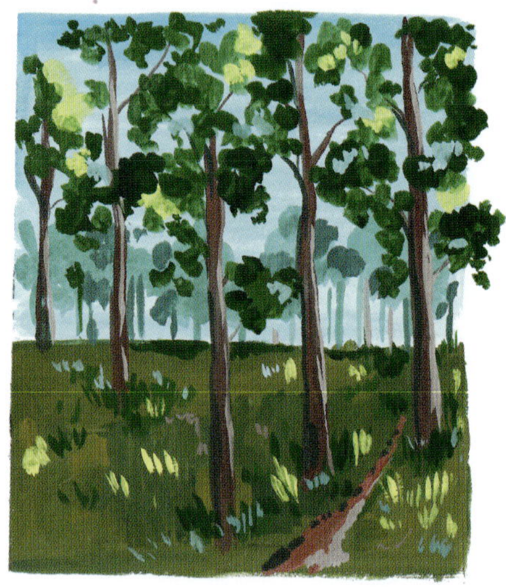

Figure 6

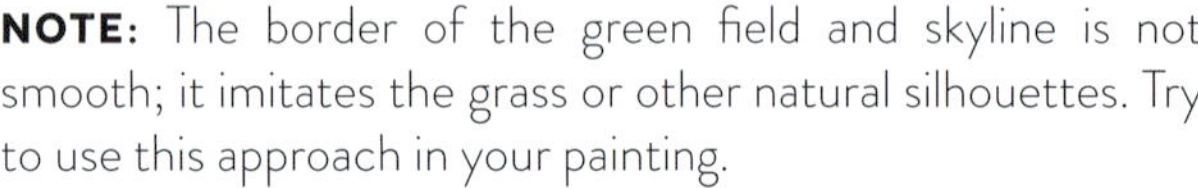

NOTE: The border of the green field and skyline is not smooth; it imitates the grass or other natural silhouettes. Try to use this approach in your painting.

Once the layer is dry, arm yourself with a medium round brush with a thin tip and paint the trunks of the trees in forest brown and the path in the tint of brown (see layering, page 11). Wait for the layer to dry and go on to the last step.

STEP 4

We've passed the hardest part in this lesson; now you can enjoy adding the final details. Throughout this step, use a variety of round brushes and a detail brush for the smallest elements.

Begin by painting the foliage of the foreground trees in green. You can overlap the branches with leaves in some areas to make the painting look natural. With the same color, add accents to the grass on the green field, as shown in Figure 5. Let the piece dry.

Now prepare the next colors: the pastel brown, the tint of green 3, the tint of green 4 and the tint of blue 2. With the pastel brown, add highlights to the trees' trunks and paint details on the path and grass. Then paint the highlights on the tree foliage in the tint of green 3 and tint of blue 2. With the tint of green 4 paint the shadows on the trunks and the path, and add some touches to the background. And finally, add more details to the grass in the tint of green 3 and the tint of blue 2. Our forest landscape is complete.

If at first glance the project doesn't look easy or if after the first attempt your painting isn't perfect, I promise that with practice you will fall in love with painting such landscapes.

For your first time through, I recommend using the same color scheme as in the lesson. You can play around with the composition and trees' shapes (see example in Figure 6). After some time, when you feel more confident in painting landscapes, change the colors. Find inspiration in nature. Don't forget to take photos during your walks in a forest for reference. Or have a look at some photos on the internet, just for inspiration. Enjoy the process of creation and be patient and you will succeed!

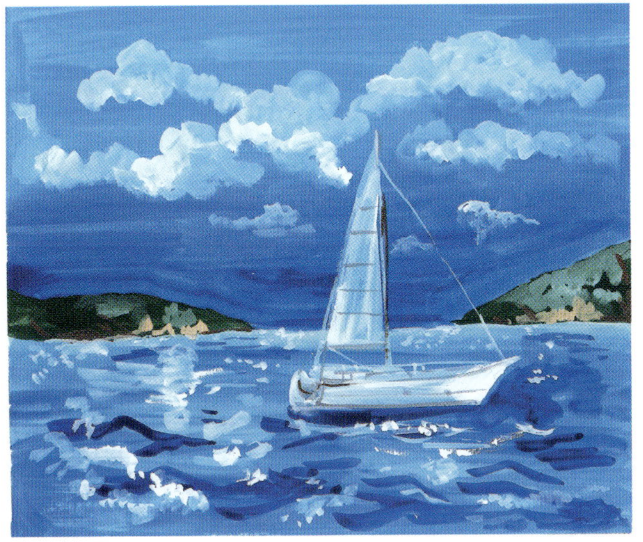

DRAMATIC SEASCAPE

This project will show you how to paint a quick and simple seascape with gouache. Painting these landscapes is pure pleasure. With gouache, we can add layers one by one and make the final painting more realistic. I hope you will enjoy painting the fluffy clouds on a dramatic blue sky or fall in love with how easy it is to make the water shimmer with gouache. I also included different techniques in this project for you to practice applying gouache in different ways.

SUPPLIES

- White paper
- Masking tape
- Pencil and eraser
- Large filbert or flat brush
- Round brushes in different sizes
- Detail brush

COLOR MIXING

- Tint of blue 1 (white + Prussian blue, proportion 1:1)
- Tint of blue 2 (white + Prussian blue, proportion 2:1)
- Pastel yellow ochre (white + yellow ochre, proportion 1:1)
- Tint of purple (violet + Prussian blue, proportion 1:1)
- Grey (black + white, proportion 1:3)

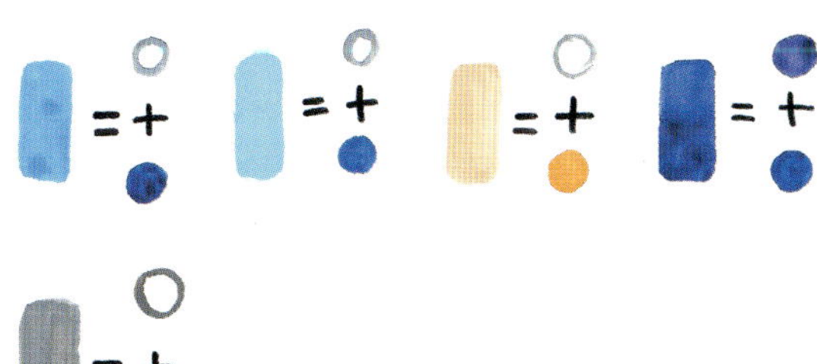

PROJECT COLORS

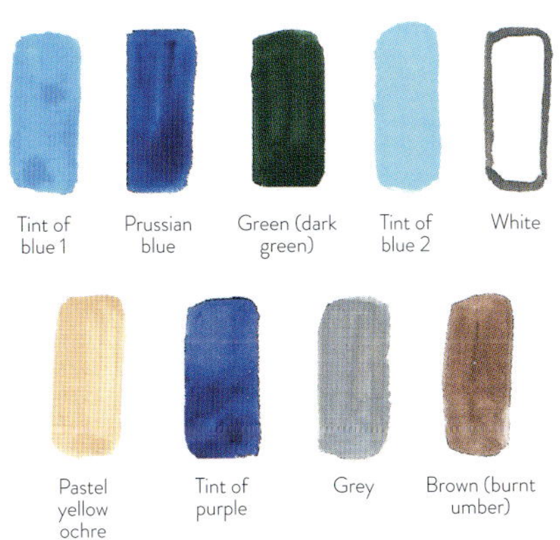

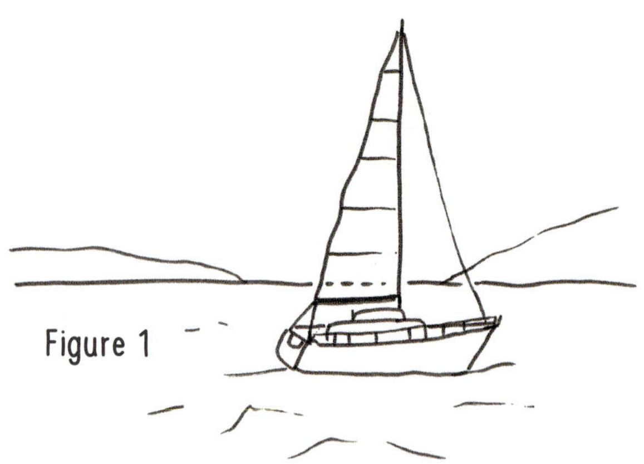

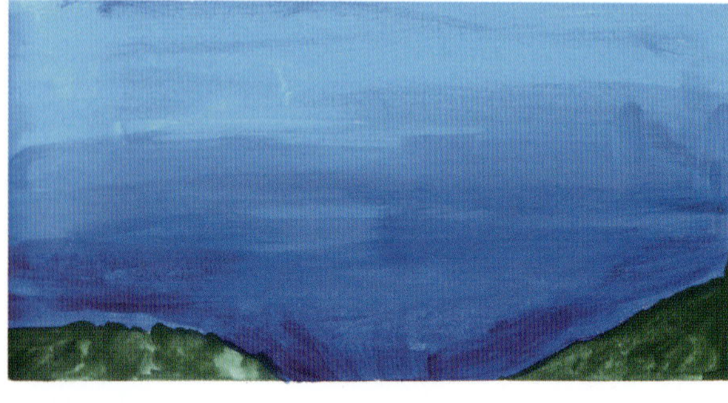

Figure 2

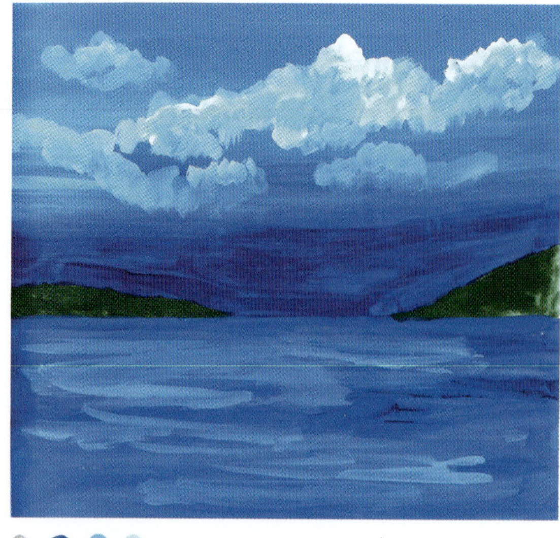

Figure 3

STEP 1

First, define the working area by using masking tape. Carefully secure the paper with masking tape on your table or board to make the horizontal rectangle area for painting. Draw a simple sketch of the landscape by using the outline in Figure 1. No details are needed, and don't draw the boat at this stage. Just mark the skyline and hills in the background.

Fill the sky area by applying the direct blending technique (page 11). Create a gradient (page 12) from tint of blue 1 at the top to Prussian blue at the bottom (Figure 2). The filbert brush will work the best for this step. However, either the flat brush or the round will work too. Let the sky area dry, then paint the hills in green with the help of a medium round brush. Allow the painted layer to dry.

STEP 2

It's time to paint the sea. Fill the sea area by using the direct blending technique (page 11) with the following colors: Prussian blue, the tint of blue 1 and the tint of blue 2.

TIP: Because gouache dries quickly, I recommend blending colors in small areas, moving sequentially from one to the next. Following this approach, start to paint from the top and go down to the bottom of the painting.

After the water is done, jump to painting the clouds in white gouache. For this, arm yourself with a medium round or filbert brush and form the clouds as shown in Figure 3.

If you would like your clouds to look fluffy and soft, apply the softening technique (page 12) and blur them a bit from the bottom side. Let the painting dry.

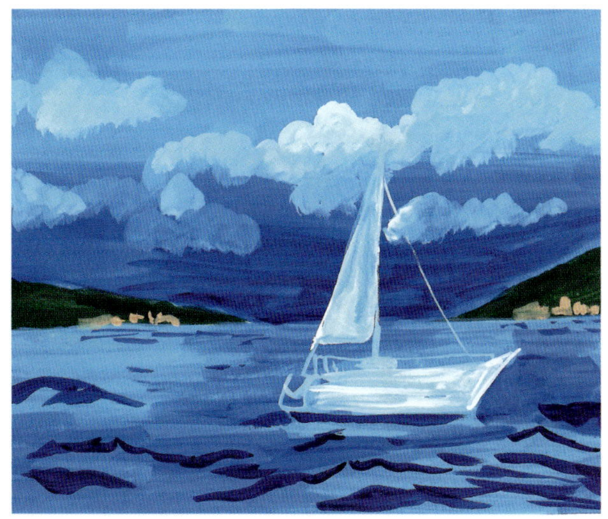

Figure 4

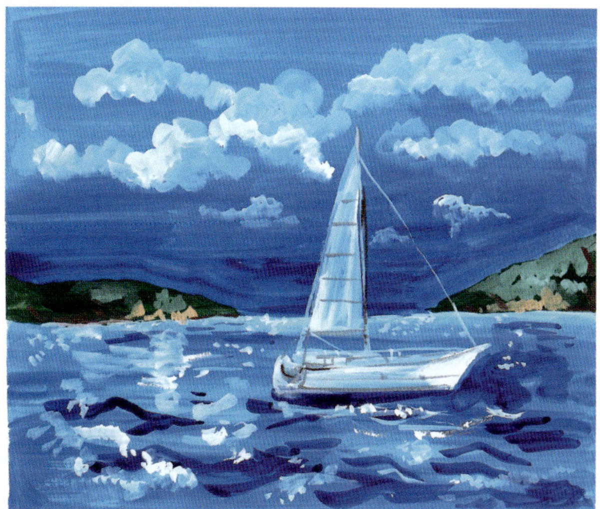

Figure 5

STEP 3

We can finally add a sailboat and some other details to the painting. Let's start with painting the boat in white gouache. Follow Figure 4 or use any reference for painting the base layer of the boat. Don't try to make it perfect; we'll add details in the next step that complete the look of the boat. Use round brushes in small sizes.

Add some accents to the hills in the pastel yellow ochre. Then, paint the dark waves on the sea in the tint of purple. Once again, let the painting dry.

NOTE: Steps 3 and 4 use the layering technique (page 11).

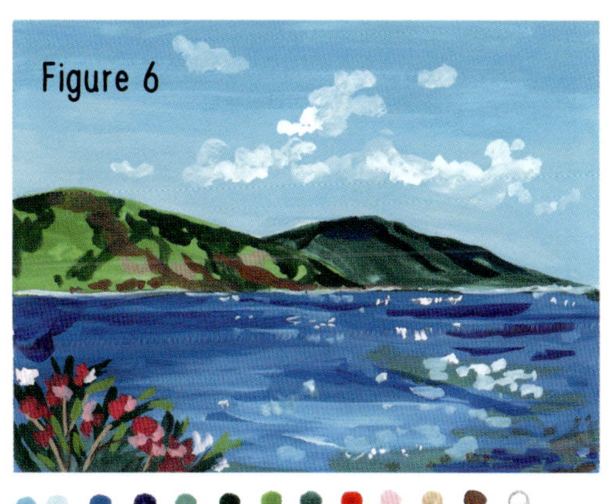

Figure 6

STEP 4

Prepare the next colors for the final step: white, grey and brown. Take the small round brush and add a shimmer to the water layer in white. You can play with the shapes of these shimmers, from spots to simplified stars.

Switch to the detail brush and add some details in brown, grey and white gouache, according to Figure 5 or the reference you use. With the same brush, paint optional details on the hills in brown and white. Note that I use a transparent white gouache for the highlights on the hill. You can get this effect by making and applying the gouache in a watery consistency. You can also add some more clouds by using a small round brush in white gouache.

After the work is done, remove the tape, and with it, everything that went beyond the area intended for your work.

This project is one in a huge variety of seascapes you can paint with gouache by using this lesson. Try creating different compositional solutions and change colors. Of course, you will need references for painting other pieces. Or you can use your own photos you have taken on vacation, or even your imagination. Figure 6 shows a picture painted using this project's methods but with modified composition and colors.

Keep practicing painting landscapes, and don't be afraid to experiment. Remember that practice makes perfect!

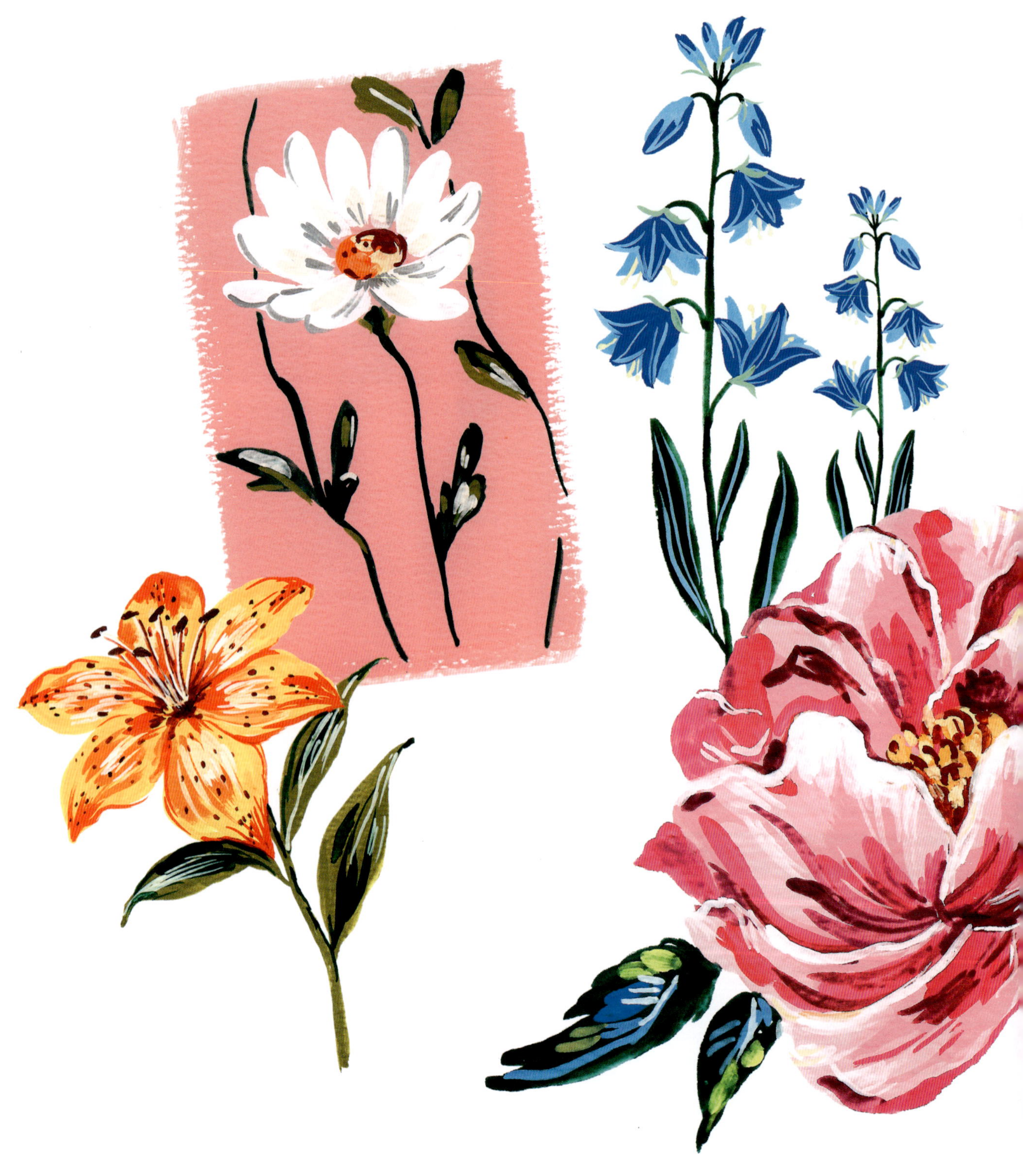

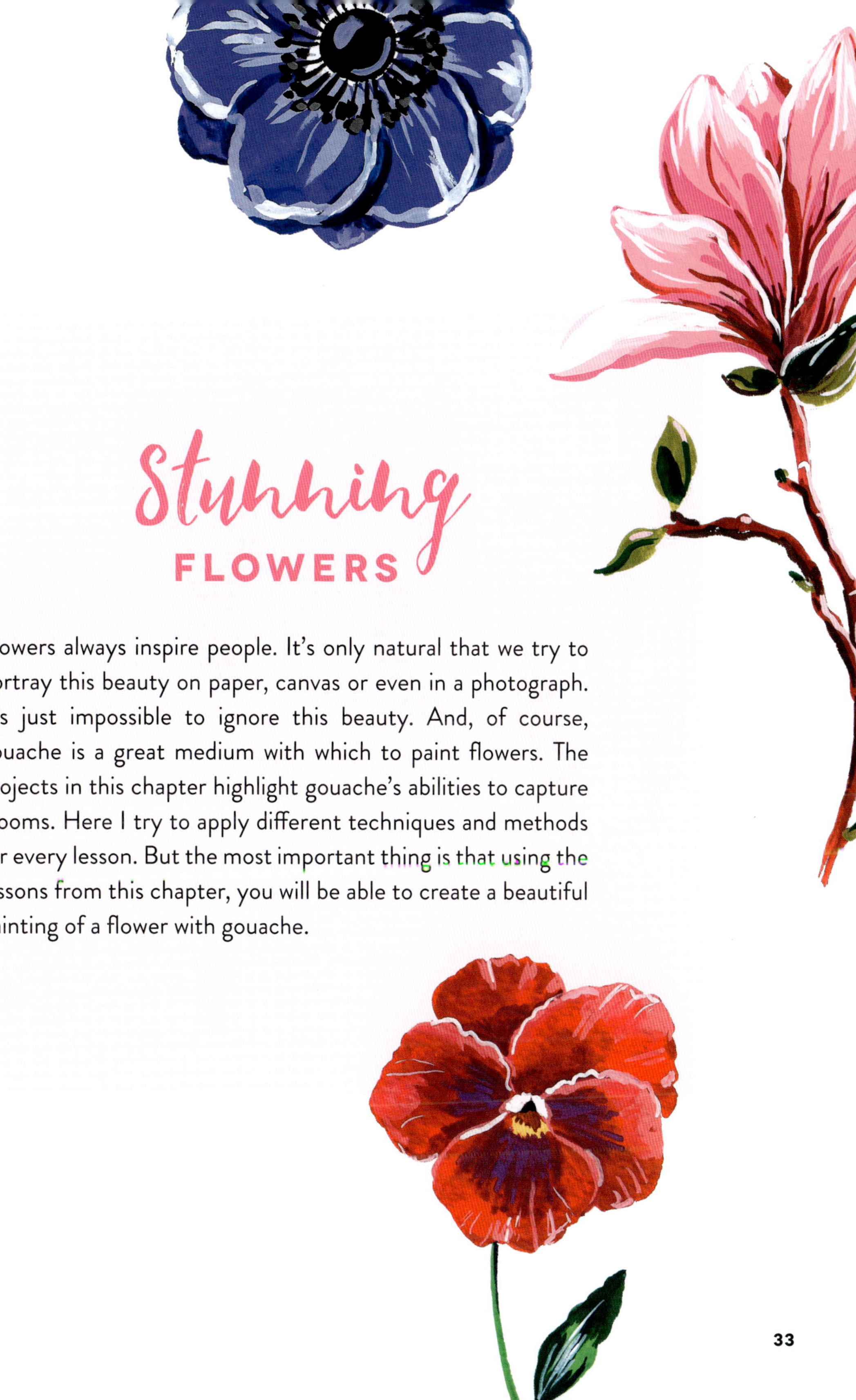

Stunning FLOWERS

Flowers always inspire people. It's only natural that we try to portray this beauty on paper, canvas or even in a photograph. It's just impossible to ignore this beauty. And, of course, gouache is a great medium with which to paint flowers. The projects in this chapter highlight gouache's abilities to capture blooms. Here I try to apply different techniques and methods for every lesson. But the most important thing is that using the lessons from this chapter, you will be able to create a beautiful painting of a flower with gouache.

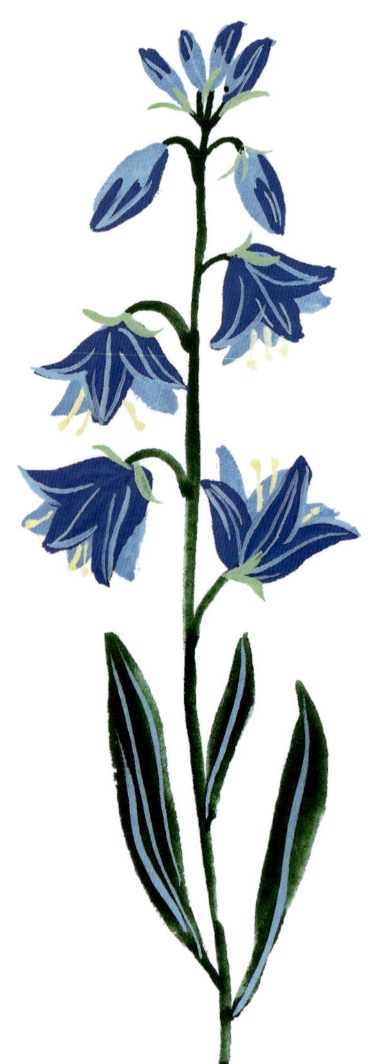

BELLFLOWER

This lesson is simple but very fun. I recommend painting it with kids or your friends, with a cup of tea and a good chat. I am sure everyone will enjoy this type of relaxing painting session with a pretty flower branch as a result. Just follow my instructions and have fun.

SUPPLIES

- White, black or craft paper
- Pencil and eraser
- Round brushes in different sizes
- Detail brush

PROJECT COLORS

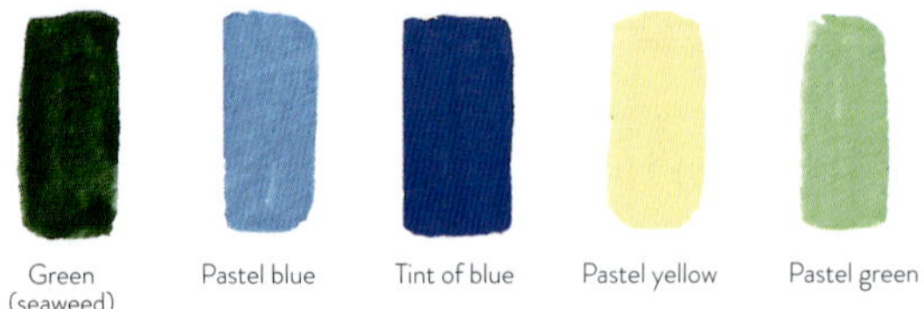

COLOR MIXING

- Pastel blue (white + ultramarine blue, proportion 2:1)
- Tint of blue (white + ultramarine blue, proportion 1:3)
- Pastel yellow (white + primary yellow, proportion 3:1)
- Pastel green (white + green + primary yellow, proportion 2:2:1)

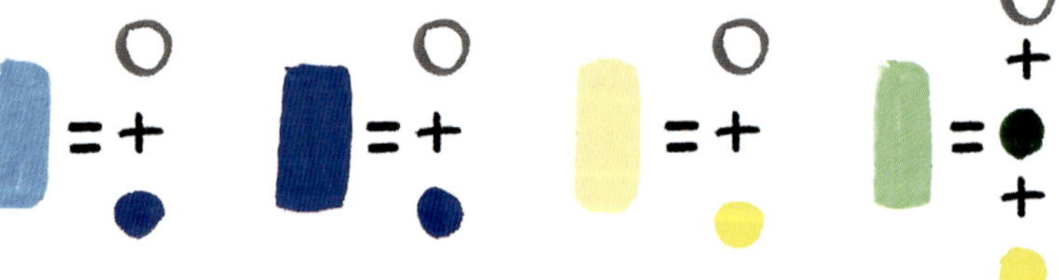

NOTE: Throughout this project, we use the layering technique (page 11).

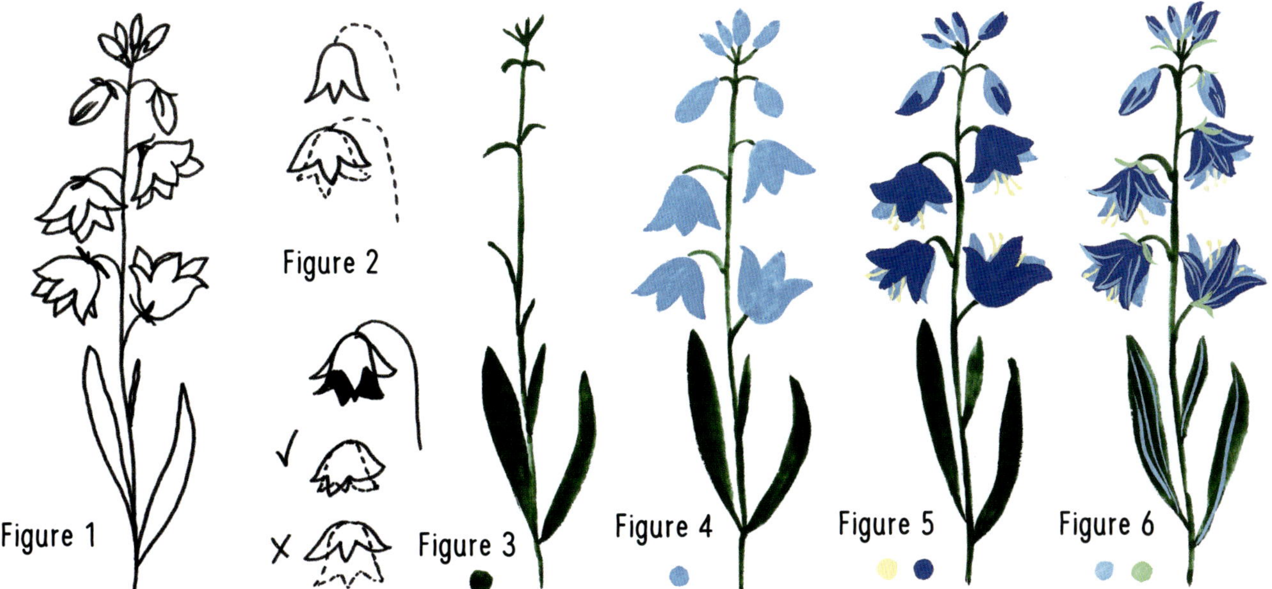

STEP 1

Make a preliminary pencil sketch, following Figure 1. I advise you to draw only the stem and then to paint the single flowers directly with gouache. However, if you feel more comfortable with the full sketch, draw it using the outline in the example.

Now let me explain how to paint the flowers in this project. This method is based on the contrast of two colors. Pay attention to Figure 2. In the image, you can see that first, you need to paint a base and then add another layer on top in a contrasting color. The one thing you need to note is that the distance of the layers should not be too long. Now we can move on to the painting itself. Let's begin.

Using a small round brush, paint the stem of the branch with green (Figure 3). Then switch to a bigger round brush and add the leaves. Allow the layer to dry and jump to the next step.

STEP 2

Time to paint the flowers and buds. Depending on the size of the brush you use, you'll get different petal dimensions (see Gouache Brushes, page 185). So, pick the round brush that suits you and paint the flowers in pastel blue (Figure 4). Once again, let the layer dry completely.

STEP 3

Now we'll make magic with color contrasting (Figure 5). As I mentioned earlier, on each flower you need to paint another layer but this time in the darker color—the tint of blue. For this, keep working with a round brush in a suitable size. Once the layer is dry, using the detail brush, add the pistils in pastel yellow.

STEP 4

Finally, we're ready to add details to the bellflower branch (Figure 6). Arm yourself with the detail brush and add some smooth stripes in the tint of blue to the flower layer, as well as on the leaves. Also, paint some small leaves on each flower and buds in pastel green.

As I promised, the project is quick and straightforward, and is very beginner-friendly. I also recommend using this method of painting bellflowers for any bell-type flower such as tulips or daylilies. You can also swap the contrasting colors, first painting the darker color and then adding a lighter one. I hope you are inspired to paint more beautiful bellflowers.

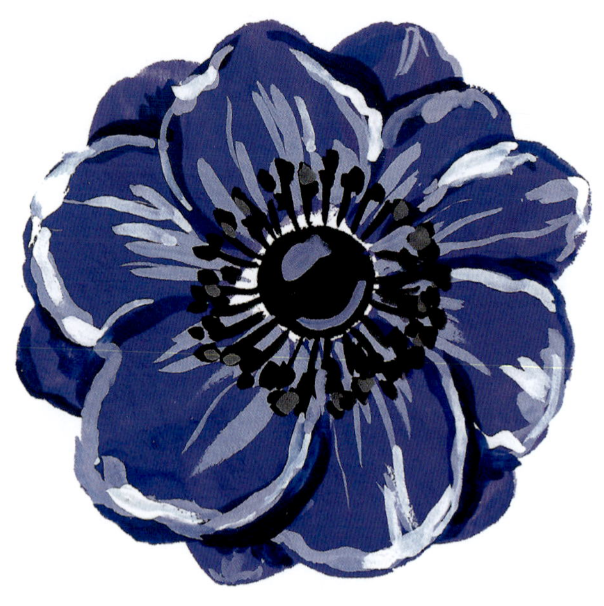

ANEMONE

The anemone flower always amazes me with its unbelievable beauty. And of course, it's a good object to paint with gouache, especially for practicing different brush strokes.

SUPPLIES

- White or craft paper
- Pencil and eraser
- Small round brush
- Large filbert brush
- Detail brush

PROJECT COLORS

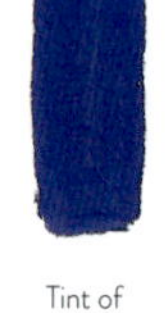
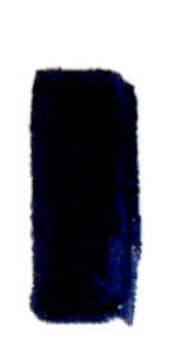
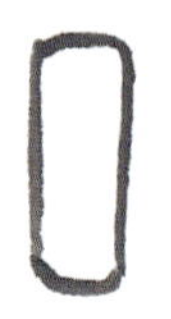
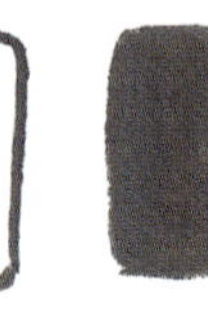

Black | Pastel purple | Tint of purple | Dark purple | White | Grey

COLOR MIXING

- Pastel purple (white + lilac + ultramarine blue, proportion 2:1:1)
- Tint of purple (white + lilac + ultramarine blue, proportion 1:3:1)
- Dark purple (black + lilac + ultramarine blue, proportion 1:2:2)
- Grey (black + white, proportion 1:3)

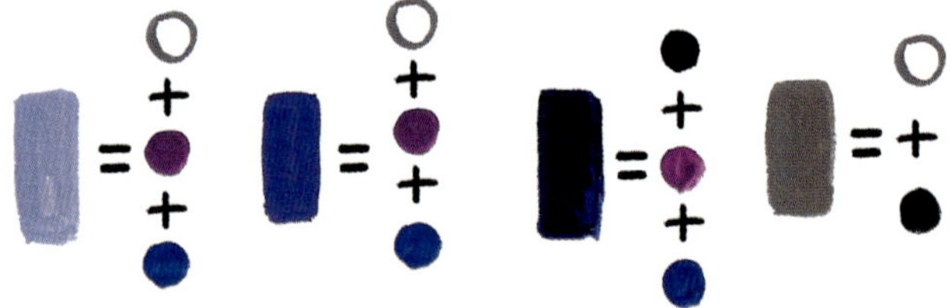

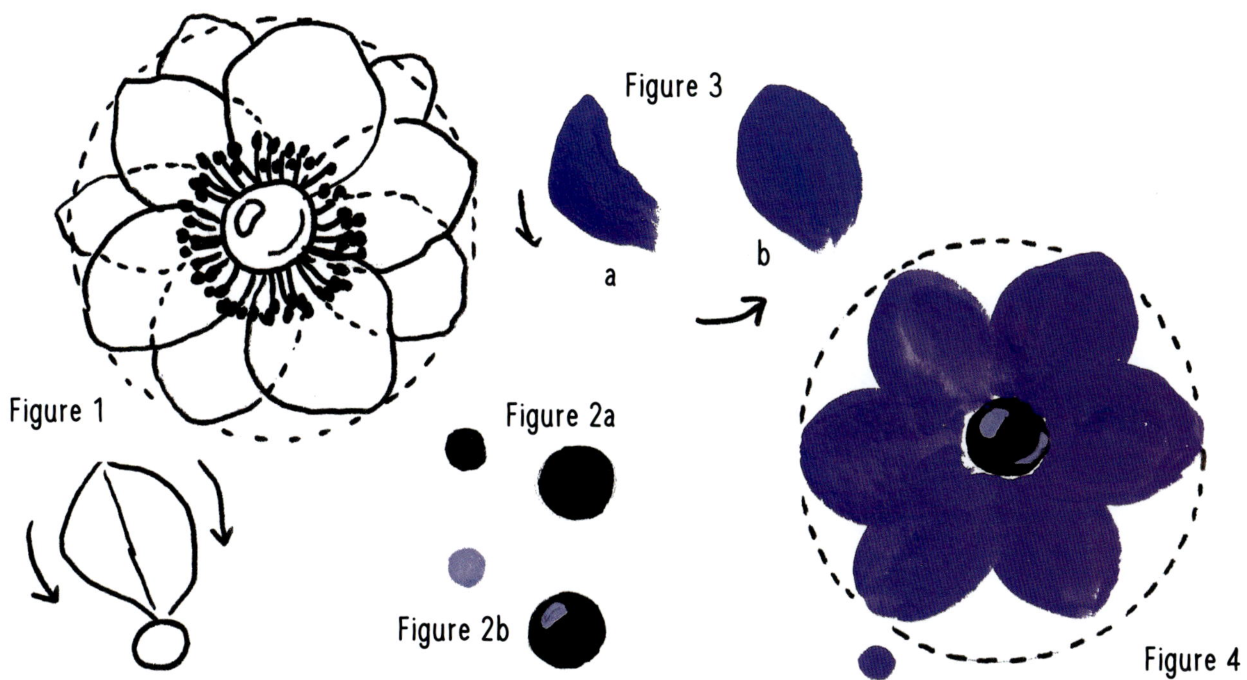

STEP 1

NOTE: During each step of this project, we will use the layering technique (page 11).

Before starting this project, have a look at the sketch (Figure 1). Notice that the flower fits in the circle. I recommend you not draw the full sketch, but instead very lightly sketch the circle and also mark the center of the flower. This will be enough to start the painting.

However, if you want to be even more confident about your painting, you can make a more detailed sketch.

TIP: Before painting, take the eraser and try to make the circle's line as soft as possible and almost invisible.

Arm yourself with the small round brush and paint the center of the flower in black (Figure 2a). Once it dries completely, add the highlights in the pastel purple (Figure 2b).

Let the layer dry completely.

STEP 2

It's time to add the petals. For this, take your filbert brush and prepare the tint of purple. Paint each petal in two stages (Figure 3). First, paint one half and then continue by adding another half beside. Start each stroke from the circle line, press the brush on the paper, move it a bit toward the center and lift it up near the center of the flower. Paint the petals close to one another, as shown in Figure 4.

TIP: I recommend practicing this brush stroke on another sheet of paper before painting the main piece.

Don't wait for the layer to dry. Jump to step 3.

NOTE: Leave a bit of space between the flower center and each petal. It will provide contrast at the end. If you are painting on craft paper, however, I recommend you use the small round brush to paint with the tint of purple and to connect each petal with the flower center. Or add the white layer with white gouache.

Figure 5

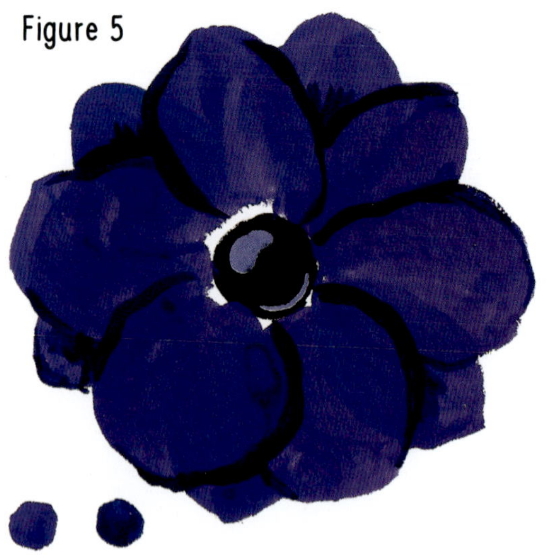

Figure 6

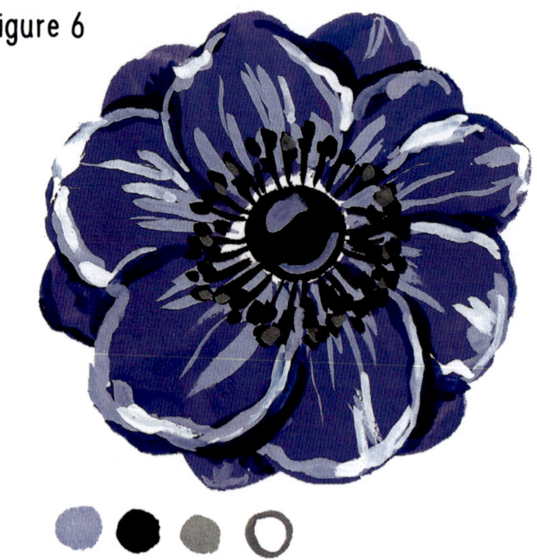

STEP 3

We already have the first level of petals. Let's move on. Paint the lower-level petals in the tint of purple by using the same method of brush stroking we used in step 2. Add the petals to the emptiest places to make the flower full and more realistic.

Let the layer dry.

At this moment, all the petals should look merged in one solid layer. Don't panic, we'll separate it into two levels of petals, and the painting will resemble an actual flower. To do this, switch to the small round brush and add a layer of shadow in the dark purple, according to Figure 5. Once the freshly painted layer dries, go to the next step.

STEP 4

We are ready to add the final details (Figure 6)! Use the small round brush or a detail brush. Add the highlights in the pastel purple and white gouache. Don't overdo the highlights; less is more. But still, they should show contrast with the petals and shadows.

As soon as the previous layer dries, paint the pistils of the flowers in black. As accents, add a few touches of grey to the pistils.

Thanks to the anemone's variety of colors, you can practice the project with any colors you would like. See the example in Figure 7 of my anemone variation in magenta-crimson shades.

Moreover, there are different variations of the flower. Explore different references and take photos for painting more anemones.

Figure 7

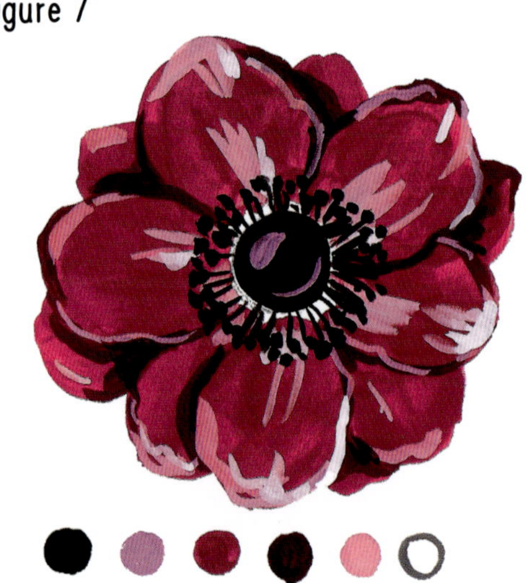

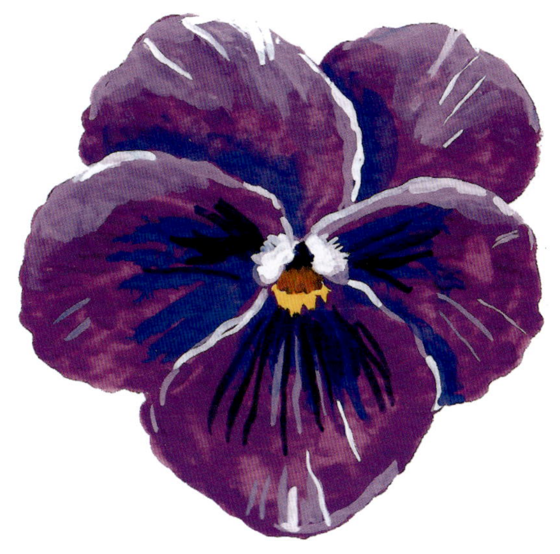

PANSY

The pansy was the first flower I painted with gouache. At first glance, the flower doesn't look simple, and it seems difficult to replicate all the details and structure. But it's much easier than it seems! The flower has five petals: two upper overlapping petals, the two side petals and the single bottom petal. As for the coloring, there is a wide range of pansy flower colors. In this project, we will paint a beautiful purple pansy flower. Afterward, you will be able to pick any colors by yourself and to paint the flower with them.

SUPPLIES

- White, craft or black paper
- Pencil and eraser
- Round brushes in different sizes
- Detail brush

PROJECT COLORS

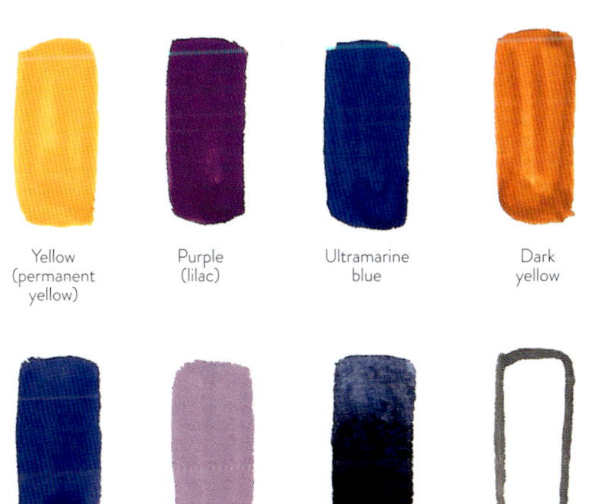

COLOR MIXING

- Dark yellow (permanent yellow + burnt sienna, proportion 3:1)
- Tint of violet (ultramarine blue + lilac, proportion 2:1)
- Pastel purple (lilac + white, proportion 1:3)
- Dark blue (ivory black + ultramarine blue, proportion 1:4)

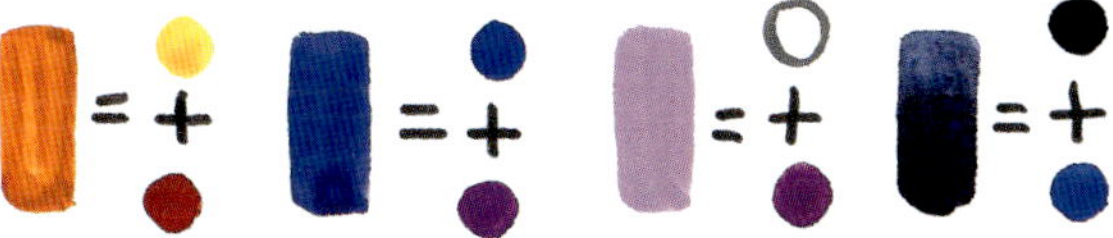

TIP: If you don't have this particular purple color, mix ultramarine blue and crimson red. Also, add a bit of white to the mix to get the matte finish.

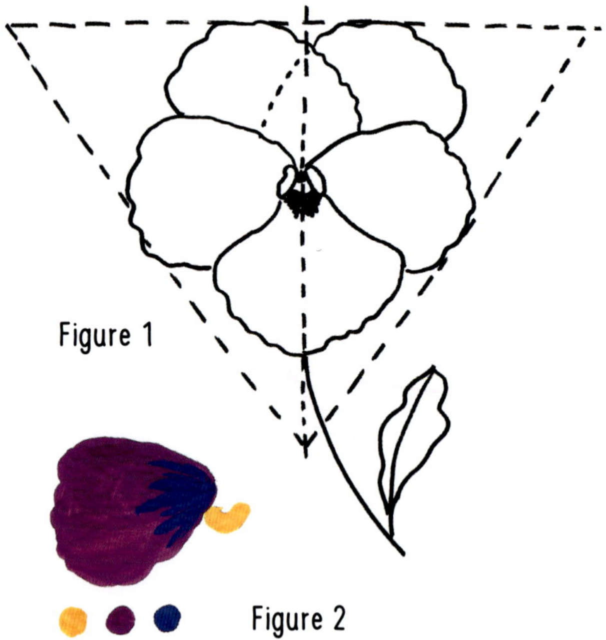

Figure 1

Figure 2

STEP 1

To make your work easy and relaxing I suggest you make a sketch. As I mentioned before, the pansy flower consists of five petals. Figure 1 shows an outline. Reference it to draw your pencil sketch of a pansy flower.

TIP: Because the flower fits into a triangle, start with a light sketch of it and then draw all the petals inside.

Paint the center of the flower with yellow by using a thin-tipped round brush in a small size. Allow it to dry. Now paint the left-side petal in purple with a medium round brush. Without waiting for it to dry, apply ultramarine blue as shown in Figure 2 (see direct blending, page 11).

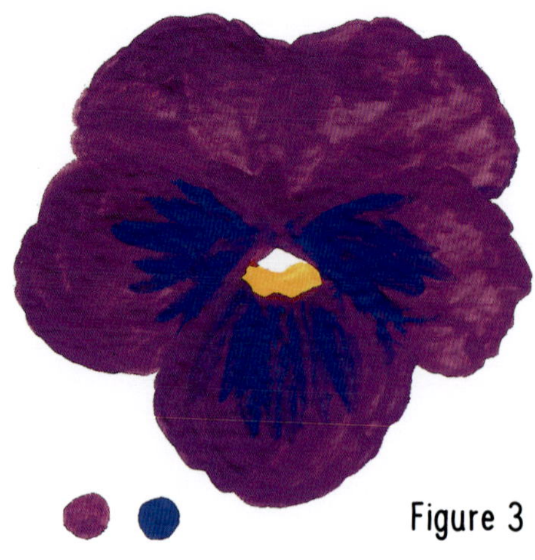

Figure 3

STEP 2

In the same way as described in step 1, paint the right-side petal and the single bottom petal of the flower. Also with the purple, fill in the shapes of the two upper, overlapping petals. Allow the painted elements to dry.

TIP: To make the shape of a petal look natural and interesting, use your brush to make its edge wavy.

STEP 3

Now let's make the flower's first layer look like a flower and not so flat (Figure 4). For this, we need to add shadows and some accents. Arm yourself with a small or medium round brush with a thin tip. First, paint the upper part of the flower center with dark yellow. Then add shadows with the tint of violet. To make the shadows look softer, use a clean and wet brush to gently blur the shadows from inside the shapes (see softening, page 12). To avoid spoiling the previously painted layer, make sure that your brush is not too wet. Let the painted layer dry completely before adding the next.

Keep working with the brush you previously used in this step. With the pastel purple shade, emphasize the edges of each petal as shown in Figure 4. Then, use the softening technique (page 12) to make the painted layer look softer. Finally, add details using pastel purple. After the painting is dry, move on to step 4.

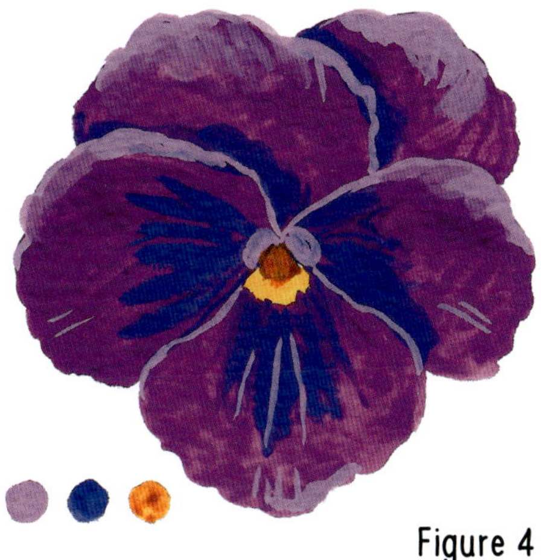

Figure 4

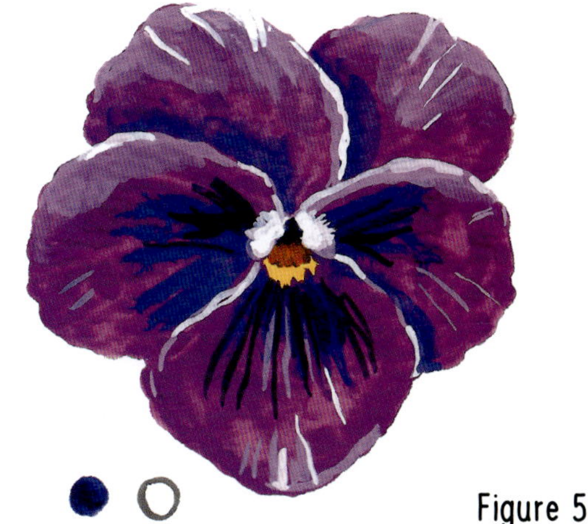

Figure 5

STEP 4

In this step, we'll add more details. Take a detail brush and use dark blue to paint details on the pansy flower. Add a few last touches of white gouache and your painting is done (Figure 5).

NOTE: The layering technique (page 11) was used in this step.

Because there is a wide range of pansy flower colors, you can paint the pansy in any other colors, not just those shown in this project. Figure 6 shows one example of how the colors can be changed. By using this method, you can experiment with colors and practice painting this beautiful flower. Moreover, you can easily add leaves and a stem to the plant or even create a floral composition featuring the pansy.

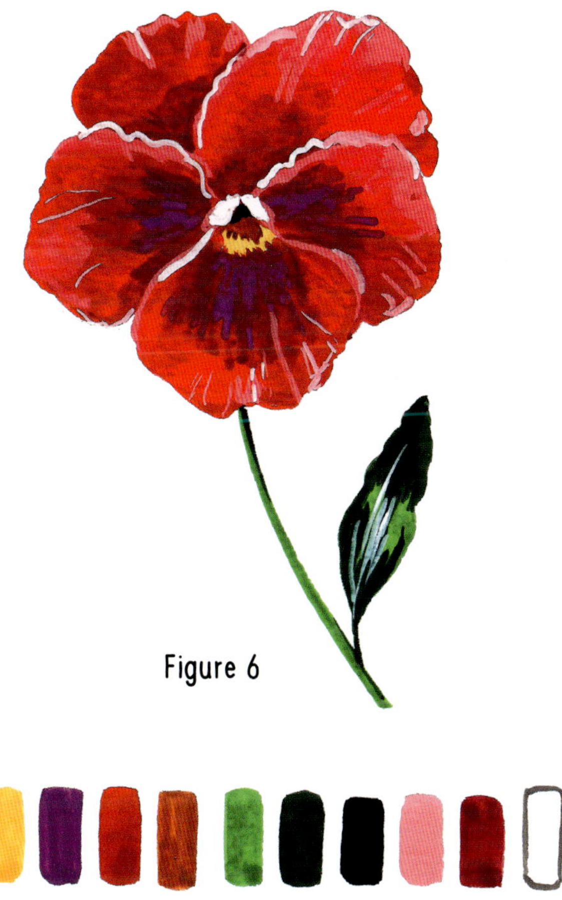

Figure 6

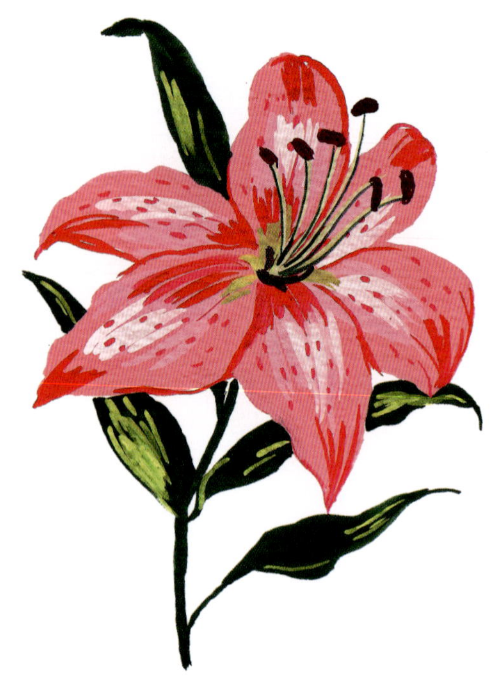

LILY

Lilies depict beauty and purity, and in this project—with the help of gouache—I will show you how to portray these flowers on paper in just a few steps. We'll paint in a realistic style, but it's still a straightforward project that everyone can paint. Now, let's begin painting step by step!

SUPPLIES

- White, black or craft paper
- Pencil and eraser
- Round brushes in different sizes
- Detail brush
- Liner brush (optional)

PROJECT COLORS

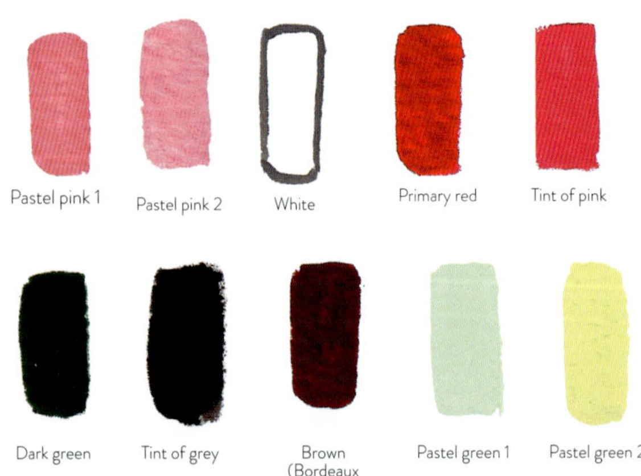

TIP: If you don't have primary red, use crimson red or any other cool tone of red.

COLOR MIXING

- Pastel pink 1 (primary red + white, proportion 1:1)
- Pastel pink 2 (primary red + white, proportion 1:2)
- Tint of pink (primary red + white, proportion 2:1)
- Dark green (permanent green + brown + ultramarine blue, proportion 4:1:1)
- Tint of grey (primary red + permanent green, proportion 1:1)
- Pastel green 1 (white + primary yellow + permanent green, proportion 4:1:1)
- Pastel green 2 (white + primary yellow + permanent green, proportion 2:3:1)

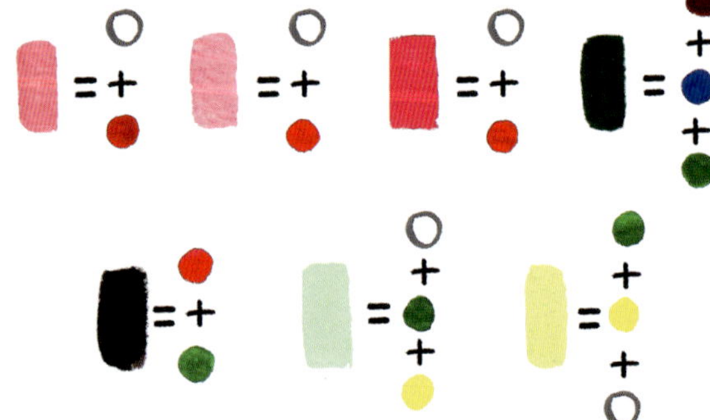

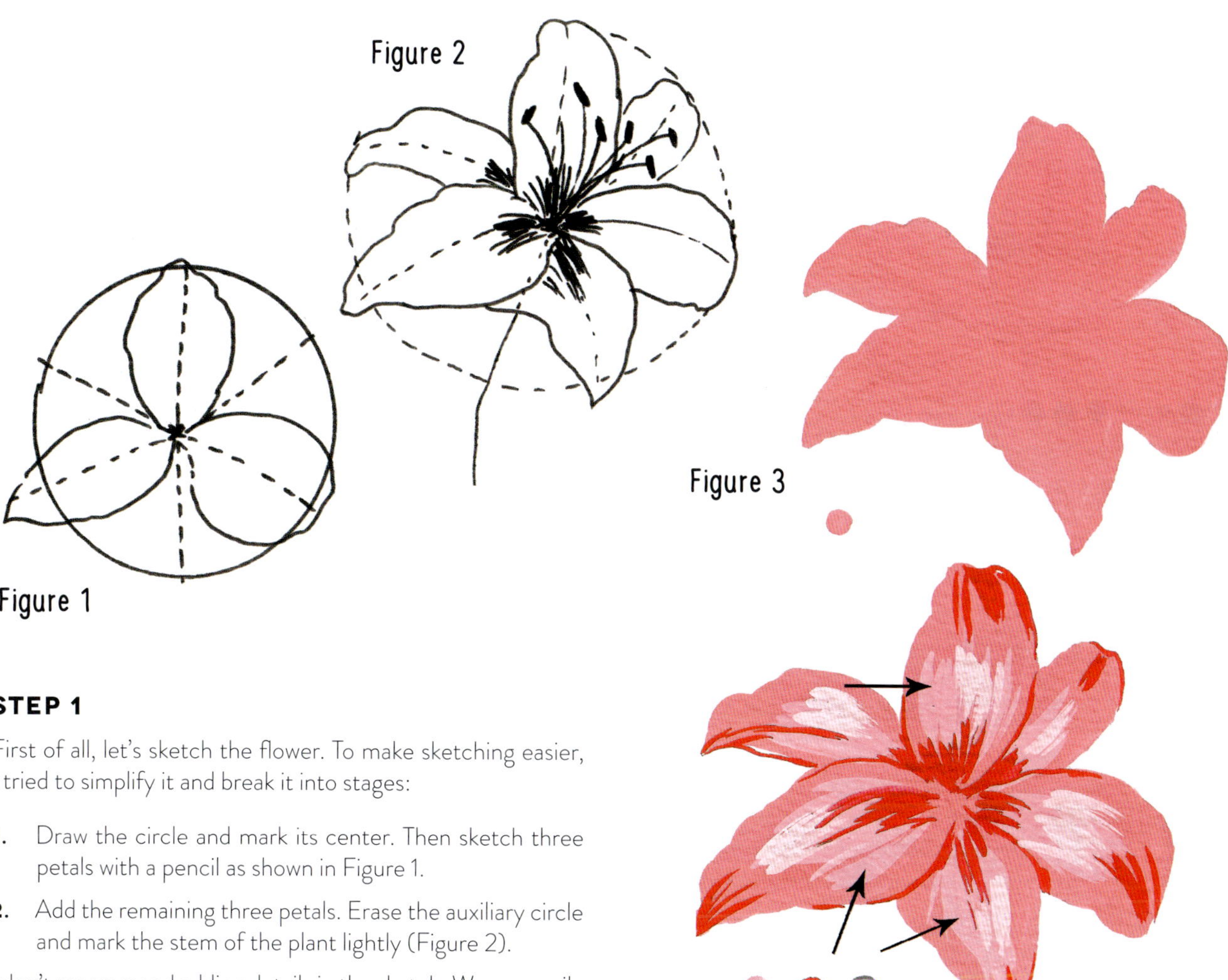

STEP 1

First of all, let's sketch the flower. To make sketching easier, I tried to simplify it and break it into stages:

1. Draw the circle and mark its center. Then sketch three petals with a pencil as shown in Figure 1.
2. Add the remaining three petals. Erase the auxiliary circle and mark the stem of the plant lightly (Figure 2).

I don't recommend adding details in the sketch. We can easily add them later with gouache.

NOTE: In this project, we will apply only the layering technique (page 11).

Once the sketch is ready, you can begin painting. Take a large round brush and fill all the petals with pastel pink 1 (Figure 3). Wait until the painted layer is completely dry before moving to the next step.

STEP 2

In this step, we will make the first layer look not so flat. Switch to a medium brush and paint the mid-tones on the center of each petal with pastel pink 2. Let it dry. Now prepare white and primary red and with the same brush, paint simplified shadows and highlights, as shown in Figure 4. Allow the painting to dry.

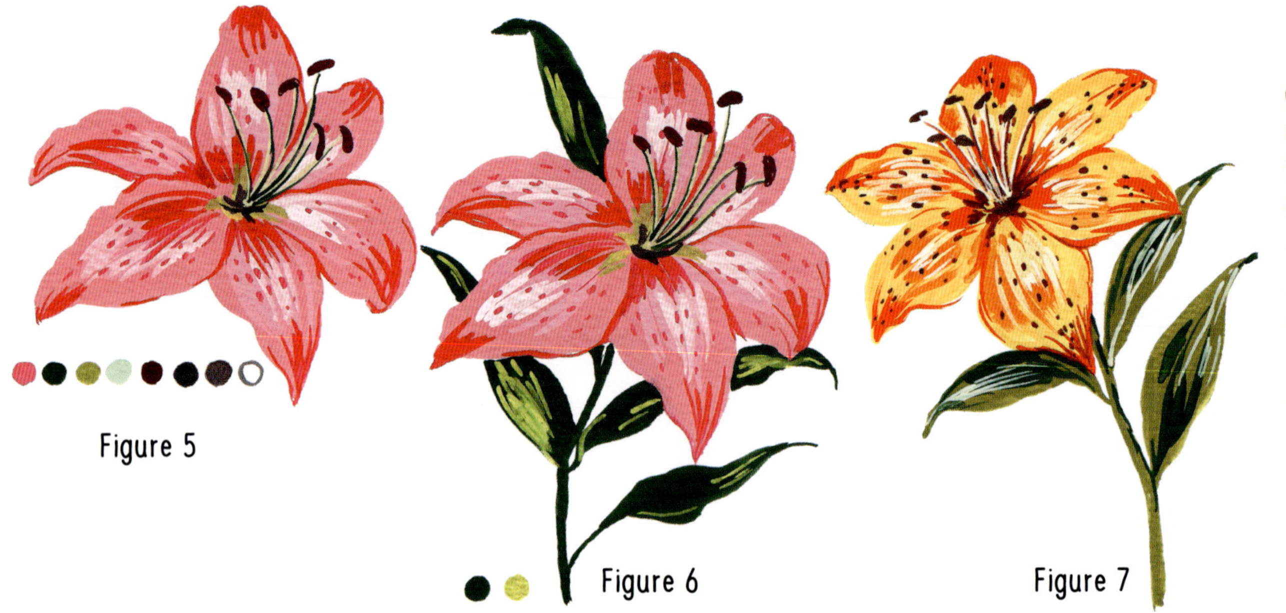

STEP 3

Now it's time to add details to the lily (Figure 5). Prepare medium-thick paint in the following shades: tint of pink, dark green, tint of grey, brown, pastel green 1 and pastel green 2. Take a detail brush and randomly add a pattern of spots on the petals in the tint of pink.

TIP: For making the spots, you can use the tip of the brush. This technique allows you to create simple and soft strokes, in just one touch (for more about brush strokes, see page 10).

Now paint the center of the flower in pastel green 2. Once it's dry, add the tint of grey. It will give even better contrast and the illusion of depth in the center. The last touch is painting the stamens and filaments of the flower. So, using your dark green, brown and pastel green 1, paint details on the petals in their corresponding colors. For this part, use the detail brush or the liner. Try to make the filaments thin. It makes the painting look neat and elegant.

STEP 4

Now let's add the stem and some leaves (Figure 6). With a large round brush, paint the base layer of leaves in dark green. Once again, let the painting dry. Now add small strokes in pastel green by using any round brush with a thin tip. Your painting is complete.

In Figure 7, you can see another example of a lily painting. I have chosen completely different colors, but this bright and sunny lily is painted using the same methods and steps as in this lesson. I've changed the angle and position of the flower slightly, but that didn't influence the principles of the lesson. I hope you enjoyed this beautiful project and that it will inspire you to paint other flowers!

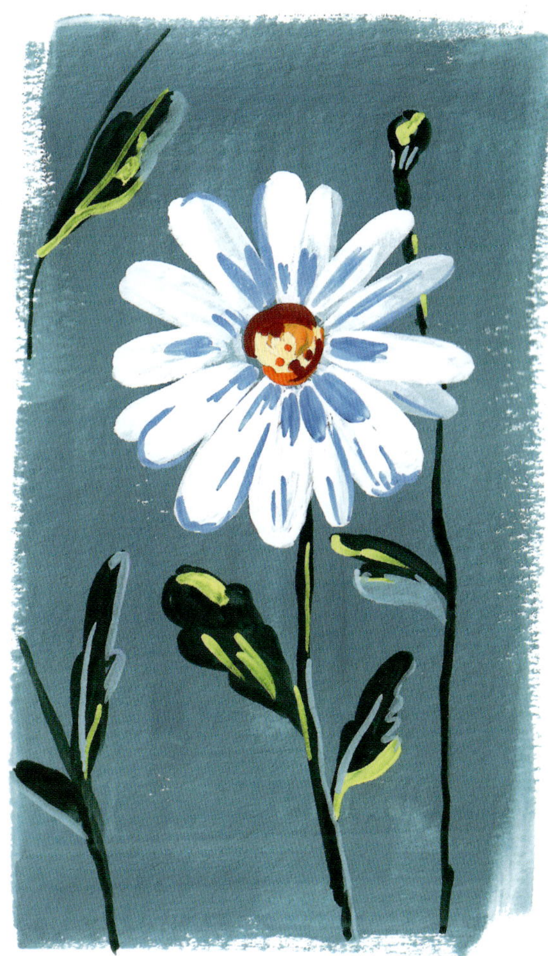

LAWN DAISY

This straightforward project gives a super pretty result and shows the power of gouache. We'll paint daisies! I have chosen a daisy because it has white petals and a very simple structure. This lesson will be a great start for painting any white flowers with gouache. You can also paint this project with children. I am sure the little ones will enjoy painting daisies.

SUPPLIES

- White paper
- Pencil and eraser (optional)
- Masking tape
- Flat brush (optional)
- Round brushes in different sizes
- Filbert brush
- Detail brush

PROJECT COLORS

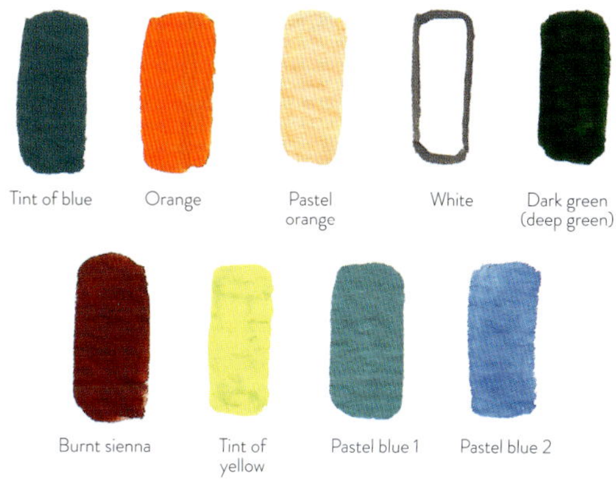

COLOR MIXING

- Tint of blue (permanent green + crimson red + primary blue + white, proportion 1:1:12:1)
- Pastel orange (orange + white, proportion 1:2)
- Tint of yellow (sap green + primary yellow, proportion 1:3)
- Pastel blue 1 (permanent green + crimson red + primary blue + white, proportion 1:1:12:3)
- Pastel blue 2 (ultramarine blue + white, proportion 1:1)

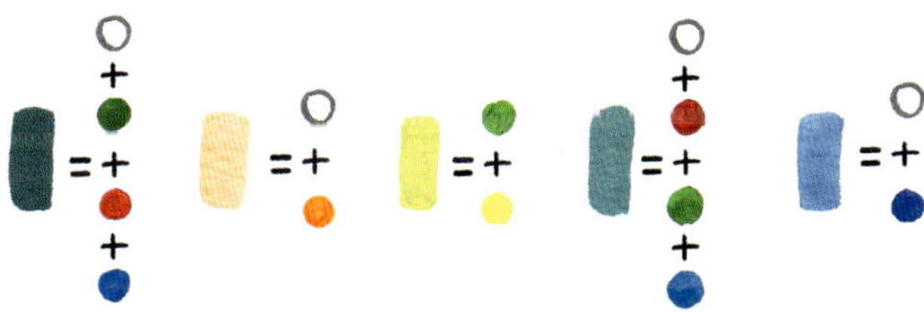

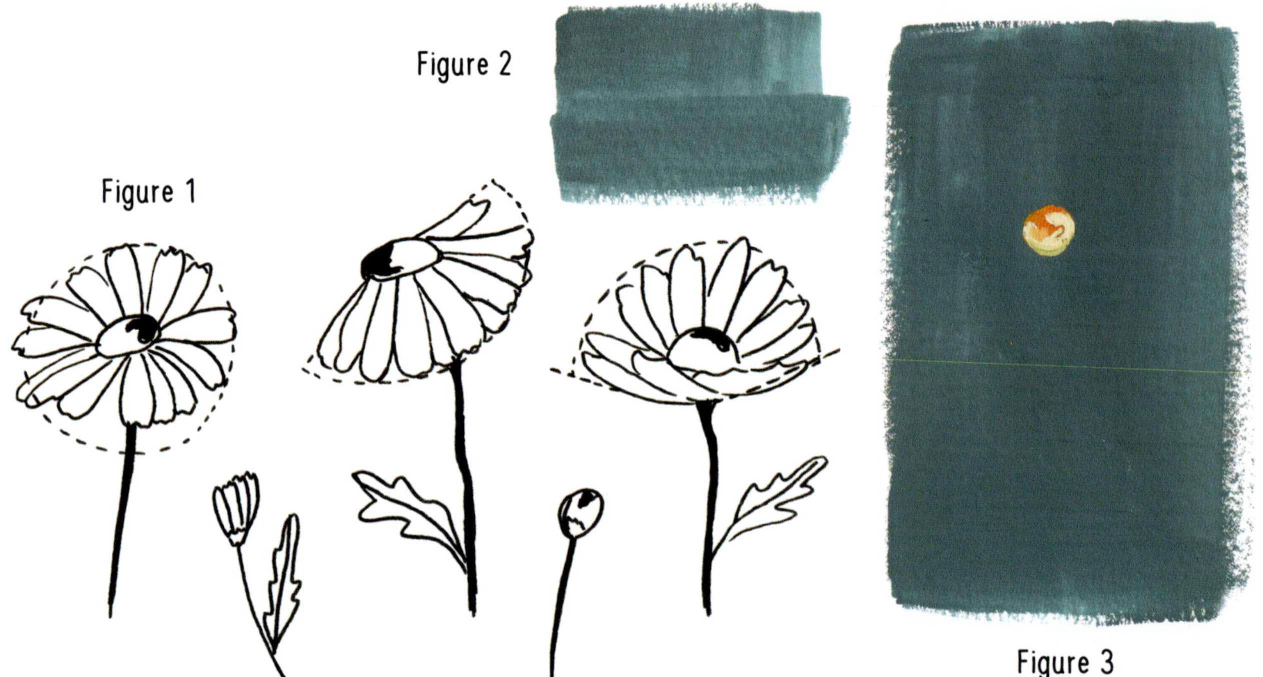

STEP 1

Let's first understand the shape of the daisy flowers.

You can see in Figure 1 two types of daisy flower shapes: the whole flower with all petals and with petals partially shown. In the whole flower, the flower fits into a circle. In the partly-shown petals, it fits into a circle sector or semicircle. Also, the flowers can be shown from different angles. Pay attention to all these nuances to better understand this object as you paint. As for the buds and leaves, I simplified forms and we will not focus on these parts in this project.

For this project, a sketch is not required. However, you need to define the area of the painting. You can either draw a vertical rectangle with a pencil and paint inside or paint in a rectangular area without any borders. I recommend the last option and using the dry-brush forming technique (page 12).

NOTE: Before starting, secure your paper with masking tape to your table or board. This will keep the paper from curving.

Paint the vertical background in the tint of blue (Figure 2). I recommend a flat brush for painting such areas, especially in dry brushing. But if you don't have it, work with a large round brush. Let the layer dry.

Take the small round brush and paint the core of the flower with orange (Figure 3). Then add a bit of the pastel orange to this area using the blending technique (page 13).

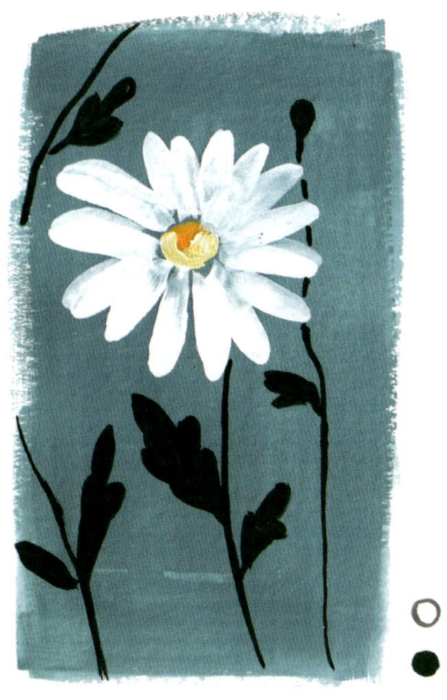

Figure 5

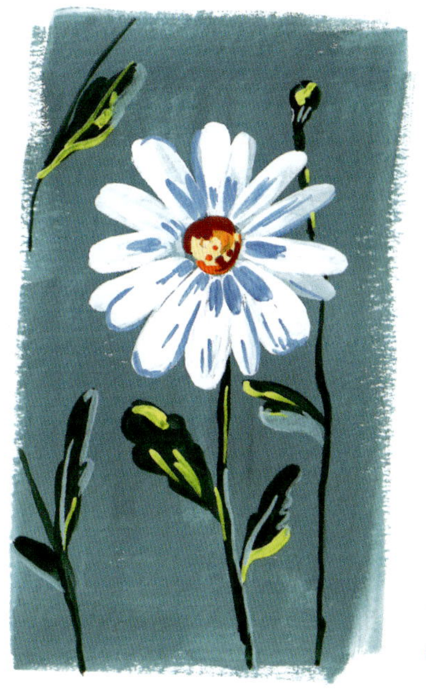

Figure 6

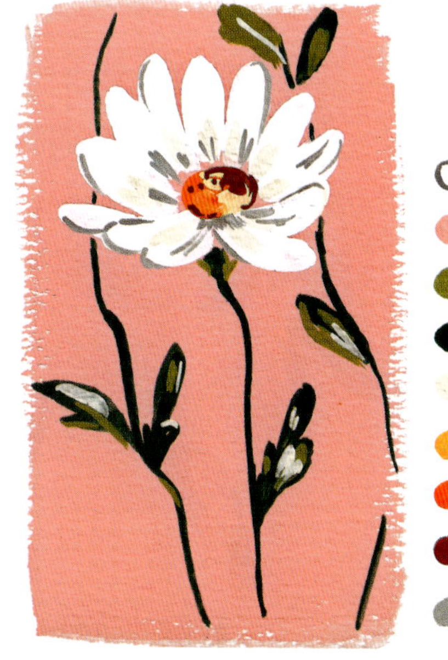

Figure 7

STEP 2

It's time to add petals. To do this, you can use a medium round brush, but a filbert brush is best for these strokes.

Figure 4 shows an example of the petal painted with the help of a filbert brush (see Brush Strokes, page 10). Press the brush, with white gouache on it, to the paper in the direction of the flower's center, then move it forward a little on the surface of the paper and lift it up. Paint all the petals one by one with this method. The petals should not be perfect or all the same. Some of them can cross over others. Let the painting dry completely.

NOTE: If, after drying, the white petals of the daisy look transparent, you can add another layer of white gouache.

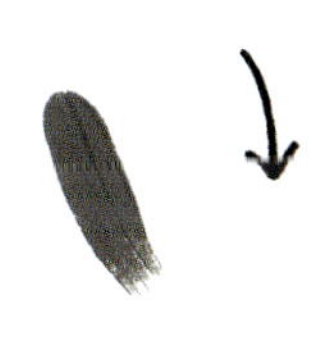

Figure 4

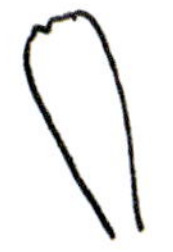

Now switch to a small round brush and paint the leaves, stems and buds of the plants in dark green (Figure 5).

STEP 3

The painting is almost finished. Take a detail brush and paint the details using the following colors: orange and burnt sienna on the center of the flower; tint of yellow and pastel blue 1 on the leaves and the stem; pastel blue 2 on the petals as shown in Figure 6. We're using the layering technique here (page 11).

Using the concepts from this lesson, try to play with background and flower position, the structure of the plant and the composition of the painting itself (Figure 7). Why not paint a few daisies at the same time? There are so many different options to experiment with, using this project as your foundation. Enjoy the process.

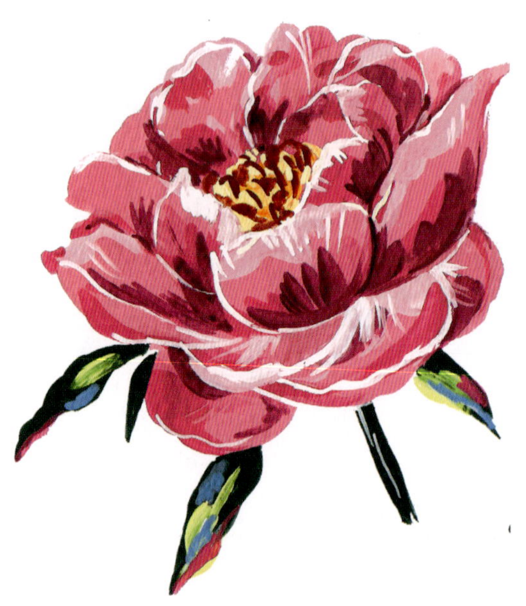

PEONY

If you asked me what my favorite flower is, I'm not sure I could pick just one. But one of my top flowers is a peony. These flowers are just incredible. They come in a range of colors, such as pink, red, white, yellow and even purple.

I can't say that painting the peony is an easy task. But gouache makes painting even such complicated objects much easier.

I have broken down the process of creating this wonderful flower so that you can re-create the work step by step.

SUPPLIES

- White, black or craft paper
- Pencil and eraser
- Round brushes in different sizes
- Filbert brush (optional)
- Detail brush

PROJECT COLORS

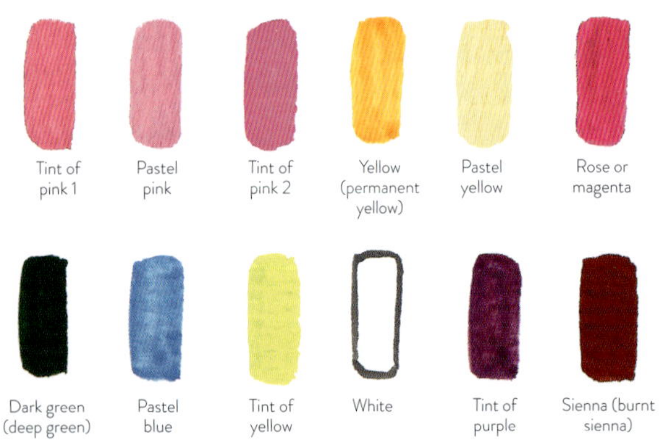

COLOR MIXING

- Tint of pink 1 (crimson red + white, proportion 1:2)
- Pastel pink (crimson red + ultramarine blue + white, proportion 2:1:5)
- Tint of pink 2 (rose + white, proportion 4:1)
- Pastel yellow (permanent yellow + white, proportion 1:3)
- Pastel blue (ultramarine blue + white, proportion 1:2)
- Tint of yellow (sap green + primary yellow, proportion 1:4)
- Tint of purple (rose + ultramarine blue, proportion 3:1)

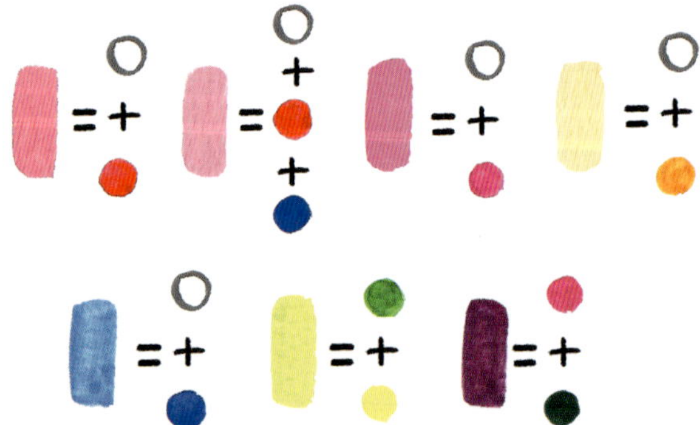

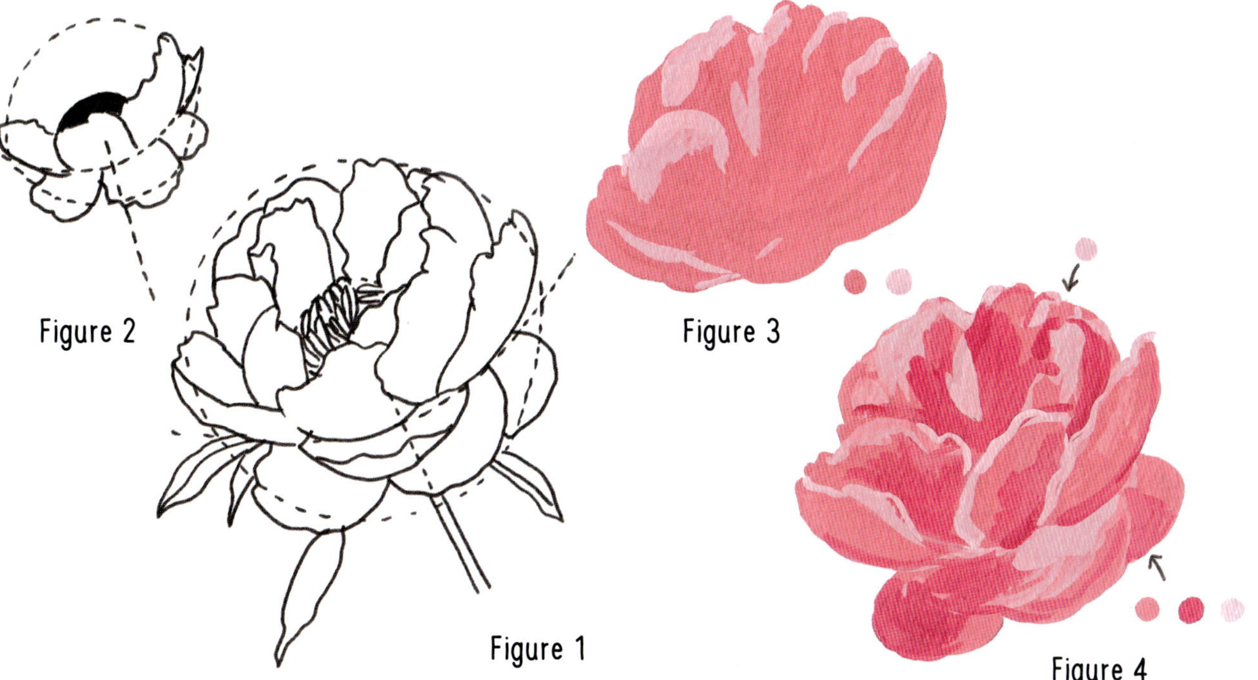

STEP 1

Before starting to paint this project, I would like to draw your attention to the structure of this pretty complicated flower. Figure 1 shows a full sketch of the peony with all petals. And in Figure 2, you can see a simplified version of it. Roughly speaking, the flower can be fitted in the circle. In the center, it has a core within numerous stamens. The petals form the flower itself.

So, to make a sketch, draw the circle and mark the stalk of the flower. Then, I advise drawing only an outline of the flower's shape and the petals in the lower part of the flower (also called guard petals). We'll add the stamens and all the details later with gouache.

Now we will begin painting the peony by filling the shape with the tint of pink 1 using a medium round brush (Figure 3). Then add pastel pink to the still-wet layer using the blending technique (page 13).

NOTE: The lower part of the petals are not painted in this step.

STEP 2

NOTE: In this and the following steps, we will use the layering technique (page 11).

With the same brush, add the petals of the lower part in the tint of pink 1. Let the painting dry completely. Now we'll make the peony look less flat. For this, take the filbert brush and paint the mid-tone areas in the tint of pink 2. These should not be symmetrical or perfect.

NOTE: If you don't have a filbert brush, you can use a round one.

Let the paint dry.

Now make the highlight areas in pastel pink, as shown in Figure 4. And once again, the highlights should not be symmetrical. Try to add them randomly in those areas where you want to emphasize the lighter parts of the petals. When the painting is dry, move on to the next step.

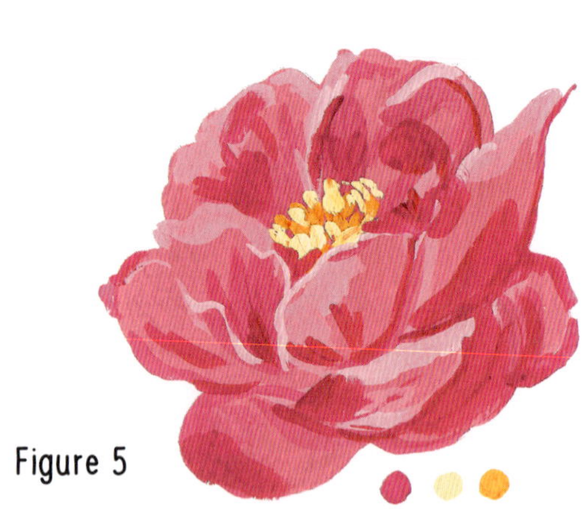

Figure 5

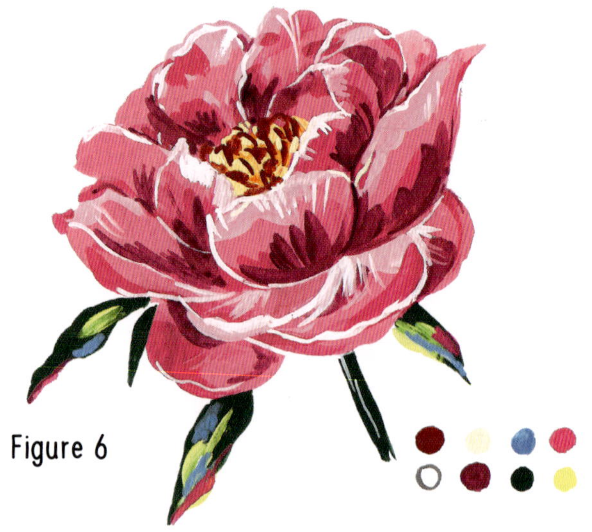

Figure 6

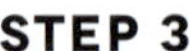

STEP 3

Arm yourself with a small round brush and paint the peony stamens first in yellow and then pastel yellow. Use the blending technique (page 13) to achieve a smooth effect.

Allow the painting to dry.

Now switch to a medium round brush and add the rose color, as shown in Figure 5. This brings an even deeper, 3D effect to our peony painting. After the freshly painted layer dries, go on to the last step.

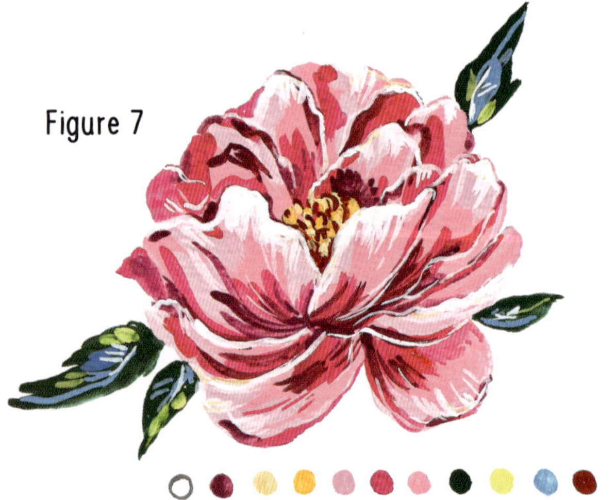

Figure 7

STEP 4

Finally, we get to the last step (Figure 6). We'll use the layering technique (page 11) at this stage as well.

First of all, let's paint the leaves and stalk of the plant. Because the flower takes the main role, I don't focus on painting leaves and the stalk in this project. But still, some greenery makes the painting fresher and more harmonious. Take a medium round brush and paint the stalk and leaves in dark green. Once the layer has dried, add some details in pastel blue, the tint of yellow and rose.

It's time to add more details. Using a detail brush, paint highlights in pastel yellow and white. Now add the shadows in the tint of purple. For the last touch, paint some details on the center of the flower with sienna. Let the painting dry completely.

It's important not to overdo the details. Less is more here, but for this project it is important to create contrasts and 3D effects.

Look at Figure 7. It is very similar to the work in this project. I just changed the colors of the flower and leaves slightly, and the petals are also in different locations. As I mentioned, the peony is not easy to paint, but practicing this lesson will help you accomplish your goals.

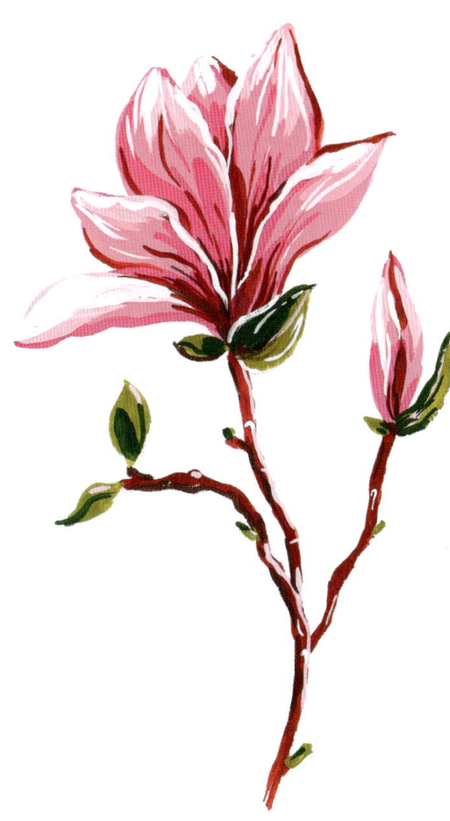

BRANCH OF MAGNOLIA

The blossoming of the magnolia trees is one of the most incredible things I have seen in my life. The flowers and buds are so big and beautiful. These trees in bloom look like they were plucked from a fairy tale. And I think that gouache is the perfect medium to portray this beauty and tenderness on paper. Let's get started.

SUPPLIES

- White, craft or black paper
- Pencil and eraser
- Large filbert brush
- Round brushes in different sizes
- Detail brush

NOTE: I highly recommend painting this project on thick craft paper, as this tone of paper will make the pastel pink and white tints of the magnolia flowers pop.

COLOR MIXING

- Tint of pink 1 (rose + white, proportion 4:1)
- Tint of pink 2 (rose + white, proportion 8:1)
- Tint of pink 3 (burnt sienna + rose, proportion 1:2)
- Tint of green (green + yellow ochre, proportion 1:1)
- Pastel pink (rose + white, proportion 1:3)

TIP: If you don't have a rose tint of gouache paint, use any tint of red with a cool tone, such as magenta or crimson red.

PROJECT COLORS

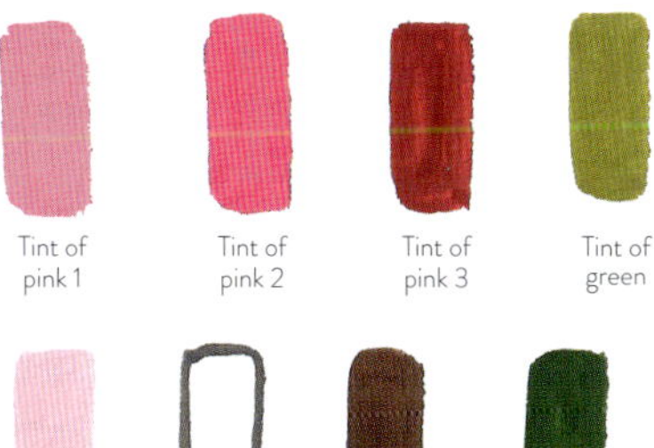

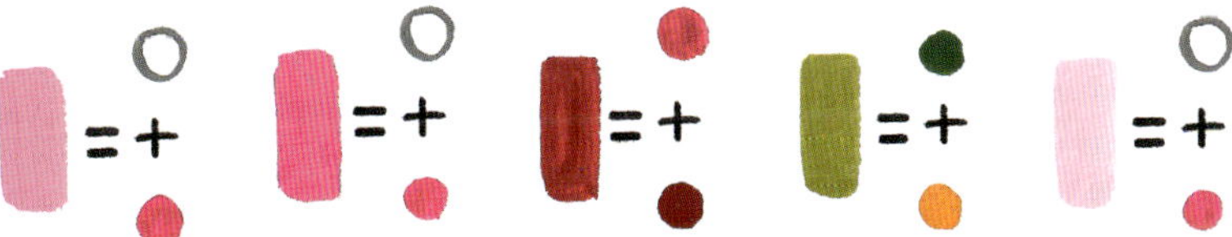

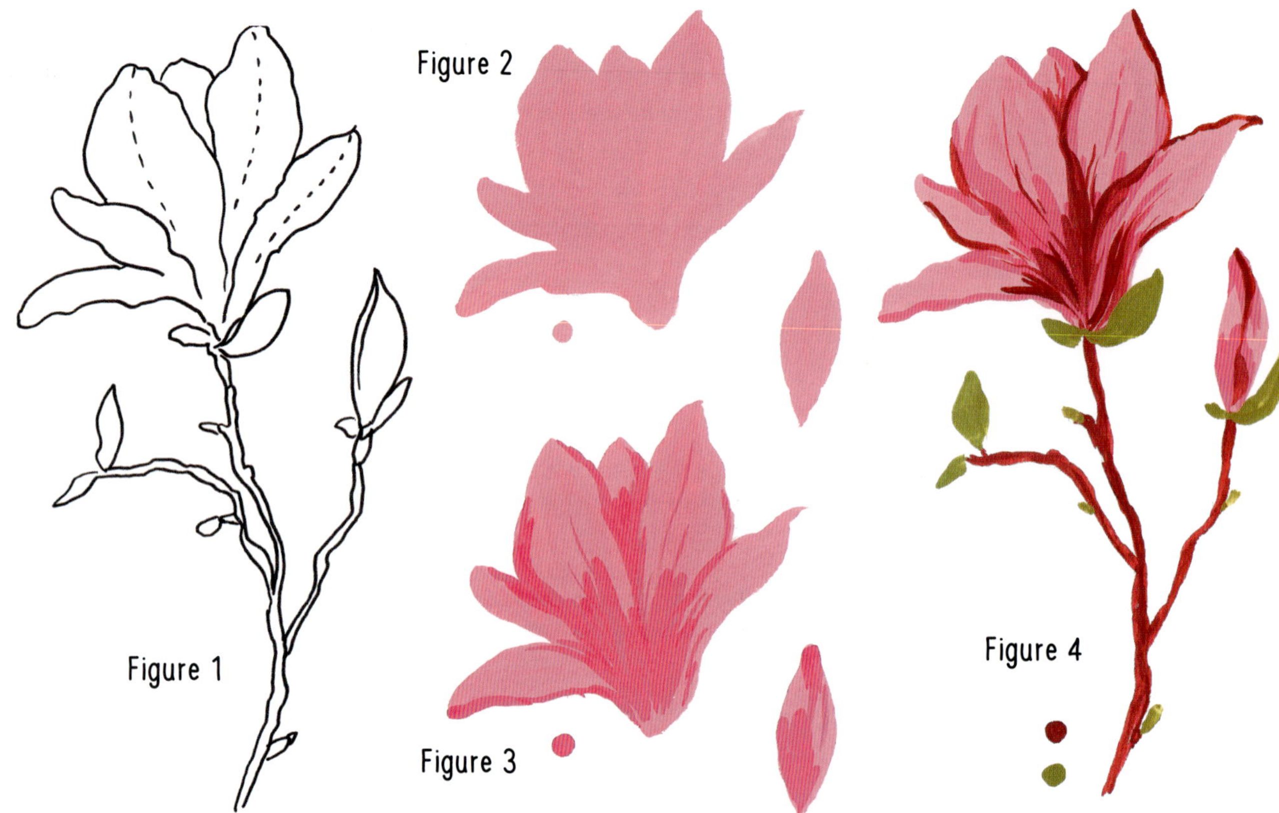

STEP 1

Start by making a light sketch of the flowery branch following the drawing outlines in Figure 1. Once the sketch is ready, move on to the painting itself.

Using the filbert brush, paint the flower and the bud in the tint of pink 1, as shown in Figure 2. Allow the layer to dry (see layering technique, page 11).

STEP 2

Let's make the flowers more realistic (Figure 3). For this, add the layer of shadows in the tint of pink 2. Use a medium round brush for painting bigger areas and a detail brush for some single strokes. Once again, allow the freshly painted layer to dry.

STEP 3

In this step, we'll combine the composition. Take a small round brush and add the branches in the tint of pink 3, according to Figure 4. Then, with the same color, paint deep shadows on the flowers. I advise you to follow Figure 4 for adding these shadows, at least if this is your first time painting the magnolia.

Let the painted layer dry completely.

Now you can paint the leaves and some green details in the tint of green. Use a round brush in the size easiest for you. For the big leaves, I recommend using the filbert brush. Go on to the final step once the painting is dry.

STEP 4

After all this work, we need to add the details to complete the painting (Figure 5). During this step, we'll use the layering technique, so make sure that your previous layer is dry before adding the next one. Prepare the following shades: pastel pink, white, brown and green. Use the detail brush or a small round brush, depending on the brush stroke you need.

The petals of the magnolia flower can be colored differently. The project flowers have a transition from white to deep pink at the bottom. So, first of all, paint the layer in pastel pink in the upper petals. Once they dry, add the details in white gouache. And finally, make accents at the bottom of the flower in brown.

Now let's figure out the branches and leaves. First, add additional details in green. Let everything dry completely and then paint the rest of the details in their corresponding colors: brown, pastel pink and white.

Practice this lesson to create more beautiful variations of the magnolia branch. The very first version I advise painting is the branch on craft paper or a painted background. In Figure 6, you can see such an example. It is much easier to execute a painting like this on craft paper, because you can sketch it before painting.

NOTE: If you use a craft paper, it should be pretty thick. If it's thin paper, apply as thick a paint consistency as possible, with a minimal amount of water.

For making the painting with a painted background, you need to paint the background before you start step 1 and skip the sketching stage. After this, you can proceed with the steps of the lesson. Of course, you can also play with colors and compositions to create more variations. Enjoy the process of painting the gorgeous magnolia!

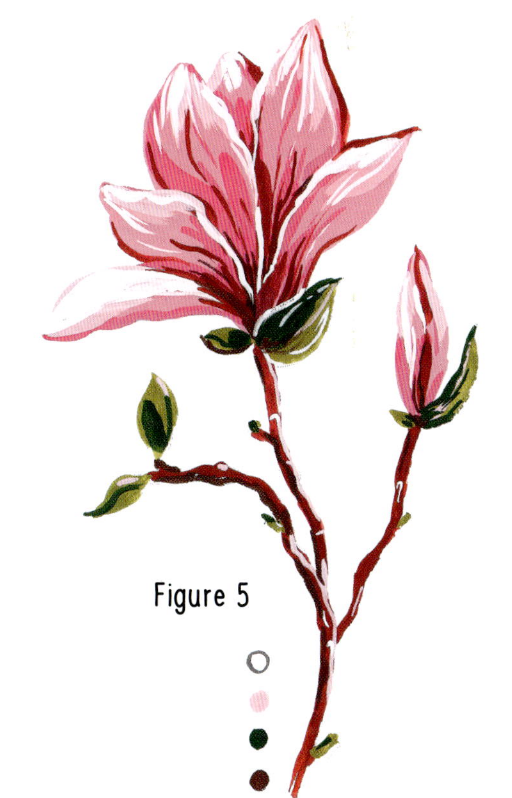

Figure 5

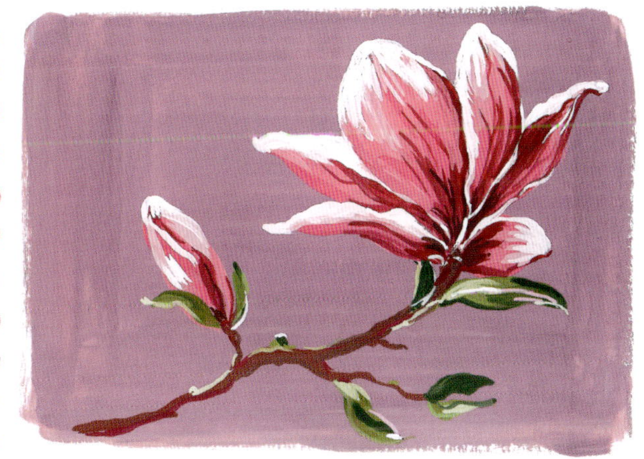

Figure 6

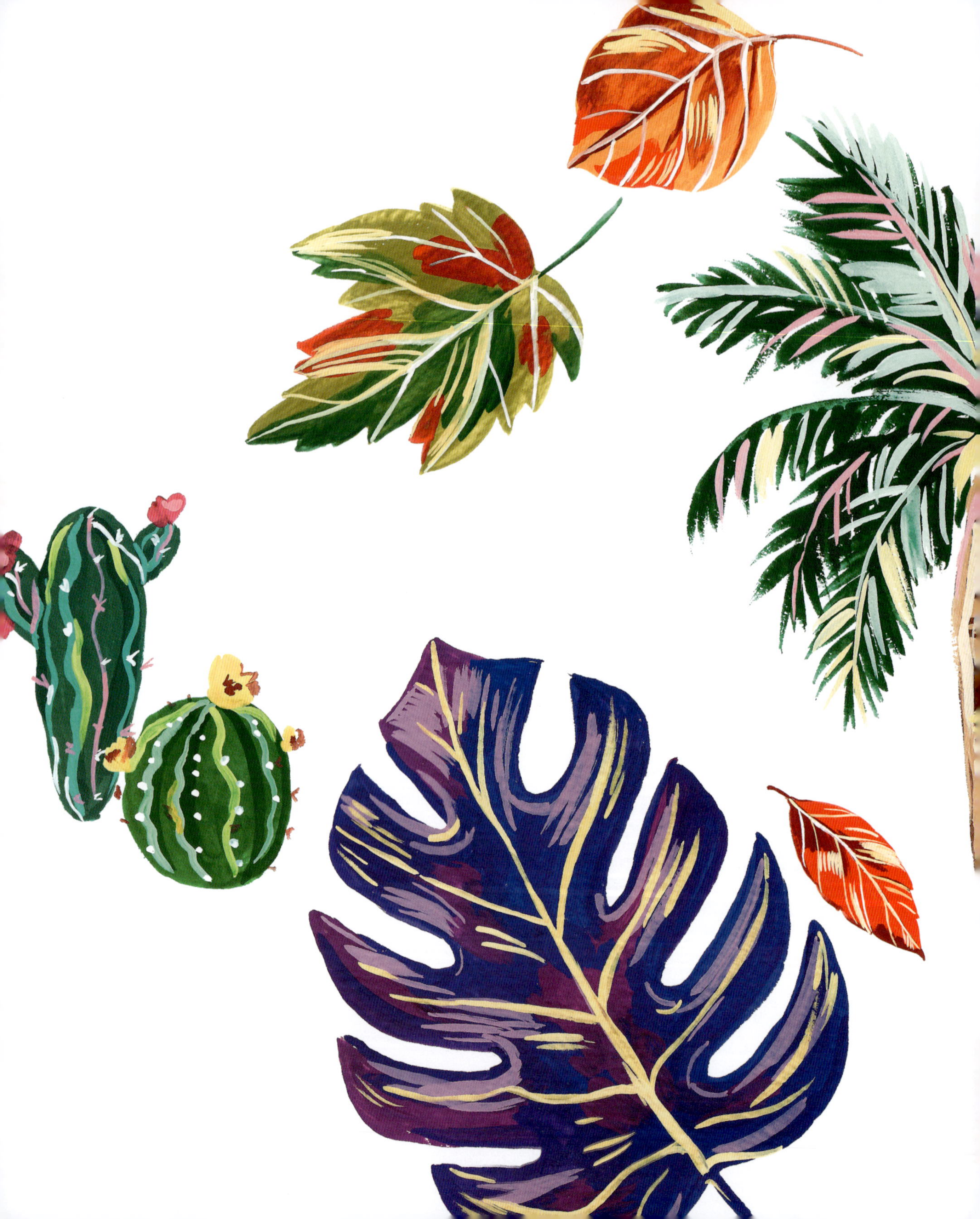

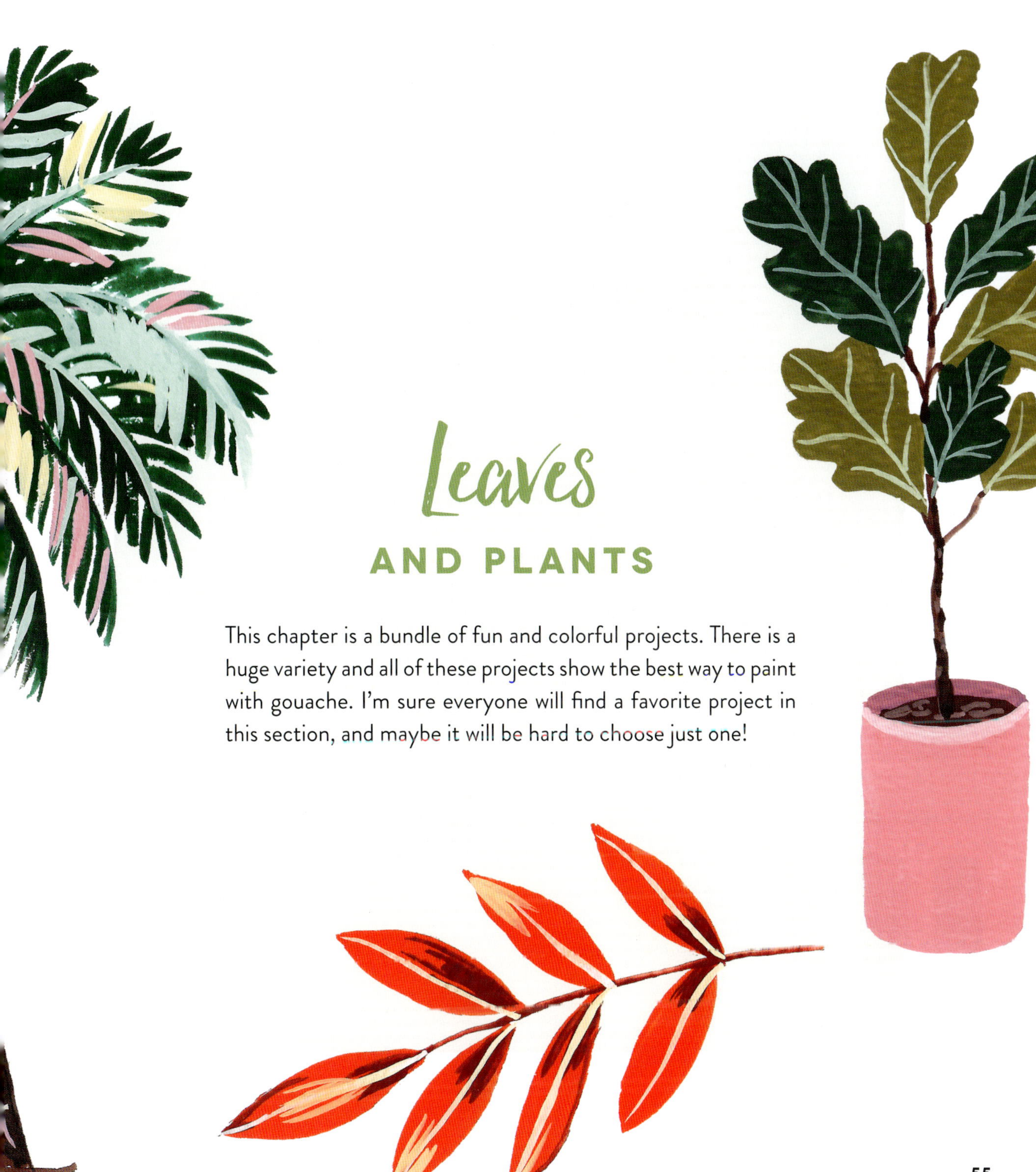

Leaves AND PLANTS

This chapter is a bundle of fun and colorful projects. There is a huge variety and all of these projects show the best way to paint with gouache. I'm sure everyone will find a favorite project in this section, and maybe it will be hard to choose just one!

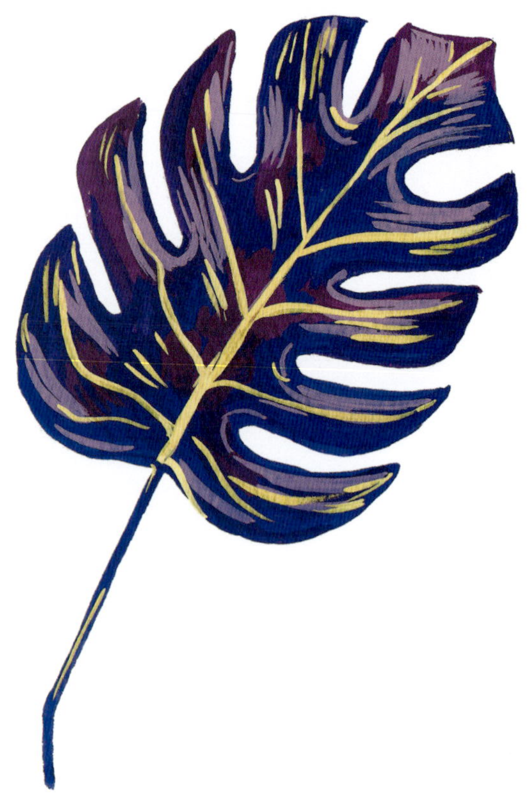

VIVID MONSTERA

In this lesson, you will learn how to paint a colorful and fancy monstera. The monstera is a trendy object to paint. Even if you have already been painting this kind of plant, I will surprise you with how fun it can be using gouache. This project is very simple and easy for anyone to create. It's also a great exercise to practice creating a clear contrast with gouache.

Let's begin!

SUPPLIES

- White or craft paper
- Pencil and eraser
- Round brushes in different sizes
- Detail brush

PROJECT COLORS

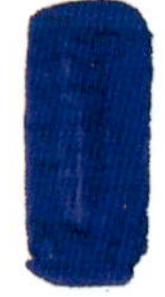
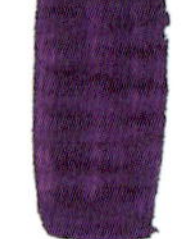
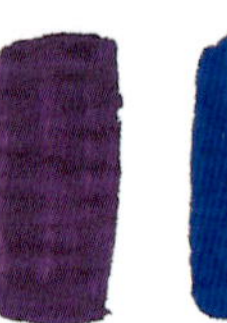
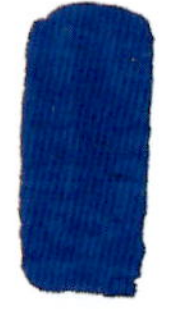
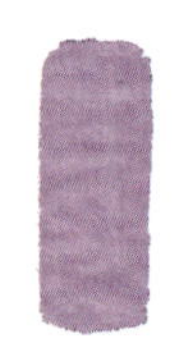
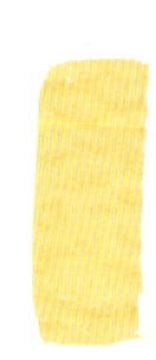

Tint of purple | Purple (lilac) | Ultramarine blue | Pastel purple | Pastel yellow

COLOR MIXING

- Tint of purple (lilac + ultramarine blue, proportion 1:1)
- Pastel purple (lilac + white, proportion 1:2)
- Pastel yellow (permanent yellow + white, proportion 1:2)

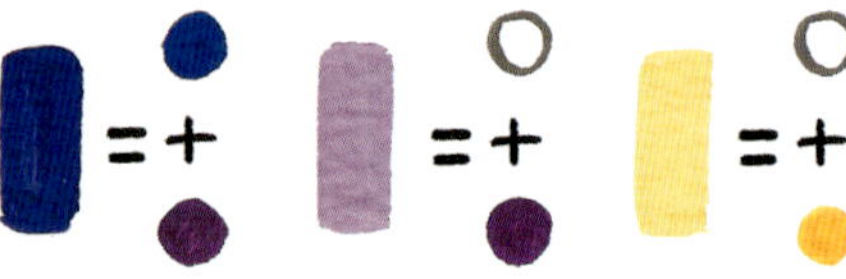

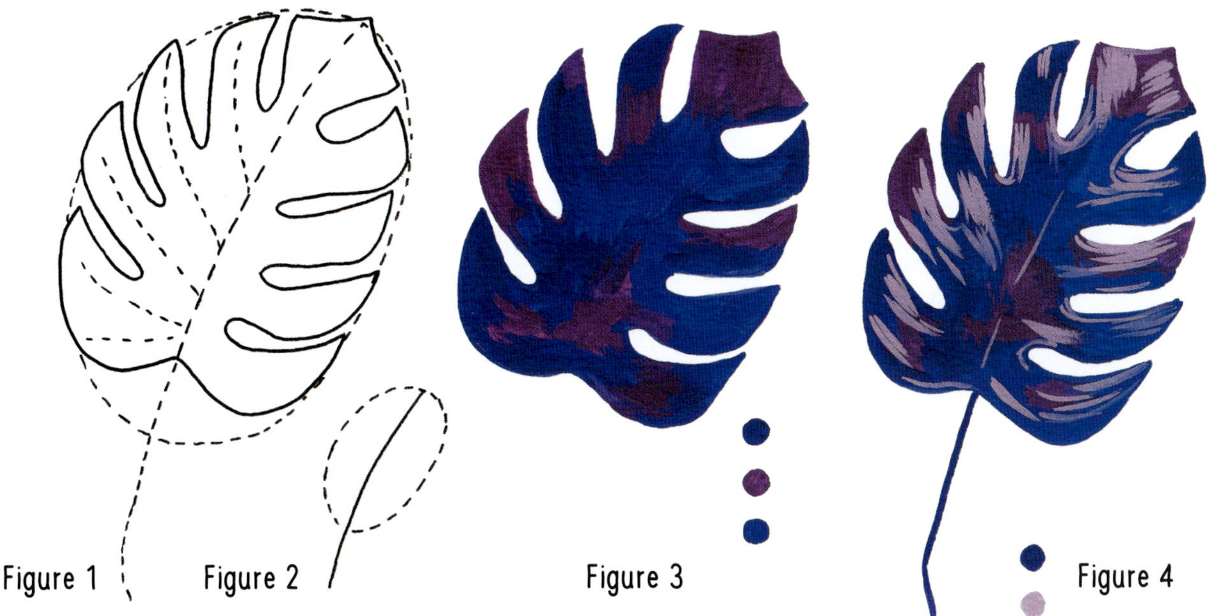

STEP 1

To paint this beautiful leaf, you have to first explore the shape of the monstera. There are different shapes of monstera leaves. I've chosen the one shown in Figure 1. You can see that if we simplify it, it fits into an oval. So, let's start by making a light pencil sketch of the oval and then turn it into the final leaf shape following Figure 2.

Prepare paint in the following shades: tint of purple, purple and ultramarine blue. Use these colors to fill in the monstera using the direct blending technique (page 11) (Figure 3).

For this step, you can use any round brush with a thin tip. However, I recommend choosing the brush depending on the size of the paper you're using. You can also switch brushes during the process. Work carefully, especially near the edges. This is very delicate work and requires your full attention. When the painting is dry, move on to the next step.

STEP 2

Paint the stem of the leaf in the tint of purple by using a small round brush.

TIP: I recommend painting the stem with a thin line and then add thickness gradually.

Now with the same brush, add another layer in pastel purple, as shown in Figure 4. Pay attention to the contrast between the base layer and this pastel tint. This is a great example of how easy and beautiful it can be to create a contrast by using gouache (see Color Contrast with Gouache, page 8).

Let the work dry completely, then move on to the last step.

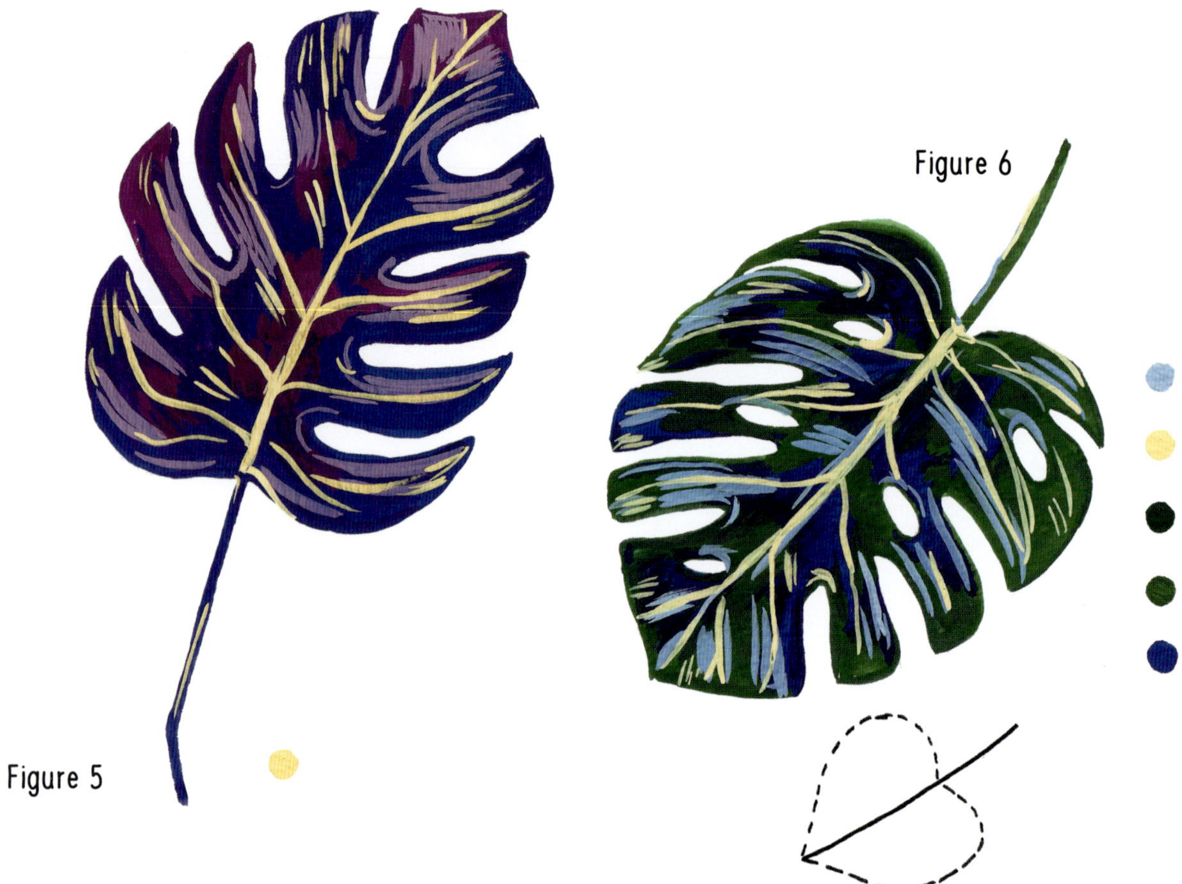

STEP 3

The last step will bring some color vibes to the painting that will make it look more interesting (Figure 5). So let's do it. Take a detail brush and with pastel yellow, paint the veins and details of the monstera leaf. We are using the layering technique (page 11). And your work is done!

As you can see, the painting looks elegant and impressive. You can also experiment with colors for this project. See the example shown in Figure 6. Selecting different shades and experimenting with the leaf shape is not only excellent practice but also a fun process. Don't be afraid to use the most unrealistic colors.

I hope you enjoyed this lesson and that my instructions and tricks allow you to create many beautiful and colorful paintings of leaves.

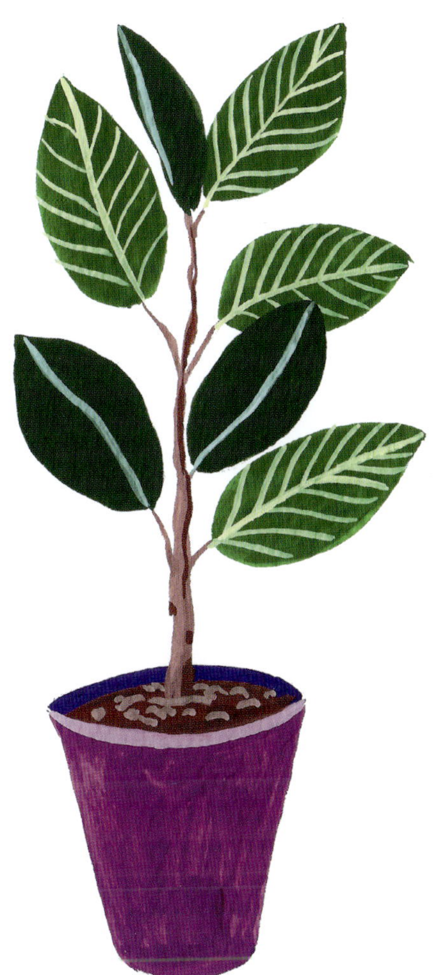

POTTED FICUS

Let's paint a potted houseplant. We'll use a super-fun illustrative style that, in this case, will mean the simplification of all the shapes and colors. Therefore, this is a simple and easy painting project. I've chosen a ficus for this project because I own one and I find it lovely and inspiring. I think, in this style—and with gouache—it will look absolutely amazing.

So, prepare your brushes and gouache and let's begin!

SUPPLIES

- White, craft or black paper
- Pencil and eraser
- Round brushes in different sizes
- Liner (size 1 or 2)

COLOR MIXING

- Tint of purple (lilac + Prussian blue, proportion 2:1)
- Tint of brown (burnt umber + Bordeaux red, proportion 1:1)
- Pastel brown (burnt umber + Bordeaux red + white, proportion 1:1:1)
- Pastel purple (lilac + white, proportion 1:2)
- Pastel green 1 (permanent green + yellow + white, proportion 1:2:6)
- Pastel green 2 (seaweed + white, proportion 1:8)

PROJECT COLORS

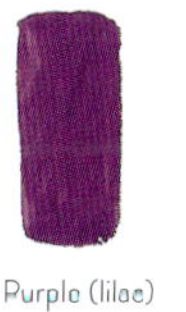
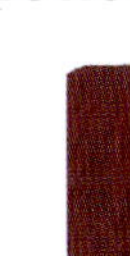
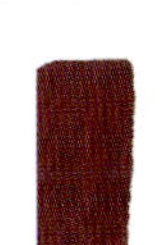
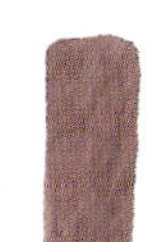
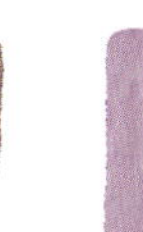
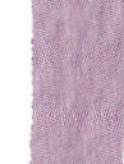

Purple (lilac) Tint of purple Tint of brown Pastel brown Pastel purple

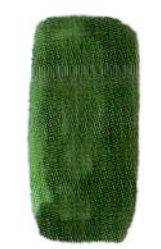
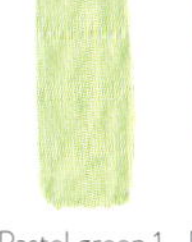
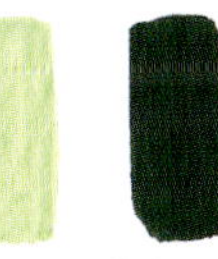
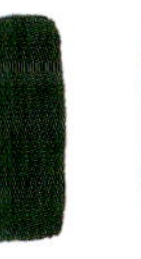

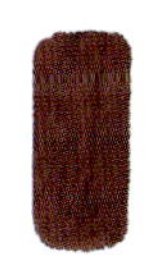

Permanent green Pastel green 1 Dark green (seaweed) Pastel green 2 Brown (burnt umber)

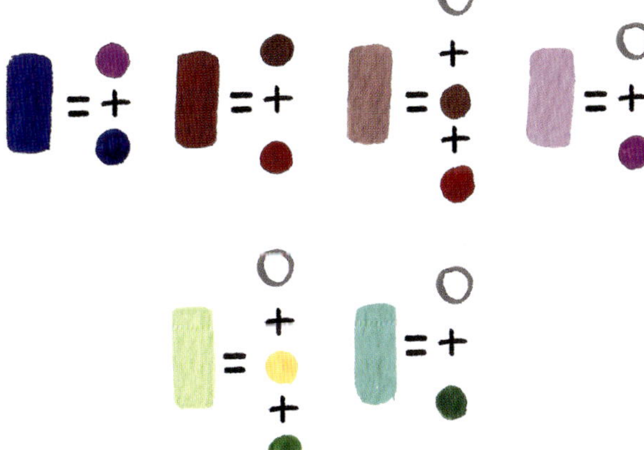

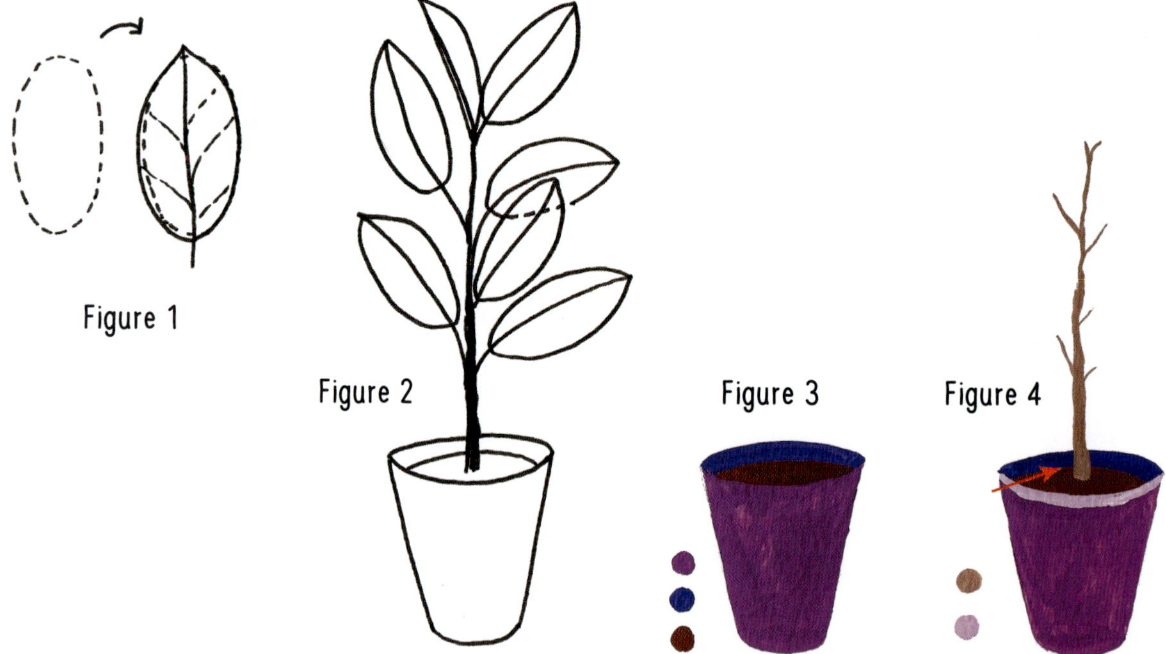

STEP 1

Before you start working with the gouache, pay attention to Figure 1, which shows a simple technique for drawing a single leaf of the plant. Draw the oval first, then add a thin tip at the front end. In Figure 2, you can see the entire sketch of the ficus. Sketch with a pencil, referring to Figure 2.

NOTE: In this project, all steps will be done using only the layering technique (page 11).

Prepare purple, the tint of purple and the tint of brown and, using a small round brush, paint all parts of the pot one by one, as in Figure 3. When the painting is dry, move on to the next step.

STEP 2

Now add a line in pastel purple onto the pot. This will give the picture more contrast and make it interesting. For this line, you can keep working with the same small round brush or use a liner. Using the small round brush, paint the trunk as well as the stems in pastel brown, as shown in Figure 4.

NOTE: To make the trunk visible on a pretty dark pot's base, it should be painted in a pastel shade. This is a great example of contrast in gouache painting (page 8).

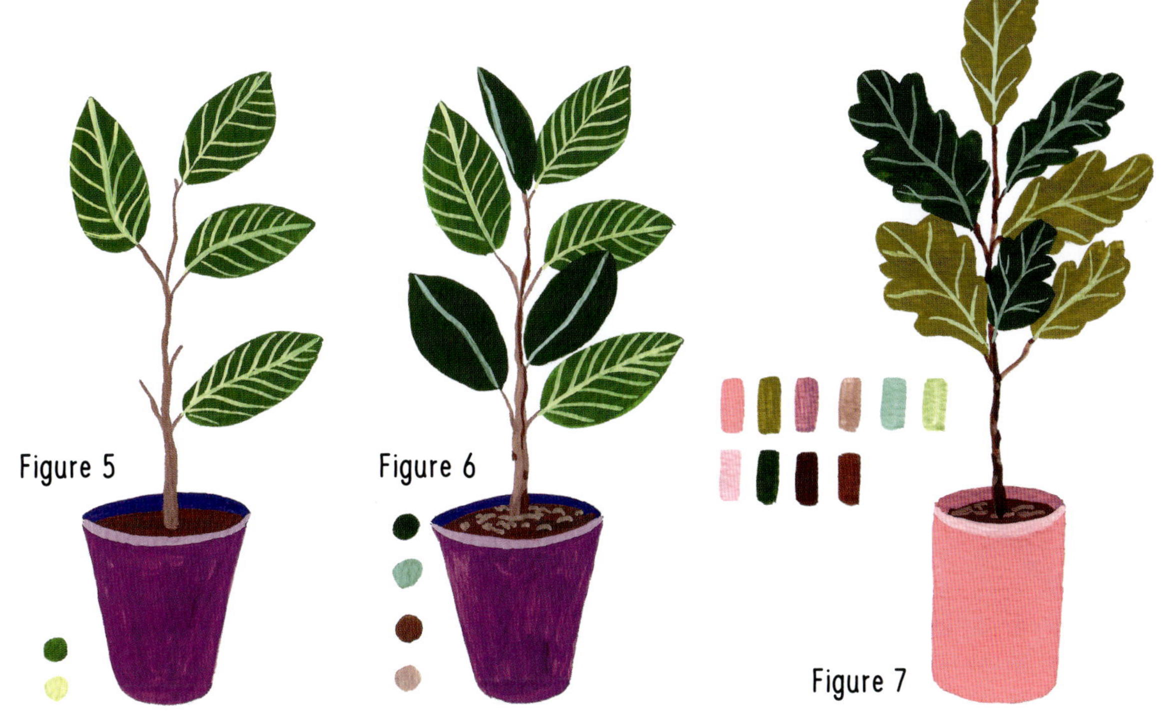

STEP 3

As I mentioned before, this project is painted in an illustrative style. This means that all the details and shapes are simplified. Nevertheless, I tried to make the illustration look interesting. For this, I decided in advance to use two types of ficus leaves, both the front and inner parts of the leaves.

With a medium round brush, paint the first type of leaves in permanent green, with a medium round brush. Once the leaves are dry, it's time to add details on the leaves. Paint some veins in pastel green 1, with the help of a liner brush (Figure 5).

STEP 4

Now paint the darker leaves using a medium round brush and the dark green color. Take a liner and paint veins on the dark leaves in pastel green 2. The final step is adding small details to the potted plant with brown and pastel brown, as shown in Figure 6.

Take a look at the contrasting details on the leaves themselves. At the same time, the darker and lighter leaves provide a nice contrast as well. So although the project is pretty simple, it looks interesting and cute.

With the principles in this lesson, you can also create different potted indoor plant projects. To do this, change the leaves' shapes and colors and experiment with the pot. I advise you to choose very bright colors for the pot to bring positive vibes to your illustration. Also, try to change the pot's shape. There are a lot of options you can play with. But remember that gouache requires consistency and patience.

Figure 7 shows a picture painted using this project's methods, but I changed the colors and shape of the pot, as well as of the leaves. Don't be afraid to be creative. Apply what you learned in this little painting to more complicated illustrations. All you need to do is try.

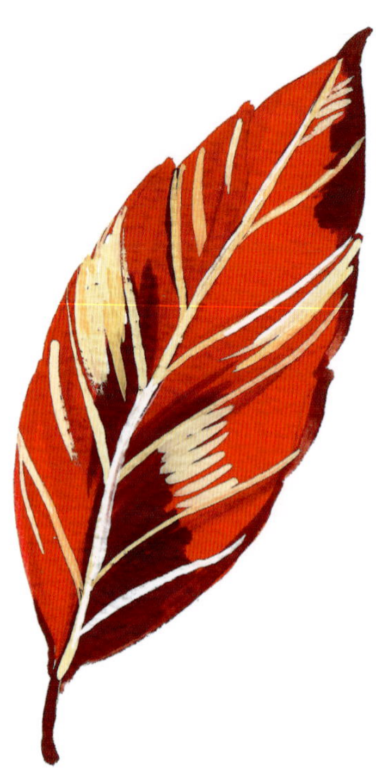

FALL LEAF

In autumn, there is nothing more inspiring than colorful fall leaves. Their shapes and hues are so varied. And I couldn't miss the chance to show you how to paint such a leaf with gouache.

This project is super easy and does not require any specific skills or knowledge, and you can even do it with kids or someone who has never painted. So let's start our creative journey!

SUPPLIES

- White or black paper (craft paper can also work for some color combinations)
- Pencil and eraser
- Round brushes in different sizes
- Detail brush

PROJECT COLORS

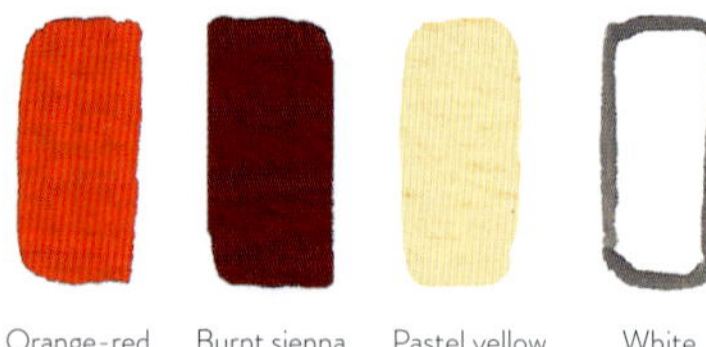

COLOR MIXING

- Orange-red (permanent yellow + scarlet red, proportion 1:1)
- Pastel yellow (permanent yellow + white, proportion 1:2)

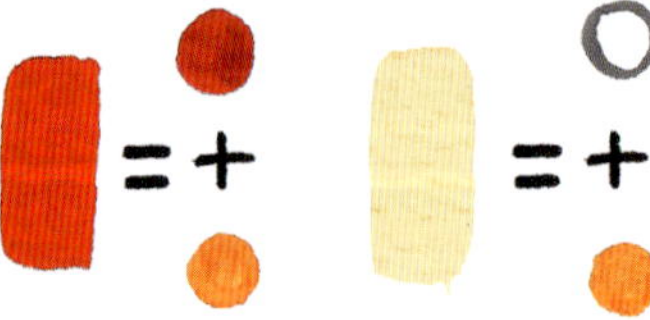

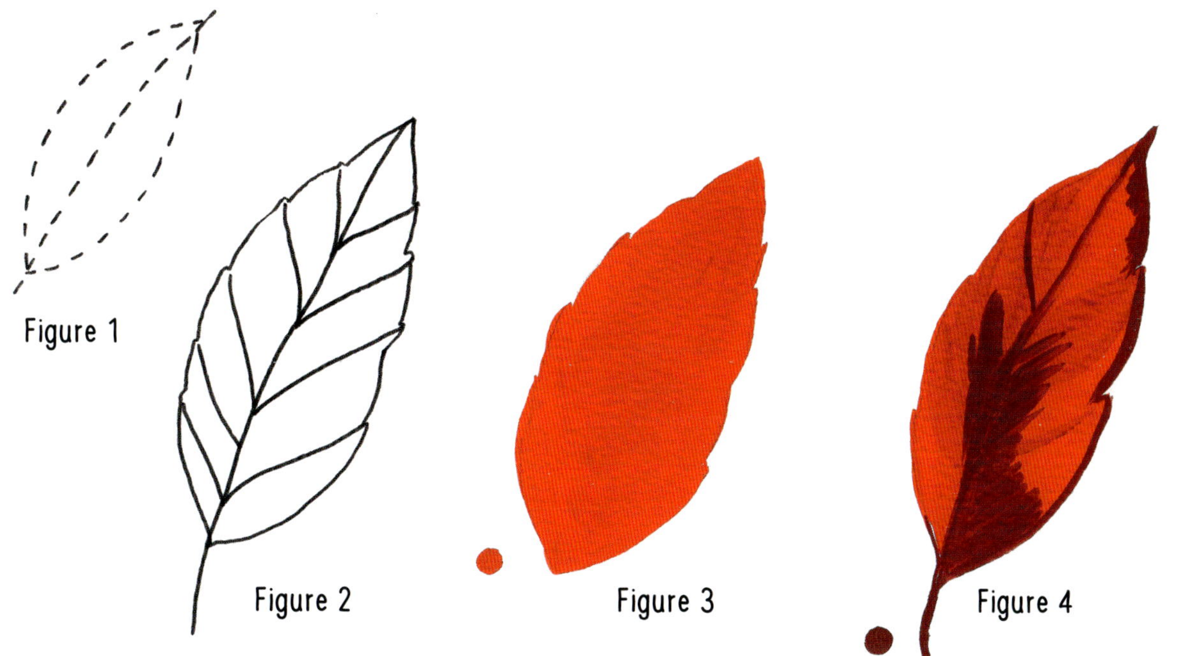

STEP 1

With a pencil, draw a light sketch of the simple leaf shown in Figure 1 and Figure 2. Once the sketch is ready, you can begin the painting process.

NOTE: In this project, we will apply only the layering technique (page 11).

First, paint the base of the leaf with orange-red (Figure 3). Use a big round brush with a thin tip for this purpose. Let the layer dry.

STEP 2

You could skip this step and go directly to the final stage, but for even deeper colors on the leaf, I recommend adding one more layer of a darker color (burnt sienna). So, with the same brush, paint the layer in burnt sienna (Figure 4). And of course, don't forget to add the stalk to the leaf in the same color.

Allow the layer to dry completely.

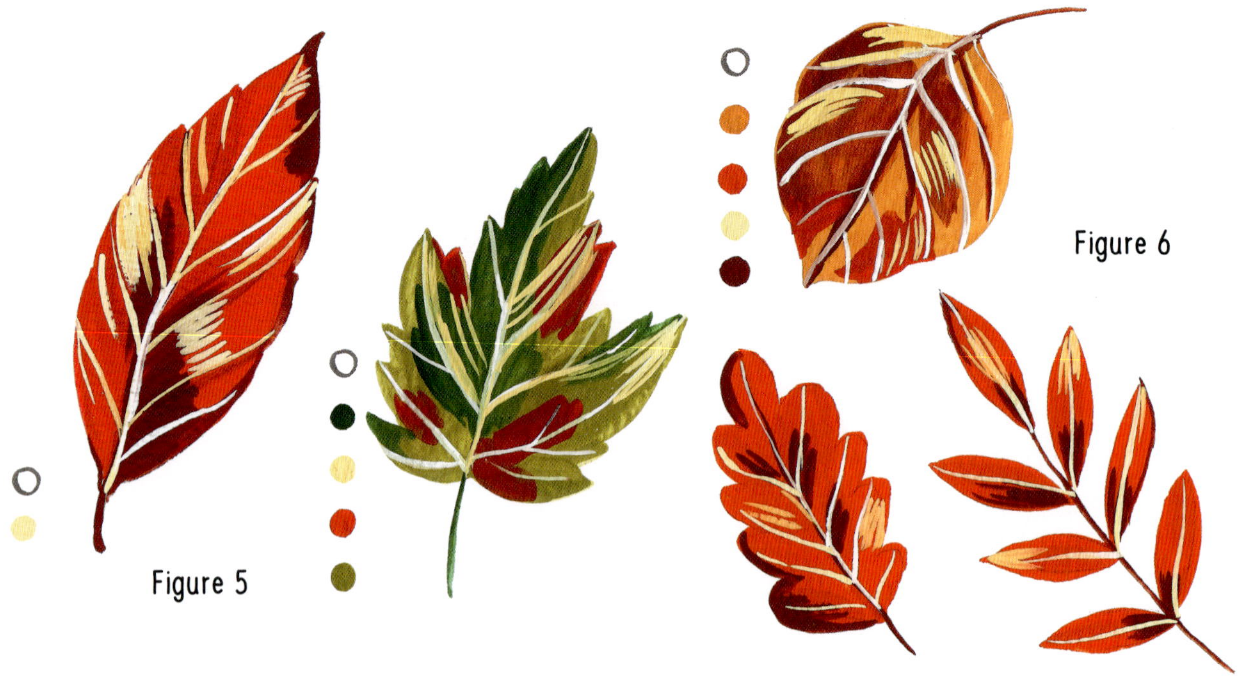

STEP 3

It's time to add details to the leaf (Figure 5). Arm yourself with a detail brush and add veins and some random strokes in pastel yellow and white gouache. The most important thing when adding details is not to overload the painting. Also, try to paint all the strokes randomly, without any order.

By following these steps, you can paint a variety of beautiful fall leaves. Choose any shape and play around with the colors. Any color combinations can be applied to this project. You can really let your creativity flourish here. And of course, be inspired by nature. If it's the fall season, go to the park or the forest and pick some leaves for reference.

In Figure 6, you can see some paintings created by following this lesson. For some leaves, I've changed the shapes and for others, both colors and shapes.

NOTE: If you change the color, the base colors should still be saturated to create contrast in step 3.

I hope you enjoyed this project, and especially in the fall, you can practice and be creative by using this lesson.

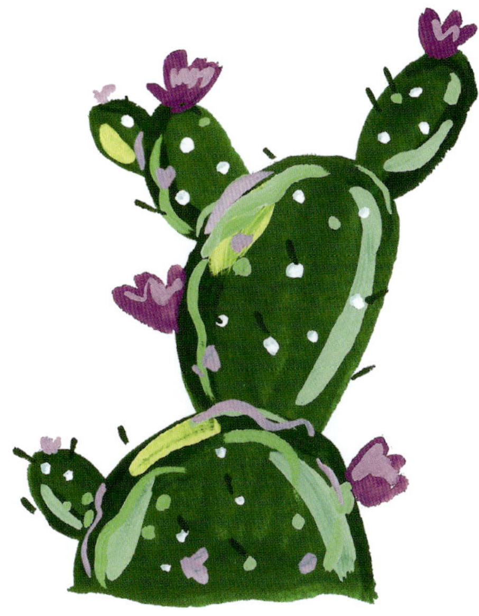

COLORFUL CACTUS

This is one of my favorite projects in this book because it's so colorful, quick and easy to do.

I will show you how to make this painting in just a few simple steps. You can use all these techniques for any botanical paintings. This is also a perfect project for the little ones. Children will definitely enjoy painting such a colorful cactus!

SUPPLIES

- White or craft paper
- Pencil and eraser (optional)
- Round brushes in different sizes
- Detail brush

PROJECT COLORS

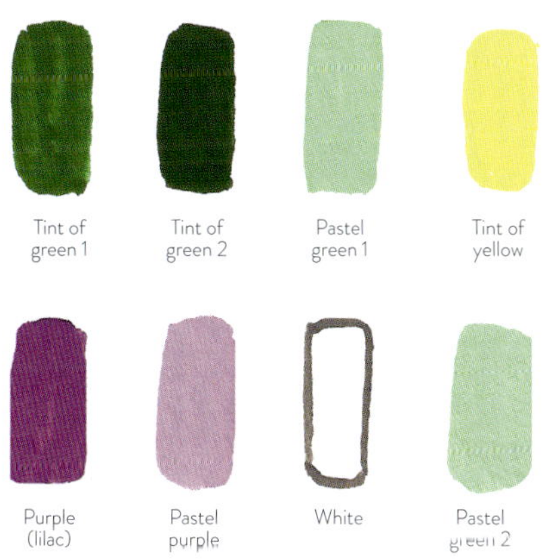

COLOR MIXING

- Tint of green 1 (permanent green + primary blue, proportion 1:1)
- Tint of green 2 (permanent green + burnt umber, proportion 1:2)
- Pastel green 1 (white + permanent green + burnt umber, proportion 2:1:2)
- Tint of yellow (yellow + permanent green, proportion 5:1)
- Pastel purple (white + purple, proportion 1:1)
- Pastel green 2 (white + permanent green, proportion 1:1)

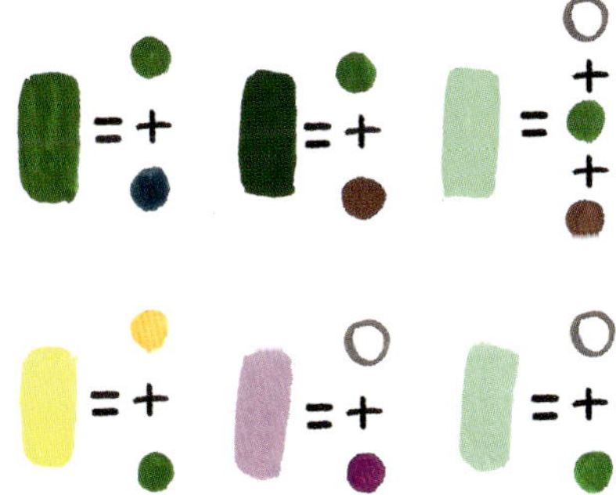

NOTE: Black paper may also work if your base green color is not too dark.

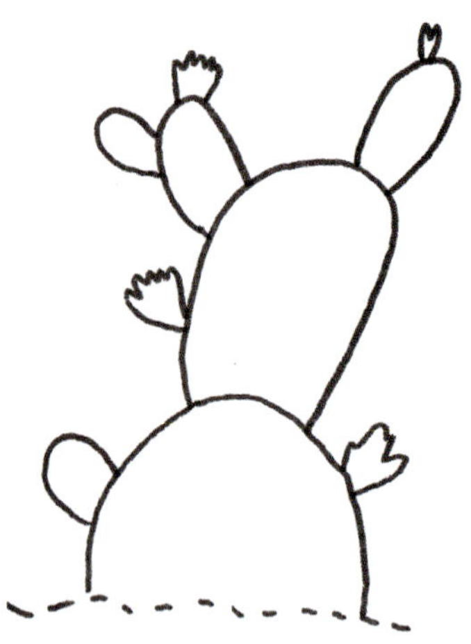

Figure 1

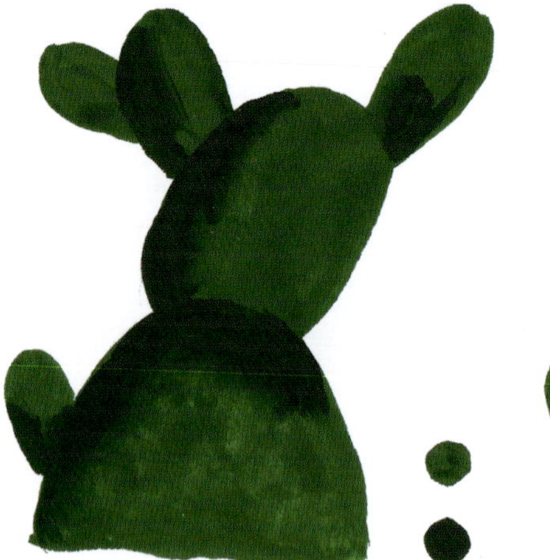

Figure 2

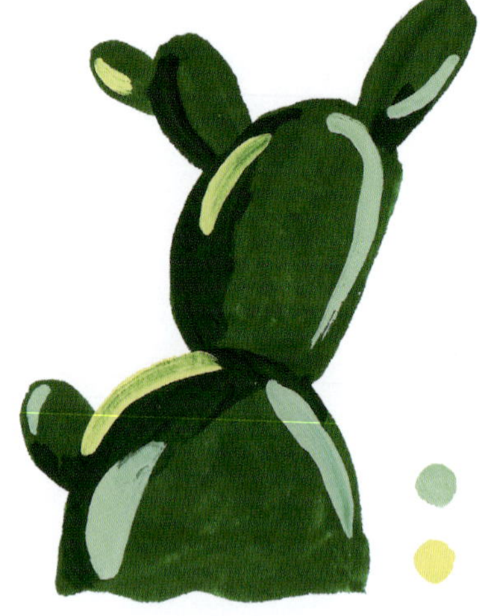

Figure 3

STEP 1

Take a look at Figure 1, which shows the outlines of the cactus. For this lesson, a sketch is not really necessary. However, you can sketch the outline of the cactus if it helps you feel more confident. Now we can move on to the painting itself. Let's begin.

Paint the base of the plant in the tint of green 1 (Figure 2). Use a medium or even big round brush for this purpose, depending on the size of paper you're painting. Don't wait for the layer to dry; add the tint of green 2 using the same brush (see direct blending technique, page 11). Once the base layer is dry, go to the next step.

STEP 2

NOTE: From now on, we'll use only the layering technique (page 11).

Using the medium round brush, add a layer in pastel green 1 and the tint of yellow, as shown in Figure 3. Allow the painted layer to dry completely.

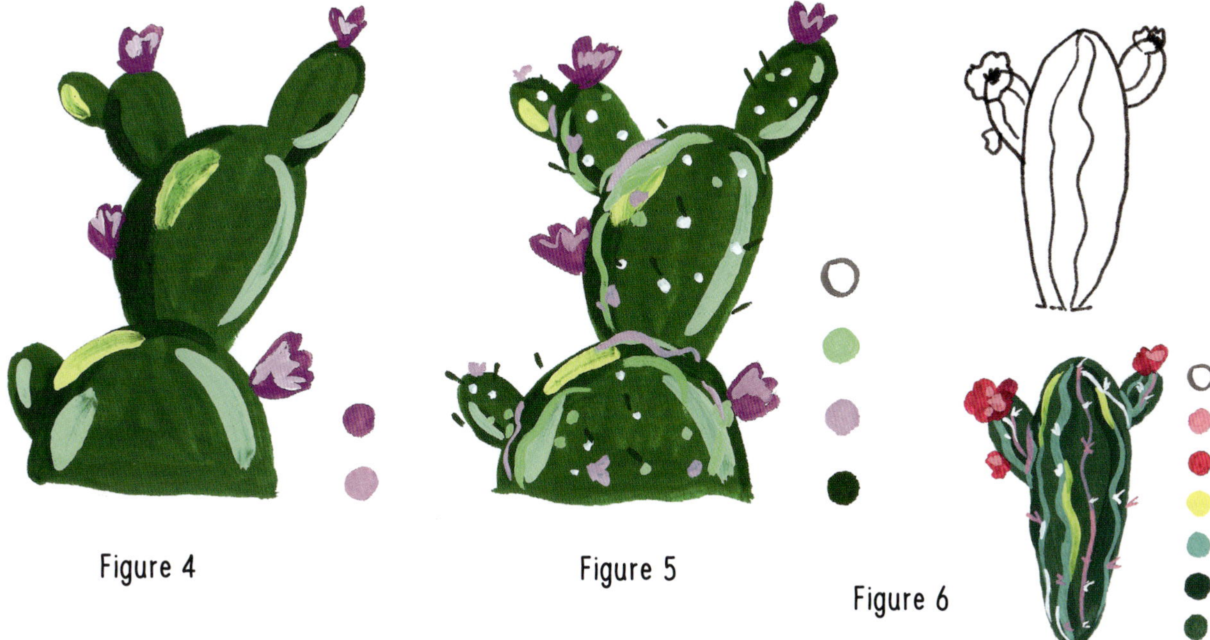

Figure 4

Figure 5

Figure 6

STEP 3

In this stage, we'll add the flowers to the cactus (Figure 4). It brings more color to the painting and makes it super cute. You can choose to paint the flowers in any color, but the most important thing to add is a second layer in a contrasting color. For example, if the flowers are purple, use pastel purple or dark purple (see Color Contrast with Gouache, page 8).

First, paint the flowers in purple. Wait until they dry and then add a contrasting second layer in pastel purple. Use a round brush for this, in a size suitable to your paper size of the project.

STEP 4

It's time to add details (Figure 5). For this step, we will use a detail brush. Paint the details in the following colors: white, pastel purple, pastel green 2 and the tint of green 2. Apply details randomly, without any order. It makes the illustration lifelike.

TIP: Because we're creating a stylized illustration, the spines of the cactus can be painted with dots, spots or ticks, or a combination of the three.

As I mentioned earlier, the techniques in this lesson work for different plants and various cacti. Choose any shape and colors, experiment with adding details and try different flowers for your cactus (Figures 6 and 7).

There is no limit to your imagination. However, I recommend using references for your experiments. It'll give you more freedom.

Figure 7

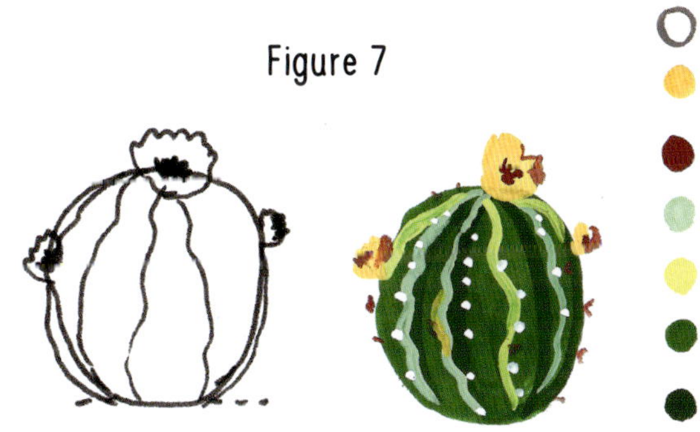

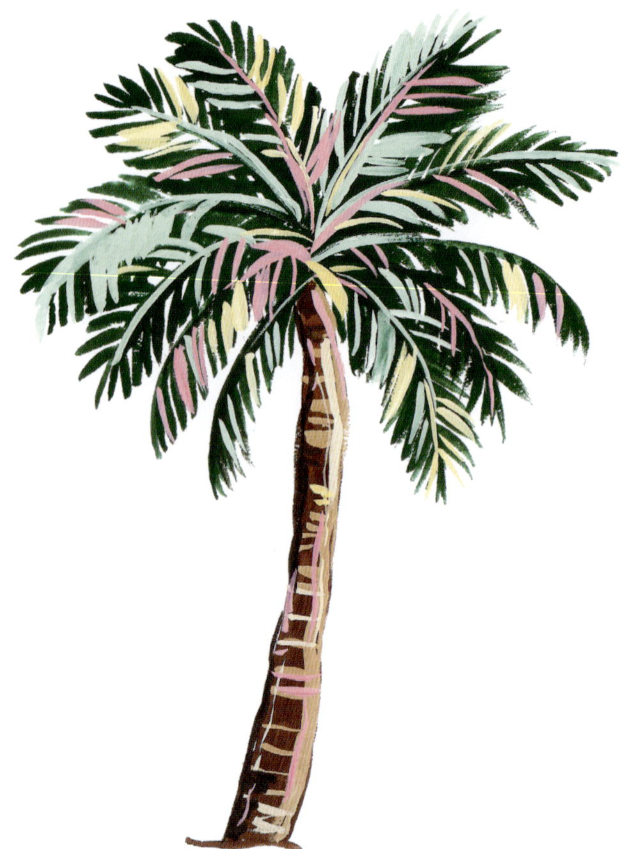

FAIRY TALE PALM TREE

I especially love this project because of its colorful and cute style. With gouache, it's so easy to add unusual colors and details. So I decided that with gouache it makes sense to show you how to paint a palm tree in a more whimsical style. This lesson is quick, and I'm sure you'll enjoy it and boost your painting skills in the process.

SUPPLIES

- White or craft paper
- Pencil and eraser
- Round brushes in different sizes
- Detail brush

COLOR MIXING

- Tint of green (green + burnt umber, proportion 2:1)
- Tint of brown 1 (white + burnt umber + yellow ochre, proportion 2:1:1)
- Pastel ochre (white + yellow ochre, proportion 2:1)
- Tint of brown 2 (black + burnt umber, proportion 1:3)
- Pastel green (white + sap green, proportion 2:1)
- Pastel pink (white + primary red, proportion 2:1)
- Pastel yellow (white + yellow, proportion 3:2)

PROJECT COLORS

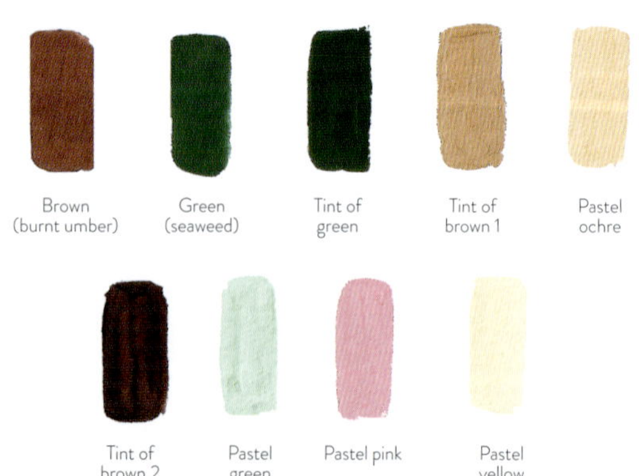

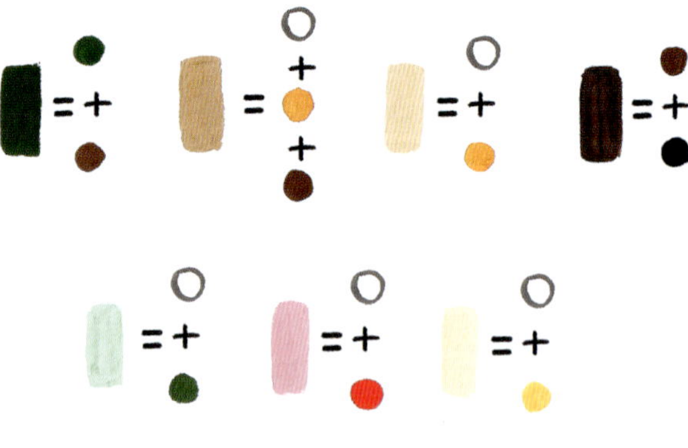

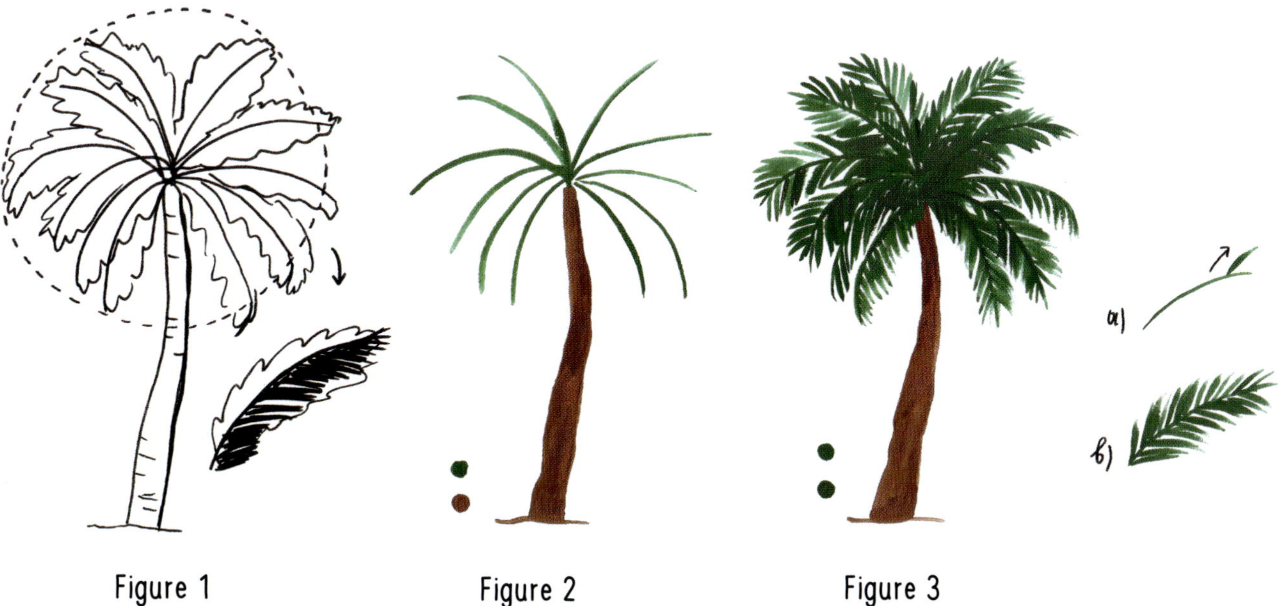

Figure 1 Figure 2 Figure 3

STEP 1

Start with a quick preliminary sketch. Sketch the palm tree with a pencil, as shown in Figure 1. The sketch doesn't need to be detailed; just mark the main lines. Also note that the crown of the tree fits into the circle. That's why I recommend you draw the auxiliary circle first.

As for the palm leaves, you need to draw the silhouette of each leaf (Figure 1). Later, we'll fill all the leaf shapes with leaflets by painting with gouache.

Finally, we can move on to the painting process itself. With a medium round brush, paint the trunk of the tree in brown, as shown in Figure 2. Keep working with the same brush. Once the previous layer has dried, paint the stems of the leaves in green, with the help of the brush tip.

Allow the layer to dry and proceed to the next step.

STEP 2

As I mentioned earlier, we need to fill each leaf with leaflets. Prepare the green color and paint every single leaflet with one brush stroke (Figure 3a and 3b). Use a small round brush for this purpose. Move the brush from the stem outward to the pencil outline (see Brush Strokes, page 10). Even though this project is painted in a cartoonish style, the leaves should look natural and not too perfect (Figure 3). Try to make the leaflets different and leave some tiny gaps between.

NOTE: The leaves in the center meet each other and that's why some leaflets overlap. If you have too many unpainted areas in the center, add extra leaflets there.

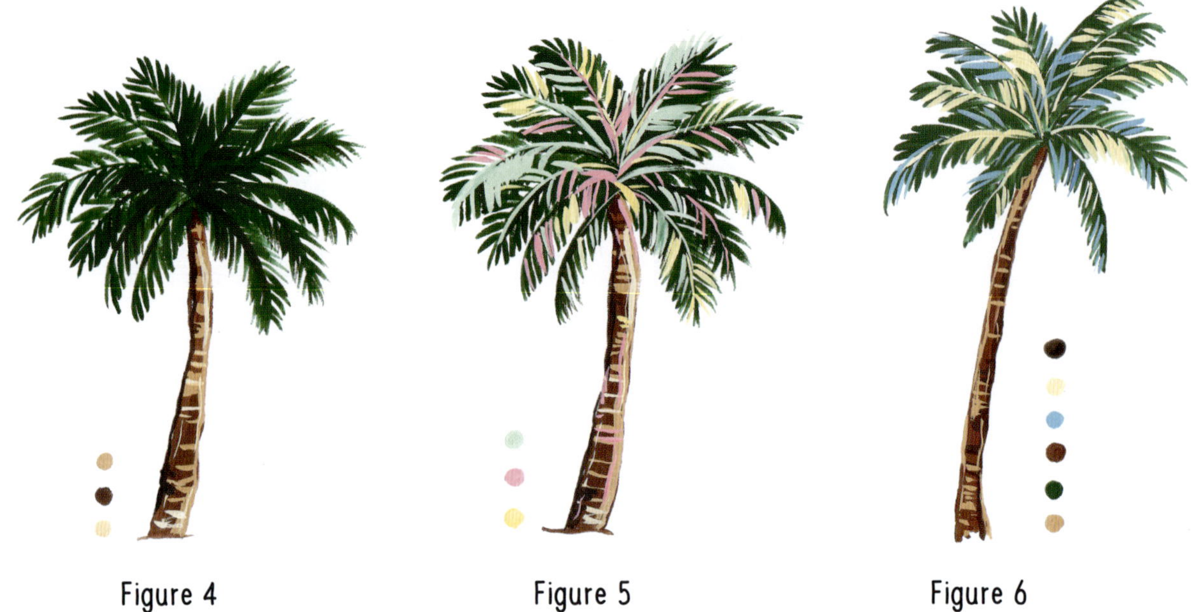

Figure 4 Figure 5 Figure 6

Let the leaves dry completely. Once the layer is dry, paint another on top in the tint of green, according to Figure 3. Use a small round brush. In this and the following steps, we are using the layering technique (page 11). Allow the illustration to dry completely.

STEP 3

We already painted the base layers and are now ready to add details (Figure 4). Prepare paint in the following tints: the tint of brown 1, pastel ochre and the tint of brown 2.

Now arm yourself with a detail brush or small round brush. On the left side of the trunk, paint the shadow layer in the tint of brown 2. Then add the layer in the tint of brown 1 on the right side. Let all the details dry completely and finally paint some additional details in pastel ochre.

STEP 4

Because we're painting a magical palm tree from a fairy tale, let's add the details in unusual colors. Again using the detail brush, add the accents on the leaves in pastel green, pastel pink and pastel yellow. You can refer to Figure 5, or add the details on the leaves in the way you prefer. The point is to add colors randomly. Also, I advise painting each color one by one and waiting until the previous layer dries.

Figure 6 shows an example of how you can paint a palm tree by using this lesson's instructions, but with some minor changes. For this example, I played with additional colors and added pastel yellow and pastel blue. I also changed the structure of the tree. Create your variations of the fairy tale palm tree and don't be afraid to experiment. Who knows, maybe these trees will inspire you to create some illustrations for fairy tales or storybooks.

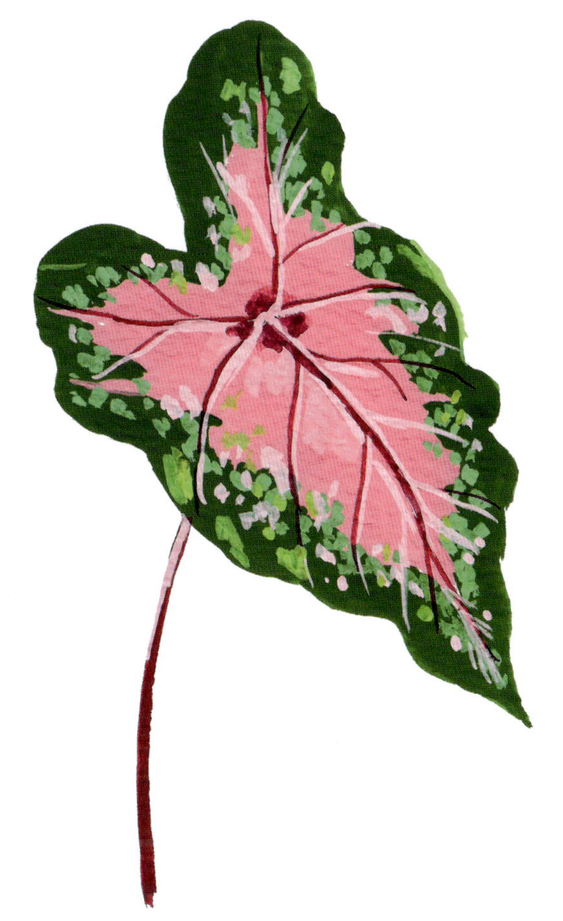

TROPICAL CALADIUM

I am a big lover of plants and flowers, and I especially admire tropical plants. When I visit the botanical gardens, I can't overlook those big and colorful leaves. These are such impressive creations of nature, and they come in a wide variety of shapes and colors. Such beauty leaves me speechless, but I can always show their beauty on paper.

For this project, I've chosen caladium plants. I'll show you how to paint this vivid and unique leaf with gouache in just a few simple steps. Let's begin!

SUPPLIES

- White, craft or black paper
- Pencil and eraser
- Round brushes in different sizes
- Detail brush

COLOR MIXING

- Pastel red 1 (white + primary red, proportion 1:1)
- Dark red (primary red + permanent green, proportion 2:1)
- Pastel green 1 (permanent green + white + permanent yellow, proportion 2:5:1)
- Pastel red 2 (white + primary red, proportion 4:1)
- Pastel green 2 (permanent green + white + permanent yellow, proportion 2:5:2)

PROJECT COLORS

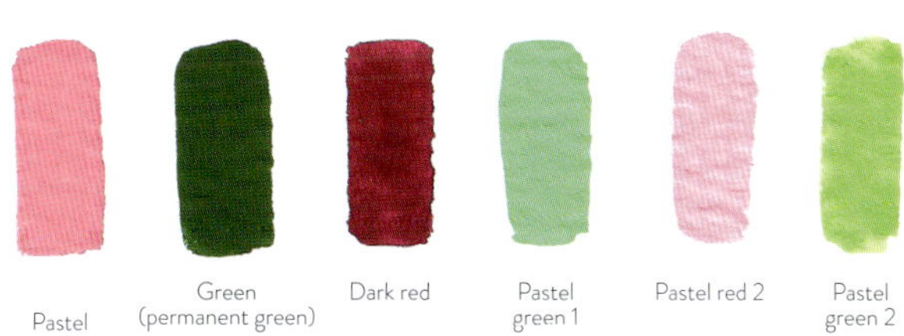

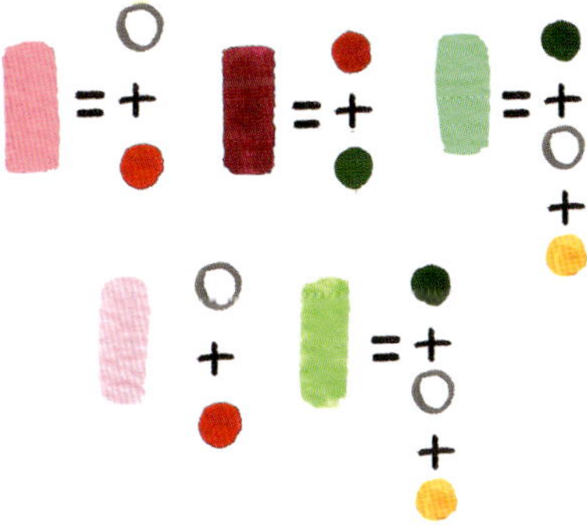

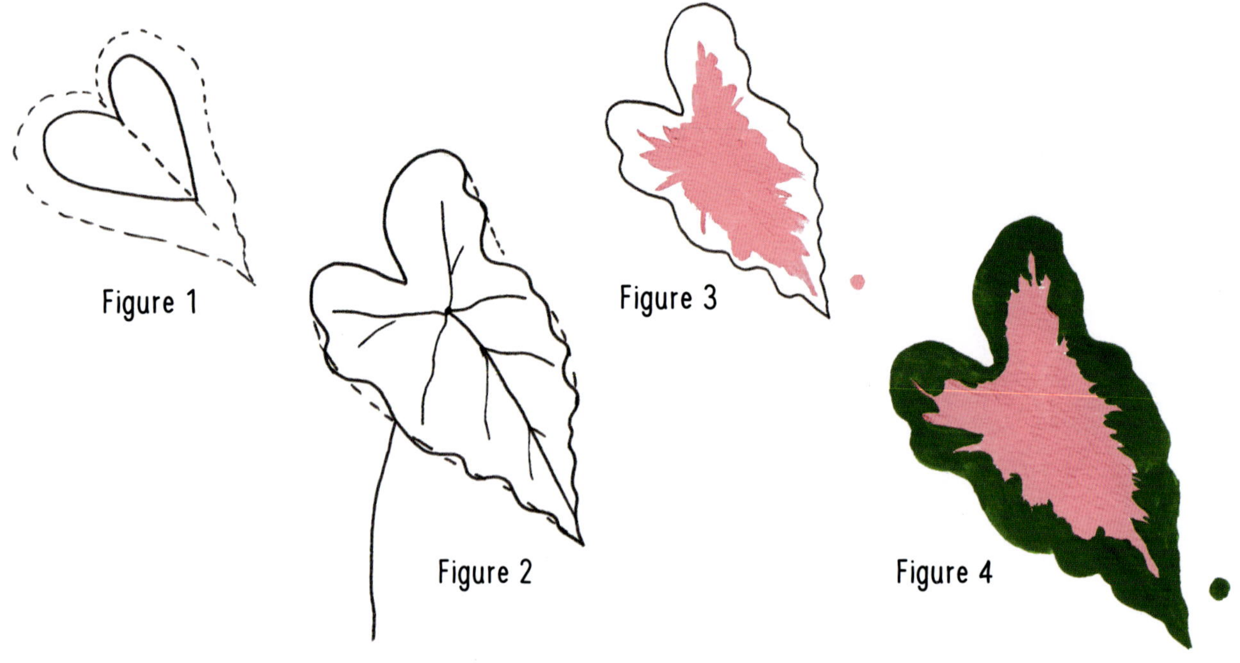

STEP 1

Before beginning this lesson, refer to Figure 1. From the figure, we can see that the leaf has a heart shape. In fact, the pattern on the leaf fits in the heart as well. The inside heart shows the area of the pattern. Also, note that the edge of the leaf is not straight. It has a wavy edge, which makes the plant look more realistic. Draw a light sketch following the outline drawing in Figure 2. When the sketch is ready, we can move on to painting with gouache.

NOTE: In this project, all steps will be done by using the layering technique (page 11) and the softening technique (page 12).

Use a large, thin-tipped round brush and pastel red 1 to paint the center area of the leaf (Figure 3). I advise you to start from the center, then move outward from the middle to add brush strokes and form the center area. Once the painting is dry, move on to the next step.

STEP 2

Keep working with a large round brush. Using green, paint the rest of the leaf (Figure 4). Try to make sure the edges are smooth. It'll make your work look neat. Let the layer dry.

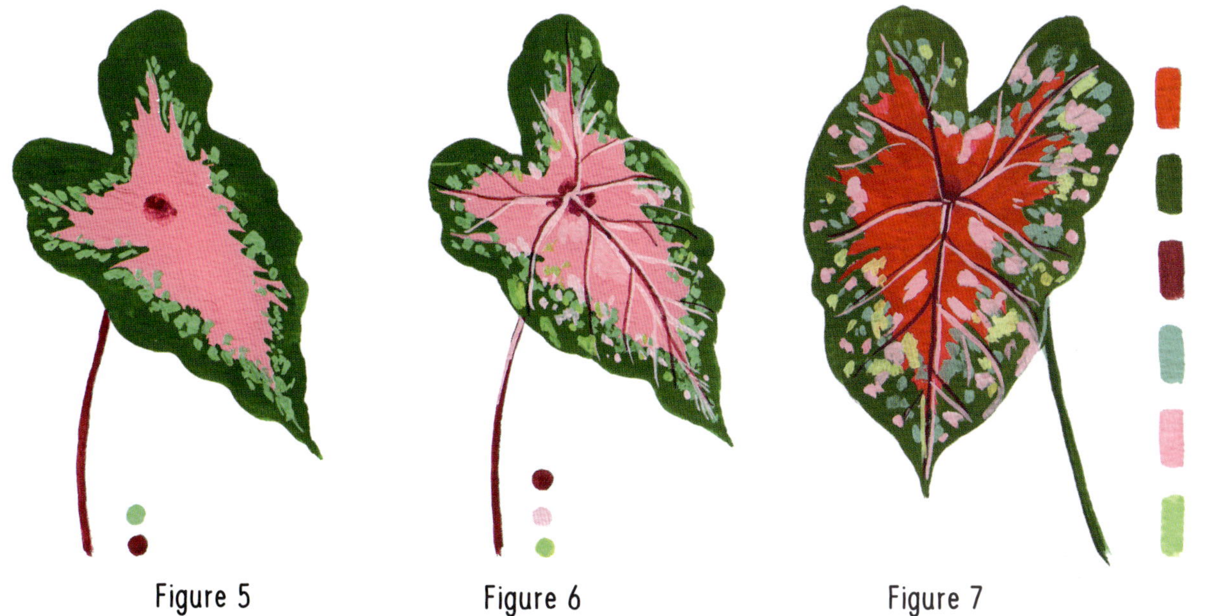

Figure 5 Figure 6 Figure 7

STEP 3

Now add the plant stem with dark red (Figure 5). Use a detail brush or a small round brush for this step. With the same color, paint the center of the leaf. To make it look softer, apply the softening technique (page 12).

Use pastel green 1 and a medium round brush to paint the details around the pastel red center, which consist of small brush strokes. Simply touch the brush's tip to the paper to form the desired pattern. Once you're done, go on to the final step.

STEP 4

It's time to add more details. For this step, we will use a detail brush. With dark red, paint the veins of the leaf, as shown in Figure 6. Allow the painted layer to dry. Now with pastel red 2 and following the already-painted veins, add one more layer of the veins in this light shade. The dark and light veins create an excellent contrast (see Color Contrast with Gouache, page 8).

Let's keep going and finish the painting. Using the small round brush, add more details with pastel red 2 and pastel green 2. It's important not to overload the painting with too many details. Less is more.

There are so many options you can play with in this project. Experiment with different shapes, colors and patterns (Figure 7). Use your imagination to create a fantastical, magical plant. Relax and enjoy the creative process.

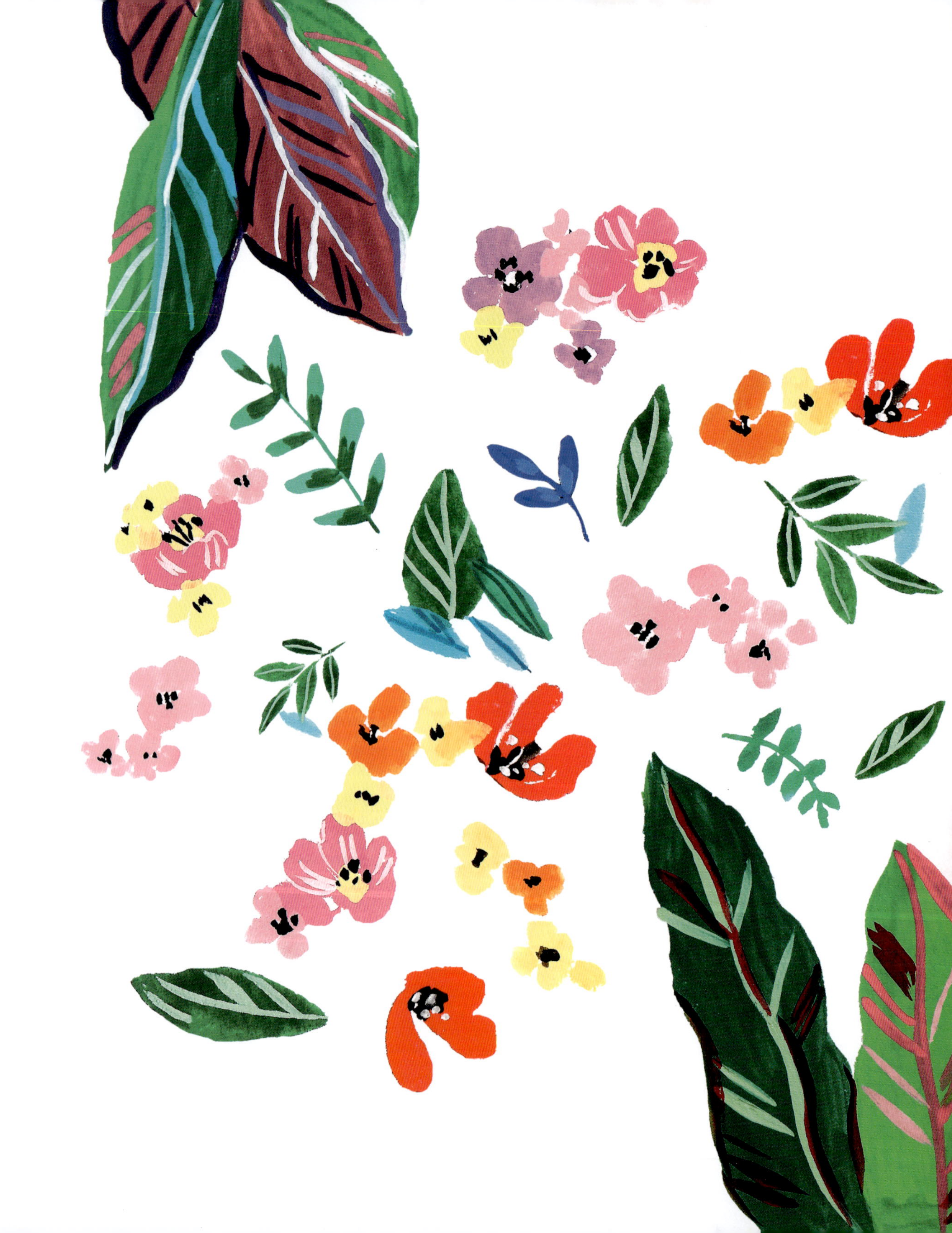

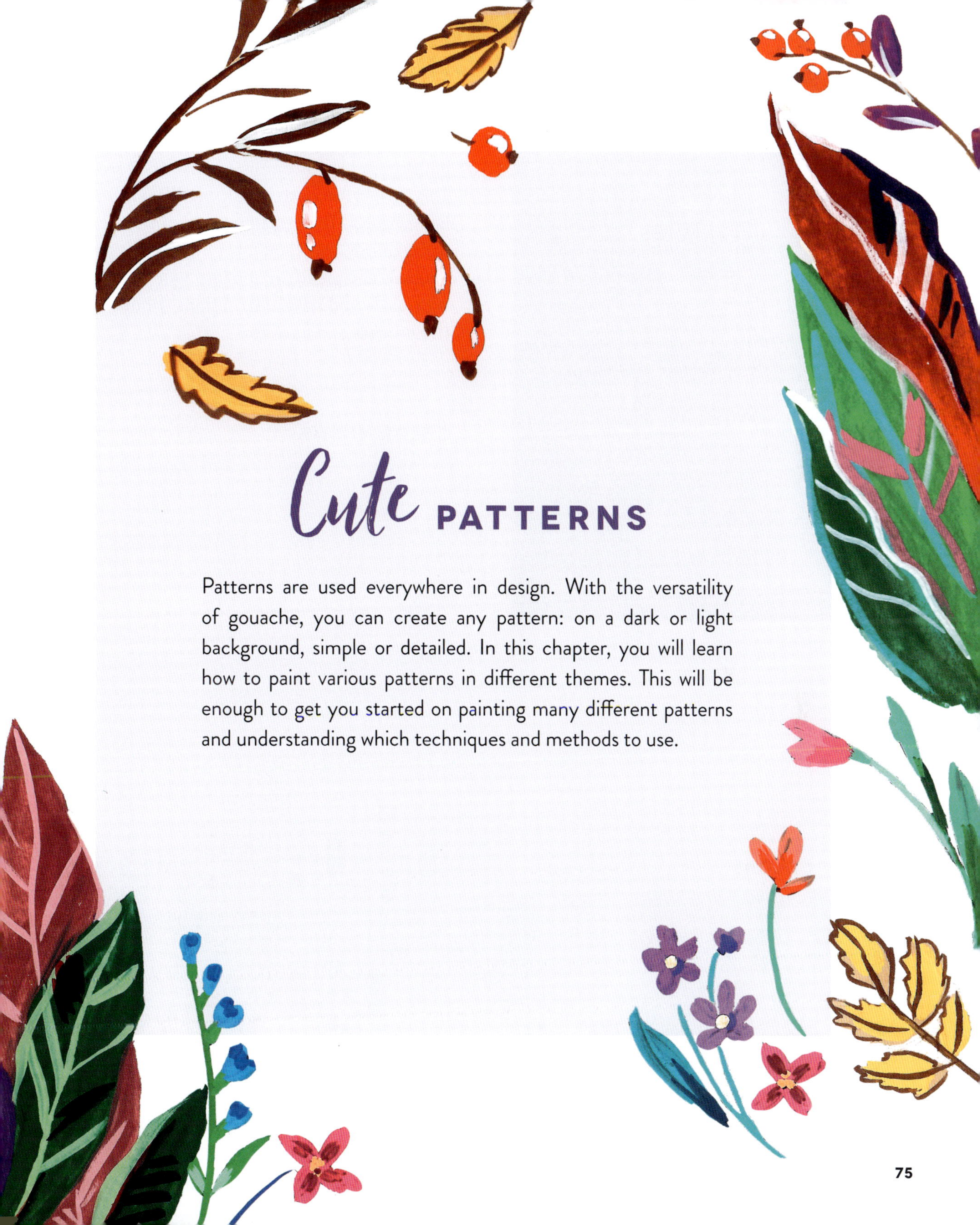

Cute PATTERNS

Patterns are used everywhere in design. With the versatility of gouache, you can create any pattern: on a dark or light background, simple or detailed. In this chapter, you will learn how to paint various patterns in different themes. This will be enough to get you started on painting many different patterns and understanding which techniques and methods to use.

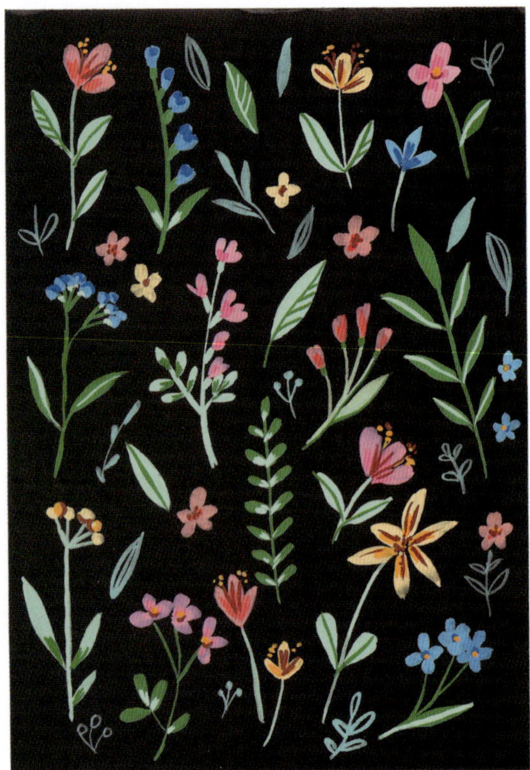

WILDFLOWERS

There are so many things you can paint with gouache, but this one is a must-try for everyone. This is a cute pattern of wildflowers on a black background. The gouache pops out on this kind of background and looks just fantastic. Don't deny yourself the pleasure of painting it. I will guide you with clear and easy instructions. I hope you enjoy the process and have fun.

SUPPLIES

- Black or white paper
- Masking tape (optional)
- Flat brush (optional)
- Round brushes in different sizes
- Detail brush

PROJECT COLORS

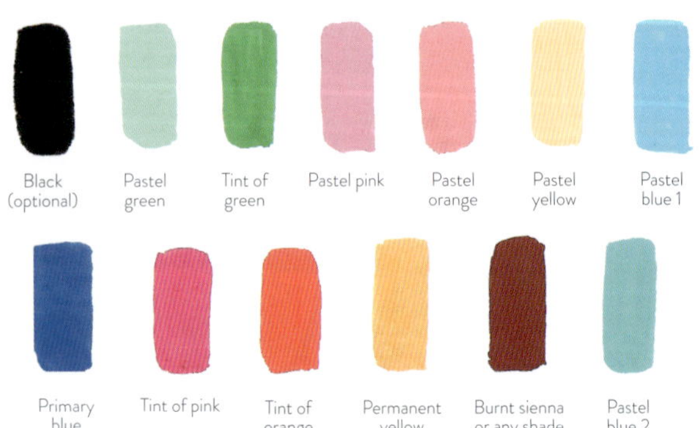

COLOR MIXING

- Pastel green (permanent green + permanent yellow + white, proportion 1:1:4)
- Tint of green (permanent green + white, proportion 8:1)
- Pastel pink (crimson red + white, proportion 1:3)
- Pastel orange (crimson red + permanent yellow + white, proportion 1:1:3)
- Pastel yellow (permanent yellow + white, proportion 1:1)
- Pastel blue 1 (primary blue + white, proportion 1:1)
- Tint of pink (crimson red + white, proportion 1:1)
- Tint of orange (crimson red + permanent yellow + white, proportion 1:2:1)
- Pastel blue 2 (primary blue + white + permanent green, proportion 2:3:1)

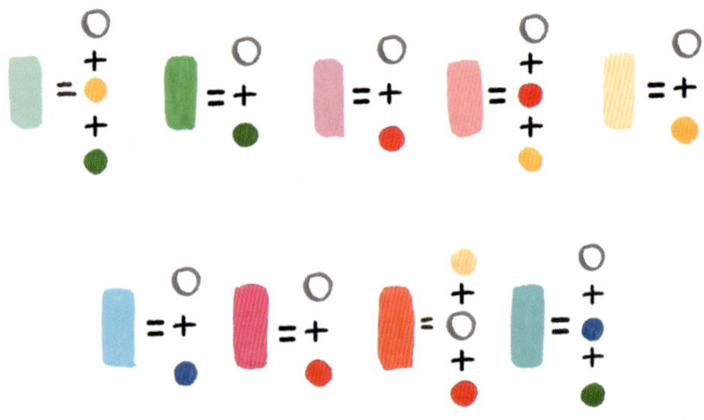

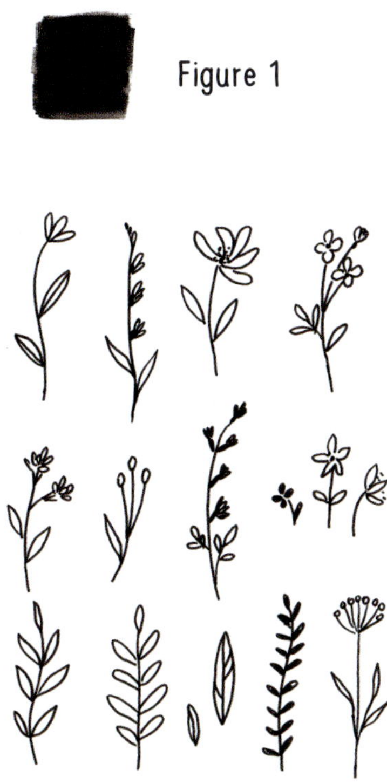

Figure 1

Figure 2

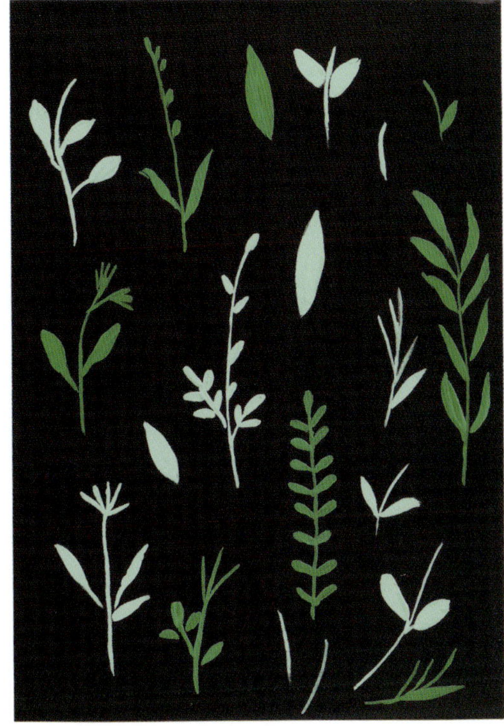

Figure 3 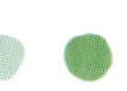

STEP 1

Before diving into the painting project, let's look at the background. There are two ways to create the black base for your painting: using black paper or painting with black gouache first.

With black paper, the process is clear. Just define the painting area with masking tape and enjoy the painting process. I use half-letter-sized sheets of black paper and paint on it without the help of masking tape.

If you don't have black paper, paint the background layer with black gouache (Figure 1). Apply the dry-brush forming technique (page 12). I recommend you use a flat brush for this purpose. Once the background is dry, you are ready to proceed.

NOTE: Make sure there are no white areas, especially in the middle of the black background. The background should be solid, except for the edges. If you use the dry-brush forming technique, the edges will look textured and make the work charming.

This project does not need a preliminary sketch. However, in Figure 2, I offer you some examples of wildflowers and wild herbs. These may offer you a reference to make painting easier.

Start by painting the leaves and stems in pastel green and the tint of green, as shown in Figure 3. Use a small round brush with a thin tip or even a detail brush at this stage. Once this layer is dry, move on to the next step.

NOTE: If you paint on the black painted layer, make sure that your gouache is thick and not watery so that you don't destroy the base coat (see layering technique, page 11).

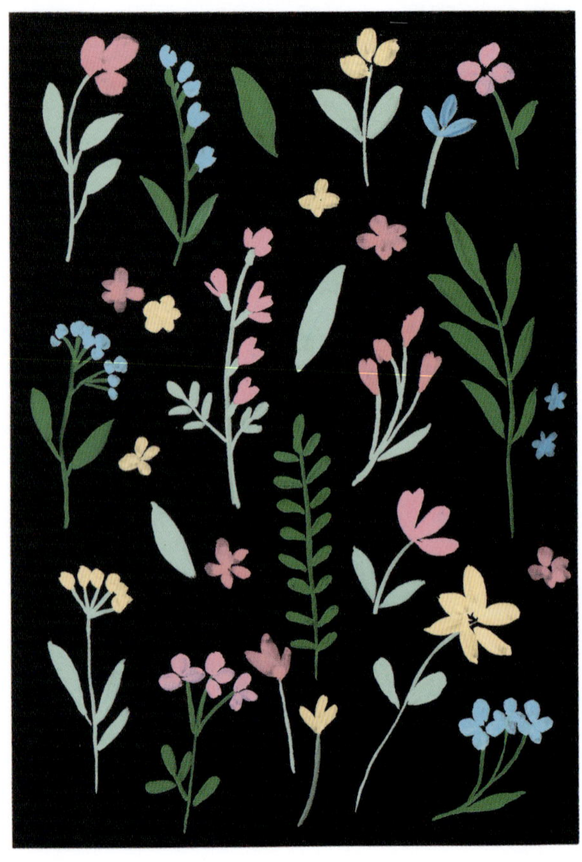

Figure 4

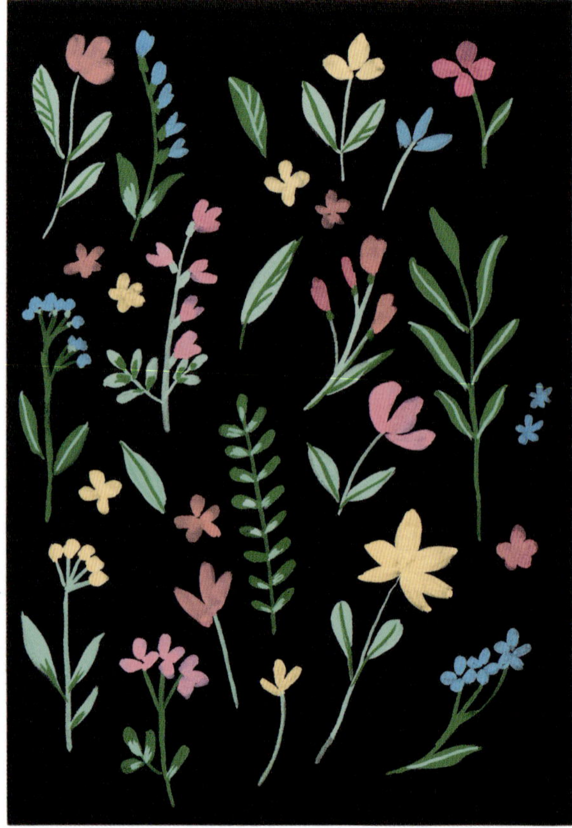

Figure 5

STEP 2

Time to add more colors to our pattern (Figure 4). With the small round brush, paint flowers and petals in the following tints: pastel pink, pastel orange, pastel yellow and pastel blue 1. When painting flowers and petals, avoid making unnecessary movements with the brush (see Brush Strokes, page 10). Allow the painting to dry completely.

STEP 3

Now take a detail brush and paint details in pastel green and the tint of green (Figure 5). For the most effective contrast, details in pastel green should be added on to the darker green (the tint of green) and vice versa (see Color Contrast with Gouache, page 8). Let the painting dry.

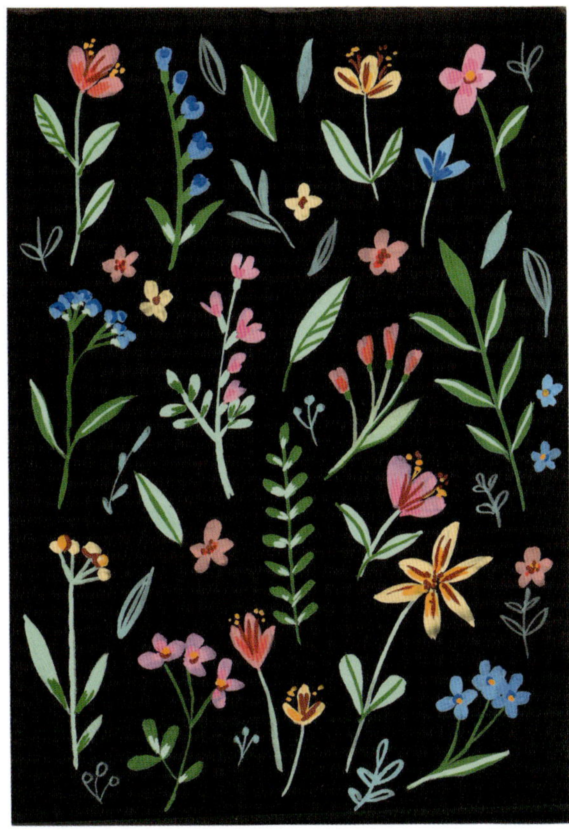

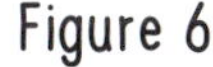

Figure 6

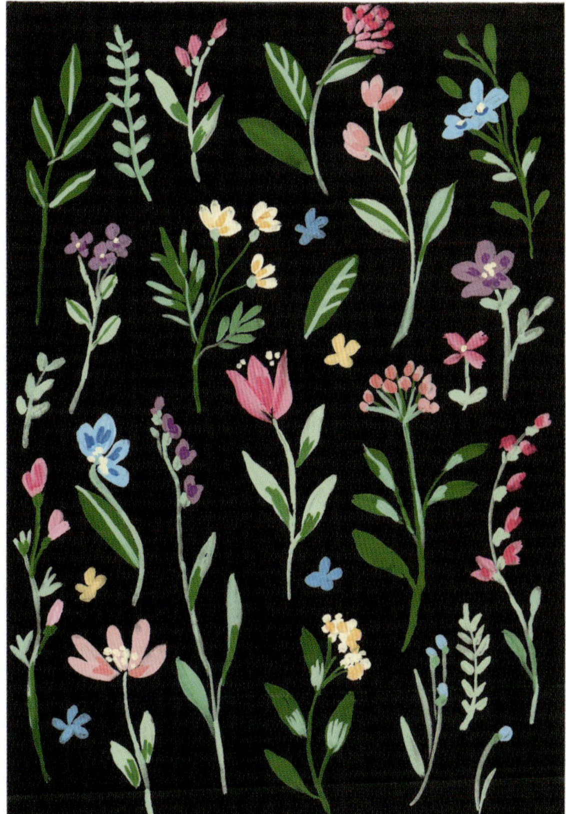

Figure 7

STEP 4

Your cute pattern is almost done. You just need to add the last details using the layering technique (page 11). Prepare paint in the following shades: primary blue, the tint of pink, the tint of orange, permanent yellow and burnt sienna. Now paint the details corresponding to those in Figure 6. Use a detail brush for this step. Now add some details with pastel blue 2. Those little doodles fill space and create a harmonious composition.

Experiment with different colors and shapes for the pattern's elements and you will be able to paint a lot of diverse and unique patterns. Figures 7 and 8 show two examples of how it works in practice. Just follow my instructions and go with your creative flow. I love this project because of how relaxing and fun it is to add all these little details while building a composition. I hope you enjoy it too.

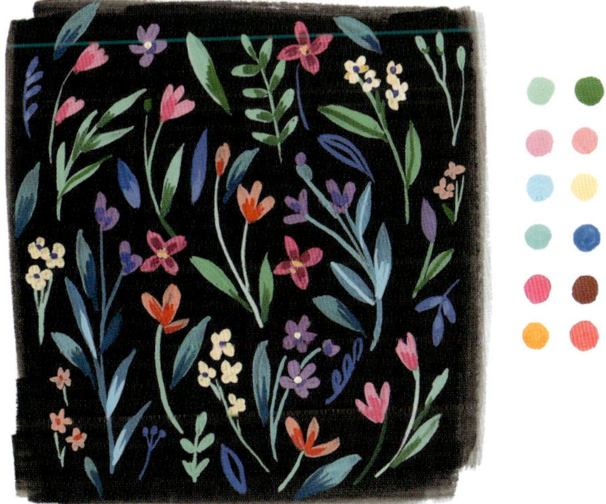

Figure 8

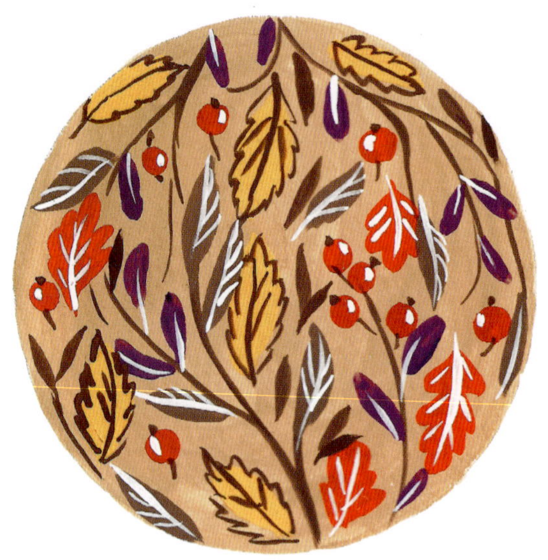

AUTUMN VIBES

This project shows how important colors are. I'm talking not only about the color combination in the piece, but also about the mood and feeling those colors give. For this autumn pattern, I picked the shades we most associate with autumn. These warm tones give the feeling of autumn and the smell of a fall forest. I hope you enjoy working on this project with me!

SUPPLIES

- White paper
- Pencil and eraser
- Compass or any round object
- Round brushes in different sizes
- Detail brush
- Liner brush (optional)

PROJECT COLORS

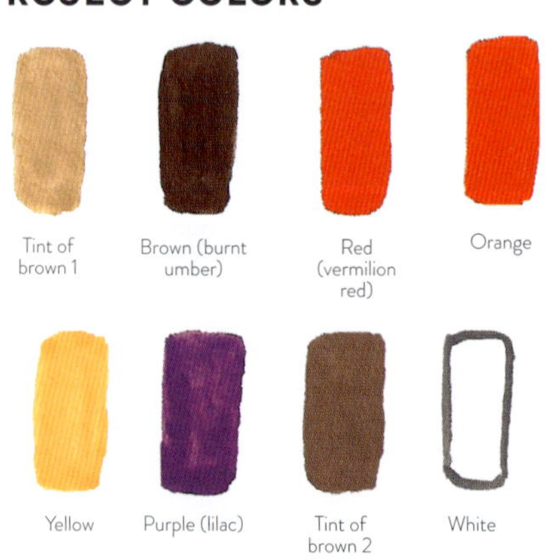

COLOR MIXING

- Tint of brown 1 (white + yellow ochre + burnt umber, proportion 1:2:1)
- Tint of brown 2 (white + burnt umber + yellow ochre, proportion 1:4:1)

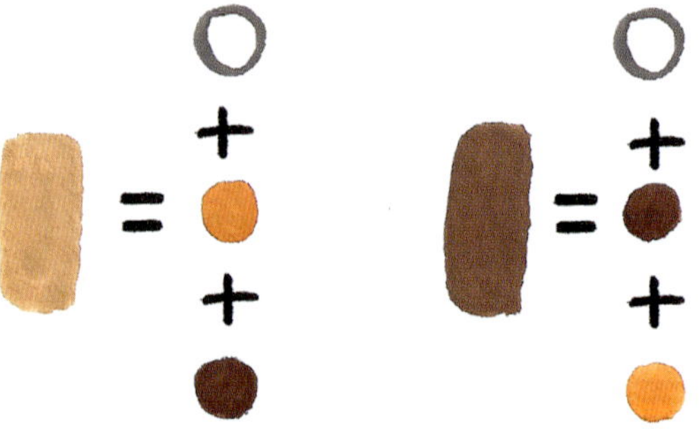

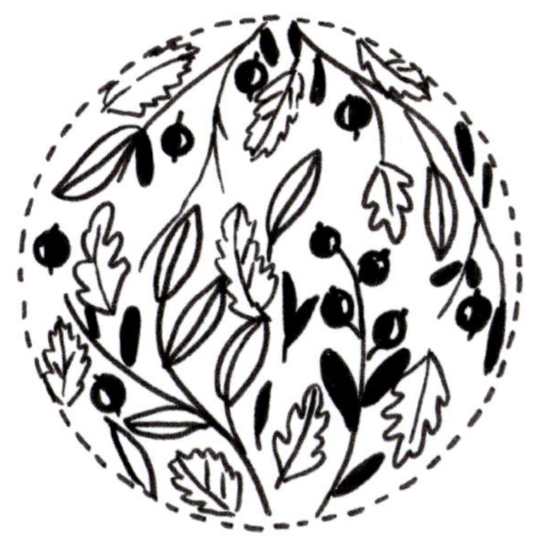

Figure 1

Figure 2

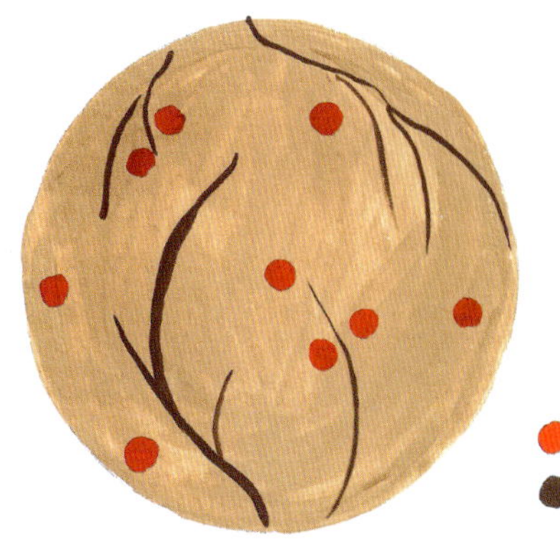

Figure 3

STEP 1

Begin by lightly sketching a circle with a pencil (Figure 1). To do this, use a compass or trace around a circular object. The diameter of the circle should be neither too small nor too big (3 to 5 inches [8 to 13 cm]). After that simple sketch, you can proceed with the painting process.

NOTE: Throughout this project, we will use the layering technique (page 11).

Using a large round brush, fill in the circle with the tint of brown 1 (Figure 2). To make the painting neater, you can use a small round brush for painting the edges of the circle. After the painting is completely dry, move on to the next step.

STEP 2

Take a small round brush and paint the branches in brown (Figure 3). Add berries in red.

The branches should not look perfect. I even suggest you paint them in different thicknesses. Let the painted layer dry completely.

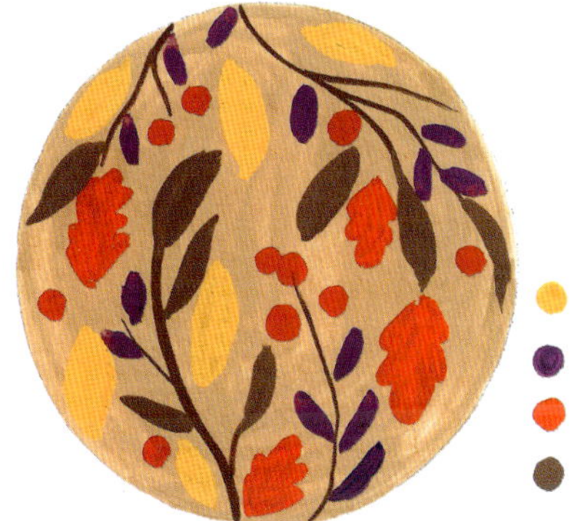

Figure 4

STEP 3

It's time to paint some leaves. The foliage will be painted in different shapes and colors. You can follow Figure 4, or paint the leaves in your own way. Prepare the next colors: orange, yellow, purple and the tint of brown 2. Use the small round brush. When you're done, allow the painting to dry.

TIP: If all elements are dried and some of them look transparent, go over them again in the same color for an opaque effect.

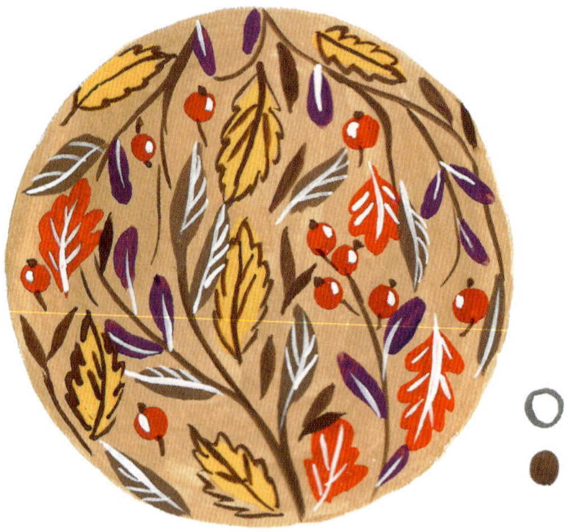

Figure 5

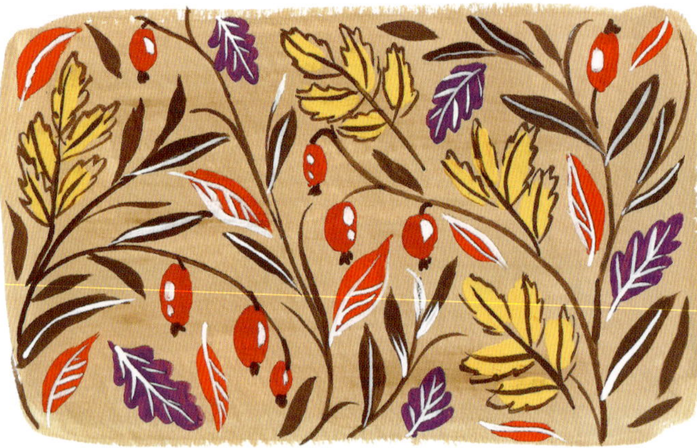

Figure 6

STEP 4

The work is almost done. All that remains is adding the final details. Using a detail brush, begin by adding the details on the berries and the outlines of the yellow leaves in brown. With the same color, add small leaves and elongate some branches to make them look more elegant.

Let everything dry completely. Finally, paint the rest of the details with white gouache, as shown in Figure 5.

TIP: For painting the branches I especially recommend using the liner brush. I have found it's the best for painting such lines.

Allow the painting to dry completely.

This project is one that you can always re-create to practice and experiment. I recommend playing with the elements and painting different ones that match the fall mood: various types of leaves and berries, apples, acorns and so forth (see an example in Figure 6).

The next level is changing the colors for the pattern. Remember, the shades should correspond to the fall mood and be in harmony with each other.

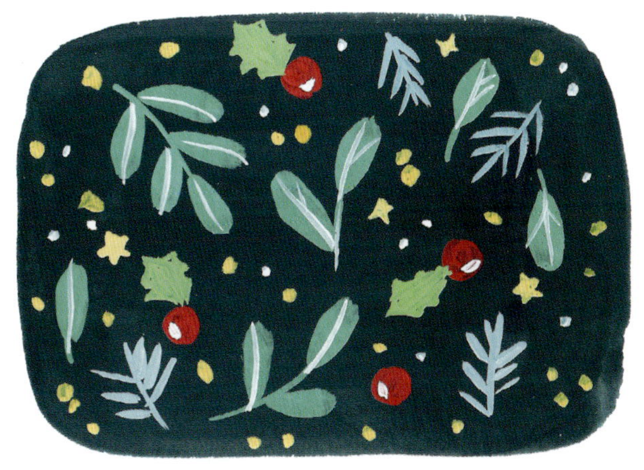

FESTIVE CHRISTMAS PATTERN

Using gouache, you can create very cute and simple patterns in just a few simple steps. Because gouache is so pigmented, it's easy to paint on top of any color—whether it's black or pastel. Gouache's matte finish also brings a unique style that's perfect for these patterns. All colors look so bold with gouache, especially when using contrasting colors. All these factors make the process of creating a pattern very straightforward and satisfying. In this project, I'll show you how to paint a fancy pattern for Christmas.

SUPPLIES

- White paper
- Masking tape
- Pencil and eraser (optional)
- Flat or filbert brush
- Round brushes in different sizes
- Detail brush

PROJECT COLORS

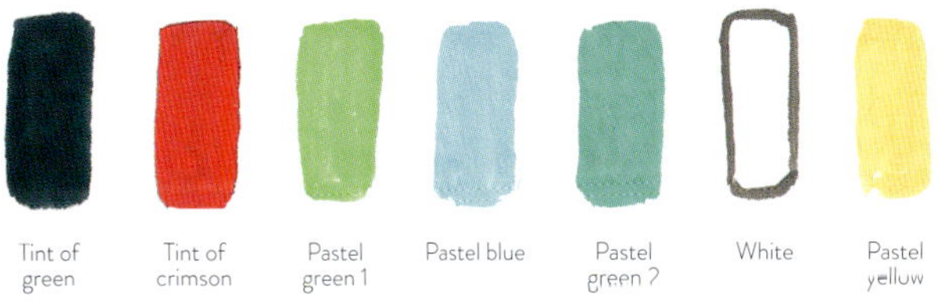

COLOR MIXING

- Tint of green (Prussian blue + viridian green + burnt umber, proportion 4:4:1)
- Tint of crimson (white + crimson red, proportion 1:8)
- Pastel green 1 (white + sap green, proportion 2:1)
- Pastel blue (white + cerulean blue, proportion 2:1)
- Pastel green 2 (white + viridian green, proportion 1:1)
- Pastel yellow (white + yellow, proportion 1:1)

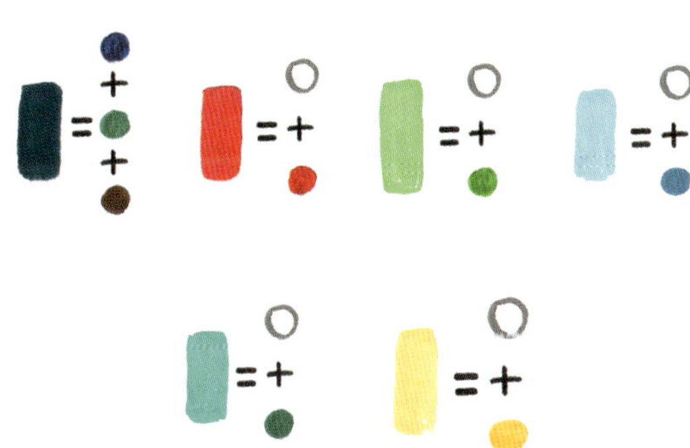

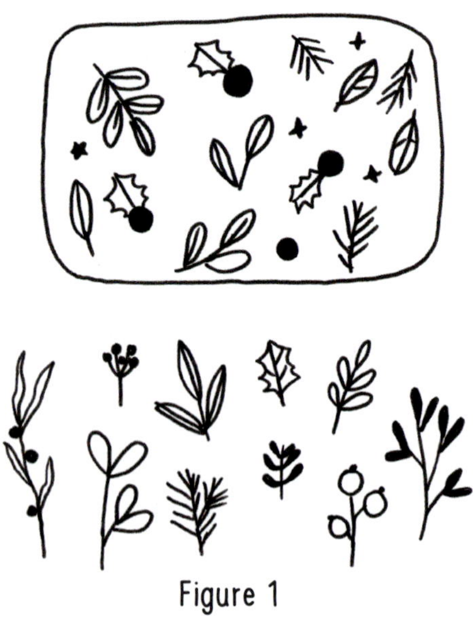

Figure 1

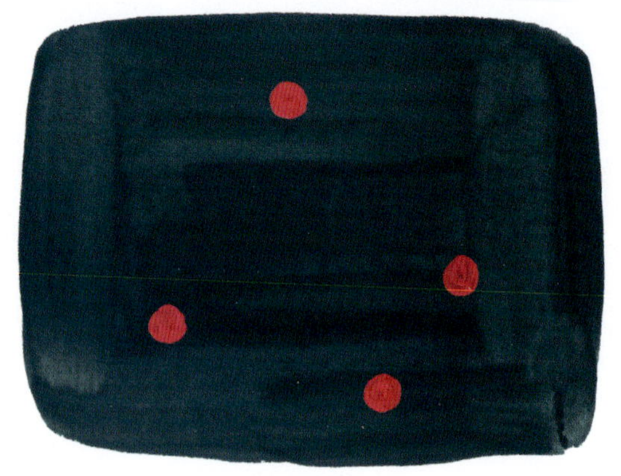

Figure 2

STEP 1

For this work, you don't need to draw a preliminary sketch (Figure 1). You do, however, have to define a work area. I offer two options for this. You can either define the rectangular border around your area with masking tape, or you can just mark the corners of the rectangle with a pencil.

I prefer the second option and will paint the background in a freehand style.

TIP: Even if you choose the second option, I recommend securing the paper to the table or board with masking tape to prevent curling.

Using the flat or filbert brush, form the background in the tint of green (Figure 2). When it dries completely, use the small round brush to paint the berries on the pattern in the tint of crimson.

If, after they dry, the berries remain transparent, duplicate the layer until it looks opaque.

Let the painting dry completely.

NOTE: Throughout this lesson, we'll use the layering technique (page 11).

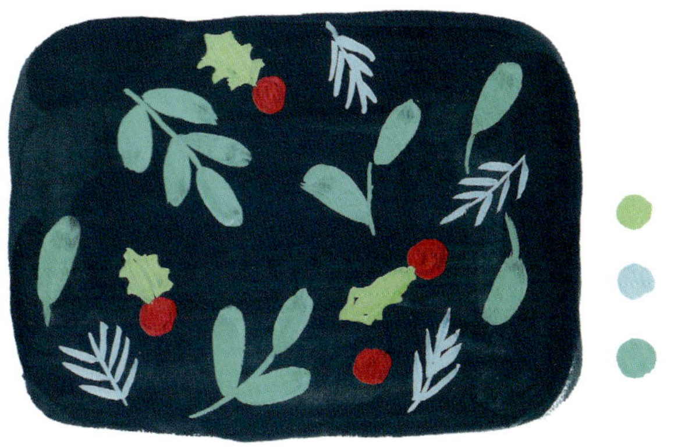

Figure 3

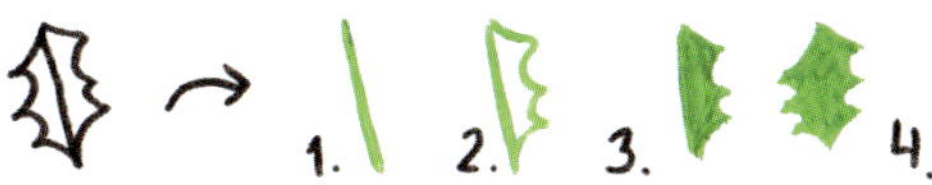

Figure 4

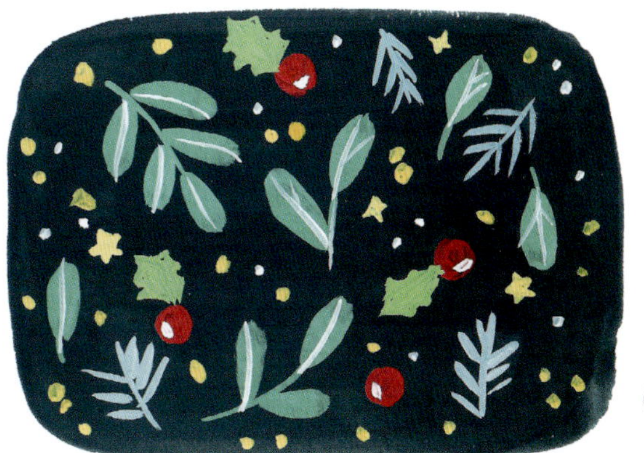

Figure 5

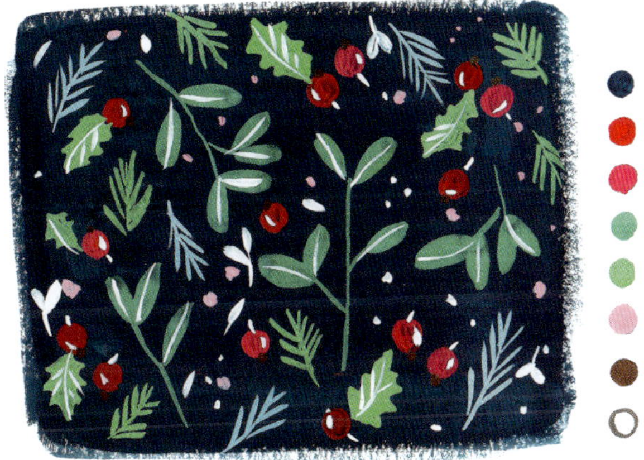

Figure 6

STEP 2

Arm yourself with a small round brush and add all kinds of leaves as shown in Figure 3 in the following colors: Paint holly leaves in pastel green 1; pine branches in pastel blue; and the other leaves in pastel green 2. For the normal leaves apply a one-stroke technique by using a round brush. For the pine branches, I suggest using the brush tip with the detail brush (see Brush Strokes, page 10). Allow all the freshly painted elements to dry completely.

You can use any leaf shape. But, because this pattern should have a Christmas mood, I recommend painting typical Christmas foliage such as holly and pine. Also, try to keep the distance between all the leaves approximately the same.

TIP: Have a look at Figure 4. It shows how easy it is to paint the holly leaf in a freehand style, in a few simple steps. Before painting these leaves onto the main painting, practice on a separate sheet of paper.

STEP 3

The main work in this simple pattern is done. Now we need to make it look complete and full. With white gouache and a detail brush, add some highlights on the berries and veins on leaves (Figure 5). Also, paint small decorative details around the leaves and berries in pastel yellow and white. These can be stars, spots or anything that matches the Christmas mood. These tiny decorative elements should be randomly spread in the pattern layout and at the same time fill all the free space. This pattern could be part of any illustration or greeting card, or perhaps you will use it to create a design for wrapping paper.

Play with the elements and don't be afraid to add any shape of leaves or other festive elements to the pattern. In Figure 6, you can find some additional outlines of such elements. Also, experiment with colors. Whenever you practice later with this project, keep to the principles of contrasting colors and balance of composition.

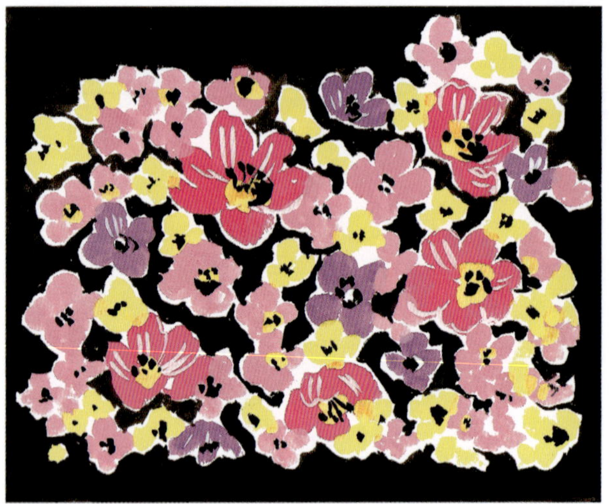

ADORABLE BLOOMING PATTERN

I called this project "Adorable Blooming Pattern" because the colors I've chosen for it are truly soft and sweet. Painting this pattern is so relaxing and meditative. The brush strokes don't have to be perfect, and all the colors contrast perfectly to make a stunning painting. Let's have a look at how to do it step by step.

SUPPLIES

- White paper
- Masking tape
- Round brushes in different sizes
- Detail brush

COLOR MIXING

- Tint of pink (white + primary red, proportion 1:1)
- Pastel purple (white + lilac, proportion 3:2)
- Pastel pink (white + primary red, proportion 2:1)
- Pastel yellow (white + primary yellow, proportion 1:1)

PROJECT COLORS

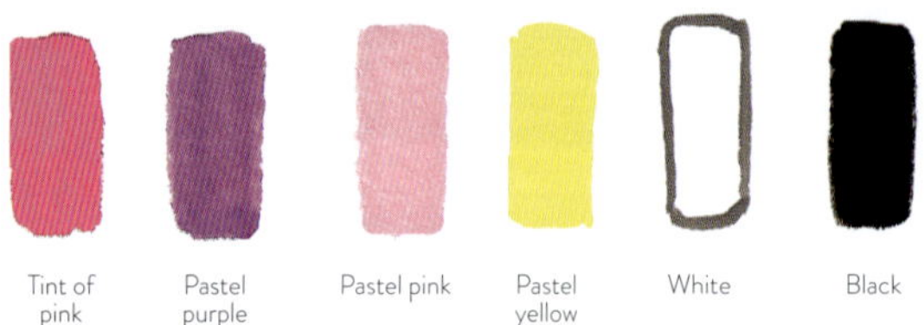

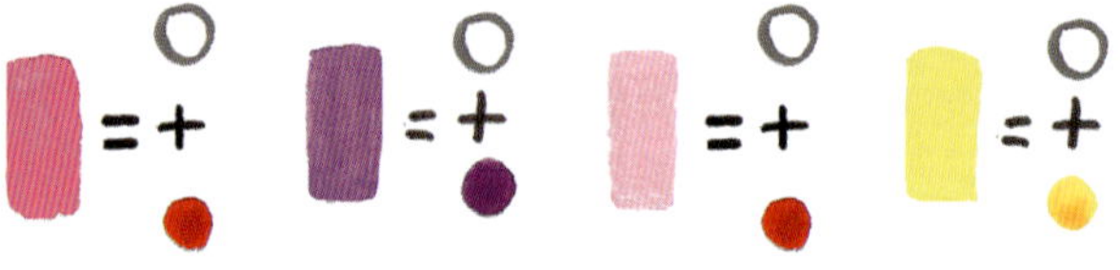

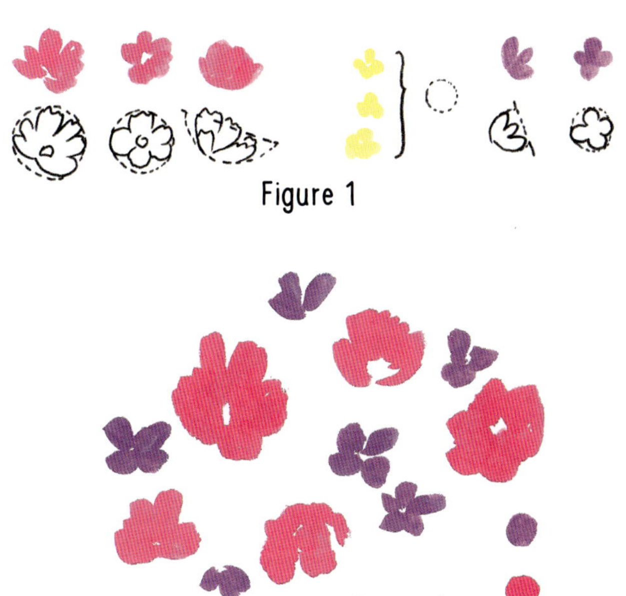

Figure 1

Figure 2

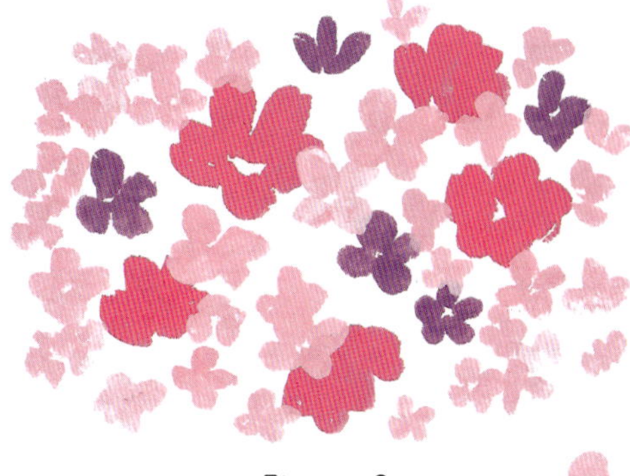

Figure 3

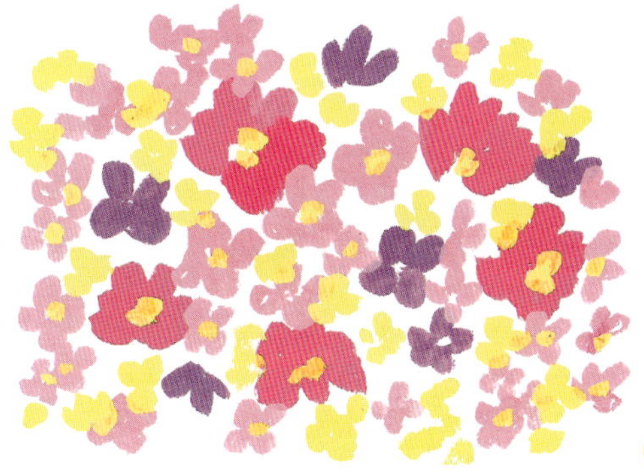

Figure 4

STEP 1

This project does not require a preliminary sketch. However, you do need to define your work area before beginning by using masking tape. So, create a rectangular border around your area with masking tape.

Basically, the first three steps in this project are adding flowers in different sizes and colors, layer by layer. We will paint such flowers in a freehand style. In Figure 1, you'll see that there are two basic types of flower shapes: open and closed. In the open shape, the flower fits into a circle. In the closed shape, it fits into a circle sector or semicircle. Now let's work out how to paint a petal with one single brush movement. Press the paintbrush against the paper and stretch it a little ahead, depending on how long the petal should be, then gently lift it up. That's it, the petal is ready. (For more about brush strokes, see page 10.)

The last thing you need to know before you start painting flowers is the brush size. The bigger paintbrush you use, the bigger brush stroke (and petal) it gives. Prepare small and medium round brushes, and with their help, paint flowers respectively in the tint of pink and the pastel purple, as shown in Figure 2. Let the painted layer dry completely.

STEP 2

By using the principles of flower painting, described in Step 1, add flowers to the pattern in the pastel pink using the layering technique (page 11). Use round brushes that are suitable for each flower size (see Figure 3).

Note that, because we are painting with gouache, even tender pastel colors cover up the more saturated colors painted previously. In this case, the petals overlap in some places, and it's easy to make one holistic composition.

STEP 3

Now add more flowers to the pattern by using the small round brush, this time with pastel yellow (see Figure 4). Once again use the principles of painting flowers freehand. With the same color, add the centers to each flower (except for the yellow flowers). Here again we are using the layering technique.

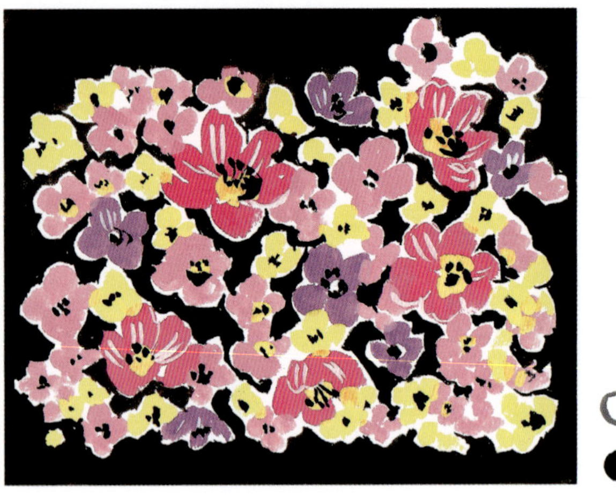

Figure 5

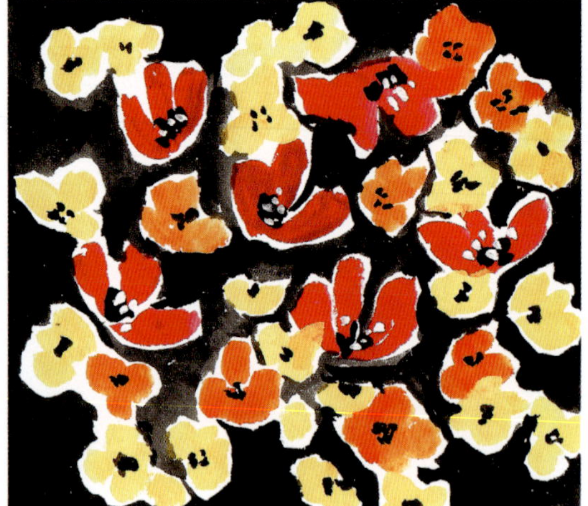

Figure 6a

STEP 4

Finally, we can add details to the pattern. Arm yourself with a detail brush and add the details in white and black as shown in Figure 5. The last thing I suggest in this step is painting a black background surrounding the blooms we created. By using a small round brush with a thin tip, paint the areas surrounding the flowers with black gouache. At the same time leave a little space between the flower and black.

This approach (I also call it the contrast trick) creates such a contrast and makes the flowers pop in the composition. At the same time, it ties all the elements together. I definitely suggest you apply this last step, and don't be afraid to paint the black background around such tender flowers. After the work is dry, remove the masking tape and *voilà*!

I hope you enjoy the process of painting this cute little pattern. This kind of pattern can be used on fabric or other surfaces. And it looks so organic if it's hand-painted. In Figures 6a and 6b you can find two other patterns based on the method of this lesson. Experiment with your own designs. And remember, because it's gouache, there are no limits or rules about the colors and their saturation. You can start with deeper shades and then add lighter and lighter layers. Also, play with the shapes. Despite the fact that it's a super straightforward project, it is flexible and gives you a wide range for your own variations.

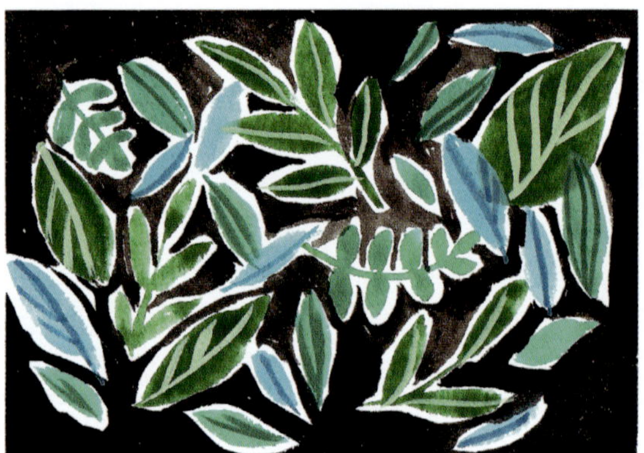

Figure 6b

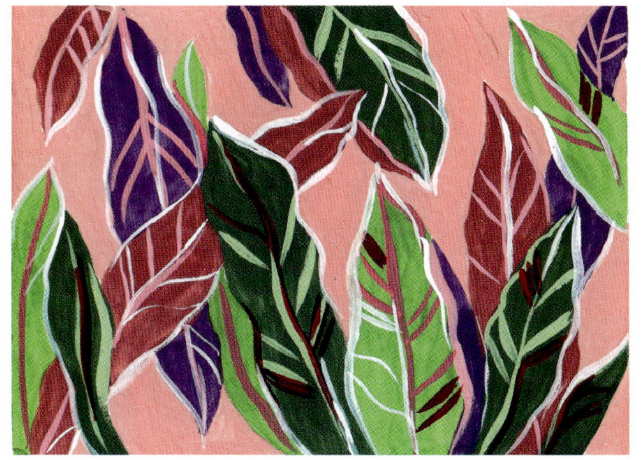

COLORFUL LEAVES

This is a project I painted when I decided to explore the ability of gouache to cover any layer, dark or light. At the same time, I was looking for a simple object to paint, and the leaves are perfect. I was so happy with how this pattern turned out! It was vivid, very creative and the process was super relaxing. Let's re-create the Colorful Leaves project using gouache. I hope you will enjoy this lesson and find it relaxing and fun.

SUPPLIES

- White paper
- Masking tape
- Pencil and eraser
- Round brushes in different sizes
- Detail brush

PROJECT COLORS

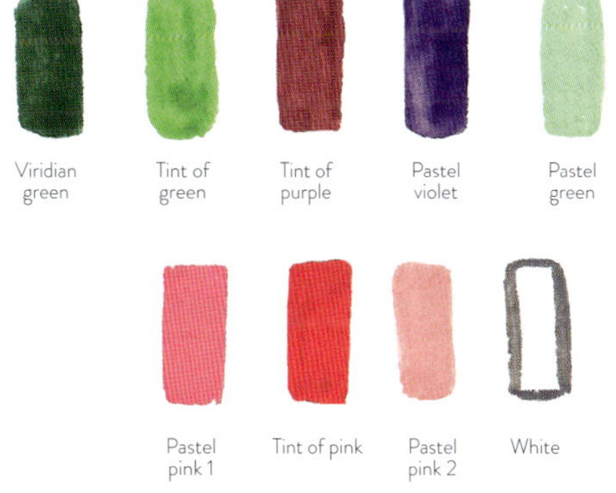

COLOR MIXING

- Tint of green (white + sap green, proportion 1:4)
- Tint of purple (purple + crimson red, proportion 3:1)
- Pastel violet (white + violet, proportion 1:2)
- Pastel green (white + sap green, proportion 1:1)
- Pastel pink 1 (white + crimson red, proportion 2:1)
- Tint of pink (white + crimson red, proportion 1:1)
- Pastel pink 2 (white + crimson red + yellow ochre, proportion 3:1:2)

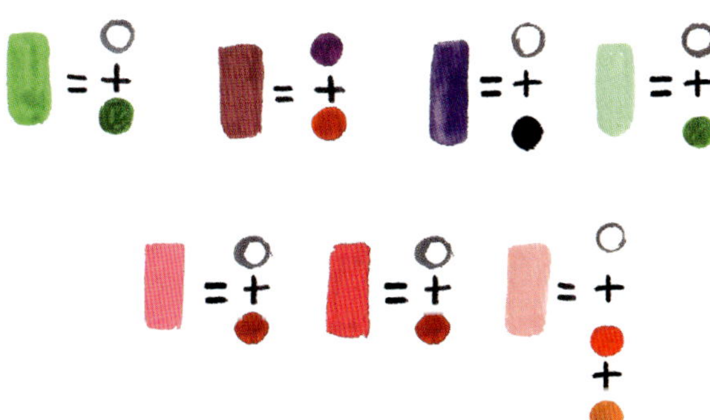

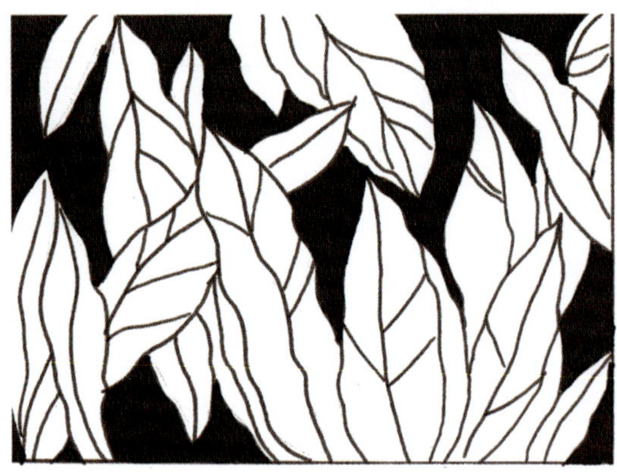

Figure 1

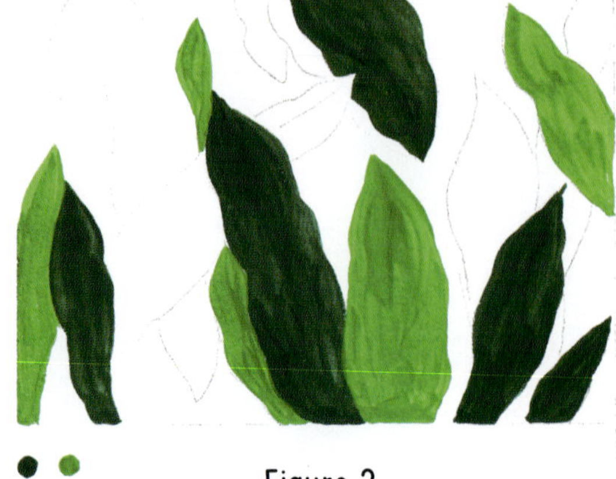

Figure 2

STEP 1

Let's begin with some preparations. To create the pattern, you need to first define an area for it. If you are using a sketchbook, the borders of the sheet can determine the painting area. If you're working with a regular sheet of paper, create a horizontal rectangular border around your area with masking tape.

Now with a pencil, draw a sketch, following the outline in Figure 1. Or draw your own variation of the leaves.

NOTE: The area filled with black on the outline image should not be showing in your sketch. It's just shown here for a better visual view and understanding of project composition.

Take a medium round brush and color some leaves on the pattern in two colors: viridian green and the tint of green (see Figure 2). You can start with either color, but I suggest you first paint in one color, let the leaves dry and then continue by using the other color. If you are using different colors for your own composition, try to distribute the colors evenly for color harmony in the piece. Once the leaves dry completely, move on to the next step.

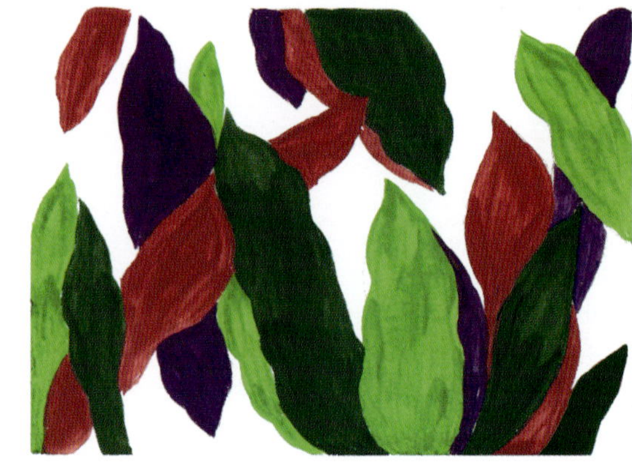

Figure 3

STEP 2

Keep working with the same brush. Paint the rest of the leaves in the tint of purple and the pastel violet by following Figure 3, or choose the colors yourself. Let the painted layer dry completely.

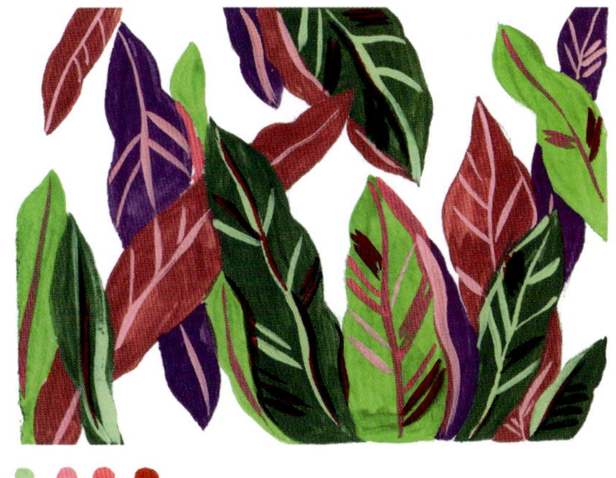

Figure 4

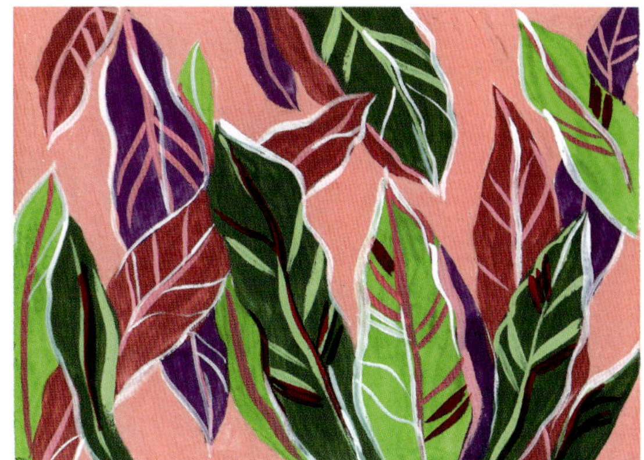

Figure 5

STEP 3

It's time to add the details to the leaves. Because initially this project was an experiment in color combinations, you can add the veins and stems of the leaves randomly in very different colors. However, I suggest that you paint details in the following tints: pastel green, crimson red, pastel pink 1 and the tint of pink. For the violet and pink leaves, use pastel pink 1. On the green leaves, use pastel green, crimson red and the tint of pink. Use a detail brush or a small round brush for this step (see Figure 4).

NOTE: The details were added in the second layer using the layering technique (page 11).

STEP 4

The pattern is almost ready, and the final touches make it look absolutely gorgeous (see Figure 5).

For this step, use round brushes in sizes appropriate to the areas you're working on. Paint the background surrounding the leaves in pastel pink 2. Let the layer dry.

Arm yourself with the detail brush and add the outlines of the leaves in some places with white gouache. Also paint additional details on the leaves themselves. The outline should not absolutely follow the leaves' shape; you can modify them a bit. For example, make them wavy.

Our pattern is complete now. Remove the tape and, with it, everything that may go beyond the area intended for your work. The background in this pattern plays a very important role, pops the leaves' colors and makes the work look complete.

To further practice the project, try different color combinations. Even unusual color combinations sometimes work great. And of course, try to apply other background colors: pastel variations, black and maybe some dark tints. Also, change the composition of the leaves. For this, you can find inspiration in nature and see how leaves overlap each other on a tree or bush. Nature always inspires us. Figure 6 shows a pattern painted using this project's methods but with other colors and with the modified composition. Gouache is a perfect medium to paint bright, fun projects like this one.

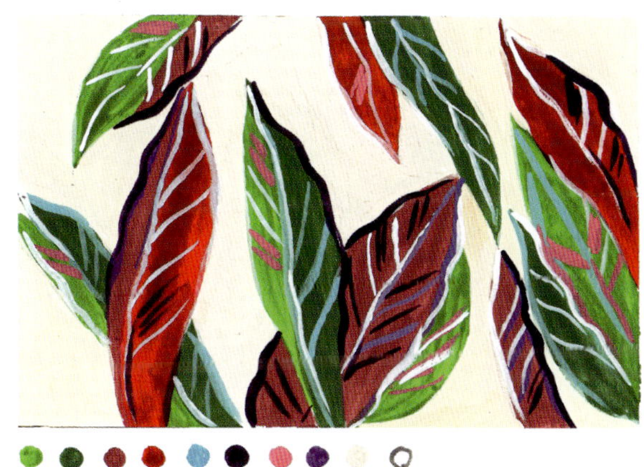

Figure 6

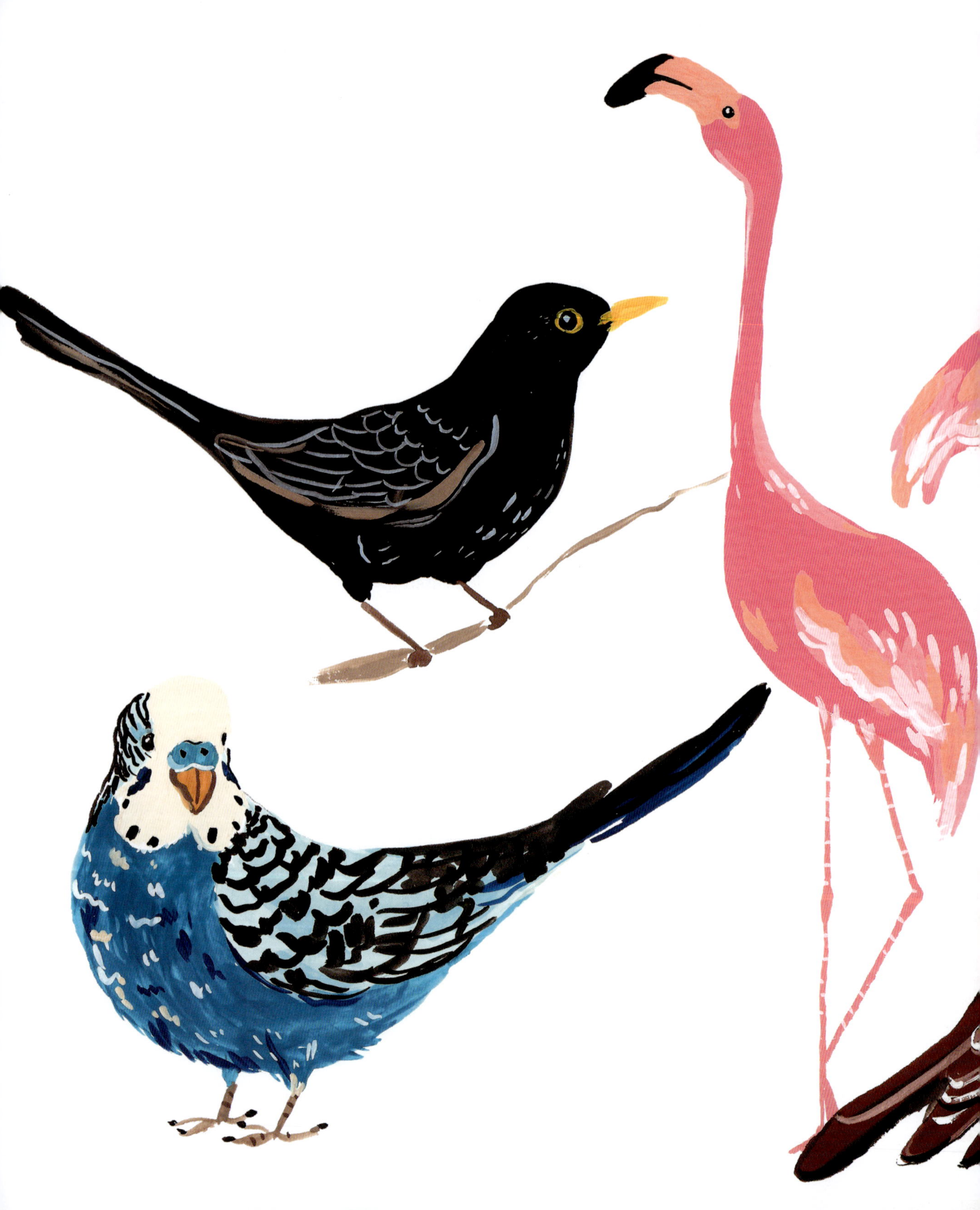

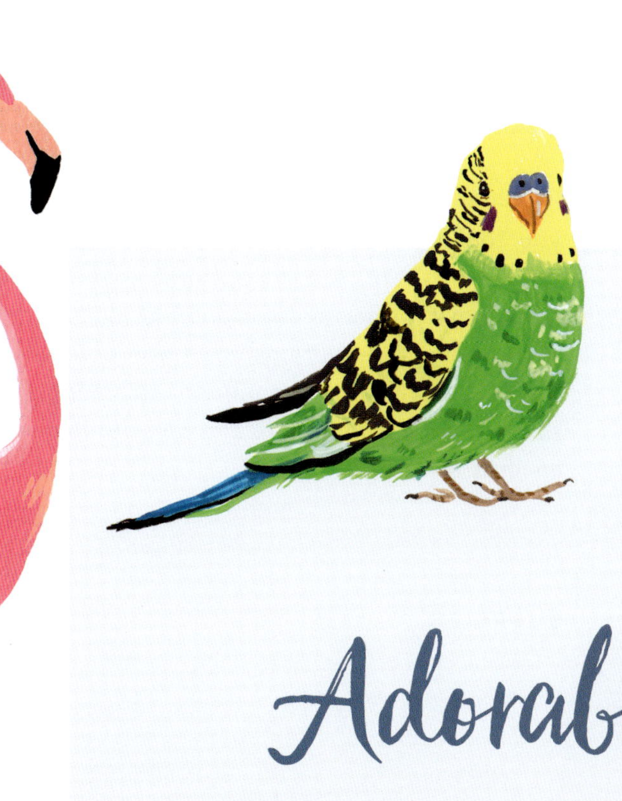

Adorable BIRDS

I love birds so much that I have dedicated an entire chapter to painting these cuties—from small garden birds to big and exotic ones. I tried to keep the projects simple while also applying different approaches for using gouache to show you all the versatility and power of the medium. I hope you enjoy painting these beautiful birds!

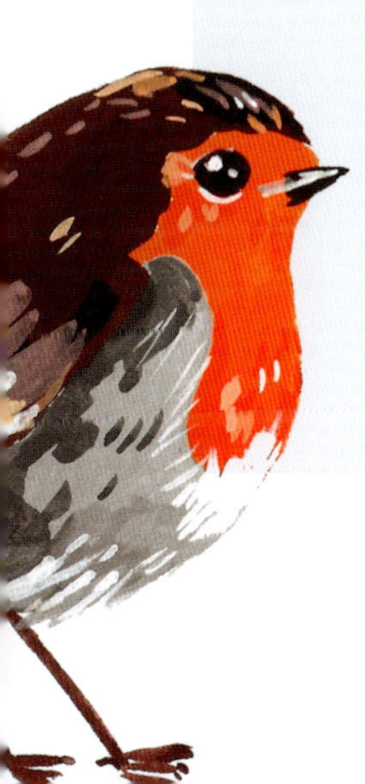

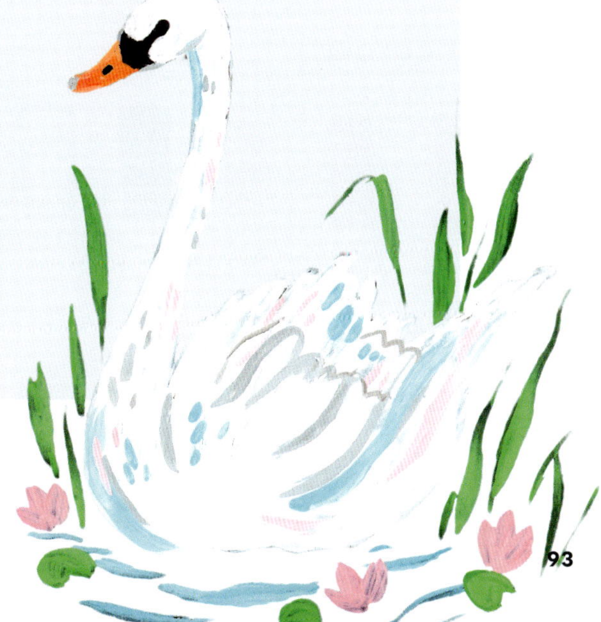

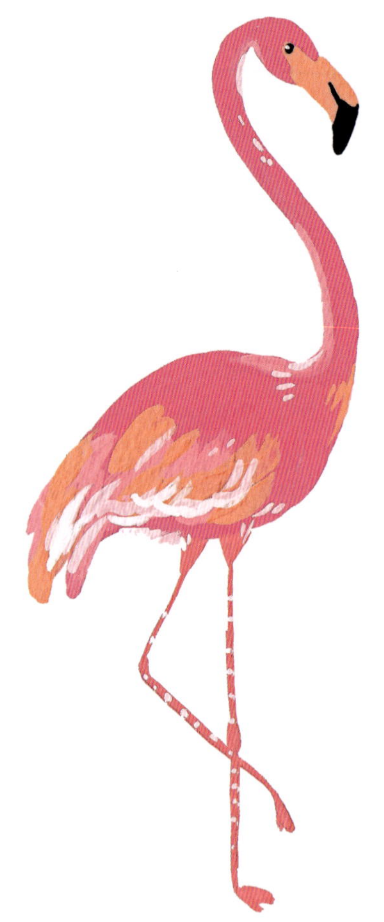

FANCY PINK FLAMINGO

If you always wanted to paint a flamingo, I assure you that you will enjoy doing so, especially with gouache. When I see illustrations or paintings of a flamingo, it makes me smile and feel more cheerful. I hope this project brings you some positivity and makes you feel more confident in your painting skills. So let's paint a cute and colorful flamingo in an illustrative style.

PROJECT COLORS

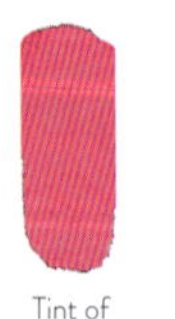
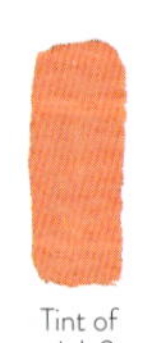
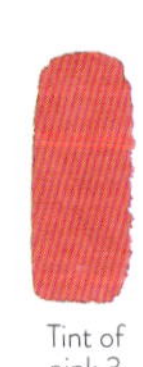
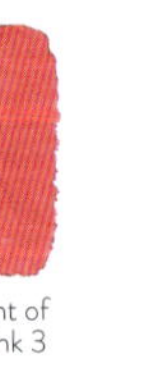
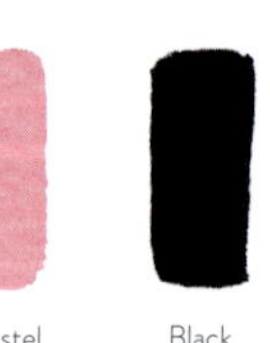

Tint of pink 1 · Tint of pink 2 · Tint of pink 3 · Pastel pink · Black (noir) · White

SUPPLIES

- White, black or craft paper
- Pencil and eraser
- Round brushes in different sizes
- Detail brush

COLOR MIXING

- Tint of pink 1 (white + rose, proportion 1:6)
- Tint of pink 2 (white + rose + permanent yellow, proportion 1:1:1)
- Tint of pink 3 (white + rose + permanent yellow, proportion 1:2:1)
- Pastel pink (white + rose, proportion 2:1)

TIP: If you don't have a rose tint, use magenta or any other tint of cool pink.

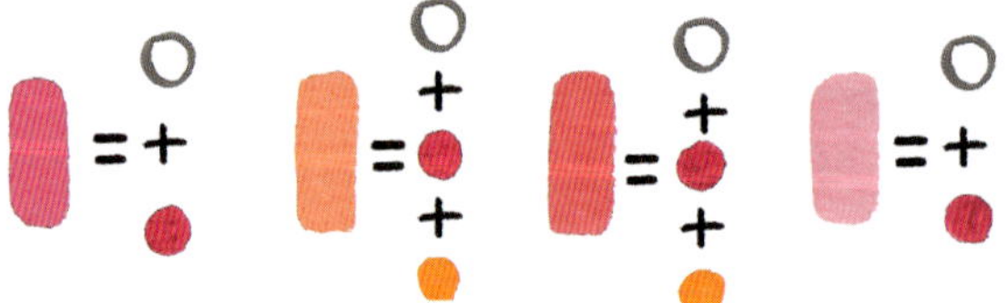

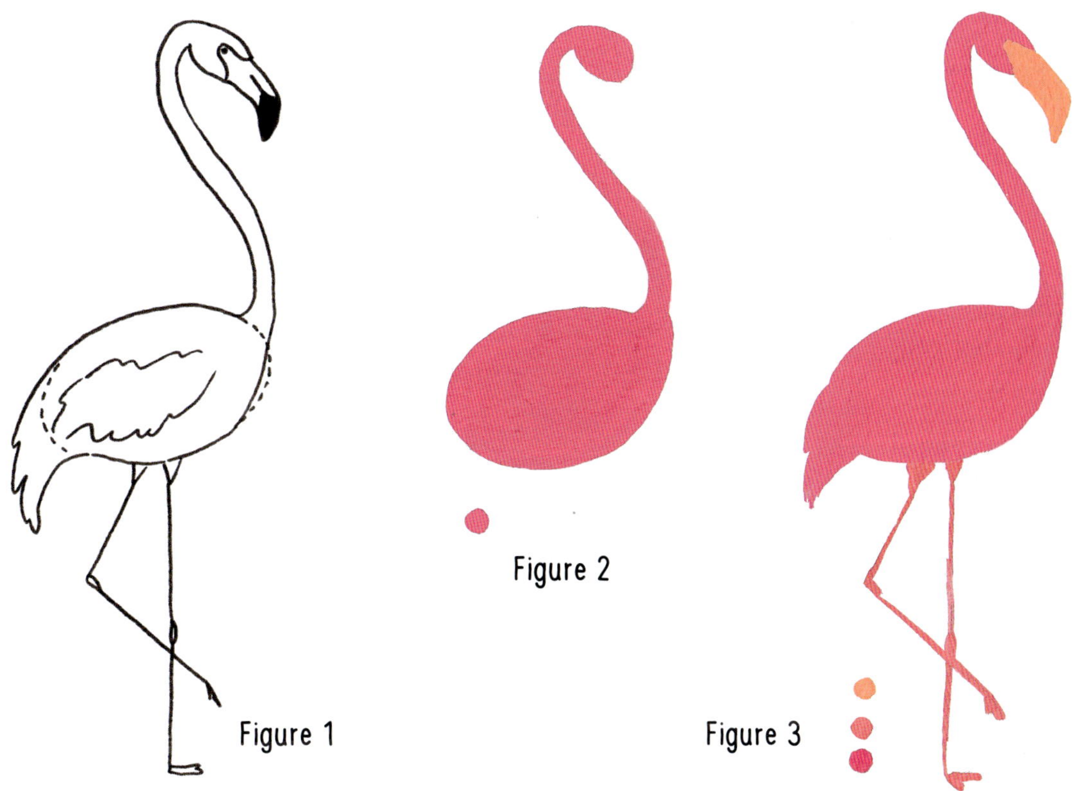

STEP 1

Let's first understand the shape of the flamingo (see Figure 1). Make a light sketch with a pencil following the outlines in Figure 1. Keep the sketch simple, just the baselines.

TIP: I suggest you start sketching by drawing the oval and then turn to the rest of the bird's body.

Take a medium round brush and, with the tint of pink 1, fill in the head, body and neck of the flamingo (see Figure 2). If the shapes' outlines look rough and not smooth, use the detail brush or small round brush to make the outline of the shapes smoother. Once the base layer is done, go to the next step.

STEP 2

Now using a medium round brush, add the tail of the bird with the tint of pink 1, as shown in Figure 3. Let the painting dry completely. Keep working with the same brush and paint the beak in the tint of pink 2. Now we can paint the legs. Flamingos have slender legs. To emphasize this you can even make them longer and out of proportion with the body. It makes sense if you paint in an illustrative or cartoon style. Take a detail brush and paint the legs in the tint of pink 3. Try to make the bird's legs look thin and elegant. I suggest you paint broken lines and then connect them. Allow the painted layer to dry completely.

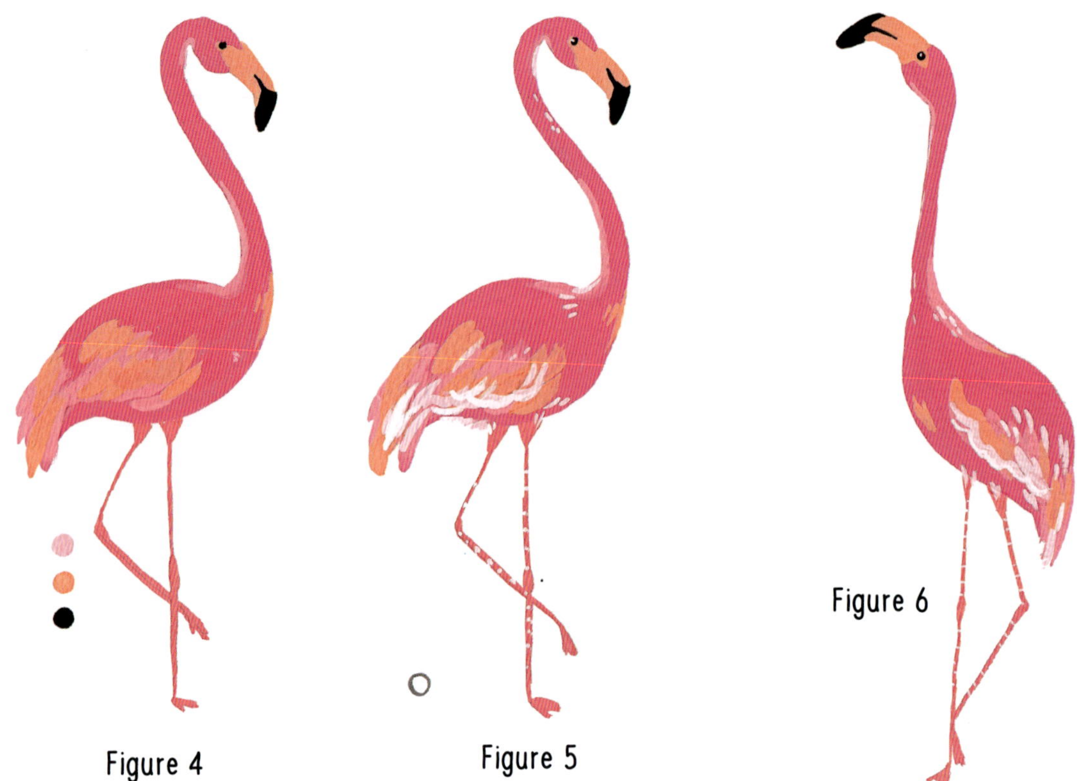

Figure 4

Figure 5

Figure 6

STEP 3

The silhouette is already recognizable, and even if you leave it in this stage, everyone will guess that this is a flamingo. Let's keep the illustration simple and just add some details, which make the painting more interesting (see Figure 4).

NOTE: For this step, we'll use the layering technique (page 11).

Add the wing and some details by using a medium round brush in the next colors: first pastel pink and then, after that layer has dried, the tint of pink 2. Add a few feather details to the plumage using pastel pink. Now paint the details on the beak and eye in black.

TIP: Use the small round brush for painting bigger areas and a detail brush for some neat work and details.

STEP 4

Time to add the final touches (see Figure 5). We'll use a detail brush for this step. Add details in white gouache to the eye and to the plumage of the flamingo. Then, paint some details on the legs with the same color.

The illustration is done and it looks charming, doesn't it? If you would like to practice painting this lesson, you can change the bird's position, as well as add more details (Figure 6). Despite the fact that it's super easy to execute and in a simple style, you can always go back to this project and enjoy painting adorable flamingos.

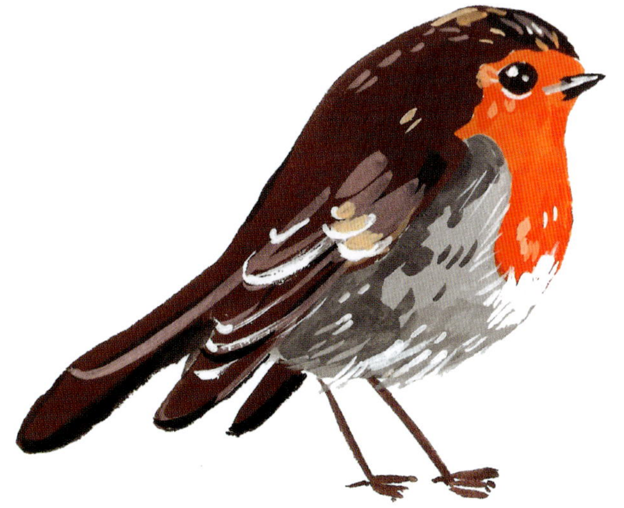

CUTE ROBIN

Let's paint a cute little bird, the robin. This is my favorite bird. Robins look so cute. Their body shape and vivid plumage make this bird such a nice object to paint. There are many styles in which you can paint birds, from very realistic to a minimalist, flat illustration. When using gouache, I suggest you paint in a cartoon style. Gouache is just the perfect medium to add layers, and it will give the perfect result quickly and easily.

SUPPLIES

- White or craft paper
- Pencil and eraser
- Round brushes in different sizes
- Detail brush or liner

PROJECT COLORS

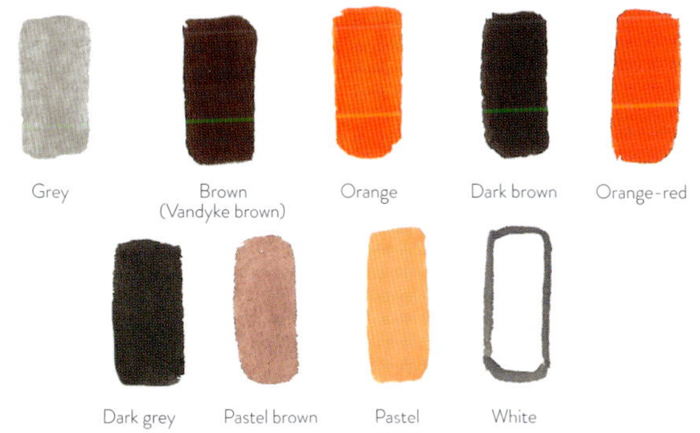

COLOR MIXING

- Grey (white + black, proportion 10:1)
- Dark brown (black + Vandyke brown, proportion 1:3)
- Orange-red (orange + vermillion red 3:1)
- Dark grey (white + black, proportion 3:1)
- Pastel brown (Vandyke brown + white, proportion 1:2)
- Pastel orange (orange + white, proportion 1:1)

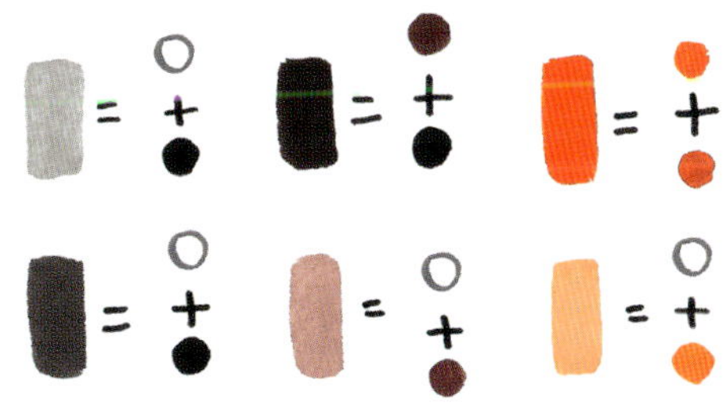

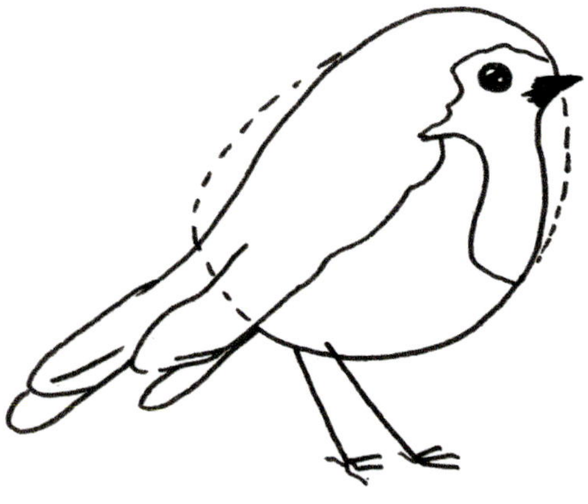

Figure 1

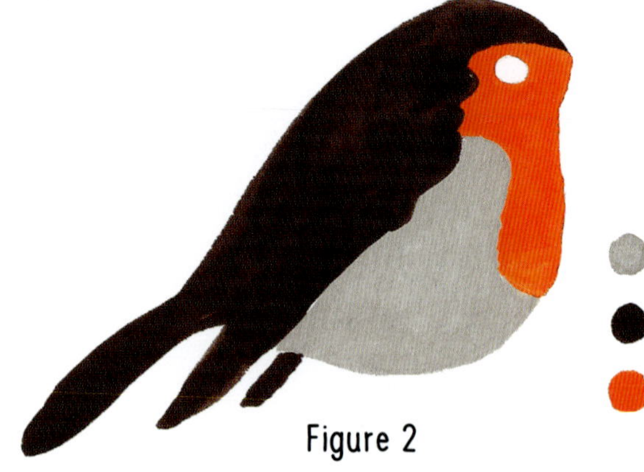

Figure 2

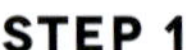

STEP 1

Let's get started with a pencil sketch. Take a look at Figure 1, which shows the outline of the bird. Follow it to make a pencil sketch on your paper.

NOTE: Because the project will be done in a cartoon style, I divided the body shape into three sections: 1) the back and wings; 2) the underbelly; and 3) the face and chest. You can use the same approach to create any bird painting.

Using a round brush, fill the areas with grey, brown and orange one after another, as shown in Figure 2. Paint each area after the previous one has dried. Let the painting dry.

TIP: If the painted shape is not perfect, you can fix it with the same color by painting over it after it's dried.

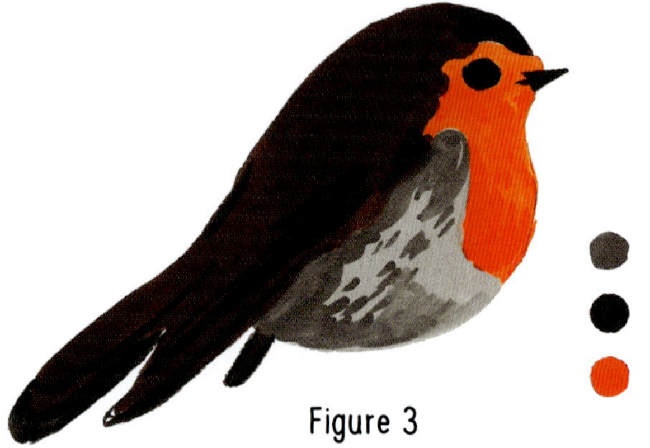

Figure 3

STEP 2

Paint the bird's eye and beak dark brown with a thin-tipped round brush in a small size. Allow the details to dry. Add the dark brown, orange-red and dark grey colors as shown in Figure 3, using the layering technique (page 11). To make the layer look softer, use the softening technique (page 12) by taking a wet round brush and blurring desired areas. I applied this technique to the dark grey and orange-red areas of the bird. Let the painting dry.

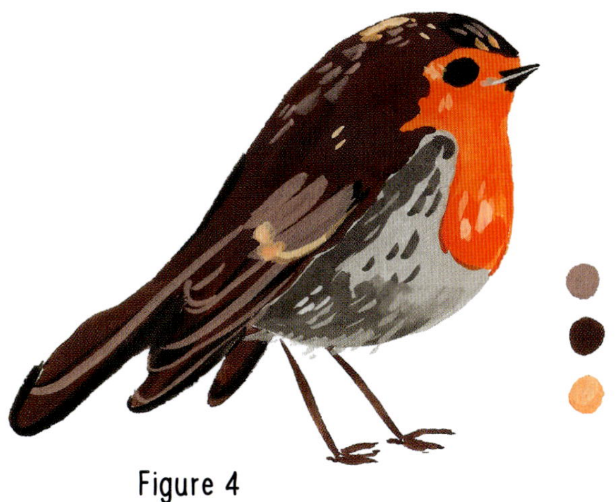
Figure 4

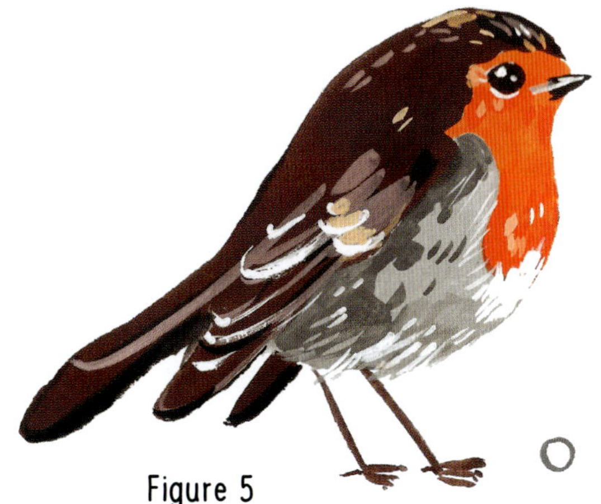
Figure 5

STEP 3

Let's continue to build the bird's body. Paint the bird's feet in dark brown by using a detail brush.

Time to add light tones and details to the painting, which we can do easily because we're using gouache. So with grey, pastel brown and pastel orange, paint the details as shown in Figure 4. Use a round brush for painting lines on the bird's plumage and a detail brush for the feather details on the back, wings, the face and chest. Let the painting dry completely, then jump into the next step.

STEP 4

As in other projects of this book, the last step turns the painting into a beautiful piece. Equip yourself with a detail brush or liner (it's best to have both brushes for different brush strokes) and add details in white, on the wings, underbelly and chest, as well as to the eye and beak as shown in Figure 5.

I suggest you use the dry-brush technique (page 12) with the white gouache to create a more interesting illustration. No need to apply this technique for all the details, but a few textured lines would be a nice final touch.

I hope you're happy with the result and would like to paint more cute birds like this one. It's very simple to do using gouache. Figure 6 shows a pink robin created using this lesson's methods. I changed the colors and the bird's position, but I followed this lesson's general principles.

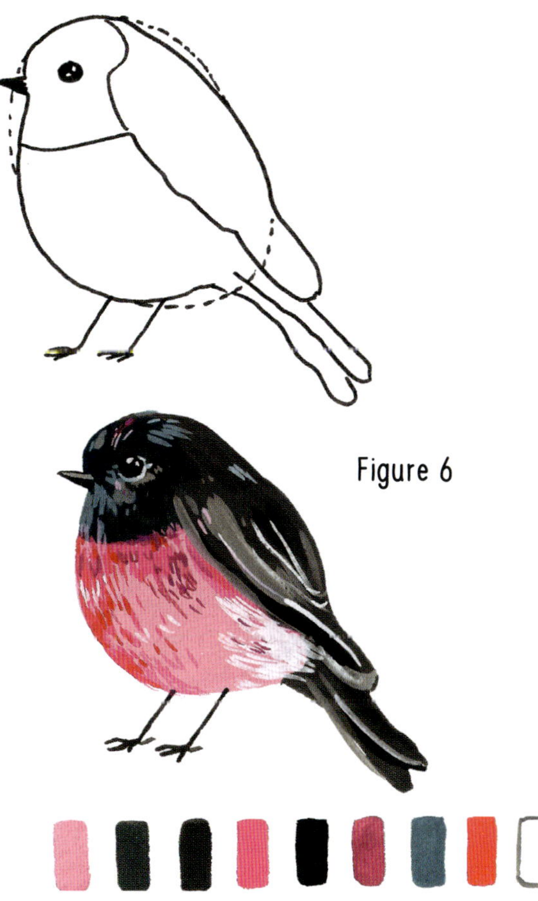
Figure 6

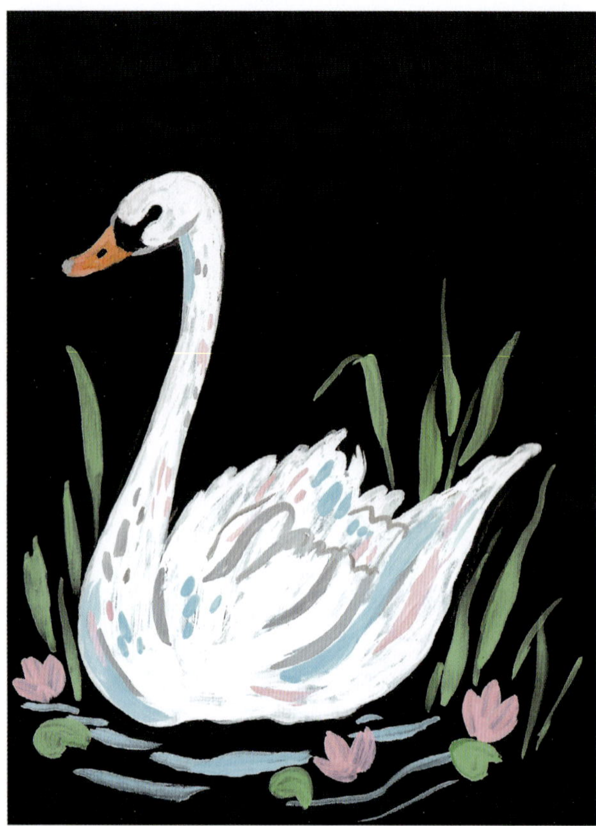

ELEGANT SWAN

This project is a great demonstration of the power of gouache. In just four simple steps, you will be able to create an incredible and elegant illustration of a swan. Let's get started!

SUPPLIES

- Black paper or white paper
- White pencil and eraser
- Flat brush (optional)
- Round brushes in different sizes
- Detail brush

COLOR MIXING

- Pastel orange (orange + white, proportion 1:1)
- Pastel blue (cerulean blue + white, proportion 1:2)
- Light grey (black + white, proportion 1:8)
- Pastel pink (primary red + white, proportion 1:5)
- Pastel green (sap green + white, proportion 1:3)

PROJECT COLORS

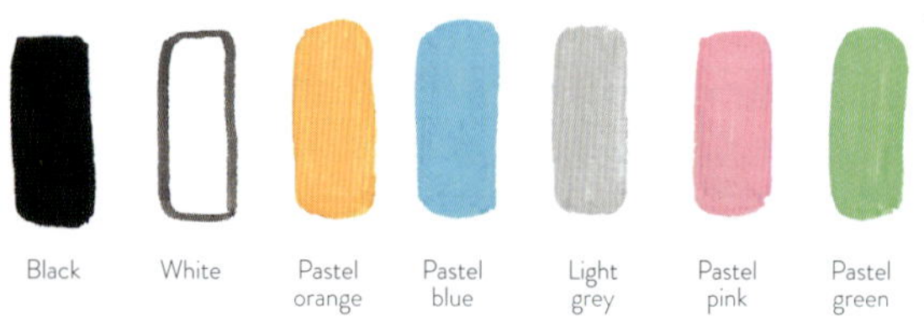

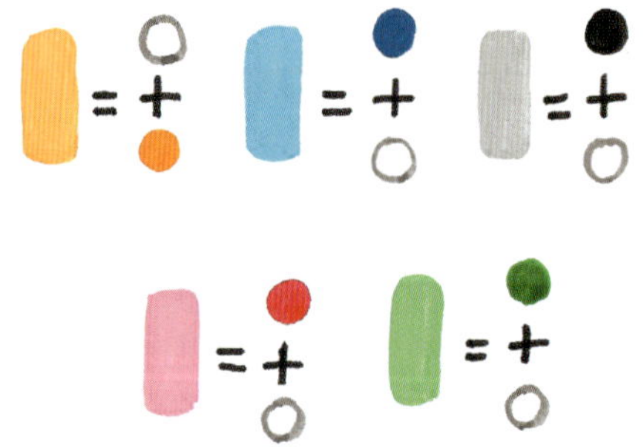

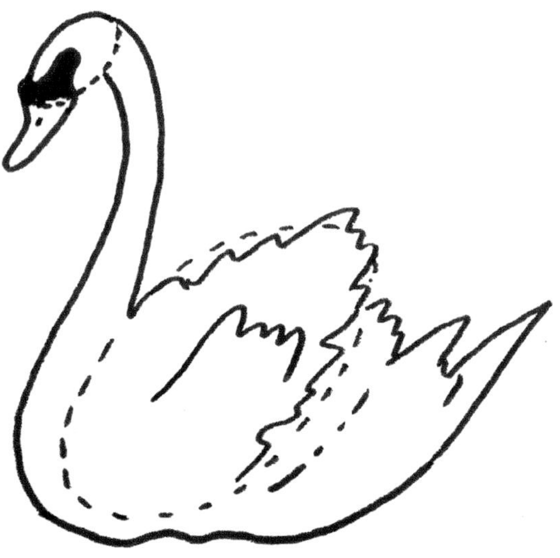

Figure 1

Figure 2

STEP 1

For this project, you will need to draw a sketch (Figure 1). Because we will paint on black paper, use a soft white pencil for preliminary sketching. While sketching, try to make the lines almost invisible and do not press too hard on the paper. Once the sketch is ready, let's turn to the main work.

TIP: It's not essential to use a white pencil. It could be any pastel tint visible on the black paper.

If you don't have black paper, you still can execute this project. Instead, paint the background in black gouache by using the flat brush. Let the layer dry, and then jump to the main painting process.

NOTE: If you painted the black background, for all the following layers make double sure your paint consistency is not watery or creamy. Also, don't apply pressure with the brush or add unnecessary movements, as you may smudge the black base layer.

Take a medium round brush with a thin tip and paint the base layer of the bird in white gouache, as shown in Figure 2. You may change the brush to the small one if it would be easier for you to paint the thinner areas.

Let the layer dry completely.

If, after it's dry, the base layer still looks transparent, feel free to add one more layer on top, with the same color.

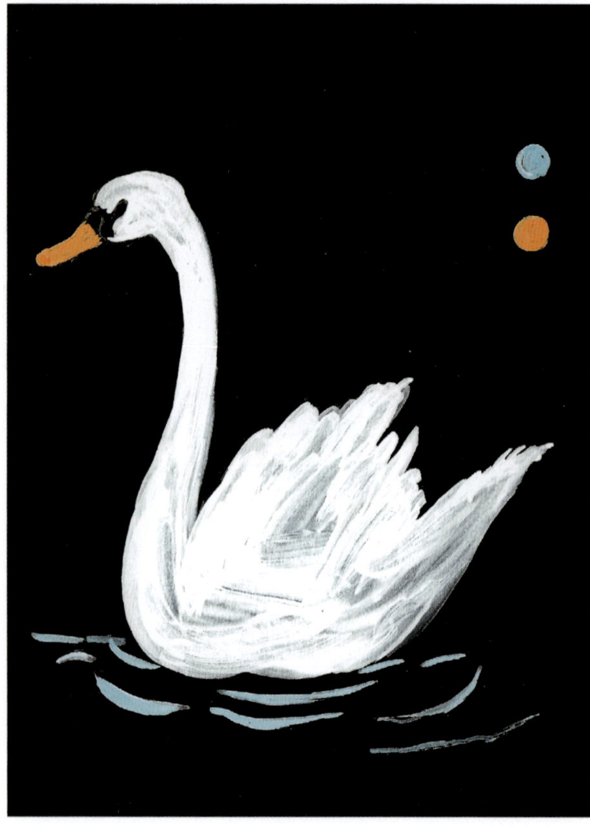

Figure 3

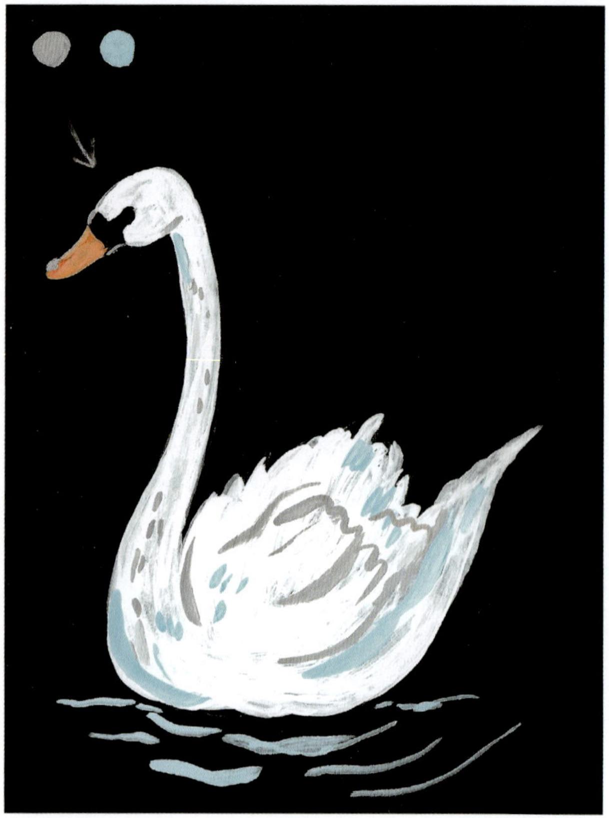

Figure 4

STEP 2

Arm yourself with a small round brush and paint the beak of the swan in pastel orange (see Figure 3). Then paint the waves in pastel blue. Allow all details to dry completely.

STEP 3

Now we are ready to add some details. Keep working with the small brush or use a detail brush for this step. By following Figure 4, paint the highlights in pastel blue and the wing and some plumage in light grey using the layering technique (page 11). After the painting is completely dry, move on to the final step.

NOTE: The area over the beak is not painted. I left it in black and just contoured it from both sides in light grey.

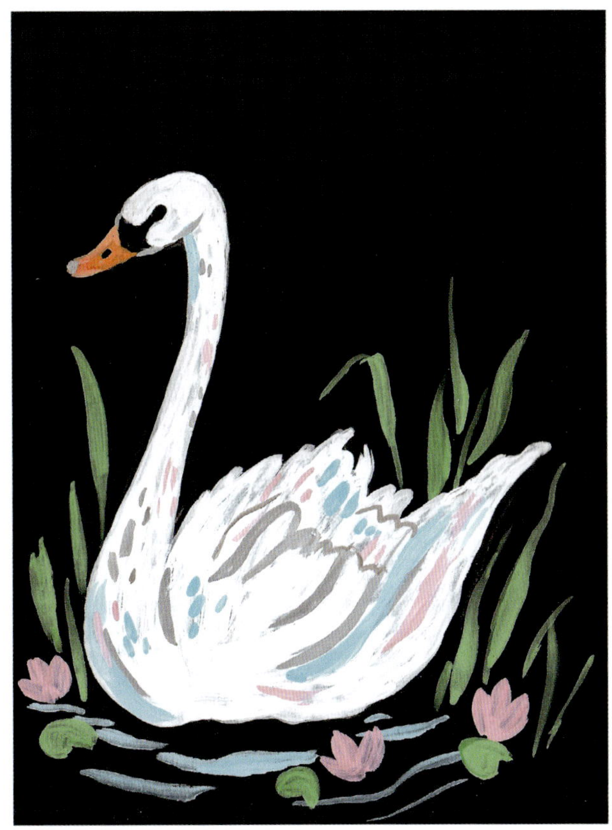

Figure 5

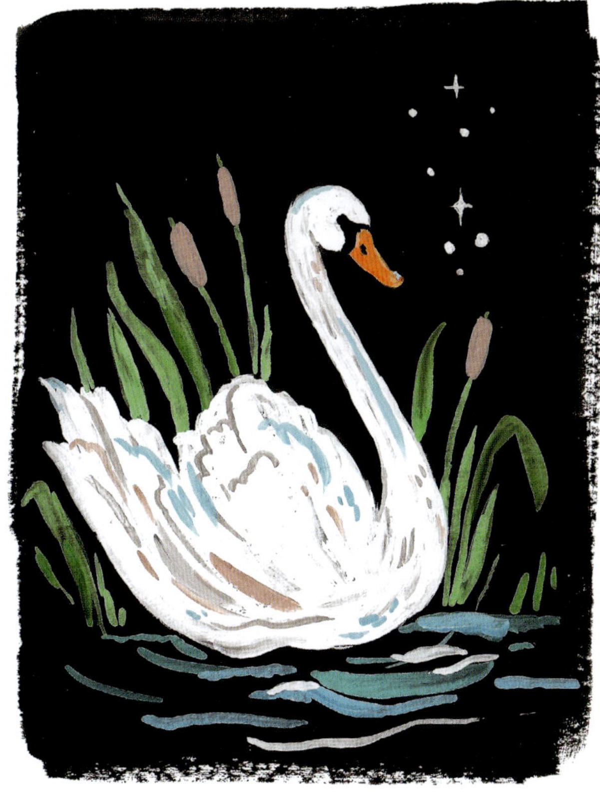

Figure 6

STEP 4

Using the detail brush, paint the nostril on the beak in black. Then paint some additional details on the bird's plumage in pastel pink. Now switch to a small round brush and paint the lotus flowers and some foliage in their corresponding colors: pastel pink and pastel green (see Figure 5).

NOTE: With the grey color, you can add a tiny eye, but I decided to skip this detail to make the illustration look more stylized.

Using these same methods, you can experiment and paint more swan illustrations. Play with the colors of the details and the project composition itself and add different decorative elements to change the scenery and the mood of the illustration. In Figure 6, you can see the scene painted by using this lesson. The stars and stylized shine add a feeling of magic and mystery. Also, I've changed the position of the bird as well as some colors. Doesn't it look charming? I hope you enjoy this lesson and will get inspired to paint with gouache on black paper.

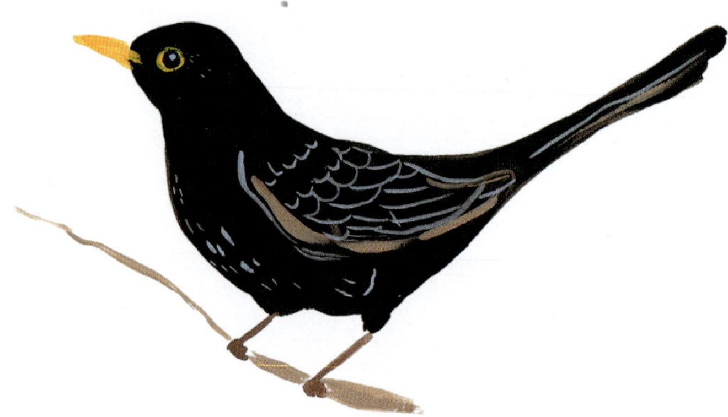

STRIKING BLACKBIRD

The blackbird is a very common bird that you can meet in parks, gardens and hedgerows. I have been so inspired every time I have seen these birds outside my studio window in Tallinn or somewhere in London. So I decided to include a painting of a blackbird in this book. I promise you it will be fun and easy. In only three easy steps you'll get a beautiful illustration of a blackbird.

SUPPLIES

- White or craft paper
- Pencil and eraser
- Round brushes in different sizes
- Detail brush

COLOR MIXING

- Dark blue (Prussian blue + black, proportion 2:1)
- Pastel brown (white + burnt umber + yellow ochre, proportion 3:2:1)
- Pastel blue (white + ultramarine blue, proportion 3:1)

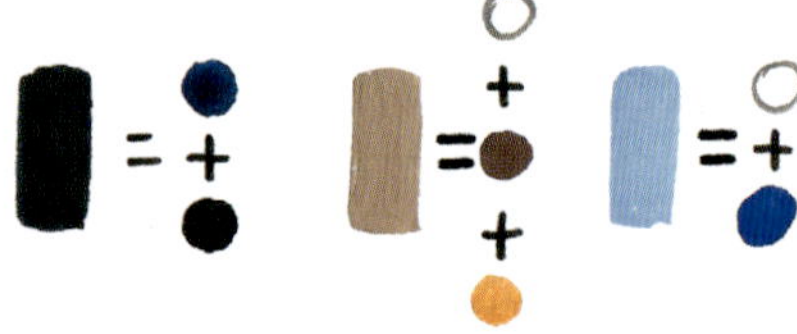

PROJECT COLORS

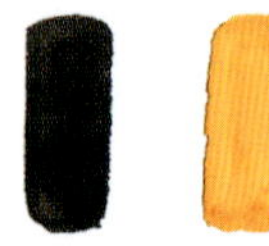

Black (ivory black)

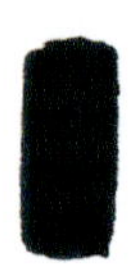

Yellow

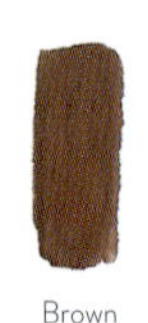

Dark blue

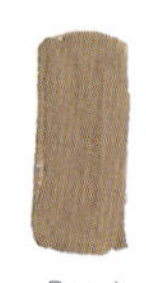

Brown (burnt umber)

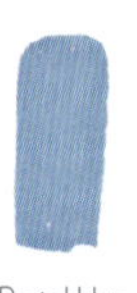

Pastel brown

Pastel blue

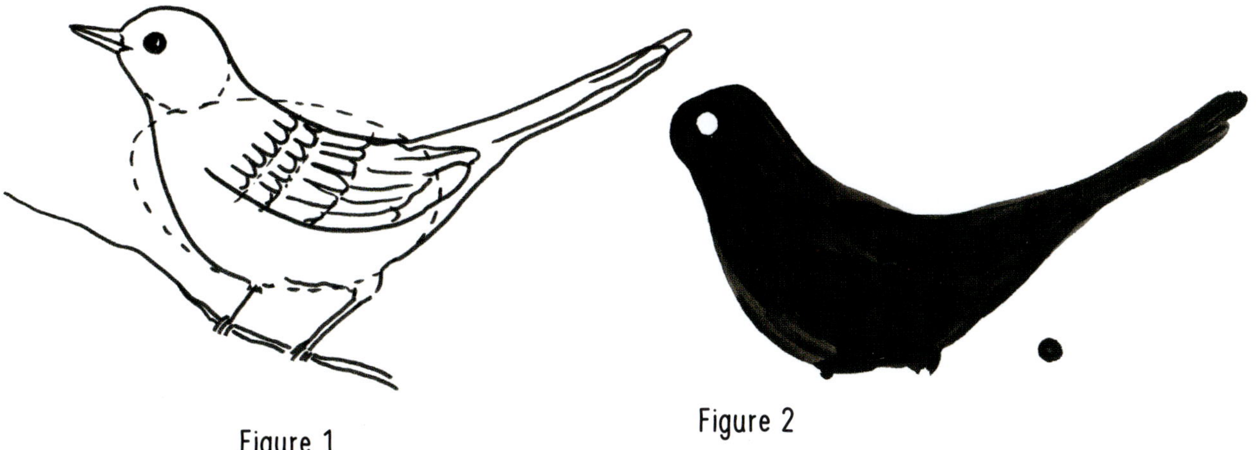

Figure 1

Figure 2

STEP 1

Let's start with perhaps the most difficult step of this project: sketching the bird with a pencil. Draw a sketch by following Figure 1. No need to draw a detailed sketch, just an outline will be enough at this stage. Draw the bird's eye very simply.

Remember that any object, even complicated ones, can be broken down into simpler shapes. You can simplify the blackbird to two ovals (head and body). Start there and then move ahead until you get the final outline.

Take a medium round brush with a thin tip and, with black gouache, fill the body shape, except for the eye area (see Figure 2). Allow the painted layer to dry completely.

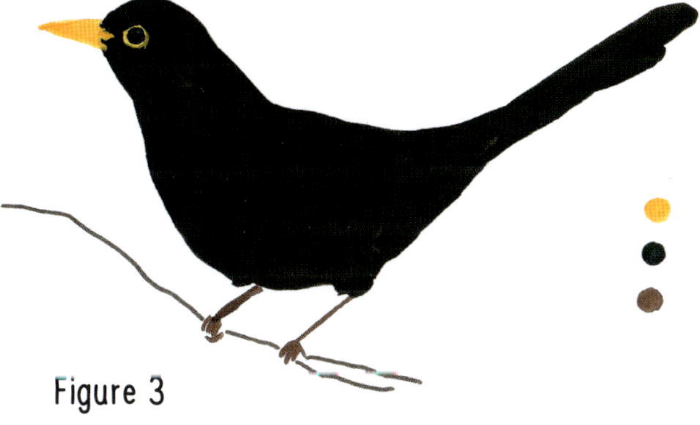

Figure 3

STEP 2

Switch to the small round brush and paint the beak in yellow (see Figure 3). With the same color but using the detail brush, paint the eye. You can paint only the ring in yellow or the whole eye. If you choose the second option, add the pupil in dark blue by using the layering technique (page 11). Finally, paint the simplified legs and feet of a bird in brown with the detail brush. Let everything dry.

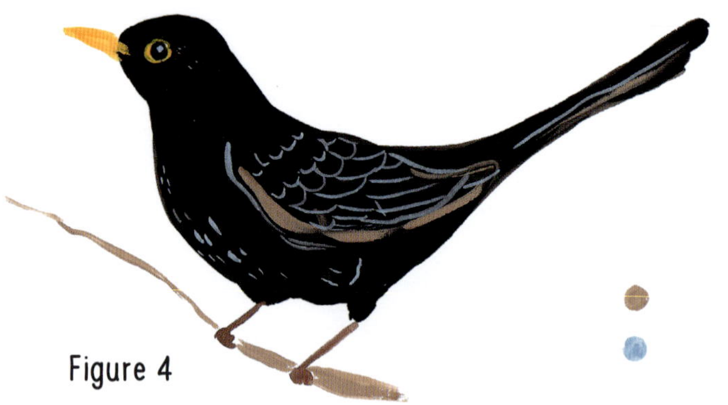

Figure 4

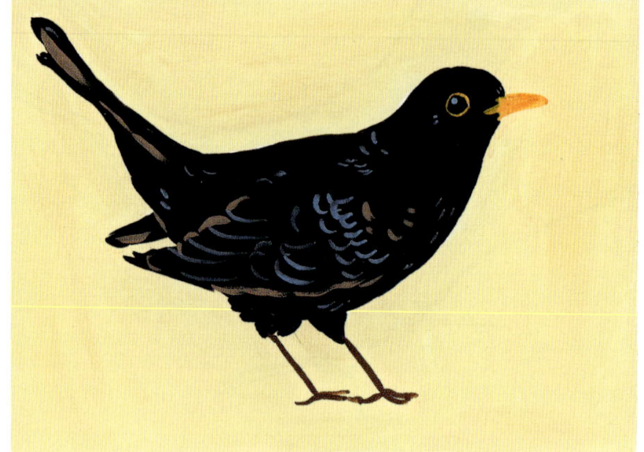

Figure 5

STEP 3

NOTE: In this step we will be using the layering technique (page 11).

We can already recognize the bird in our painting. But for now, it looks pretty flat and unfinished. So let's add the final details to the illustration (see Figure 4). Arm yourself with a detail brush and prepare the pastel brown and the pastel blue tints.

With pastel brown, underline the wing and also add some details in the bird's tail. With pastel blue, add the highlight to the eye and details to the plumage.

Finally, paint the branch the bird is set on in pastel brown. To paint the branch, I recommend applying the dry-brush technique (page 12). Use the small round brush for this purpose.

The painting is finished. You can also try this project with a pastel background. Just paint the background first—fill the background area with the desired color, except for the body shape. Then continue with all the steps and instructions of the lesson.

You can also practice this project by changing the bird's poses (see Figure 5). This is such good practice because you don't need to focus on plumage or specific details. All you need is just to determine the silhouette and then outline it on the paper. Use references on the internet or from books for this purpose. If you are willing, you can add some additional details to the background, such as blossoms, leaves or maybe some simple background scenery. Just keep practicing and don't be afraid to experiment.

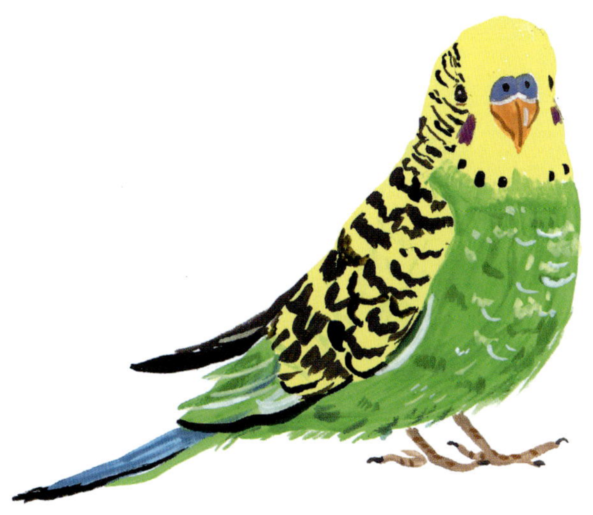

CHARMING PARAKEET

Paint a little cute, vibrant parrot with me. This project may seem more complicated than the rest in this chapter, but it's still achievable, even if you're a newbie to gouache painting. Just be consistent and patient and follow the instructions. It's a really amazing project that shows the power of the layering technique. All the simple details combine to create a vivid and pretty painting. Also, the gouache's rich colors make the illustration even more eye-catching. I hope you're excited!

SUPPLIES

- White or craft paper
- Pencil and eraser
- Round brushes in different sizes
- Detail brush

PROJECT COLORS

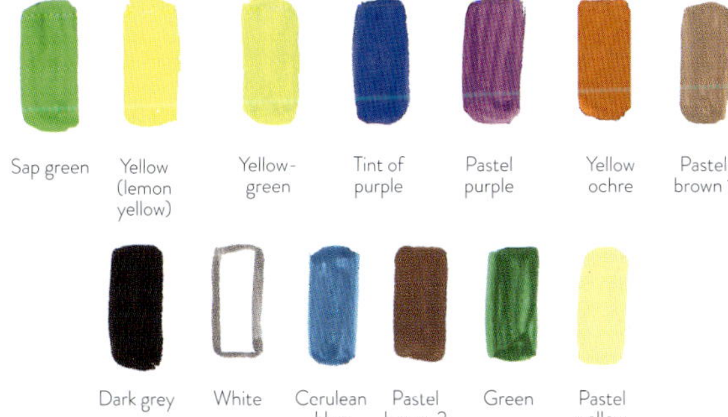

COLOR MIXING

- Yellow-green (yellow + sap green, proportion 3:1)
- Tint of purple (white + purple + ultramarine blue, proportion 1:1:2)
- Pastel purple (white + purple, proportion 1:2)
- Pastel brown 1 (white + burnt umber + yellow ochre, proportion 3:2:1)
- Dark grey (black + white, proportion 3:1)
- Pastel brown 2 (white + burnt umber + yellow ochre, proportion 3:3:1)
- Pastel yellow (yellow + white, proportion 1:1)

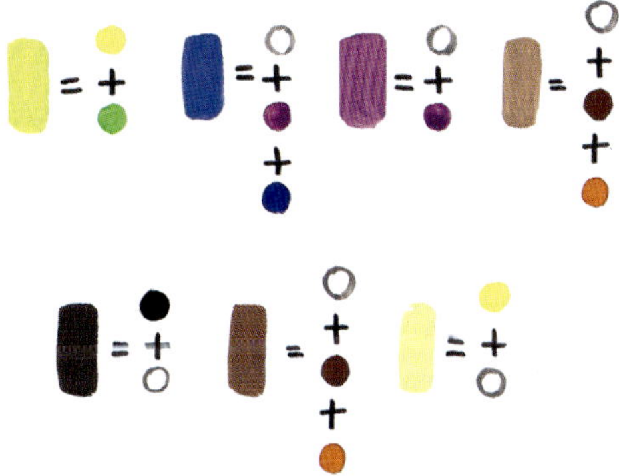

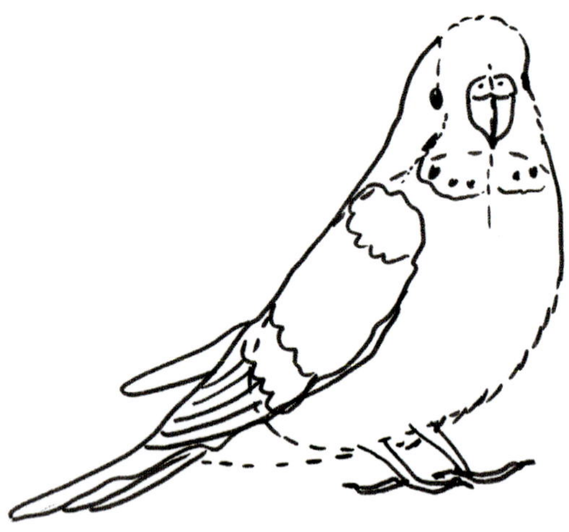

Figure 1

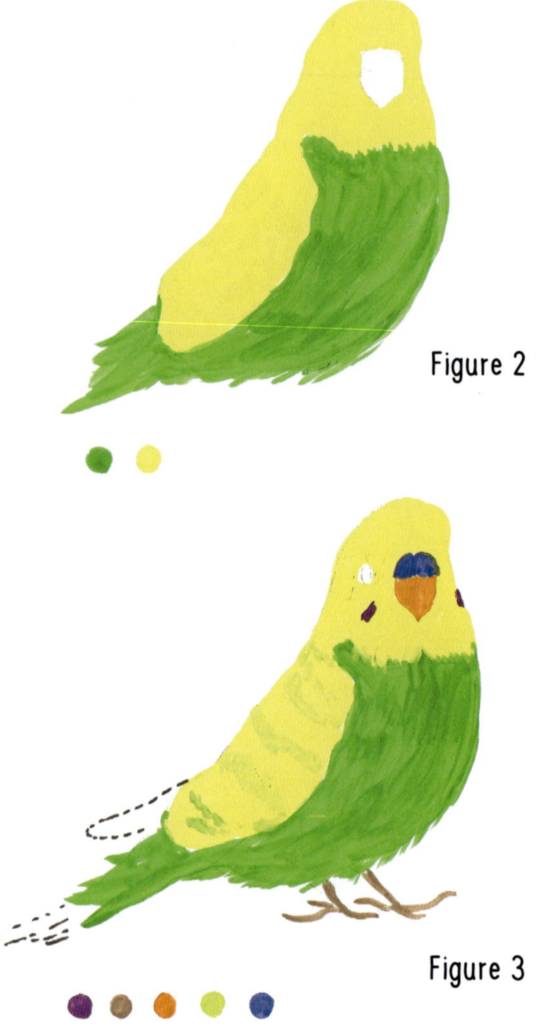

Figure 2

Figure 3

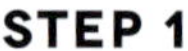

STEP 1

Start by sketching the bird following Figure 1. This time do a detailed sketch. Because we will fill particular areas with gouache paint, a detailed sketch will help.

Using the medium round brush, fill the bird's chest and part of the tail coverts with sap green. When the layer dries, apply the yellow in the head and the wing areas (see Figure 2).

Allow these areas to dry completely.

STEP 2

Next, we'll add some details to complete the base shape of the bird (see Figure 3). Use a small round brush or even a detail brush in this step. Prepare the next tints: yellow-green, the tint of purple, pastel purple, yellow ochre and pastel brown 1. First, paint the wavy pattern on the wing with yellow-green. Then add the beak in yellow ochre and the cheek patches in pastel purple. Paint the legs and feet in pastel brown 1. And finally, paint the cere (a patch at the base of the upper side of the beak) in the tint of purple.

Allow the painting to dry completely.

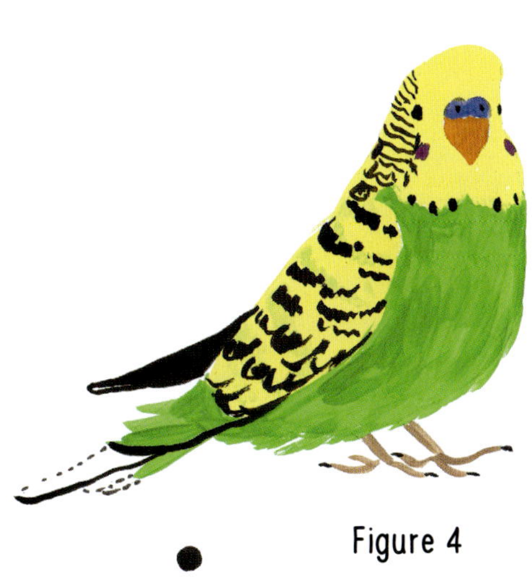

Figure 4

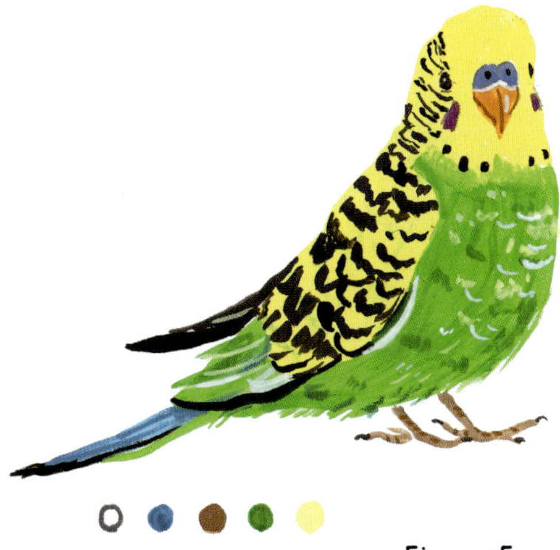

Figure 5

STEP 3

NOTE: In this step and step 4 we will be using the layering technique (page 11).

The base of the painting is done. Let's make the illustration even better by adding details in a very dark grey tint. You can use a pure black instead, but I find this rich dark grey tint much more interesting and realistic. Follow the example in Figure 4 to add all the details, such as the wavy pattern on the head and wing; the eyes; talons on the feet; spots on the neck; part of the tail; and the hidden wing. Use the small round brush or the detail brush in this step. After all the details are done, let the illustration dry.

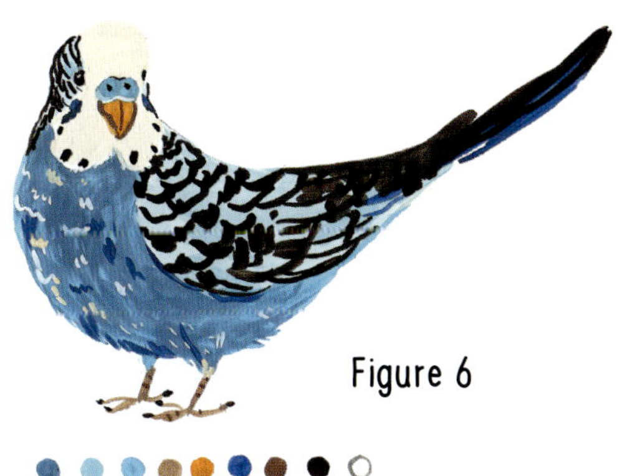

Figure 6

STEP 4

After all the work we are ready to add the final details and touches. Prepare the following colors: white, cerulean blue, pastel brown 2, green and pastel yellow. Arm yourself with the detail brush and paint the feather details and details on the feet, beak and eye, as shown in Figure 5, in their corresponding colors.

TIP: I advise you to add the green details on the plumage by applying the dry-brush technique (page 12). It'll make the illustration look more interesting and realistic.

Our cute parakeet is finished.

As you may know, parakeet plumage can be in different color combinations, so you can practice the principles of the lesson with different colors. For additional practice, choose other poses of the bird. Once again, for exploring the poses of this small parrot as well as other animals, I recommend you use references from the internet or bird guidebooks.

In Figure 6, you can find another painting of the parakeet in blue and soft yellow tones. I hope you fall in love with this project and that it shows you all the beauty of painting birds in a more realistic style.

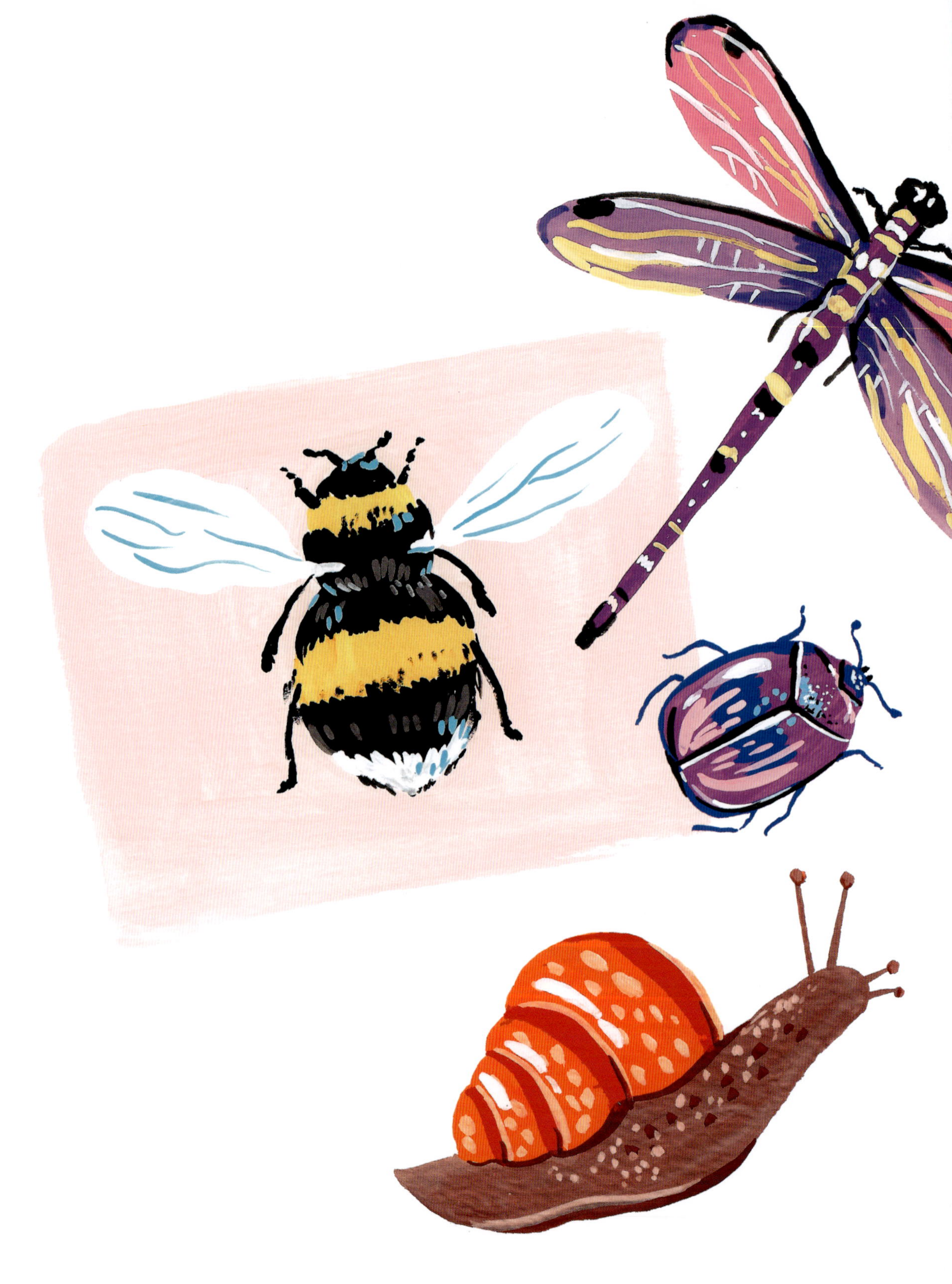

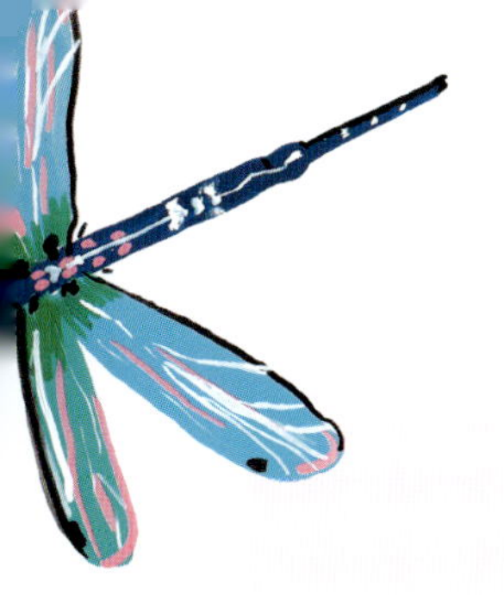
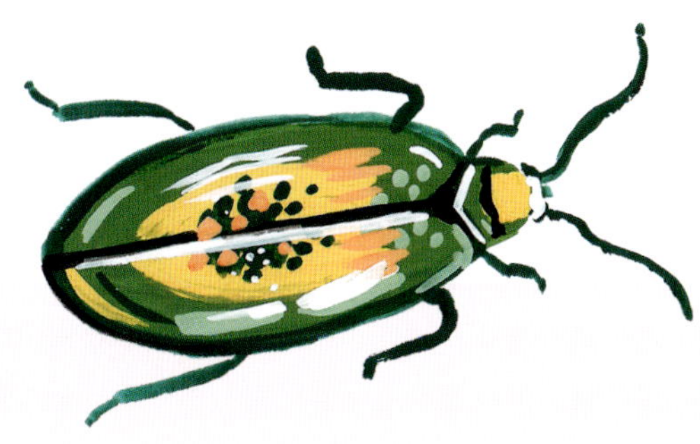
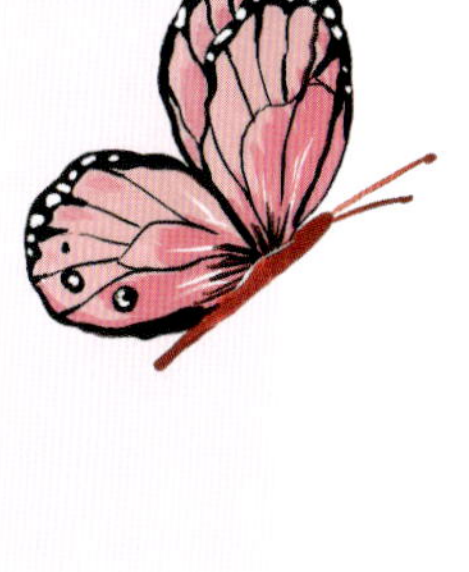

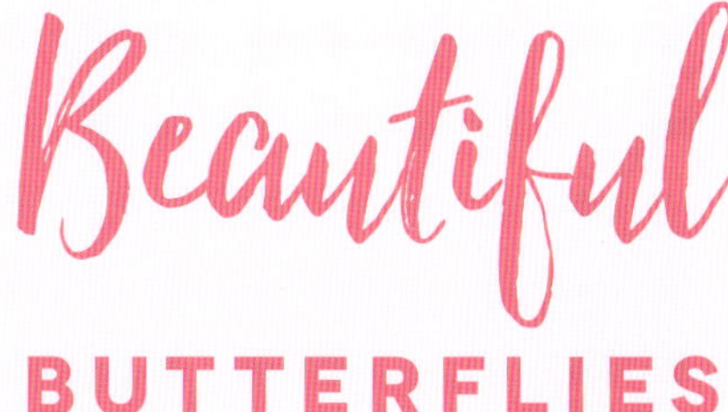

Beautiful BUTTERFLIES, BUMBLEBEES AND MORE

You may think that insects are not inspiring objects to paint, but I promise you that you will enjoy painting an elegant butterfly, gorgeous moth, colorful beetle and more. When using gouache, this is such a fun and easy process. All the details are just a pleasure to paint. And, as I say throughout this book, whatever you paint is always good practice. I hope you will like to paint these little friends as much as I do!

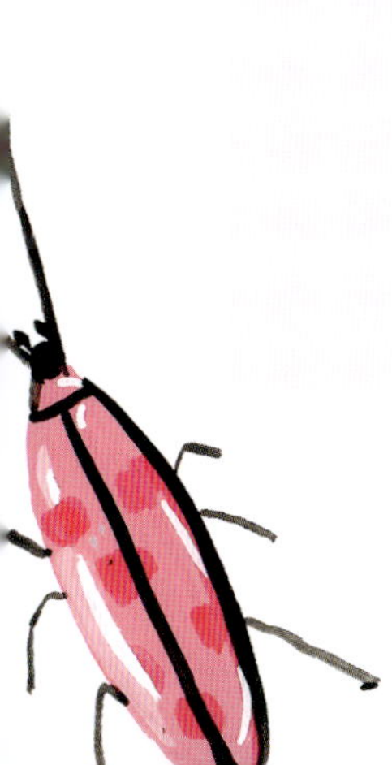
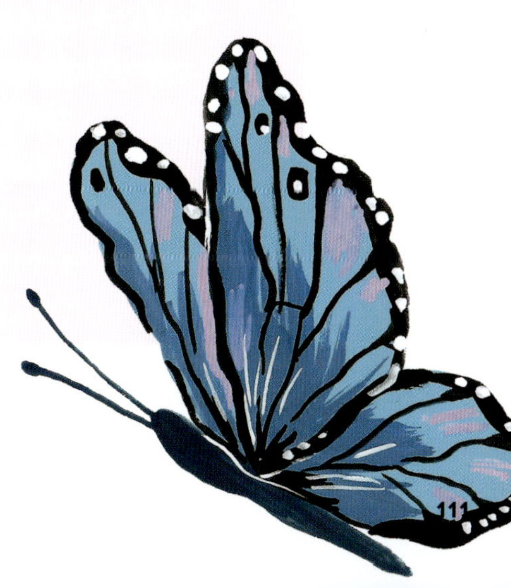

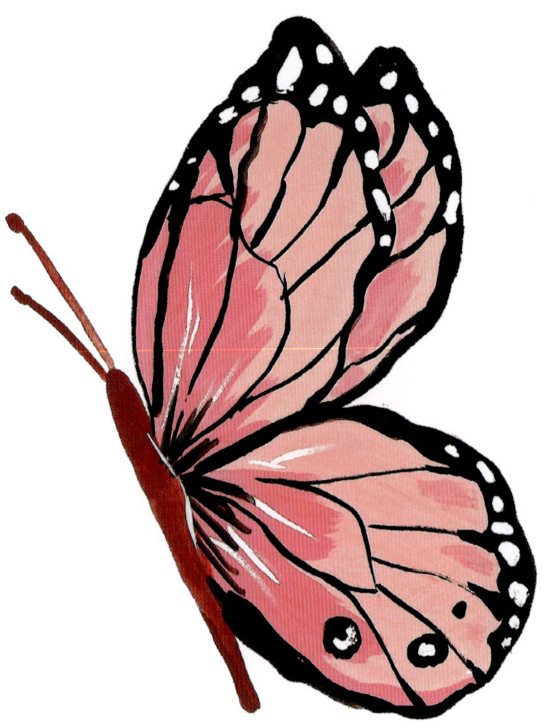

PINK MONARCH BUTTERFLY

In this project, I will explain step by step how to paint a butterfly in pastel tones with gouache. The style we'll use for this project is very simple and decorative. However, it will open our eyes to all the grace and beauty of these wonderful insects.

SUPPLIES

- White paper
- Pencil and eraser
- Round brushes in different sizes
- Detail brush
- Liner brush (optional)

NOTE: Black or craft paper may work for some color combinations, but I recommend painting on white paper for this project.

PROJECT COLORS

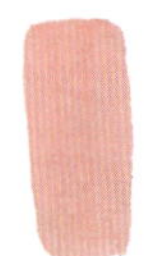

Tint of pink 1

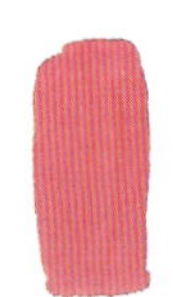

Tint of pink 2

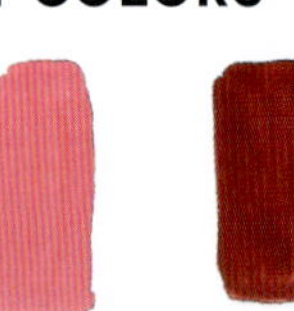

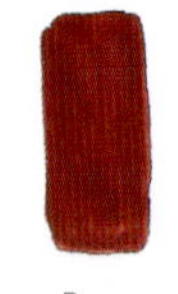

Brown (Bordeaux red)

Black (noir)

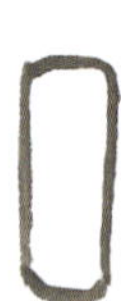

White

COLOR MIXING

- Tint of pink 1 (white + crimson red + mid yellow, proportion 4:1:1)
- Tint of pink 2 (white + crimson red + yellow ochre, proportion 1:2:1)

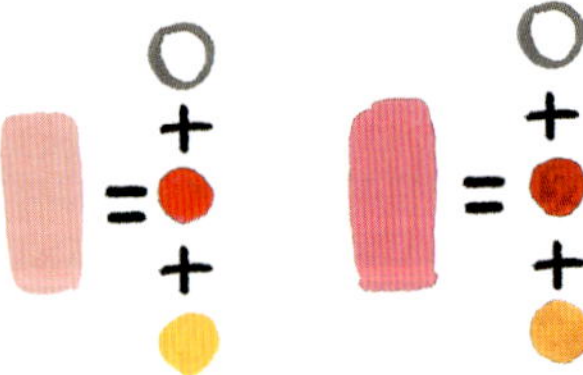

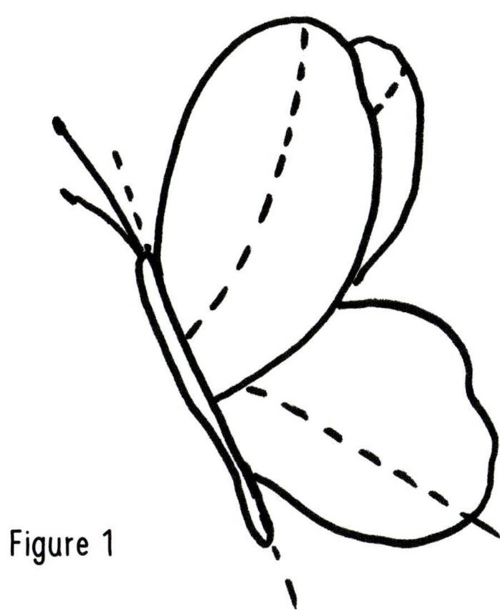

Figure 1

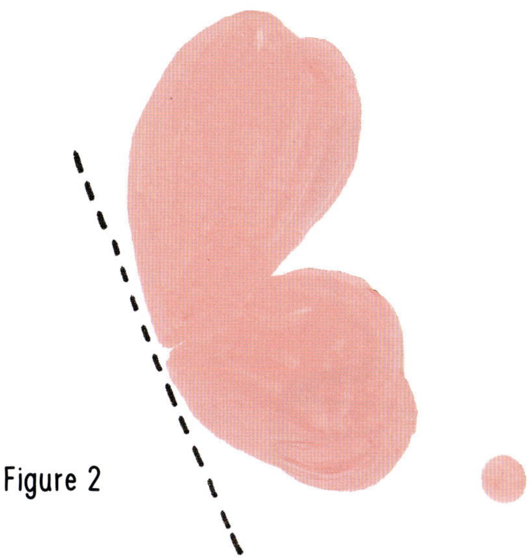

Figure 2

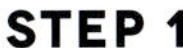

STEP 1

Because this project is very decorative, the shapes and structure of the butterfly are simplified. Draw the sketch, following the outline shown in Figure 1. I don't advise drawing the details at this stage. Because the first layer of the gouache will cover the sketch and make all lines invisible, the main outlines of the butterfly will be enough.

NOTE: In this project, we will be using only the layering technique (page 11).

Now we'll begin creating the base of the painting. With a medium round brush, fill the wing shapes with the tint of pink 1, as shown in Figure 2. Make sure that you're filling the visible wing shapes completely with paint, in one solid shape. Allow the layer to dry completely.

STEP 2

Using the same brush, paint a layer on the wings in the tint of pink 2 (see Figure 3). Try to paint this layer with rough brush strokes, adding them one by one (see Brush Strokes, page 10). Now prepare the brown paint and add the body and antennae to the insect painting. You can use a detail brush at this stage or combine the detail brush with a small round brush.

TIP: For painting antennae, the liner brush is the best. But if you don't have this type of brush, use a detail brush or a small round brush with a thin tip.

Let the painting dry.

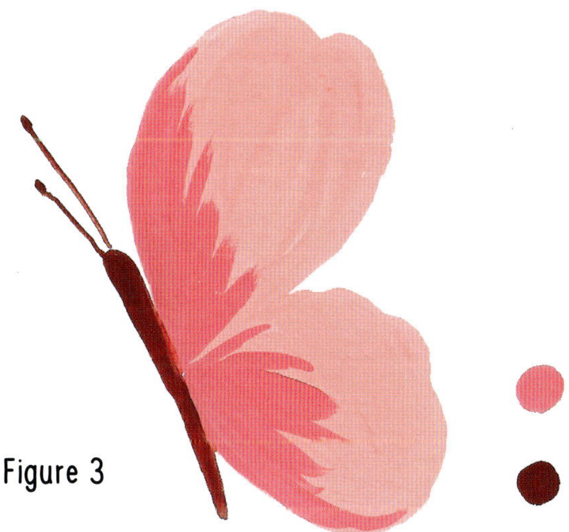

Figure 3

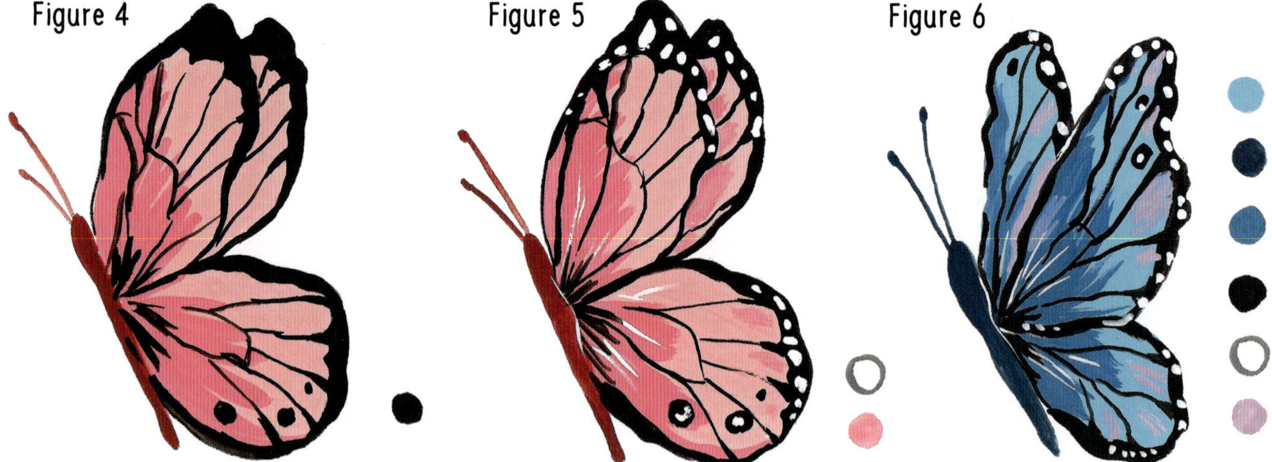

STEP 3

Time to make the butterfly look more lifelike. Arm yourself with the detail brush and carefully paint details in black paint, as shown in Figure 4. The black pattern at the edges can be painted outside the area of the pink wings. The main point is to form the wings' shapes by using black and to make them look interesting.

NOTE: The veins on the wings' pattern are thicker at the edges and thinner in the middle. I suggest you paint them as thin as possible, then make them thicker at the end.

Once again, let the painting dry.

STEP 4

We are almost finished with the painting. All you need is to add the final details. With the detail brush, add all the small details on the wings' pattern in white gouache. Let the work dry completely.

To give the picture more contrast, add shadows to the back wing according to Figure 5 in the tint of pink 2. Now our illustration is complete. It's lovely, isn't it?

This is the perfect project if you want to paint something quick and cute with gouache. By following my instructions you can create different beautiful butterflies in various colors. Also try experimenting with the shapes and patterns of the wings.

Figure 6 shows an example of a butterfly that I painted using this lesson's methods, except I chose completely different shades and changed the wing shapes. Don't be afraid to experiment and enjoy the process.

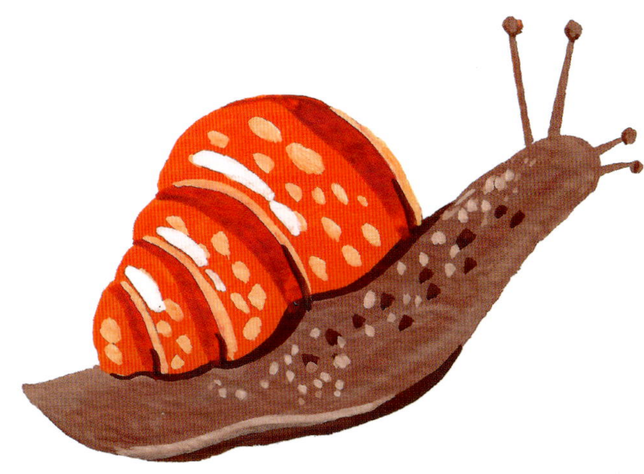

GARDEN SNAIL

In this project, I show you how to paint a cute little garden snail with gouache. This medium is excellent for creating patterns on the shell, as well as painting all the details of the body.

How fast and easy is it to paint a cute garden snail in an illustrative style? Let's look at it step by step.

SUPPLIES

- White or black paper
- Pencil and eraser
- Round brushes in different sizes
- Liner or detail brush

PROJECT COLORS

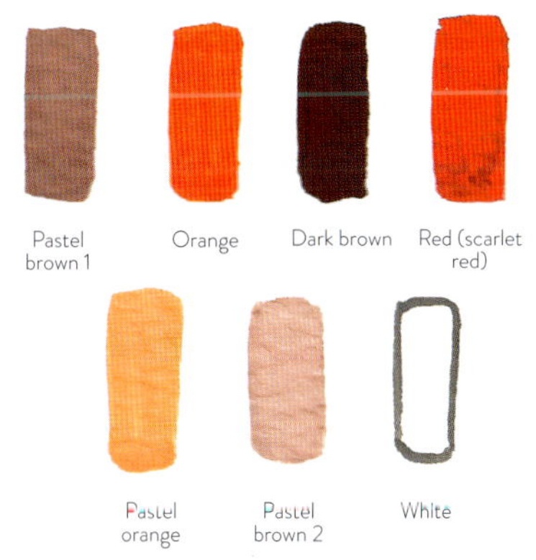

COLOR MIXING

- Pastel brown 1 (burnt sienna + white, proportion 2:1)
- Dark brown (burnt sienna + burnt umber, proportion 1:1)
- Pastel orange (orange + white, proportion 1:2)
- Pastel brown 2 (burnt sienna + burnt umber + white, proportion 1:1:3)

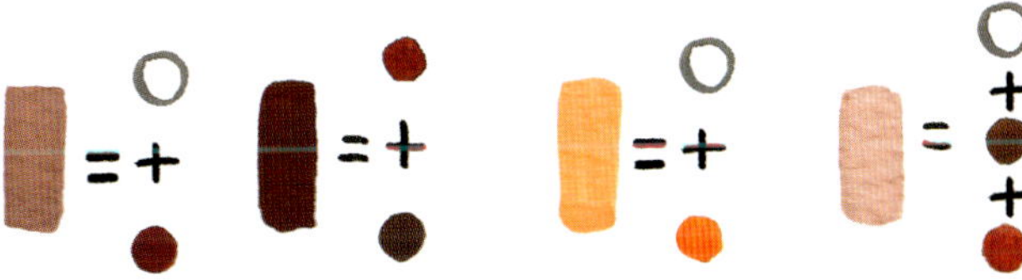

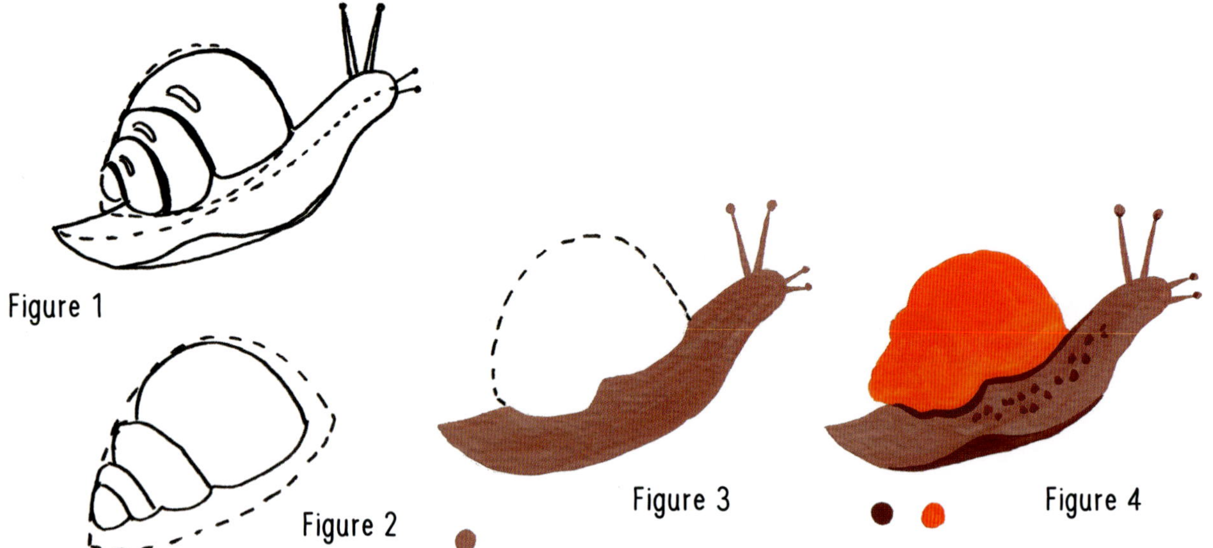

STEP 1

Make a sketch with a pencil following the outlines in Figure 1. Also pay attention to Figure 2, which demonstrates how you can simply draw a shell of the snail. The sketch doesn't need to be detailed or perfect, just mark the main lines. Once the sketch is ready, you can begin painting.

NOTE: In this project, all steps will be done by using only the layering technique (page 11). Before adding a new layer or details, make sure that the previously painted layer is dry.

Start by painting the snail's body in pastel brown 1 (see Figure 3) using a medium round brush. Afterward, take a detail brush and add eye stalks and antennae.

STEP 2

Now let's paint the shell itself (see Figure 4). For this, with the help of a medium brush, fill the shape of the snail shell with orange paint. Once the painting is dry, using a small round brush or detail brush, you can add a layer of shadow and details with dark brown.

TIP: When painting the shell, use a pretty saturated tint of orange. If your orange is too bright, add a bit of red to it. I also recommend adding white gouache to the mix. It will bring a matte finish after the paint dries.

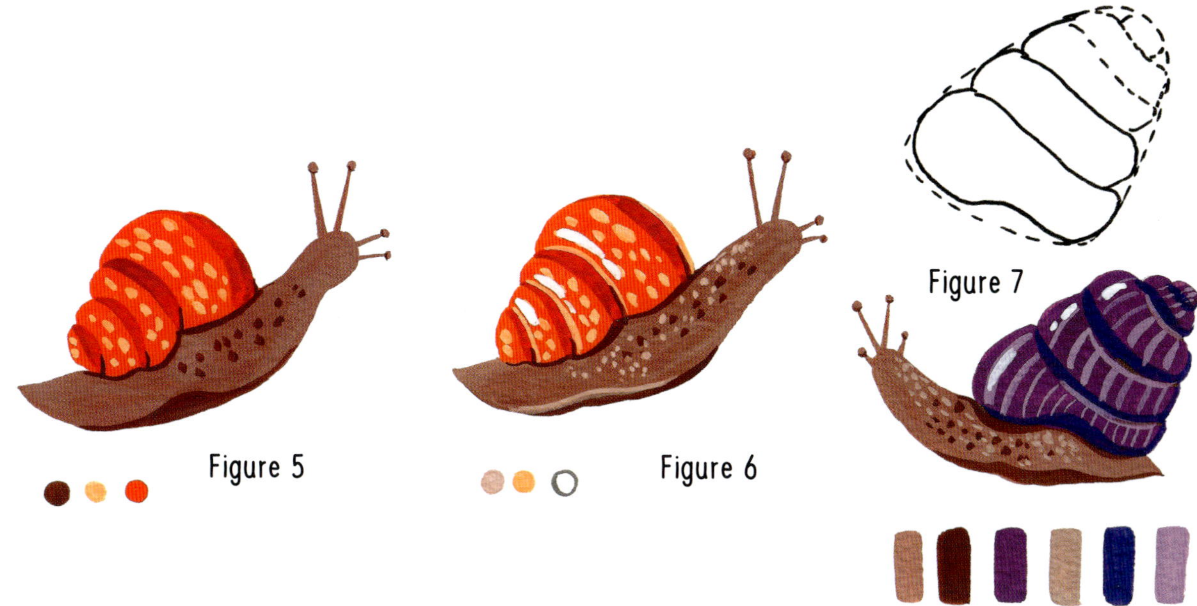

STEP 3

Now it's time to start adding the details to the snail shell (see Figure 5).

First, paint the shadow with red using a small round brush. Then, take a detail brush and paint a pattern in pastel orange. For this project, I've chosen flecks. But those could be stripes, waves, spots or anything else you would like to add. Because we're painting in an illustrative and even cartoonlike style, I think it's quite acceptable. Keep working with a detail brush and paint small strokes in dark brown at the bottom of the shell.

TIP: If, when it's dry, the shell's pattern details are not in sufficient contrast to the orange background, paint another layer of them.

STEP 4

Add more details to the snail's body and shell with a detail brush in pastel orange and pastel brown 2, as shown in Figure 6. With white gouache, paint small details to show the highlights and to make the shell look shiny. Our illustration is complete.

Snails are such wonderful objects to paint; explore gouache and enjoy each stroke with a brush. The project is effortless and anyone can do it. And despite its simplicity, the picture looks pretty.

You can practice this lesson in other color combinations and experiment with the shell structure. Take a look at the example in Figure 7. It shows an example of how you can paint the garden snail in other shapes and colors with this lesson's instructions. For your own variations, use references and your imagination.

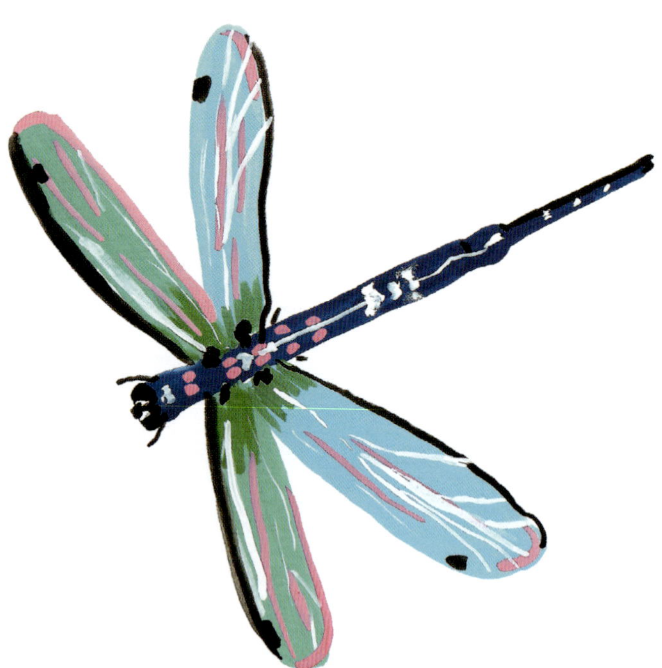

ELEGANT DRAGONFLY

Dragonflies are insects that are welcome in any garden. They're elegant and even mystical. I love to look at them and explore their structure, colors and all their details. I am personally always amazed by how wonderful the dragonfly is. And of course, I think it's a great object to portray with gouache. So, prepare your supplies and we'll paint the elegant dragonfly.

SUPPLIES

- White, black or craft paper
- Pencil and eraser
- Round brushes in different sizes
- Detail brush

PROJECT COLORS

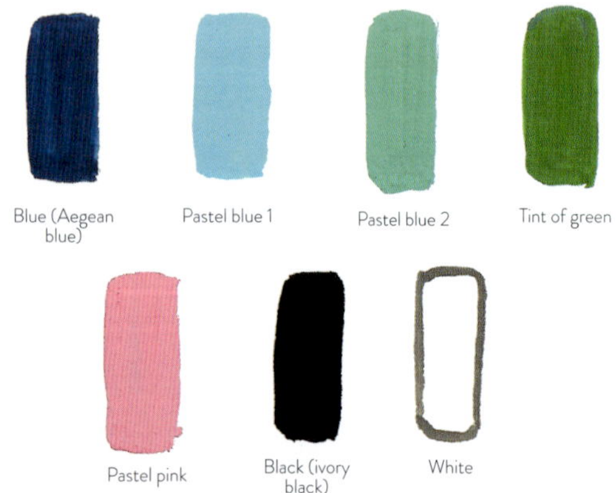

COLOR MIXING

- Pastel blue 1 (white + cerulean blue, proportion 1:2)
- Pastel blue 2 (white + cerulean blue + sap green, proportion 1:2:1)
- Tint of green (white + cerulean blue + sap green, proportion 1:2:2)
- Pastel pink (white + primary red, proportion 2:1)

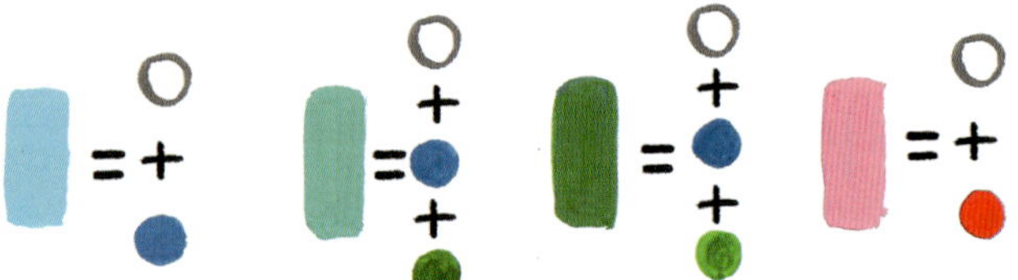

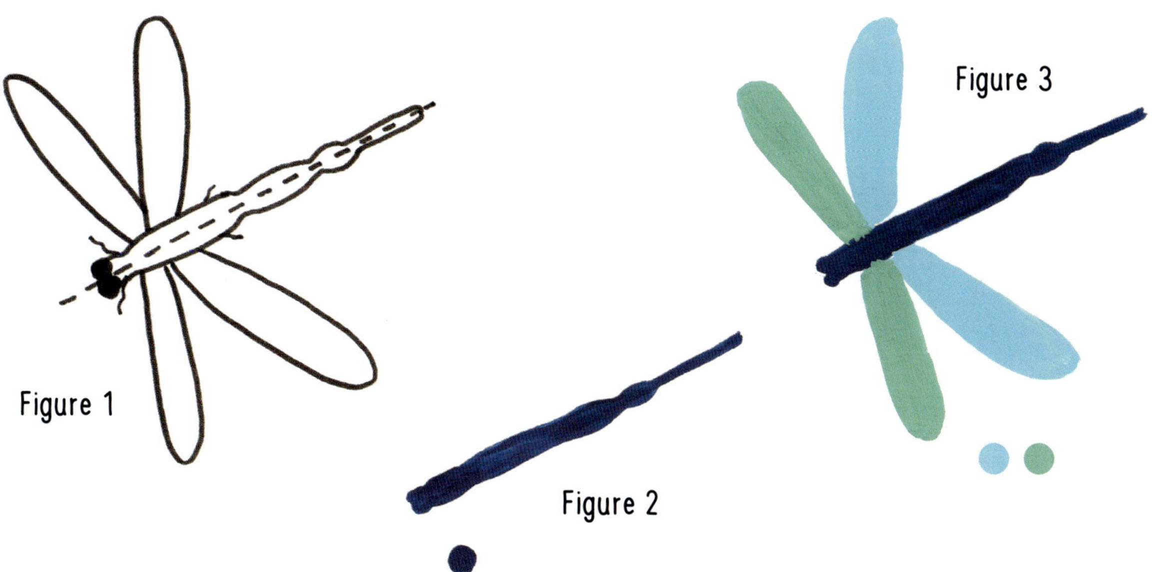

STEP 1

Let's start the project by making a sketch following the drawing outlines in Figure 1. I advise you to make a very simple sketch that includes only the main lines. We'll add the details later.

NOTE: In this project, we will be using only the layering technique (page 11).

Now we can move on to the painting itself. Paint the body of the dragonfly in blue by using a small round brush (see Figure 2). Try to keep this shape thin and elegant and don't paint outside the edges.

STEP 2

Switch to the medium round brush and fill the wings' shapes in pastel blue 1 and pastel blue 2 (see Figure 3). To make these shapes look neat, you can first paint the outline and then fill in with the paint inside the outline. Go on to step 3 once the painting is dry.

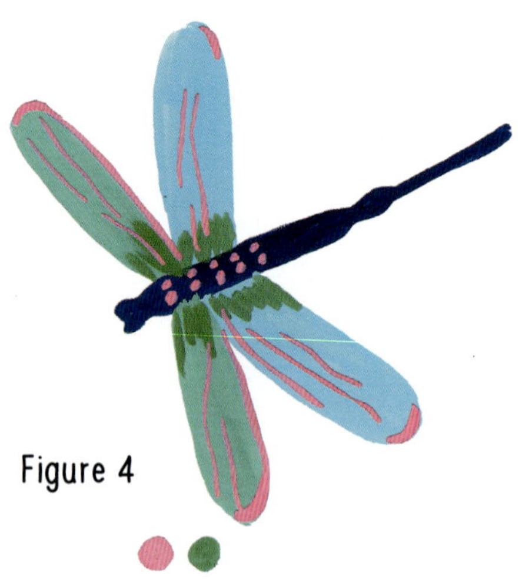

Figure 4

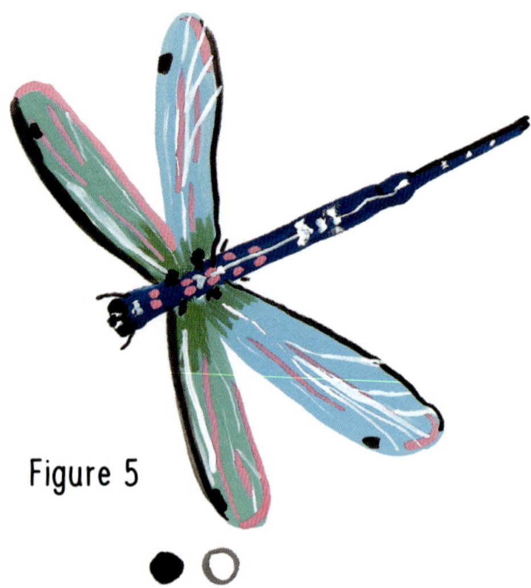

Figure 5

STEP 3

Our dragonfly is already becoming recognizable. Now we need to give it depth. To do this, paint a layer on the wings with the tint of green, as shown in Figure 4. Allow the piece to dry completely. Now take a detail brush and add some details in pastel pink. Once again, let the painting dry.

STEP 4

We are almost finished. All you need to do is add all the details onto the wings and body of the dragonfly in black and then white gouache, using a detail brush. Paint eyes and legs in black. Work carefully so that the illustration looks neat and elegant (see Figure 5). This is very delicate work and requires your patience. Remember that the dragonfly should look symmetrical, so try to add all the details one by one and consistently.

This project can easily be done in other colors. Try different and unusual color combinations, as in Figure 6. I recommend you limit the colors. Also feel free to experiment with a pattern on the body of the insect and the wing details. Enjoy the process and don't be afraid to experiment.

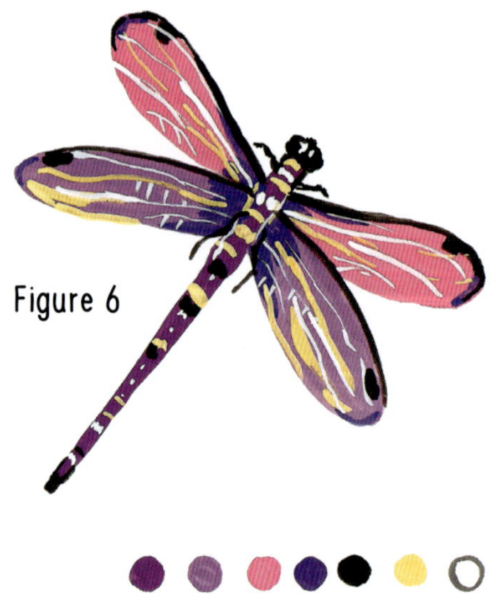

Figure 6

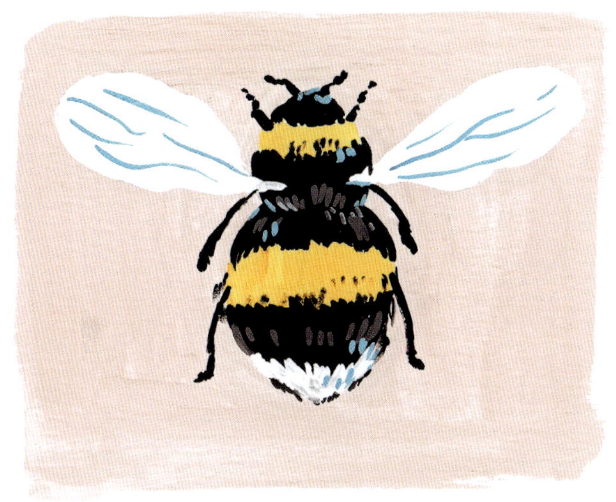

CUTE BUMBLEBEE

This project is a pure pleasure to paint with gouache. The result is so impressive, and each step is easy to execute. Pick up your brushes and paint this fuzzy and cute bumblebee with me.

SUPPLIES

- White paper
- Pencil and eraser
- Masking tape (optional)
- Round brushes in different sizes
- Flat brush
- Detail brush

PROJECT COLORS

Tint of pink

Yellow (bumble-bee yellow)

Black (noir)

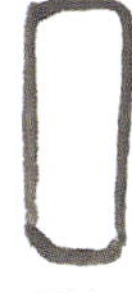

White

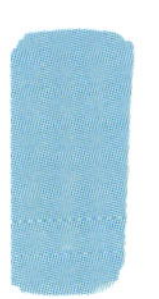

Pastel blue

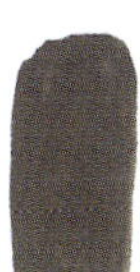

Grey

COLOR MIXING

- Tint of pink (rose + yellow ochre + white, proportion 1:2:4)
- Pastel blue (cerulean blue + white, proportion 1:1)
- Grey (black + white, proportion 1:3)

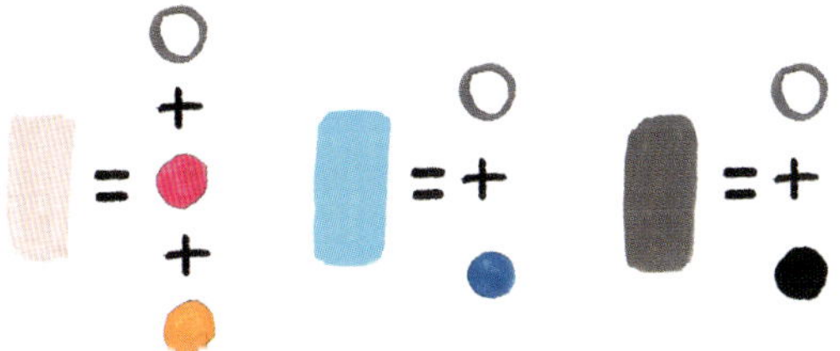

STEP 1

Before you begin painting, take a look at Figure 1, which shows the outlines of the bumblebee we will paint. Follow it to make a pencil sketch on the paper. You only need to draw the central body part of the insect (head, thorax and abdomen). Skip the wings, antennae and legs.

Because we will paint the background for this project, define your work area around the bumblebee sketch before beginning with gouache painting. I advise you to mark the corners of the background area with a pencil. You can also use masking tape to define the background on the paper.

Take a medium round brush and, with the tint of pink, start to paint the background around the central bumblebee part (see Figure 2). Then switch to the flat brush and continue working by using the dry-brush forming technique (page 12).

NOTE: If you use masking tape, just fill the working area with the paint. Use a flat brush or large round brush for this purpose.

Let the background dry completely and go on to step 2.

STEP 2

Time to paint our fuzzy buzzing friend (see Figure 3). Let's fill the central body parts with yellow and black. First, paint with yellow, and once the layer is dried completely, continue painting with the black paint. Use a medium round brush for this step. Allow the painting to dry completely.

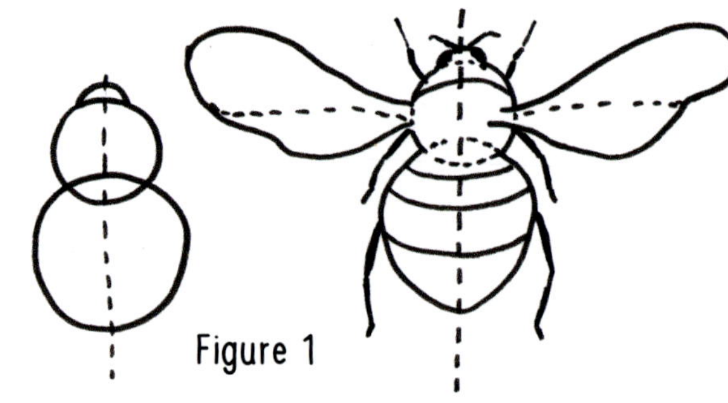

Figure 1

Figure 2

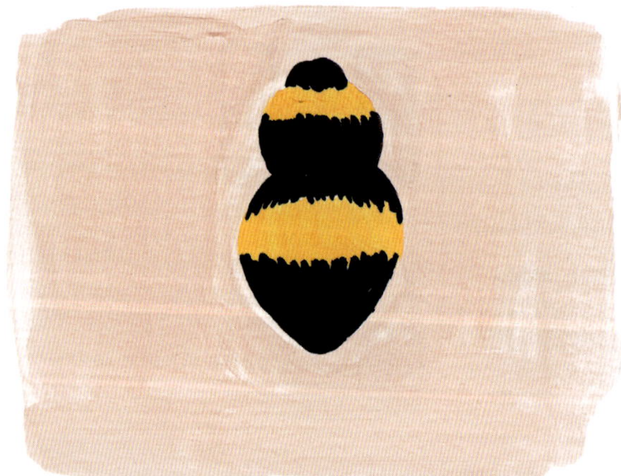

Figure 3

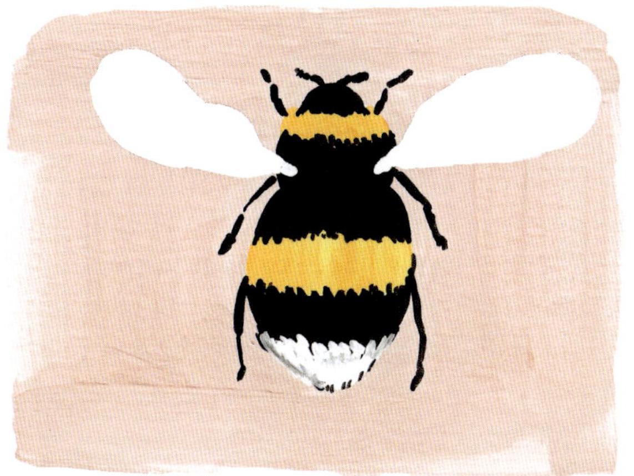

Figure 4

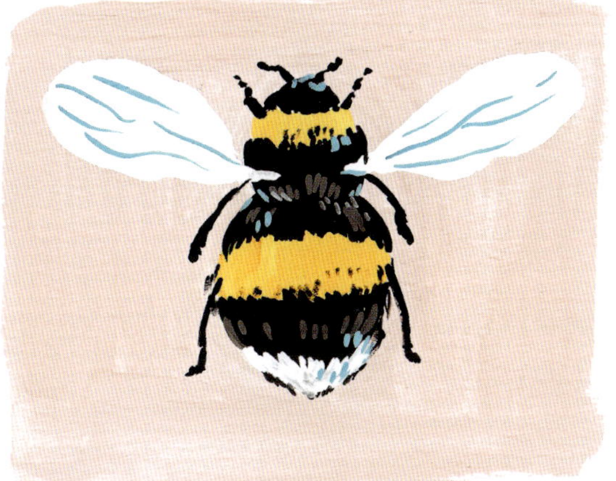

Figure 5

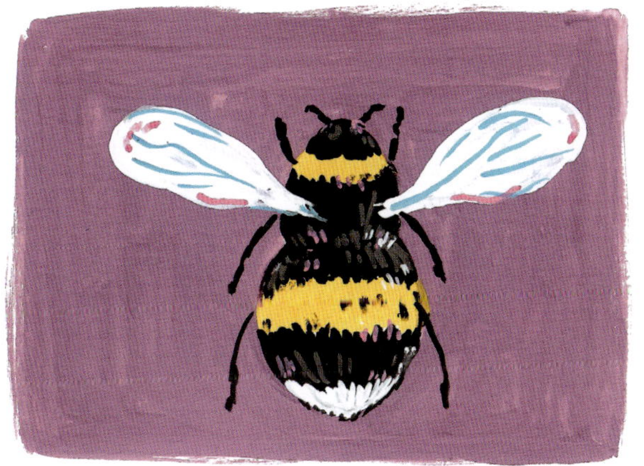

Figure 6

STEP 3

With the same brush, paint the wings and the bottom of the abdomen in white (see Figure 4). Regarding the wings, if after they dry they still look transparent, I recommend you leave them and avoid painting one more layer on top. As for the bottom of the abdomen, you can add one more layer with white gouache if it's still too transparent (see layering technique, page 11).

Now take the detail brush and with it add the antennae and legs of the insects with black gouache. Also paint some details in black on the body, if needed. Once again we apply the layering technique.

Allow the painting to dry completely.

STEP 4

The painting is almost done. The final touches and details will make it complete and perfect looking. With the detail brush and following Figure 5, paint some details on the body and wings in pastel blue and grey. Then, by using the dry-brush technique (page 12), add some strokes in black to make the fluffy texture of the bumblebee.

Let the painted layer dry.

I hope you enjoy this project. By using the principles of this lesson, you can paint any insect with a pastel or other colored background. The background pops and makes the painting pretty and more realistic. Moreover, you can experiment with painting bumblebees by changing the color of the background and playing with the details. Practice makes everything perfect, so why not paint more bumblebees? Figure 6 shows an example of how this project can be changed.

Don't miss the opportunity to practice and express your creativity!

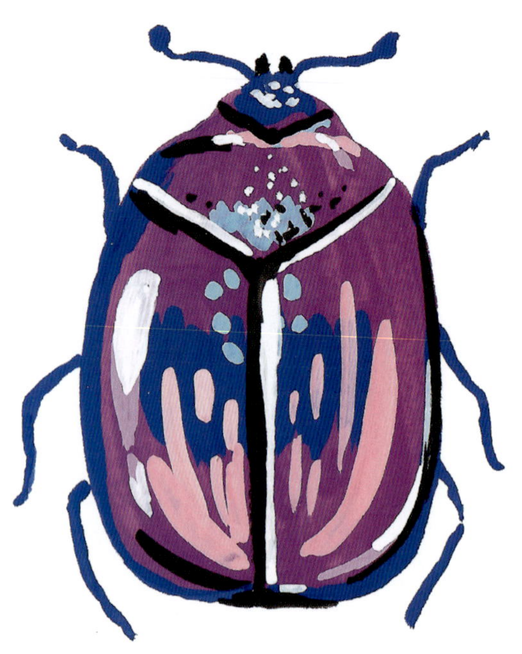

ONE GORGEOUS BEETLE

If you're looking for a quick painting session that lifts your mood, stop here. Yes, I suggest that you paint a gorgeous beetle! This will be a stylized illustration, but I also try to keep some realistic characteristics of the insect. I think such a balance of stylizing and realism is a great way to make an illustration look interesting and eye-catching. Let's get started.

SUPPLIES

- White or craft paper
- Pencil and eraser
- Round brushes in different sizes
- Detail brush

PROJECT COLORS

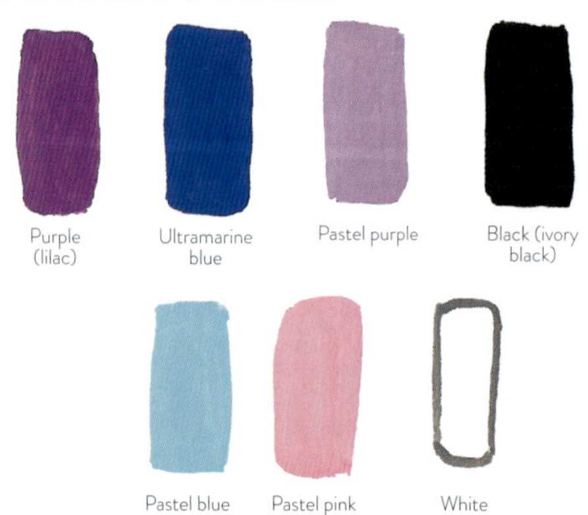

COLOR MIXING

- Pastel purple (white + purple, proportion 1:1)
- Pastel blue (white + cerulean blue, proportion 1:1)
- Pastel pink (white + rose, proportion 2:1)

TIP: If you don't have a rose tint, use any other tint of pink for mixing the pastel pink.

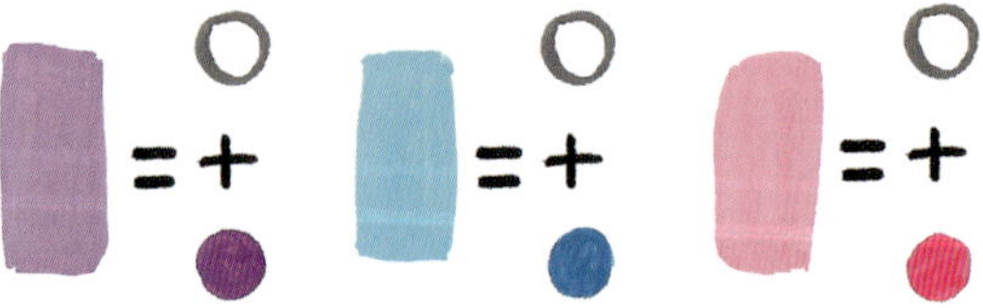

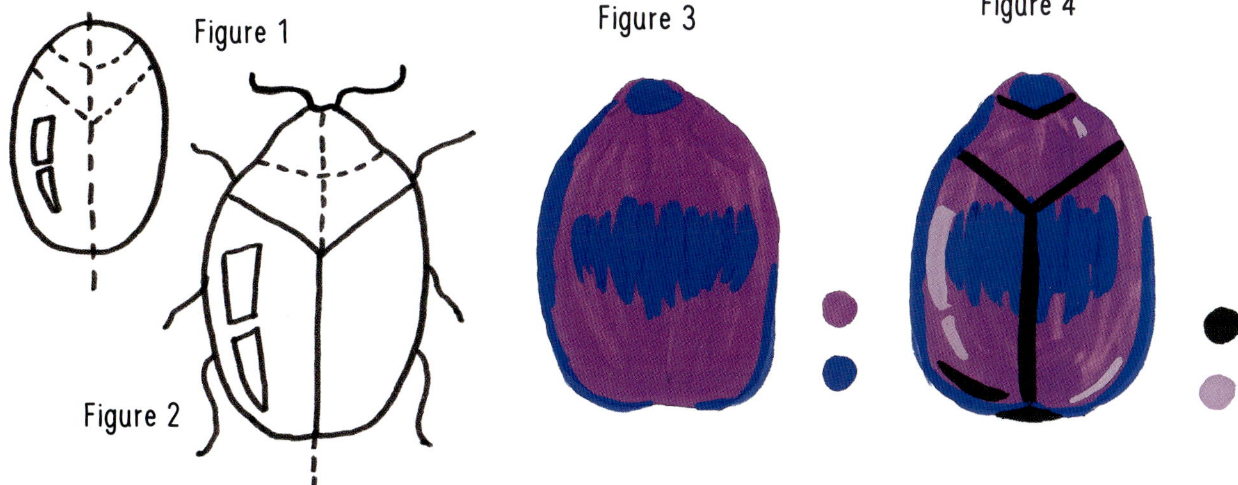

STEP 1

Start with a light pencil sketch before moving on to the gouache. For this, take a look at Figure 1, which shows the outline of the beetle we will paint. I suggest you draw an oval for your sketch first, and then modify it to the beetle's outline (Figure 2). Once the sketch is ready, you can begin painting.

NOTE: In this project, we will apply only the layering technique (page 11).

Fill the base shape with purple paint, as shown in Figure 3, by using a medium round brush. If the edge of the painted shape doesn't look accurate and smooth, try to fix it with the detail brush and paint with a pretty balanced consistency. The consistency of the paint should not be watery, but not too thick (see Consistency of Gouache Paint, page 7). Once it's dry, add an ultramarine blue layer. Allow the painted layer to dry.

STEP 2

In this step, we'll bring those realistic characteristics to the illustration I mentioned earlier: some shadows and highlights (see Figure 4). Take a small round brush and add details one by one, first in pastel purple and then in black. Let the painted layer dry completely, then go to the next step.

STEP 3

It's time to add a pattern and decorations to the beetle. Take a detail brush or a round one with a thin tip and paint spots, lines and dots with pastel blue and pastel pink, as shown in Figure 5, or use your imagination and add any decoration you like. There is only one thing to take into consideration: do not cover the highlights and shadows we added in the previous stage. Allow the painting to dry completely.

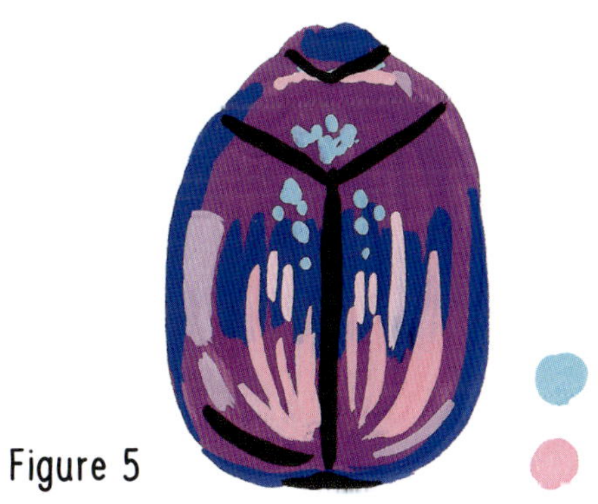

Figure 6

STEP 4

Finally, we get to the stage where this project turns into a gorgeous illustration. Keep working with the detail brush. Prepare the following colors: white, black and ultramarine blue. Paint all the details with the colors corresponding to the ones in Figure 6. Add antennae and legs using ultramarine blue; also paint highlights in white on the beetle's body and the mandible in black. Most important, the legs and antennae of the beetle should look symmetrical. Our illustration is complete.

Using the steps in this lesson, I suggest you continue painting different types of beetles. You can find some examples in Figures 7 and 8. This is a great exercise for your imagination to practice your gouache painting skills. Experiment with a color combo, as well as with the shapes of the insects. It's very simple and does not take much time. I hope you enjoy the project and return to it often.

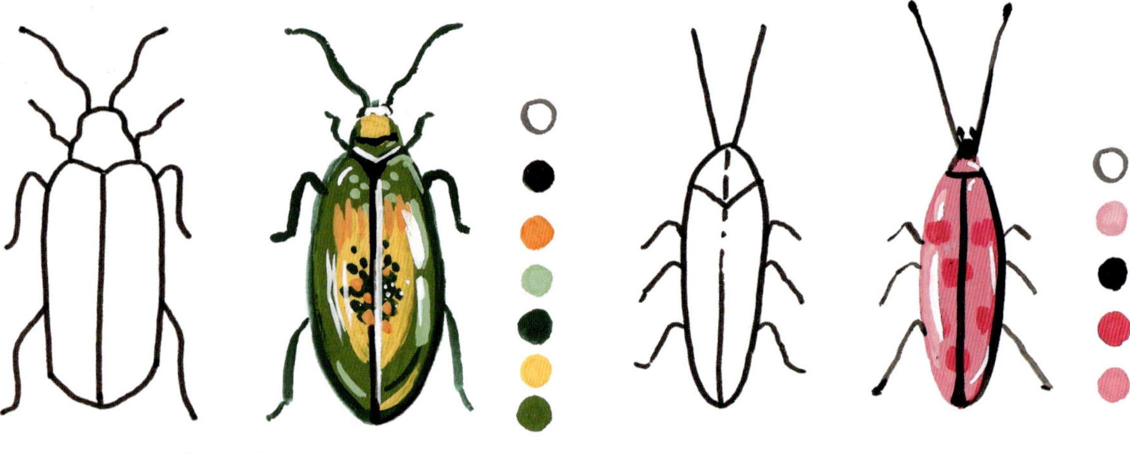

Figure 7

Figure 8

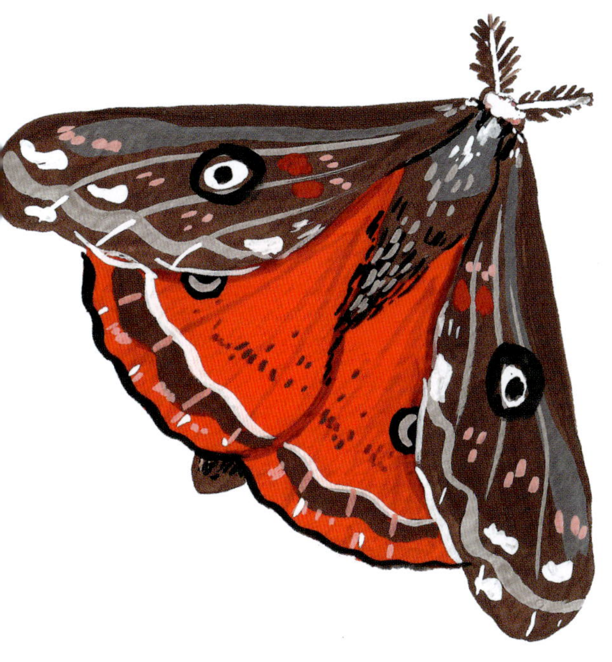

MYSTERIOUS MOTH

The world around us inspires. And even the things that at first glance are not so pretty can open our imagination and creativity. The moth is a great example of this.

Not everyone loves moths. But have you ever looked closely at these insects? They're just wonderful. The patterns and color combinations just amaze. And there is no more suitable medium than gouache to paint a moth. So, prepare your brushes and paints and let's paint it!

SUPPLIES

- White or craft paper
- Pencil and eraser
- Round brushes in different sizes
- Detail brush

PROJECT COLORS

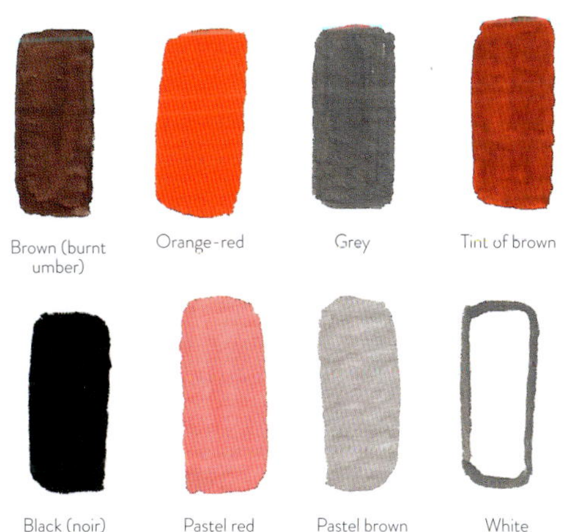

COLOR MIXING

- Orange-red (orange + vermilion red, proportion 2:1)
- Grey (black + white, proportion 1:2)
- Tint of brown (burnt sienna + vermilion red, proportion 1:1)
- Pastel red (vermilion red + white, proportion 1:3)
- Pastel brown (burnt umber + white, proportion 1:3)

STEP 1

For this project, the preliminary sketch is especially important. You need to make the halves of the moth as symmetrical as possible. I know it's not the easiest task, but do your best. Figure 1 shows a base sketch and a more detailed one. I recommend you begin by sketching the sector shapes and then move to the exact moth sketch. Once the sketch is ready, we can paint.

NOTE: In this project, we will apply only the layering technique (page 11). Before adding a new layer or details, make sure that the previously painted layer is dry.

Prepare the brown and orange-red paints. Now with the help of a medium round brush, use these tints to fill the moth's wing shapes (see Figure 2).

Let the layer dry.

TIP: Because we're painting with gouache, if you need to correct any painted shape, you can easily change it. For this, you can paint over the layer with the same color.

STEP 2

Now switch to a small brush and paint the moth's central body with the brown and grey colors, as shown in Figure 3. Also add the lines on both wings with grey. Once the painted layer is dry, take a detail brush and add the following parts: the antennae and head in brown; the wing shadows in the tint of brown; and the details in black. After the freshly painted layer dries, go on to the next step.

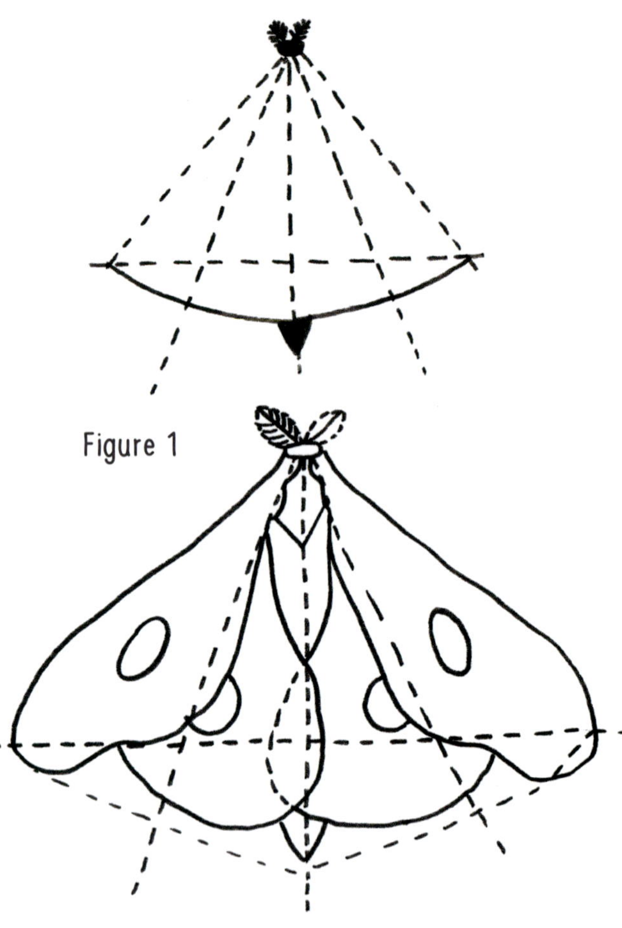

Figure 1

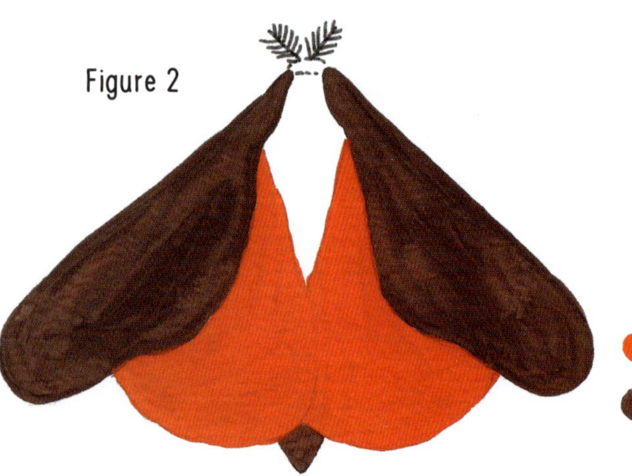

Figure 2

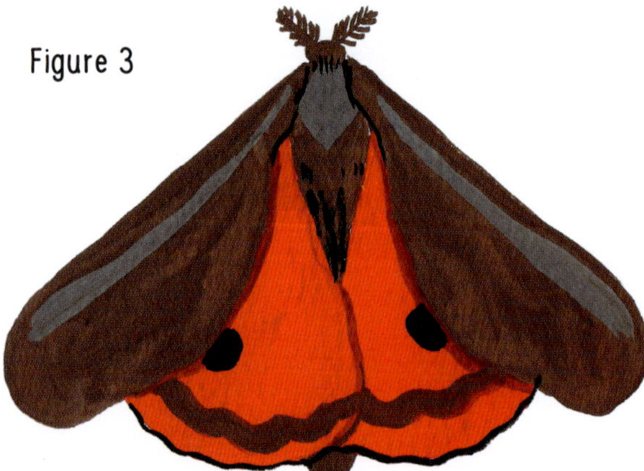

Figure 3

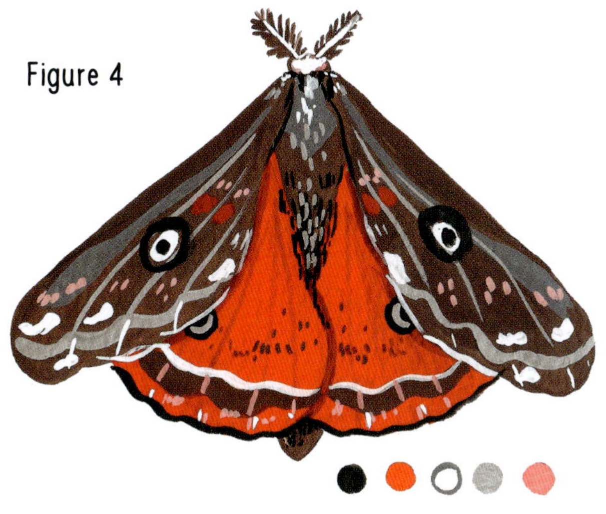

Figure 4

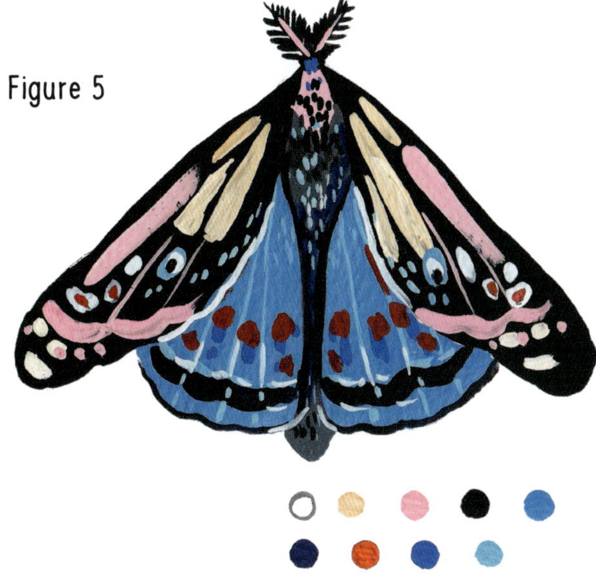

Figure 5

STEP 3

We are ready to add details. This is the most pleasant stage in the project, so relax and enjoy the process. Remember that you need to make the moth as symmetrical as possible.

Prepare paint in the following shades: black, pastel red, pastel brown, orange-red and white. Now add all the details of the insect with the colors corresponding to the ones in Figure 4. Add details in pastel brown and white onto the abdomen and thorax; the forewings and hindwings pattern by using black, pastel red, pastel brown, orange-red and white; and details on the head and antennas in white. Feel free to add your own details. But remember to maintain balance and not overload the painting.

In this project, we painted an abstract moth, not a particular specimen. But, of course, you can illustrate any real insect you would like with the help of references. Or keep working with a decorative style. Use the instructions and principles of the lesson to achieve the desired result. Also, experiment with colors and shapes. Note that you can illustrate the moth with its wings in different stages of opening.

Figure 5 shows a moth made using this lesson's techniques, but with the colors changed. I also slightly modified the shapes. The colors I've chosen are crazy and unreal. I just wanted to emphasize that you can feel free to be creative when experimenting with this lesson.

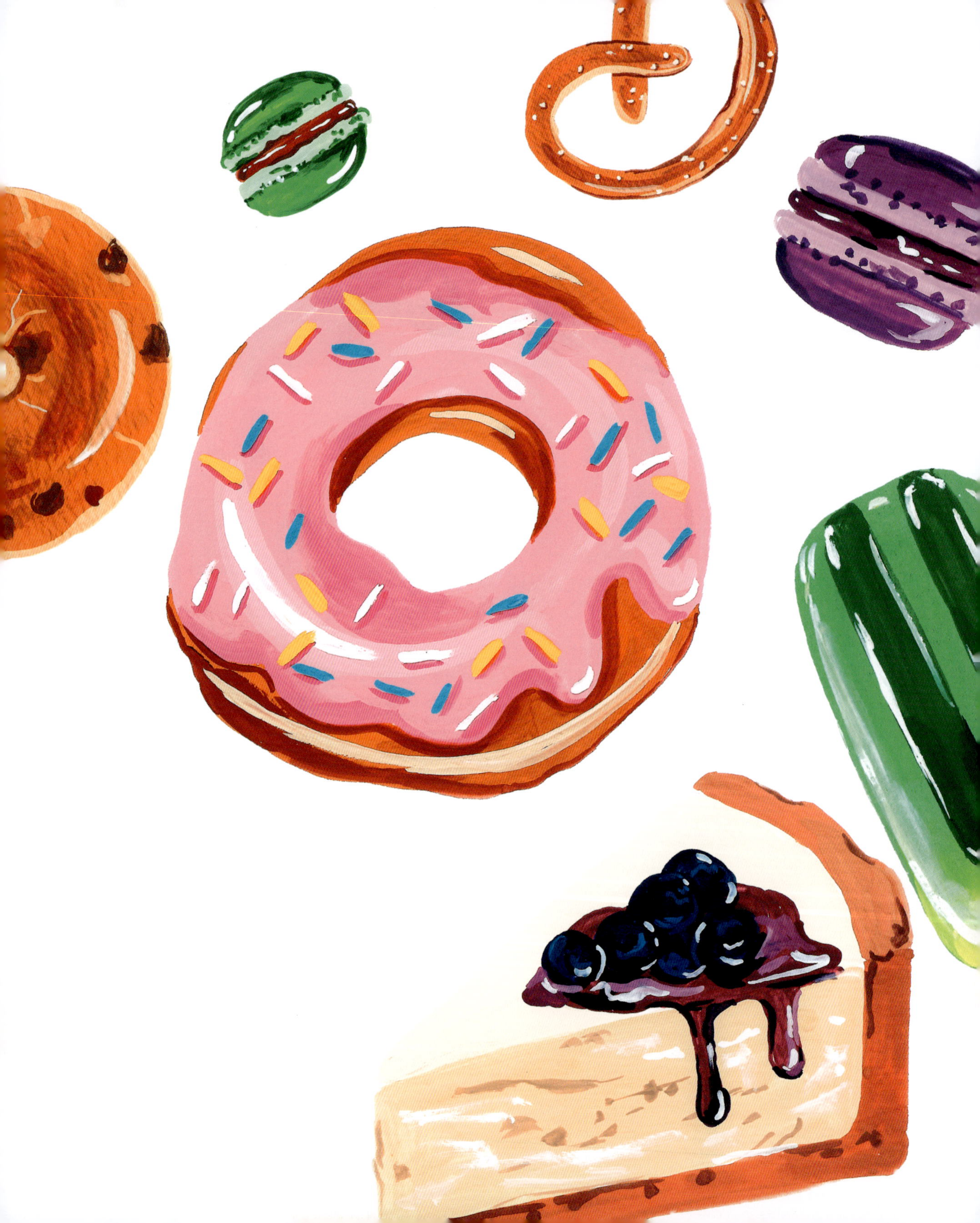

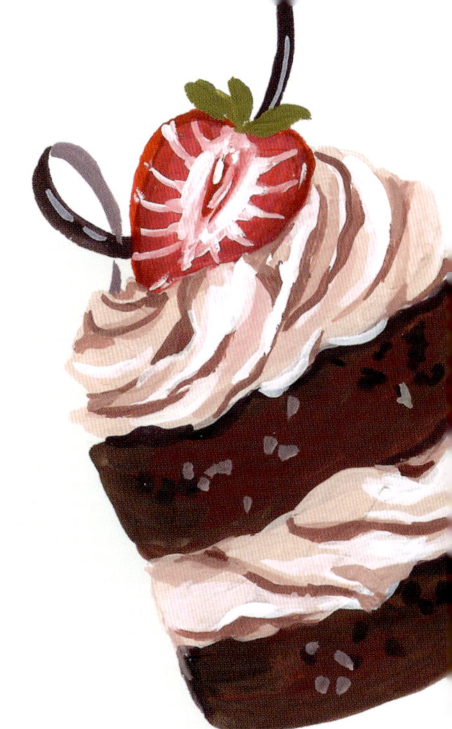

Delicious DESSERTS

This is my favorite chapter in the book because I love painting food, especially sweets. There are so many different desserts you can easily paint with gouache. I've prepared a few super-fun and varied projects that will open up the world of food illustration.

Maybe you will fall in love with food painting as much as I have. These projects will be a good start for your food-painting journey.

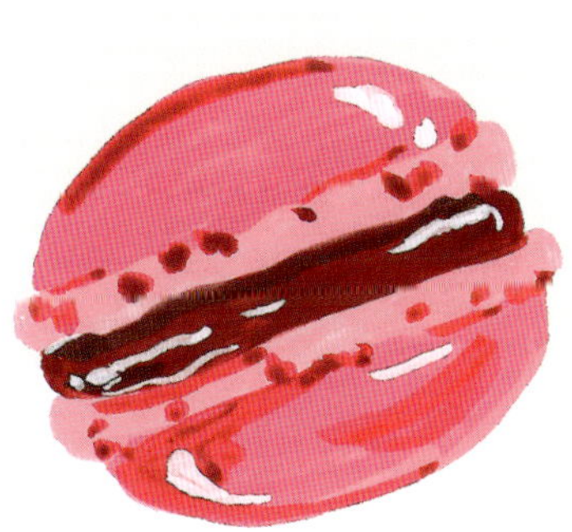

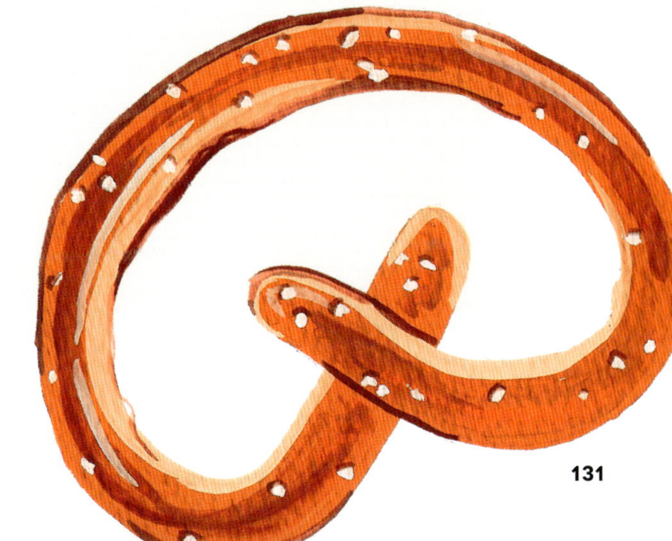

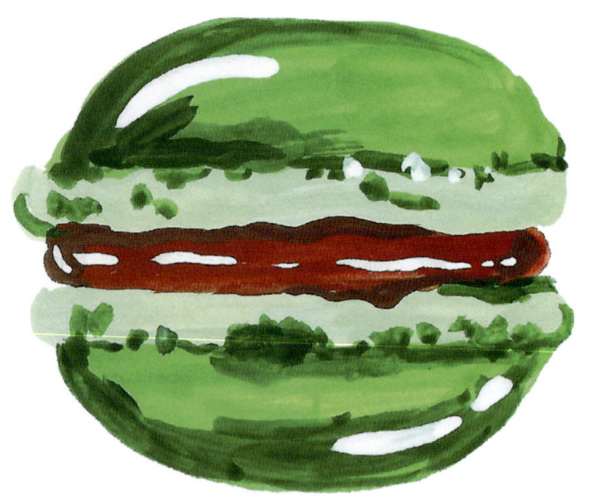

MACARON COOKIE

What is your favorite dessert? If I needed to pick just one, I would definitely choose the box of colorful macarons. The macaron is also just perfect as an object to paint and for practicing gouache. If you have no time to paint a full piece, but you would like to do a quick little painting session, this project is for you. I also recommend executing this project with children. They will love to paint such colorful elements. Let's get started.

SUPPLIES

- White, craft or black paper
- Pencil and eraser
- Round brushes in different sizes
- Detail brush

COLOR MIXING

- Tint of green (white + sap green + primary yellow, proportion 1:5:1)
- Pastel green (white + sap green + primary yellow, proportion 2:5:1)
- Dark green (sap green + Prussian blue, proportion 2:1)

PROJECT COLORS

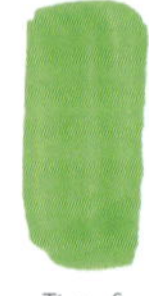

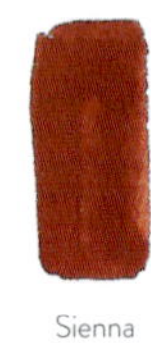
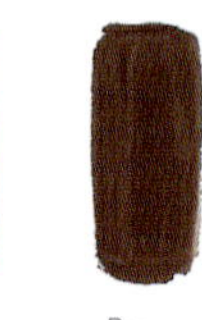
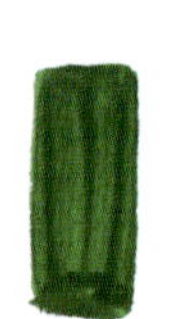
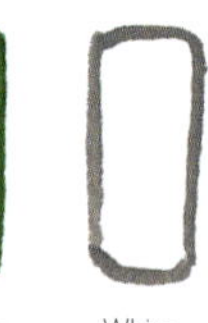

Tint of green · Pastel green · Sienna (burnt sienna) · Brown · Dark green · White

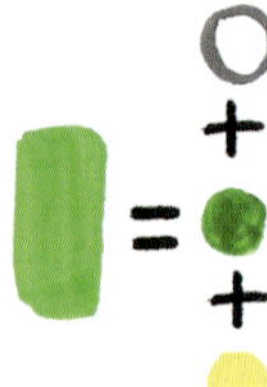
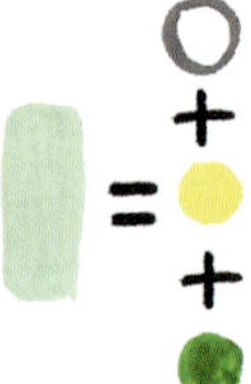
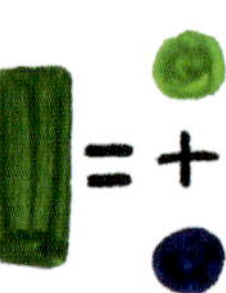

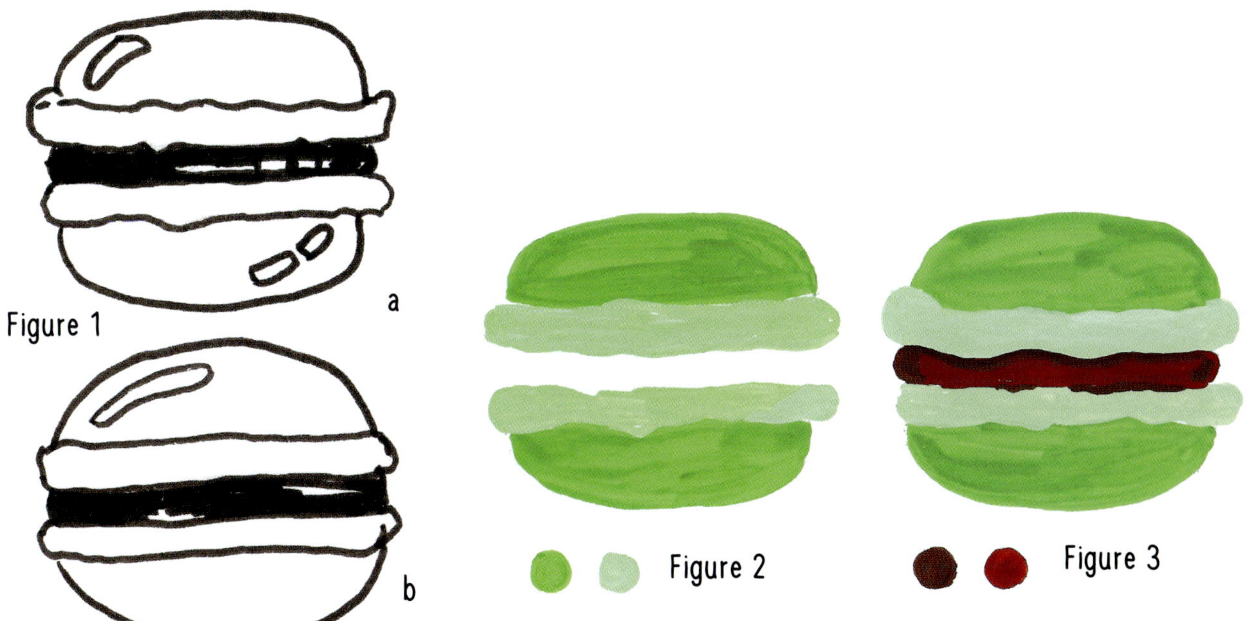

STEP 1

Let's start by making a pencil sketch. Draw a sketch following one of the outline drawings in Figure 1. As you can see, there are two options, depending on the shape of the cookie. I chose the first variation and will execute the project based on it. I don't make a detailed sketch; instead, I draw only baselines. Once the sketch is ready, jump to the painting itself.

NOTE: All steps in this project are done with the layering technique (page 11).

Arm yourself with a small or medium round brush (depending on the size of painting you would like to paint) and paint the top halves of the cookie in the tint of green (see Figure 2). Let the paint layer dry completely and then proceed with coloring the "feet" of the cookie in pastel green.

Once again, let the painted layer dry completely.

NOTE: This project can be executed in different dimensions, from a small size, like a real macaron, to one that is larger than life. Depending on this choice, pick the most suitable and handy brush sizes at each step.

STEP 2

Let's get to the filling of the cookie (see Figure 3). It can be any yummy filling in many colors. I selected a chocolate filling for my macaron, so, paint the base layer in the sienna color, and once it is dry, add the shadow in brown. If you use your own colors, you also need to use two colors: the base and the shadow.

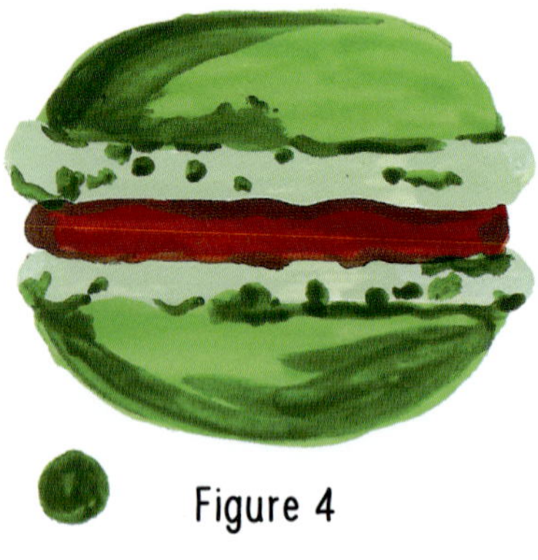

Figure 6

Figure 4

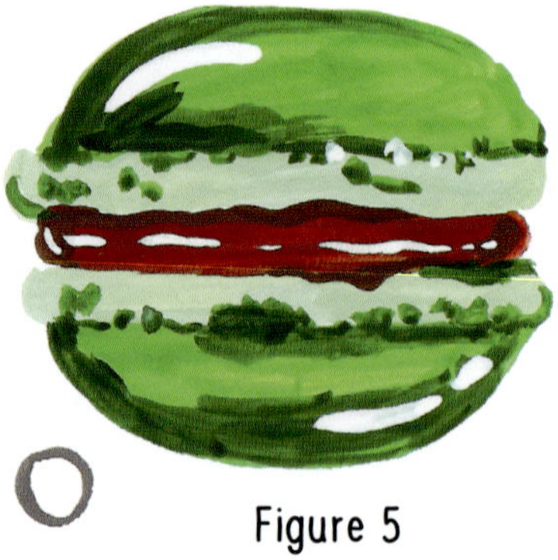

Figure 5

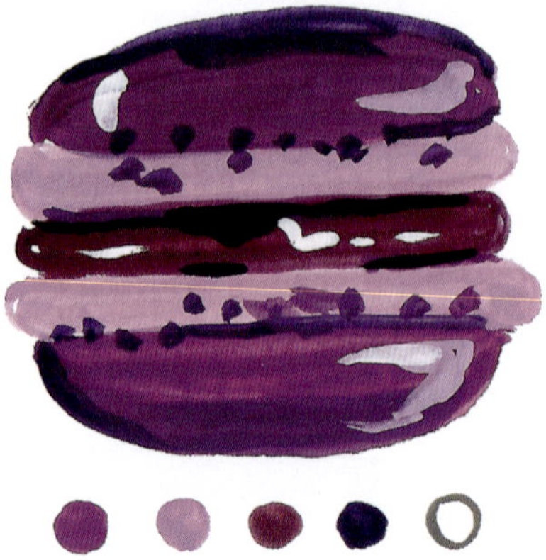

STEP 3

To make the cookie more realistic, add a layer of shadow in dark green. Then paint the details on the "feet" of the macaron as shown in Figure 4. Use a detail brush or a small round brush.

TIP: If you want to make the painting softer and smoother, use the softening technique (page 12) to blur the shadow a bit.

Allow the painting to dry.

Figure 7

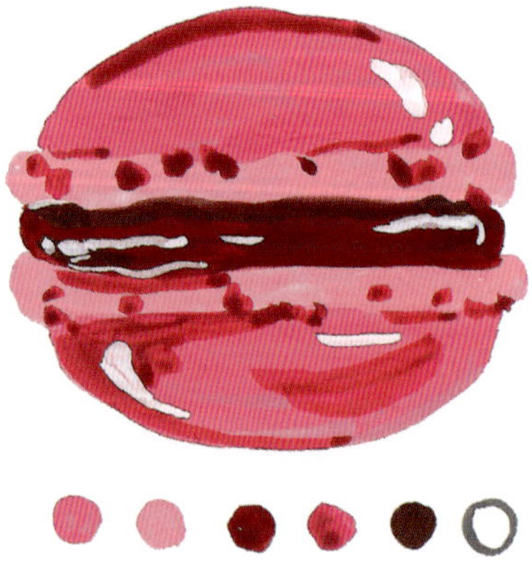

STEP 4

It's time to add some shine to the delicious and stunning French dessert (Figure 5). Using the detail brush, paint the highlights with white gouache. Try to not overdo the illustration with details. Sometimes less is more. Our little painting is done.

Take a look at the examples in Figures 6 and 7. Both of these cookies were painted using the step-by-step instructions in this lesson. I only changed the colors and used both of the outline types of the preliminary sketches (see Figure 1).

Practice based on this lesson. Experiment with colors. Because the macarons are so vivid and colorful, you can truly let your creativity flourish here. Design your own unique macaron "flavors" and enjoy the process of painting.

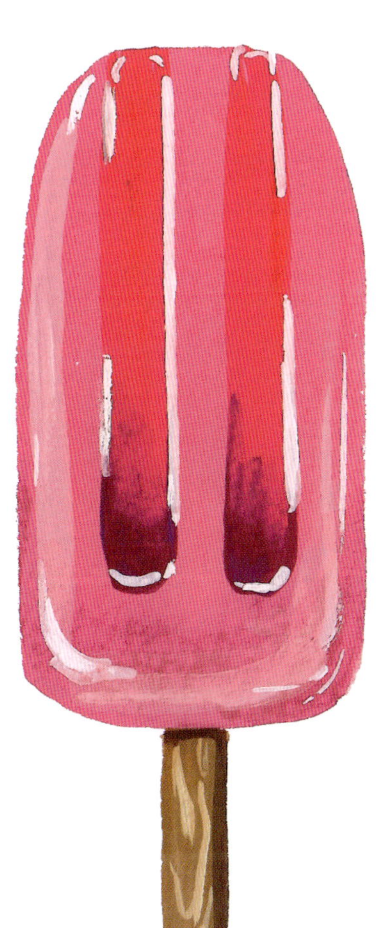

COLORFUL POPSICLE

Painting with magical gouache is easy, and this project is excellent proof. In the lesson, I will show you how to paint a colorful and yummy popsicle in just a few simple steps. It might seem challenging to paint an object with some highlights and keep it vivid at the same time. But with gouache, it can be done by glazing layers one by one. Now, let's take our brushes and create a yummy and juicy popsicle illustration.

SUPPLIES

- White, craft or black paper
- Pencil and eraser
- Round brushes in different sizes
- Detail brush

PROJECT COLORS

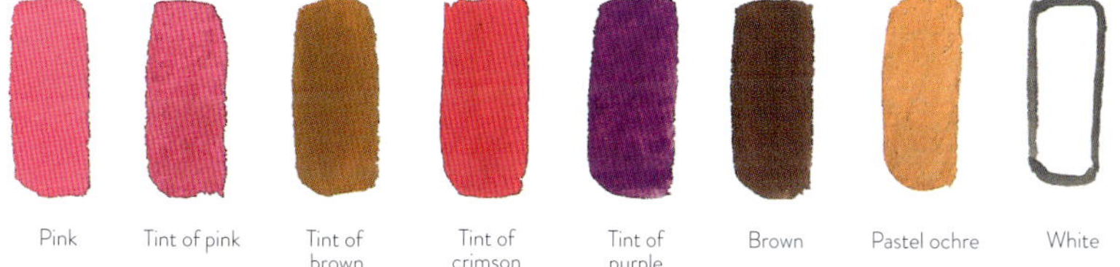

COLOR MIXING

- Pink (white + crimson red, proportion 1:1)
- Tint of pink (white + crimson red + ultramarine blue, proportion 1:2:1)
- Tint of brown (white + yellow ochre + Vandyke brown, proportion 1:2:2)
- Tint of crimson (white + crimson red, proportion 1:3)
- Tint of purple (white + crimson red + ultramarine blue, proportion 1:1:2)
- Brown (white + Vandyke brown, proportion 1:5)
- Pastel ochre (white + yellow ochre, proportion 1:1)

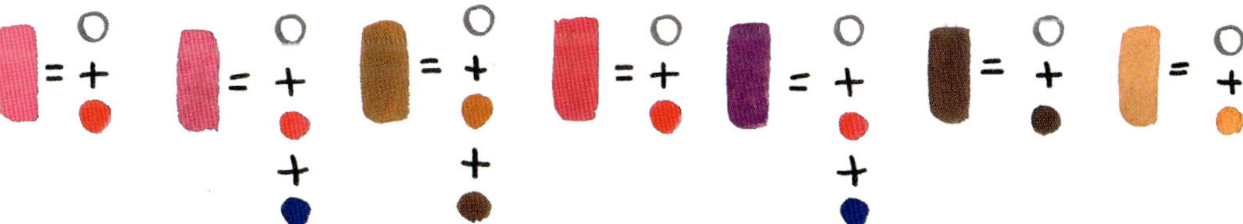

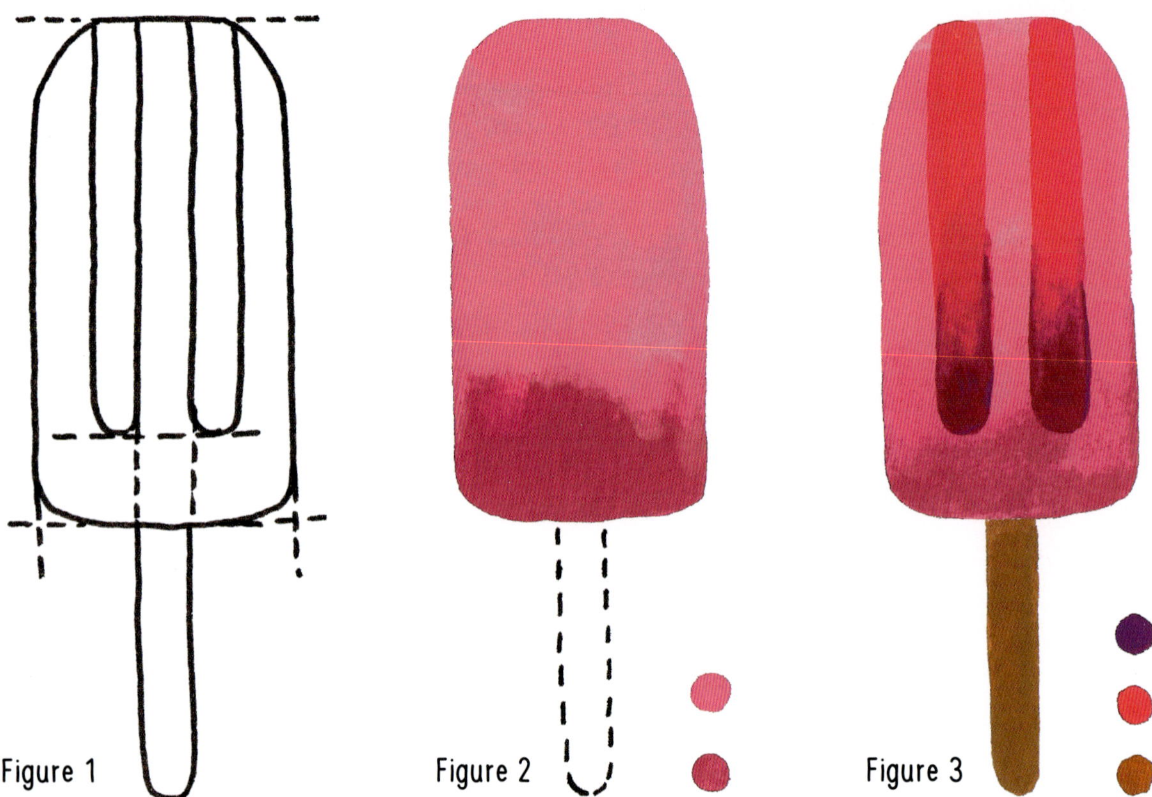

STEP 1

Draw a light sketch with a pencil following Figure 1. Because gouache is opaque, the paint will cover the sketch in the first step, so don't draw the details at this stage. Just the outline is enough.

Take a suitably sized round brush (depending on how big you want the painting to be) and fill the upper part of the popsicle with pink and the bottom part with the tint of pink (see Figure 2). Using a clean wet brush, blur the transition of the colors (see softening, page 12). In this case, you will get a beautiful transition from one color to the other. Let the layer dry.

STEP 2

Start by painting the wooden stick with the tint of brown. Now add two vertical rectangular shapes with the tint of crimson and the tint of purple as shown in Figure 3. For the rectangles, apply the gradient technique (page 12) to make a soft gradient of the two colors. We're also using the layering technique (page 11) in this step.

Allow the layer to dry.

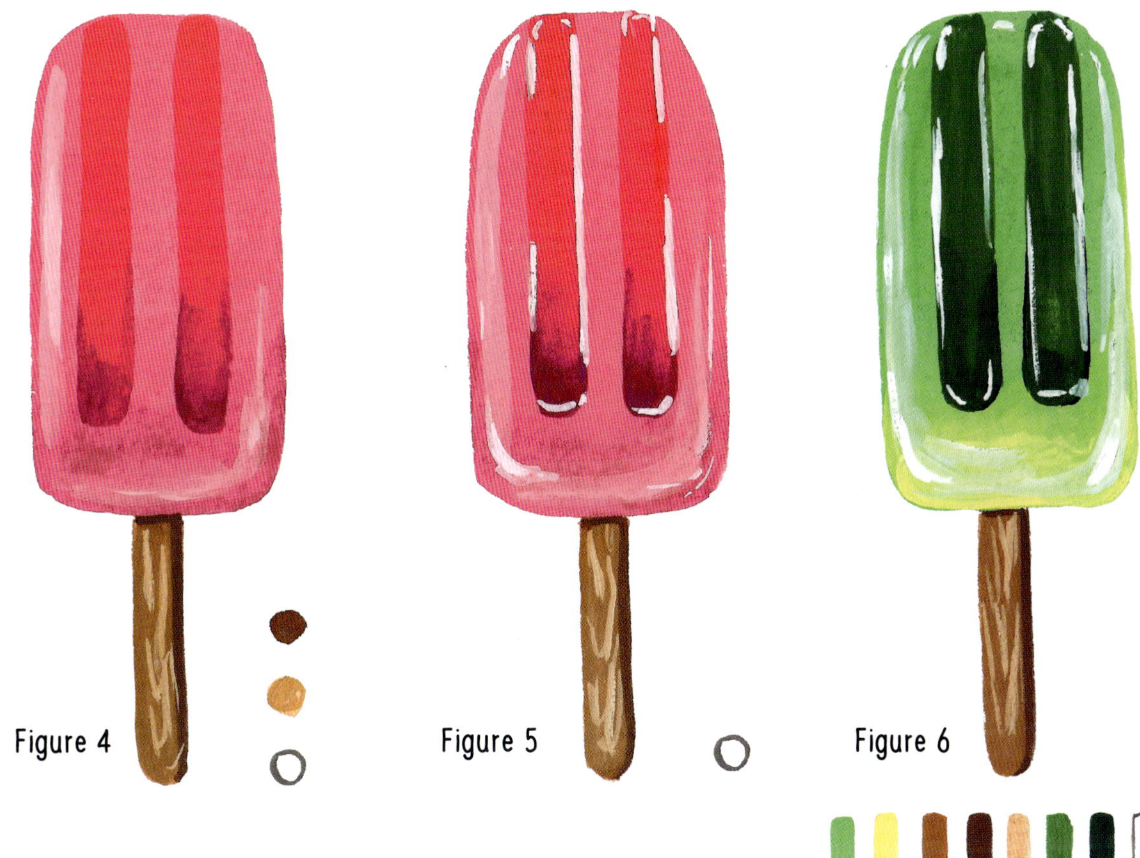

STEP 3

Let's add some details to our popsicle (see Figure 4). Paint a shadow of the wooden stick with brown. Let the layer dry. Then add a pattern on the wooden stick with pastel ochre. Now, with white, paint some highlights on the popsicle that imitate frost. For this, I suggest using a dry-brush technique (page 12). Let the newly painted layer dry. At this step work with a detail brush or thin-tipped round brush.

STEP 4

The last touch is to add white to make the illustration look shiny and more realistic. Using a detail brush, paint highlights as shown in Figure 5. And, *voilà*! Your painting is done!

TIP: Try to paint broken glow lines that are not perfect. It will make your object look more natural.

Of course, using the lesson's principles, you can paint any popsicle or lollipop. Change colors, experiment with the shape and choose different details. Just don't forget to add the shine. In Figure 6, you can see a painting created by following this lesson. I believe it looks like a pineapple and kiwi popsicle.

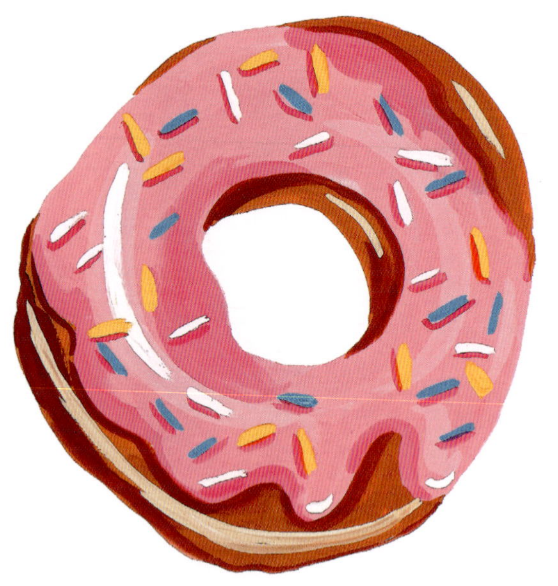

PINK GLAZED DOUGHNUT

This is such a great project, and one of my favorites in this book. I love the happy colors and how, in just a few easy steps, you have such an impressive painting. Let's figure out how to do it step by step.

SUPPLIES

- White, craft or black paper
- Pencil and eraser
- Filbert brush
- Round brushes in different sizes
- Detail brush

PROJECT COLORS

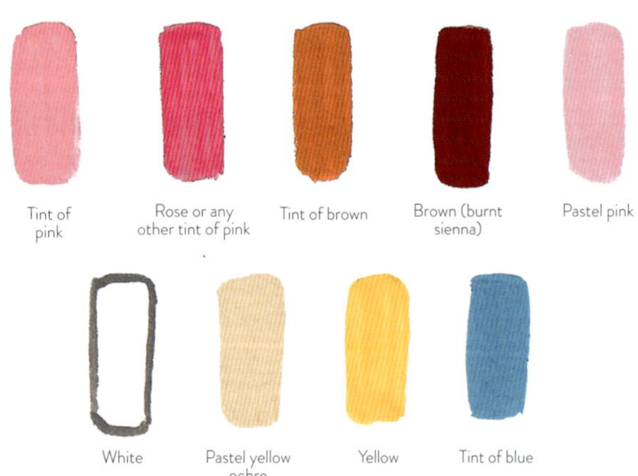

COLOR MIXING

- Tint of pink (white + crimson red, proportion 1:1)
- Tint of brown (burnt sienna + yellow ochre, proportion 1:1)
- Pastel pink (white + crimson red, proportion 2:1)
- Pastel yellow ochre (white + yellow ochre, proportion 1:1)
- Tint of blue (white + cerulean blue, proportion 1:4)

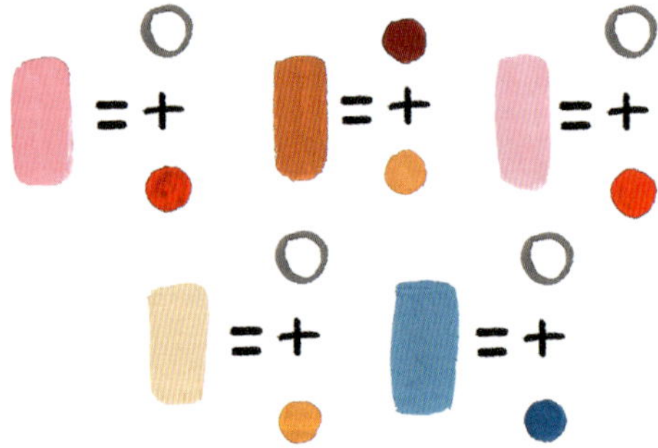

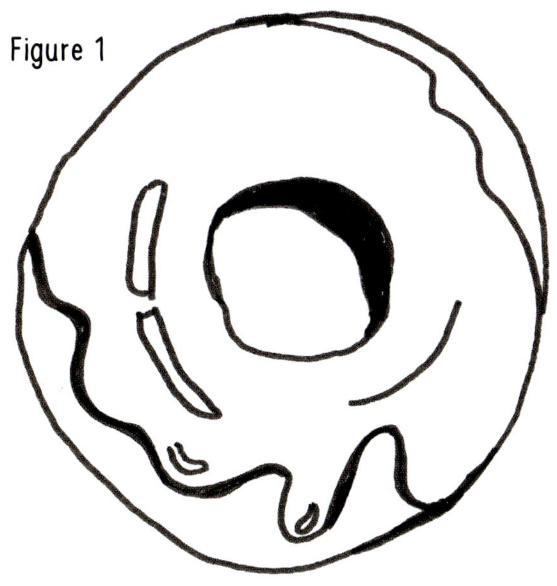
Figure 1

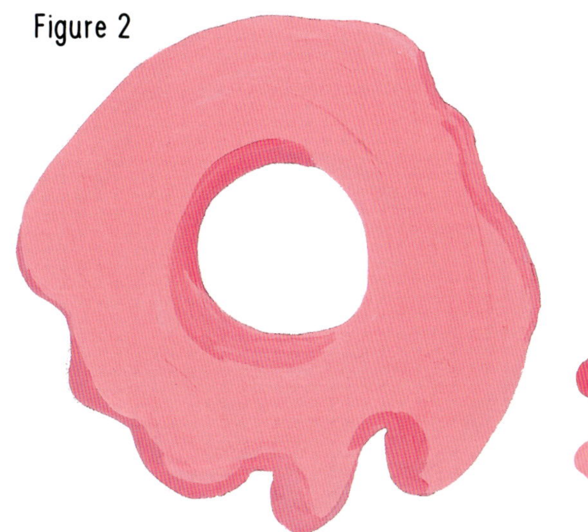
Figure 2

STEP 1

Start by creating a sketch. Following the outline in Figure 1, sketch the doughnut with a pencil. I suggest you not draw the details and instead make a very simple sketch of the main lines. All the details will be added later.

For painting the pink glaze of the doughnut, use the direct blending technique (page 11). Take the filbert or round brush in a medium size and paint the glaze layer in the tint of pink and rose colors at the edges (see Figure 2). Allow the painted layer to dry completely.

STEP 2

Our doughnut painting needs some dough. Switch to the small round brush and first paint the base in the tint of brown (see Figure 3). Once it's dry, add the shadows in brown (see the layering technique, page 11). Work especially carefully at the edges for a neat final result.

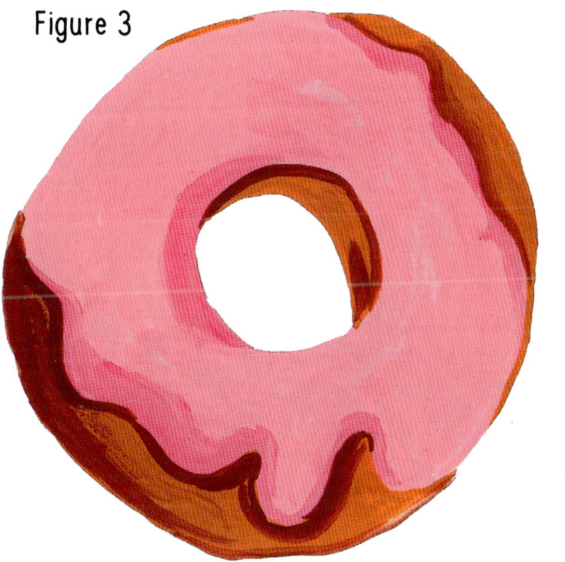
Figure 3

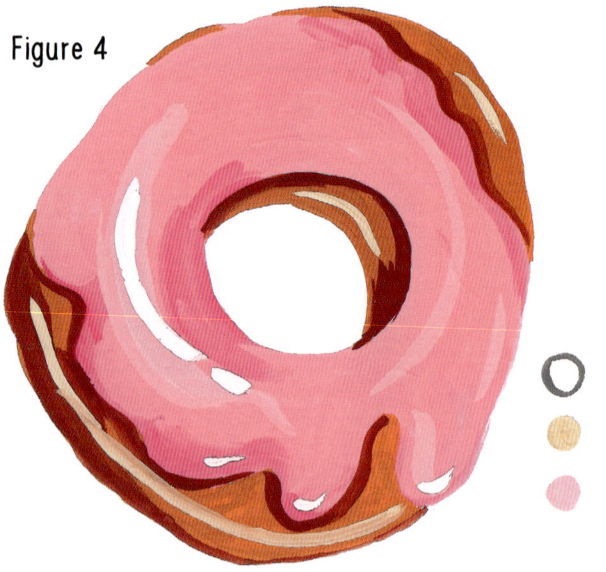

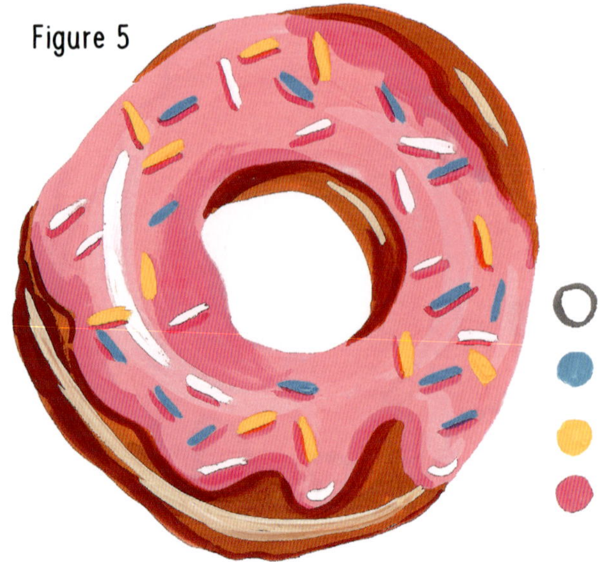

STEP 3

It's time to add some gloss to the glaze. Arm yourself with the small round brush and first paint the highlights in pastel pink, and then, when the previous layer is dry, add the accents in white gouache. Follow Figure 4. Also, add the details to the dough in pastel yellow ochre.

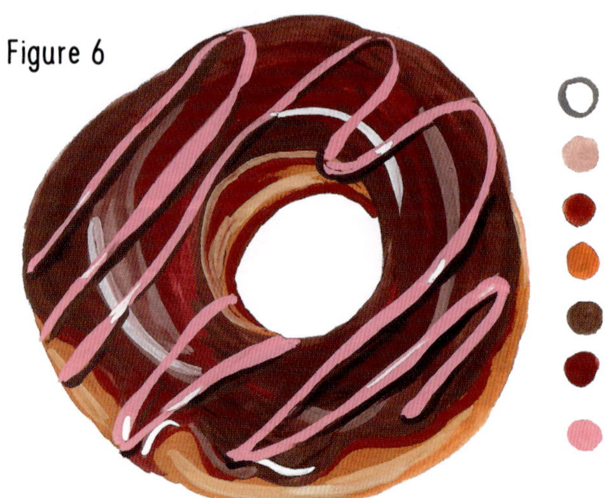

STEP 4

We already have a yummy pink glazed doughnut. But is it a proper doughnut without colorful sprinkles? Let's paint them (see Figure 5). Take a detail brush and paint decorative sprinkles in yellow, the tint of blue and white. Try to add them randomly without any order. Once the sprinkles have dried, paint the shadows with rose.

That's it, and here is a painting of a yummy glazed pink doughnut. I hope you fell in love with this project as much as I did and that it inspires you to paint more doughnuts with gouache. There are so many flavors and different decorations, and you can illustrate all of them just by following the principles of the lesson. It may be a chocolate one with some jam drizzle or maybe a Christmas doughnut. You can find my variation in Figure 6. Doesn't it look delicious? Whatever you choose, don't forget to add some gloss for a more realistic effect.

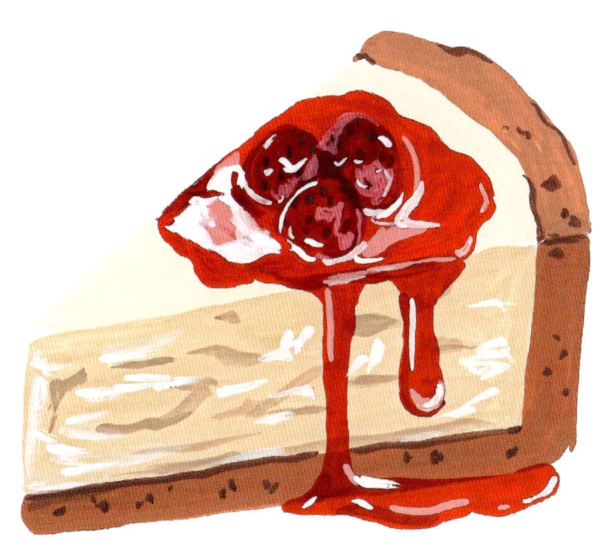

CHEESECAKE WITH BERRY TOPPING

Painting desserts with gouache is such a pleasure. You don't need to think too hard or plan in advance to show the glow of chocolate, jam or glaze. Gouache allows you to add all the details in any color anytime. And gouache makes it possible to paint even complicated pastries, so you can truly enjoy the process and maybe feel a bit like a baker.

Prepare your gouache, brushes and paper. We'll paint a piece of cheesecake with yummy berry topping.

SUPPLIES

- White or black paper
- Pencil and eraser
- Round brushes in different sizes
- Filbert brush (optional)
- Detail brush

PROJECT COLORS

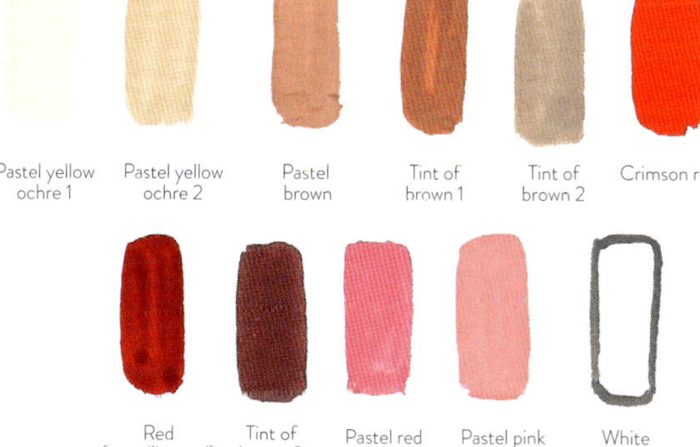

COLOR MIXING

- Pastel yellow ochre 1 (white + yellow ochre, proportion 4:1)
- Pastel yellow ochre 2 (white + yellow ochre, proportion 1:1)
- Pastel brown (white + yellow ochre + burnt sienna, proportion 2:1:1)
- Tint of brown 1 (white + yellow ochre + burnt sienna, proportion 1:1:1)
- Tint of brown 2 (white + yellow ochre + burnt umber, proportion 1:1:1)
- Tint of brown 3 (crimson red + burnt umber, proportion 2:1)
- Pastel red (white + red, proportion 1:1)
- Pastel pink (white + crimson red, proportion 1:1)

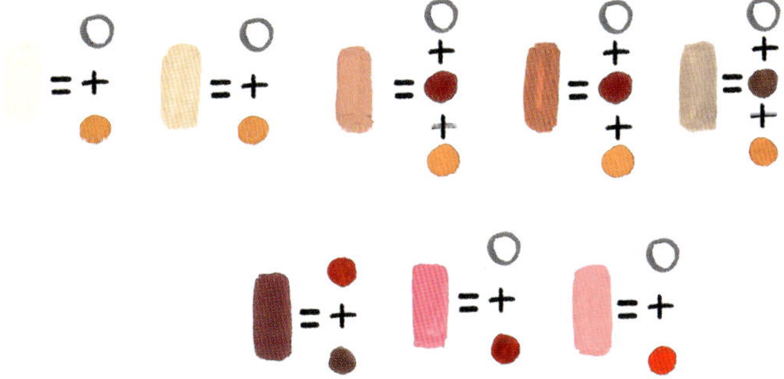

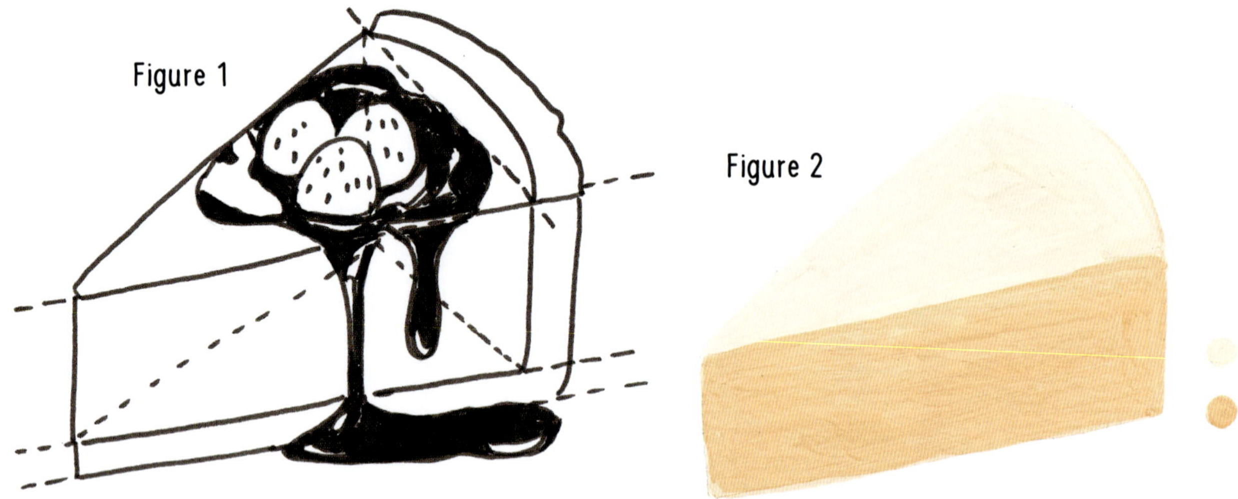

STEP 1

Make a sketch with a pencil following the outlines in Figure 1. After the base layer is covered with paint, the pencil lines may not be visible, so it's not necessary to make a detailed sketch. The main lines of the cake will be enough.

NOTE: Keep in mind that this project will use the layering technique (page 11) at all stages. Before adding a new layer, wait until the previous one is dry.

Take a big round brush and paint the base layers. First, paint the top of the cake in pastel yellow ochre 1, then proceed to color the cheesecake layer in pastel yellow ochre 2. As you can see in Figure 2, the colors differ by a few tones and make a visual contrast and 3D effect. Allow the layer to dry.

STEP 2

Now switch to a small round brush and accurately paint the graham cracker crust, the top part in pastel brown and the bottom in the tint of brown 1. Also add some details on the cheesecake layer with the tint of brown 2 (see Figure 3). These details imitate the texture of the cake on the cut side. For this purpose, I recommend using a filbert brush in a small size and making horizontal brush strokes.

TIP: You can also apply the dry-brush technique (page 12) to add texture and to make the cake piece look more realistic.

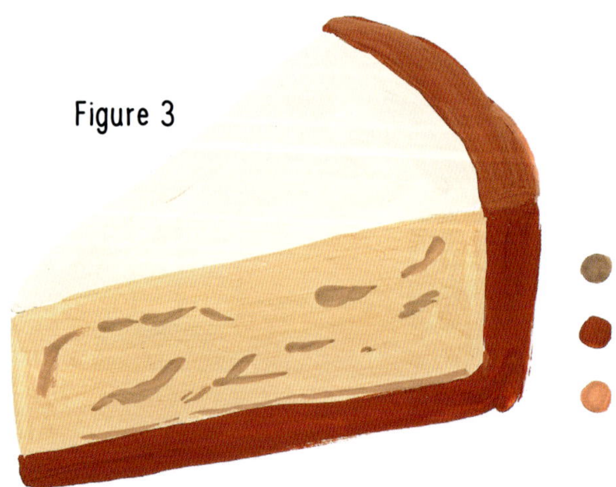

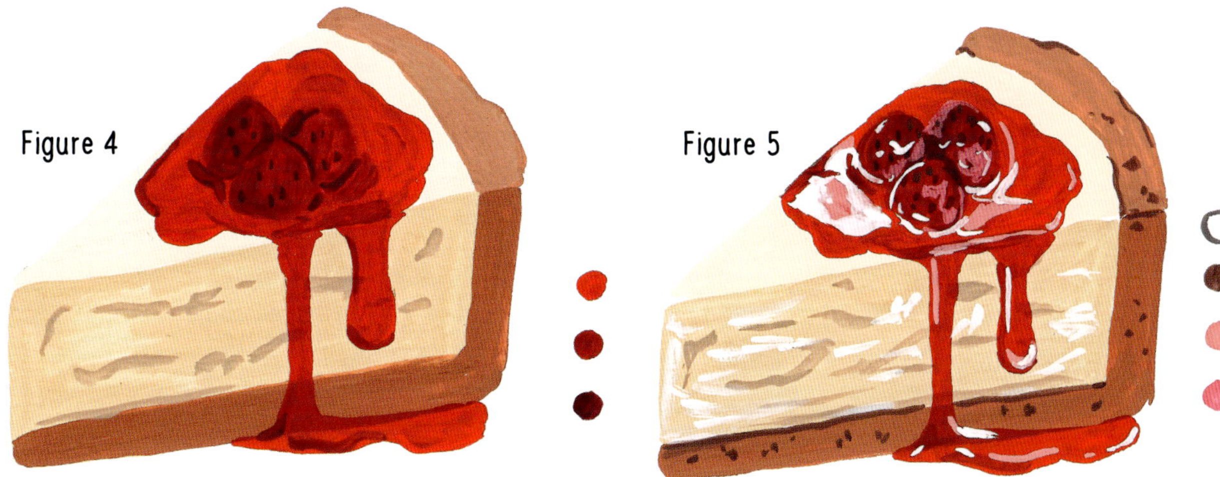

STEP 3

It's time to add the topping on the cheesecake (see Figure 4). I recommend following the next sequence: First, paint the berries in crimson red; next, add the glaze in red; and finally, proceed to the shadows in crimson red and the tint of brown 3. Because we use the layering technique in this project, let each layer dry before adding the next one. Use round brushes in handy sizes for each element while painting this step.

STEP 4

After all that work, we are ready to add the highlights and final details. Prepare a small round brush or a detail brush. Paint the gloss on the glaze in pastel red and add highlights on the berries in pastel pink.

Once the layer is dry, add the final highlights with white gouache, as shown in Figure 5.

And finally, complete the painting by adding details to the graham cracker crust in the tint of brown 3. Let the work dry completely.

When you want to practice painting some desserts with gouache, paint a piece of cheesecake. I promise you will never be disappointed. Paint your own yummy topping, or add some fresh fruits and berries on top. You can find my variation in Figure 6. Here I have chosen a blueberry glaze topping, and for the rest I just followed the principles of the lesson. I hope this project has filled your heart with positive vibes and boosted your gouache-painting skills.

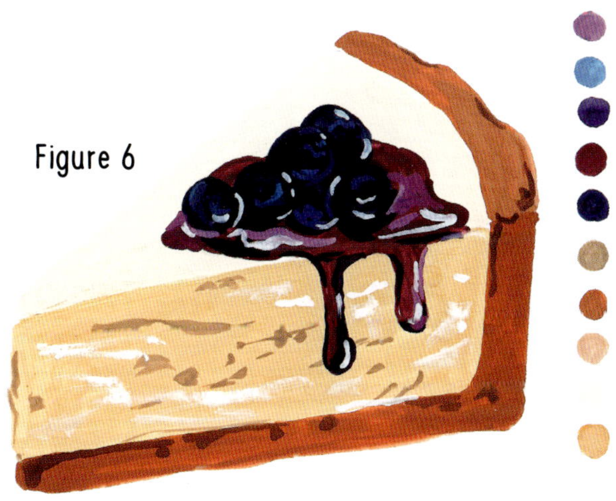

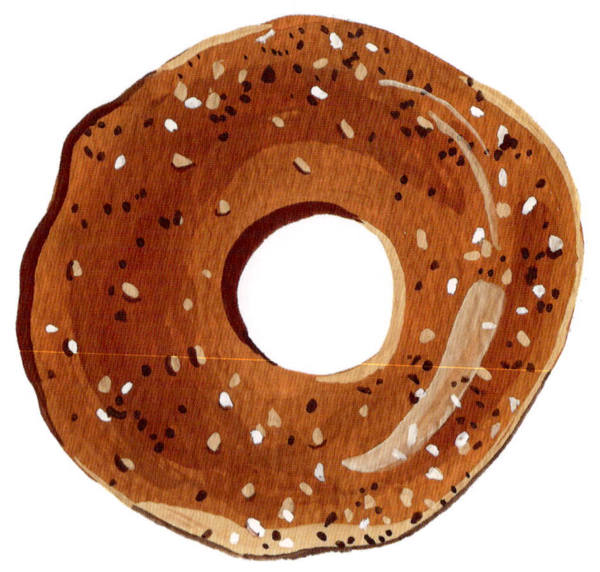

FRESH AND DELICIOUS BAGEL

There's nothing better than the smell of freshly baked croissants or bagels in the morning. For this lesson, I've chosen the bagel.

I love the golden and crispy crust and, of course, the sprinkling of the bagel. Bagels can be topped with poppy, sesame or any other seeds. Some may have salt sprinkled on top. Whichever your favorite, I can assure you that it will be fun and easy to paint, especially with gouache.

Let's do it step by step.

SUPPLIES

- White or black paper
- Pencil and eraser
- Round brushes in different sizes
- Detail brush

PROJECT COLORS

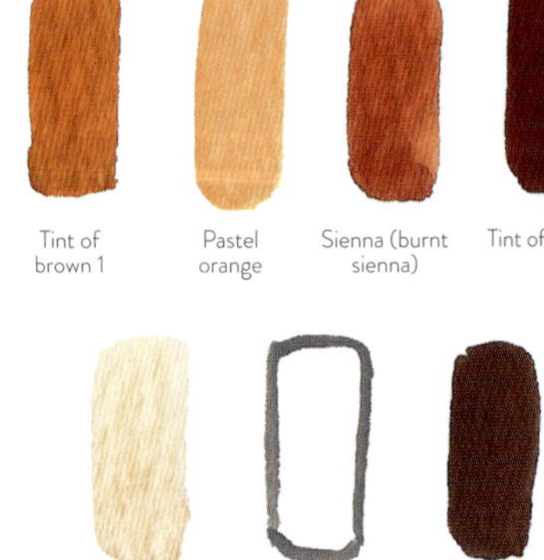

COLOR MIXING

- Tint of brown 1 (burnt sienna + yellow ochre, proportion 1:3)
- Pastel orange (orange + white, proportion 1:3)
- Tint of brown 2 (burnt sienna + burnt umber, proportion 2:1)
- Pastel ochre (yellow ochre + orange + white, proportion 1:1:3)

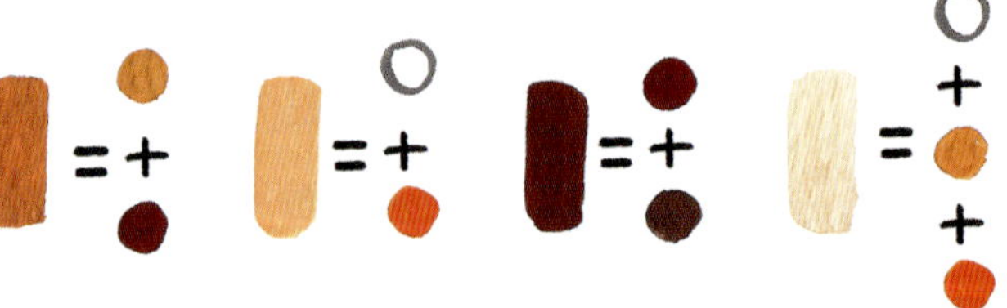

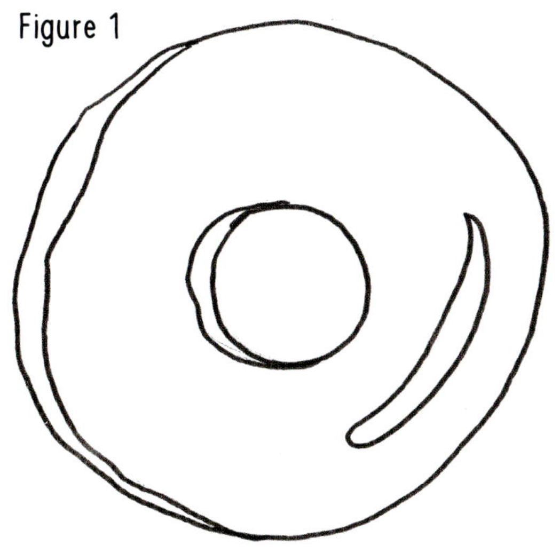
Figure 1

STEP 1

Let's start by making a pencil sketch. It should not be perfect (see Figure 1). A slightly crooked shape will make the illustration more realistic and give it charm.

Take a big round brush and fill the bagel shape with the tint of brown 1. You can see that for now, the basic shape looks pretty flat. To make it look more realistic, add a layer in pastel orange, as shown in Figure 2.

NOTE: You can use the pastel orange in two ways. The first one is by applying the layering technique (page 11), and the second is painting while the first layer of paint is still wet. Either will work nicely. But the latter will provide a smoother effect.

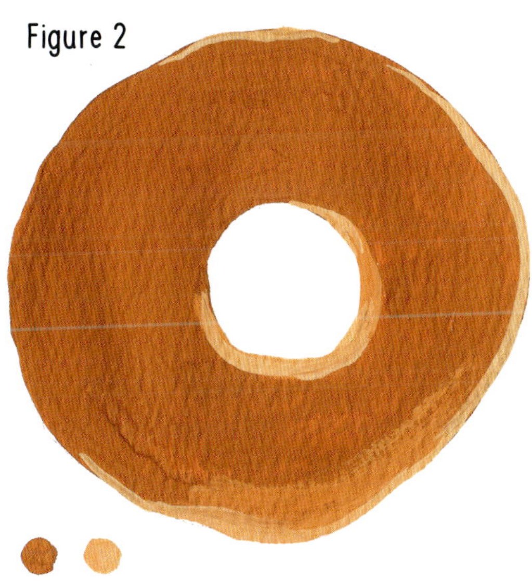
Figure 2

STEP 2

Let's make the bagel even more realistic (see Figure 3). With the same brush, add the middle layer in sienna. Then soften it (page 12) with clean water. Allow the painted layer to dry.

Switch to a smaller round brush and add shadows in the tint of brown 2. Then paint some highlights in the pastel ochre. Let the painting dry.

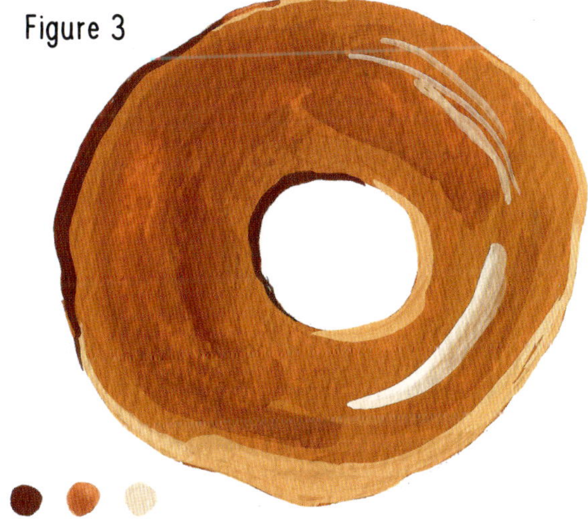
Figure 3

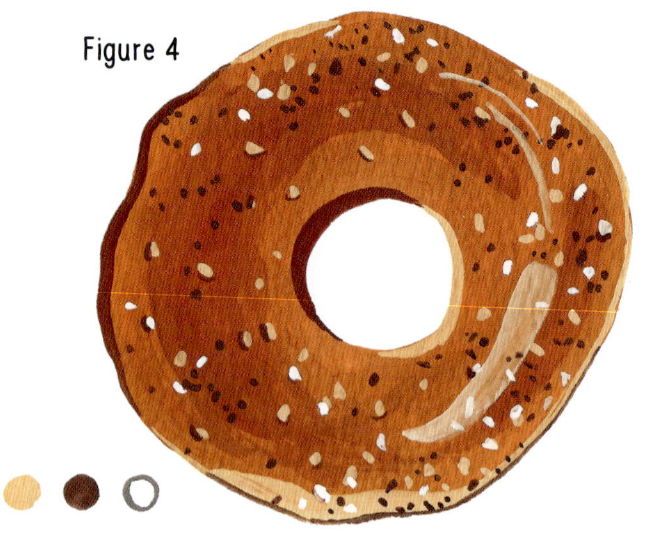

Figure 4

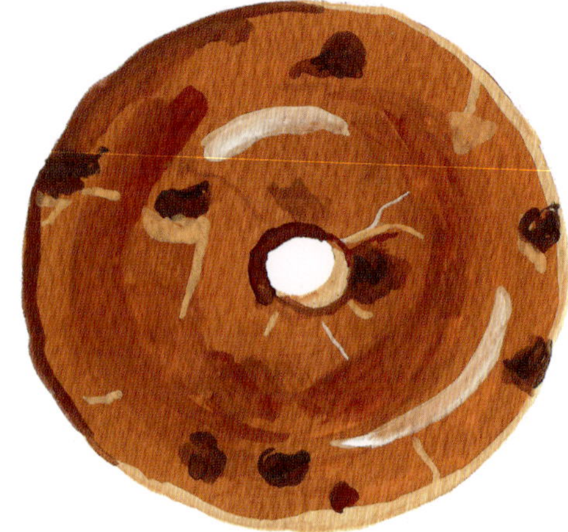

Figure 5

STEP 3

Time to add toppings to the bagel (see Figure 4). By using a detail brush, paint small details in the following colors: pastel ochre, white and brown. Add them randomly to imitate real sprinkled seeds. You can refer to a real bagel or an image from the internet. It may help you to paint it more realistically. I also added a few minor details to emphasize the edges and some shadows. They're optional. Ordinarily, I'd say that there is no need to overload the painting with details. For the bagel, I can't say that. Add as many details as you want. And our painting is done!

With the help of instructions from this lesson, you can paint any other bakery product. It could be a croissant, baguette or cinnamon bun. Anything you like and that inspires you. You can also experiment with the bagel and try different types, changing the shapes and topping.

Take a look at the examples in Figures 5 and 6. Both of them were painted using the step-by-step instructions in this lesson. Don't they look delicious?

I hope you like this lesson and have fun experimenting with the project.

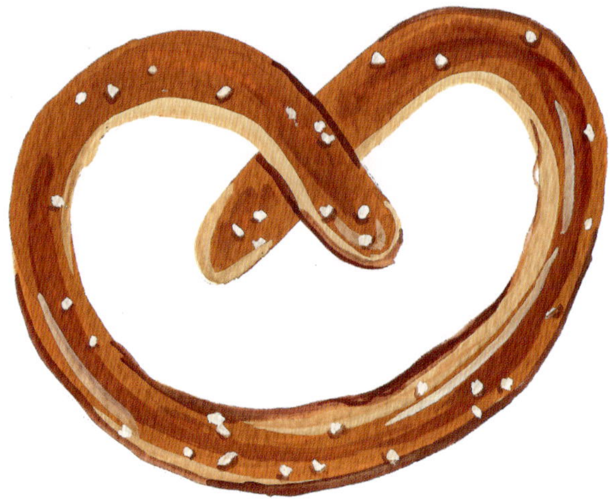

Figure 6

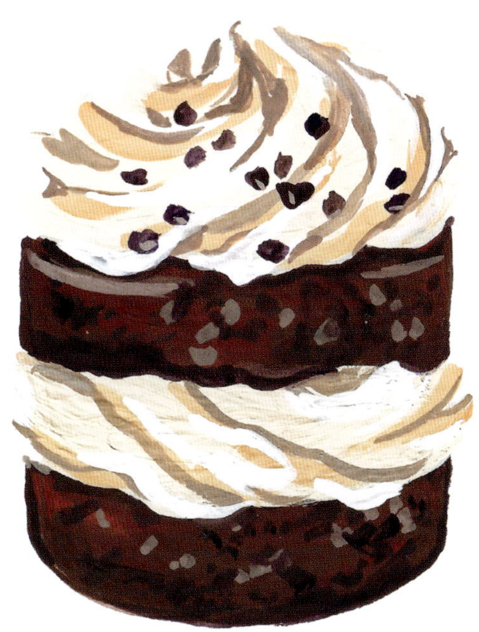

MINI CREAM CAKE

Cake painting with gouache is such an inspiring process. Gouache has such a creamy consistency, so it easily mimics the look of cream or frosting on a cake. You can even feel a little like a baker, adding layer by layer. Sounds fun, doesn't it? If you're short on time, you could paint a mini cake. And later, you can apply basically all the principles of this small cake to bigger cakes. Let's paint a mini cream cake by using gouache.

SUPPLIES

- White paper
- Pencil and eraser
- Round brushes in different sizes
- Filbert brush (optional)
- Detail brush

TIP: Instead of white paper, you could paint on craft paper, if the cream of the cake will be painted in white or some other very light pastel colors.

PROJECT COLORS

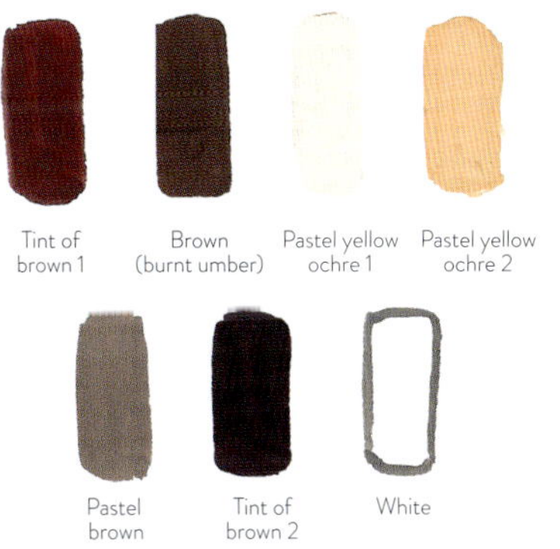

COLOR MIXING

- Tint of brown 1 (crimson red + burnt umber, proportion 2:1)
- Pastel yellow ochre 1 (white + yellow ochre, proportion 4:1)
- Pastel yellow ochre 2 (white + yellow ochre, proportion 1:1)
- Pastel brown (white + burnt umber, proportion 2:1)
- Tint of brown 2 (violet + burnt umber, proportion 1:3)

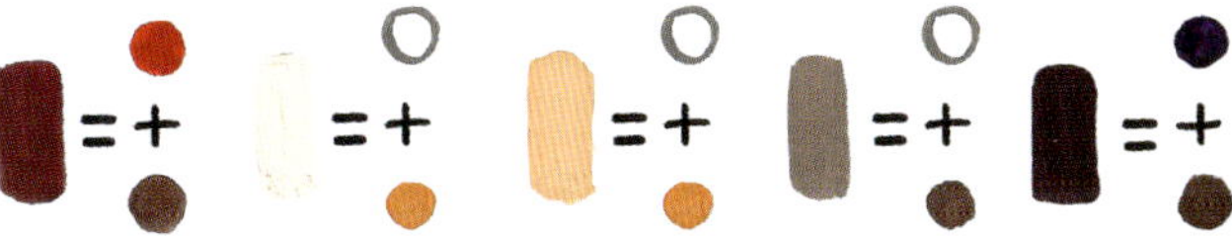

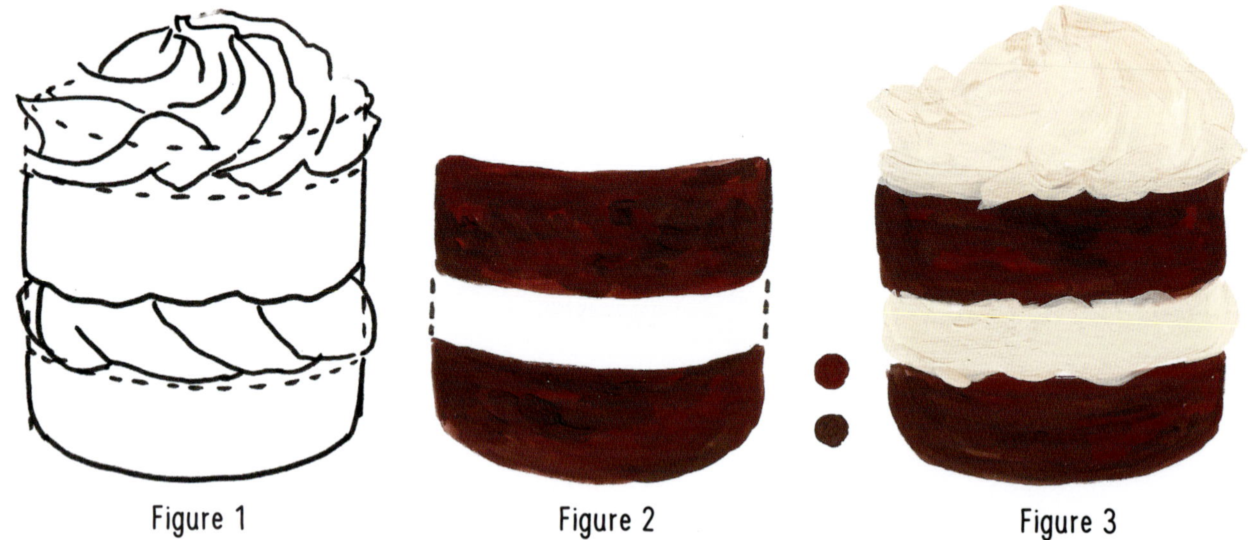

Figure 1 Figure 2 Figure 3

STEP 1

Before you begin painting, make a sketch with a pencil, referring to Figure 1. It's enough to put down just several basic lines. I suggest not drawing the details, especially in the cream area, as the base gouache layer will cover the pencil lines.

Take a medium round brush, or even better, use a filbert brush, and fill the cake in the tint of brown 1 and brown (see Figure 2). For this, apply the direct blending technique (page 11). Allow the painted layer to dry.

STEP 2

It's time to put the cream on the biscuit layers of the cake (see Figure 3). Arm yourself with a medium round brush with a thin tip and paint the cream in pastel yellow ochre 1. Pay attention and note that in some places the cream covers the biscuit layer. If, after drying, these areas still look transparent, you can add one more layer of the same color on top for a full opaque effect. Allow the painting to dry.

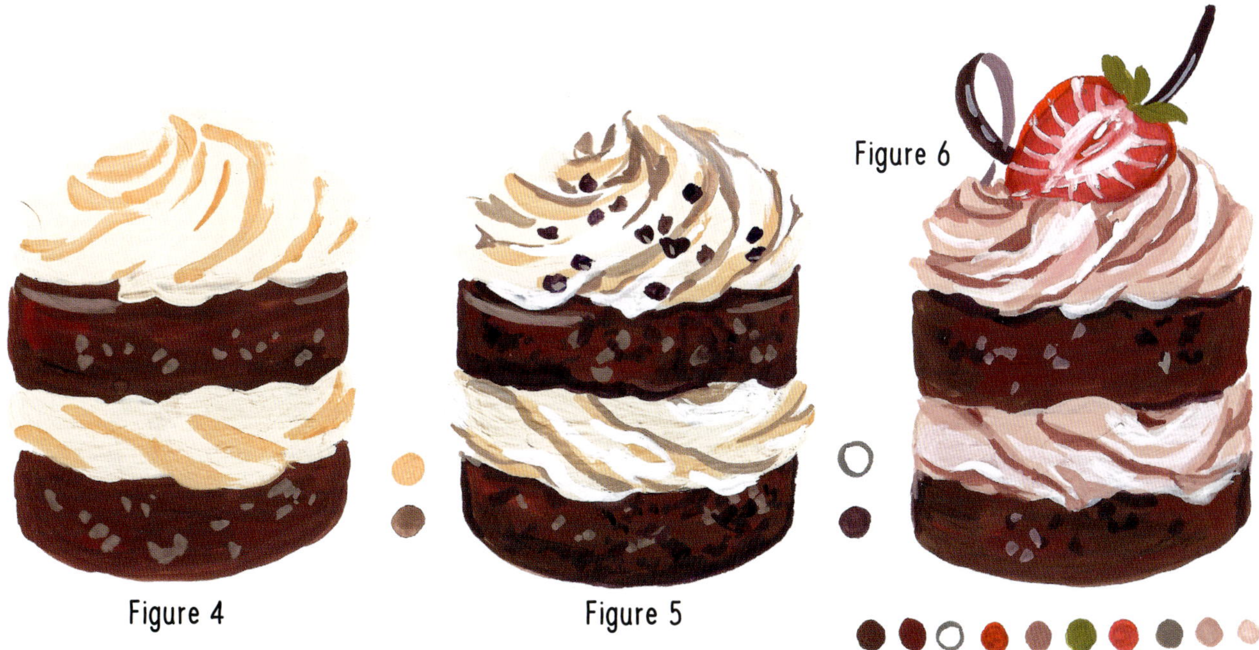

STEP 3

NOTE: In steps 3 and 4, we will be using the layering technique (page 11).

With a small round brush, paint the shadows onto the cream in pastel yellow ochre 2. For this, you can follow Figure 4 or reference a photo of a real cake. Also add the details to the cake layers in pastel brown. Once again, let the painting dry.

STEP 4

Switch to a detail brush and prepare the tint of brown 2 and white. When the paint dries, add the highlights to the frosting with white gouache, as shown in Figure 5. Next, randomly paint some chocolate pieces on the cream in the tint of brown 2 and, with the same color, paint the details on the biscuit layers. Allow the work to dry completely.

Finally, add highlights on the chocolate pieces in pastel brown. Now our painting is complete, and I hope you enjoyed the lesson. Figure 6 shows an example of how its methods can be used to create another painting of a small cake. Experiment with cream colors, toppings and decorations. There are so many options for practicing this project. And as I mentioned earlier, you can apply these principles for painting a big cake as well. Why not?! Practice and enjoy the process!

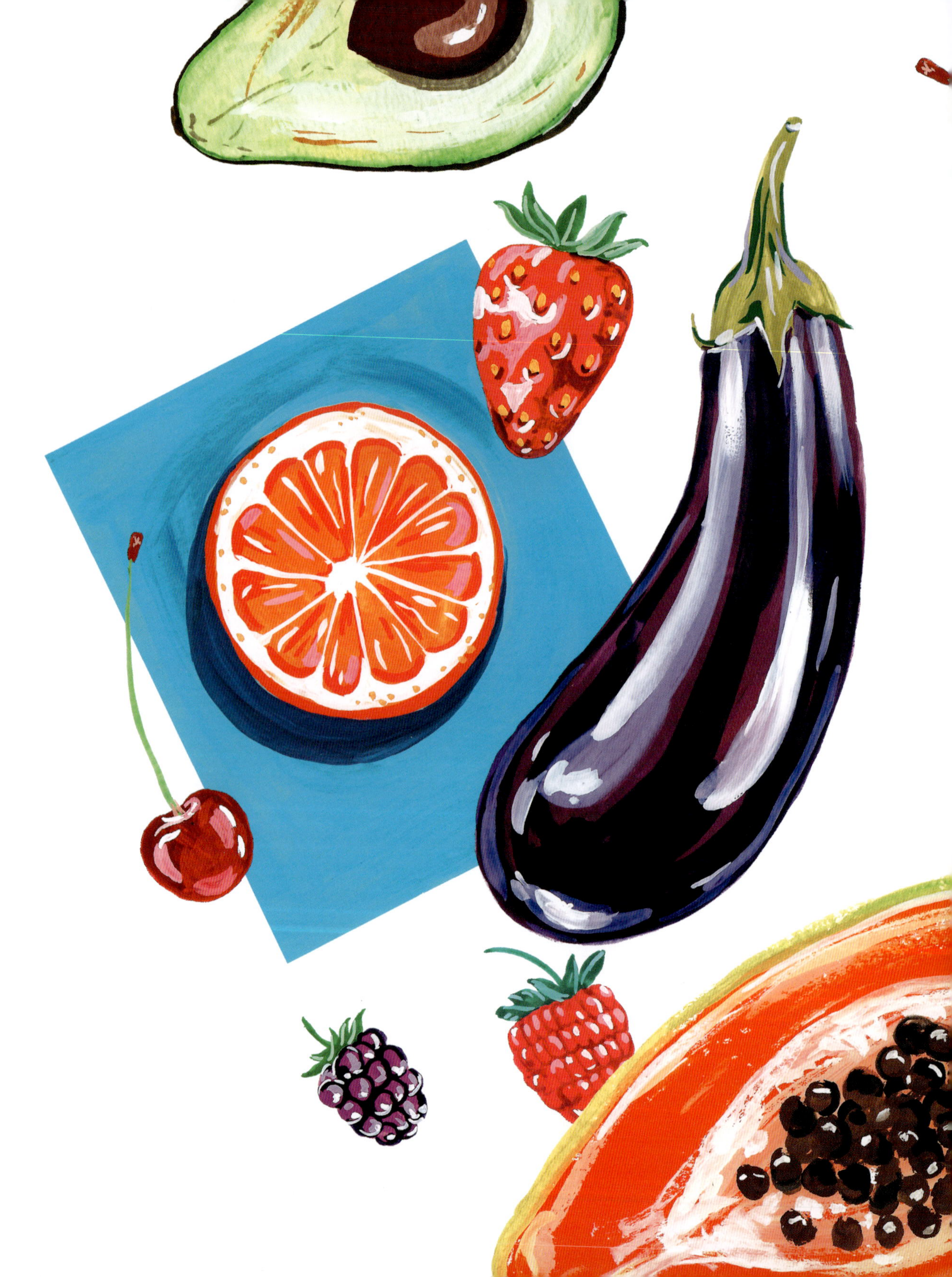

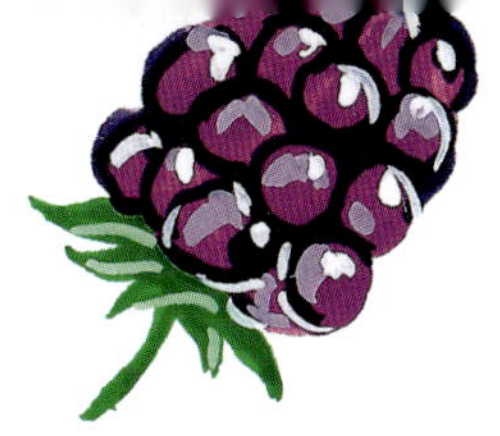

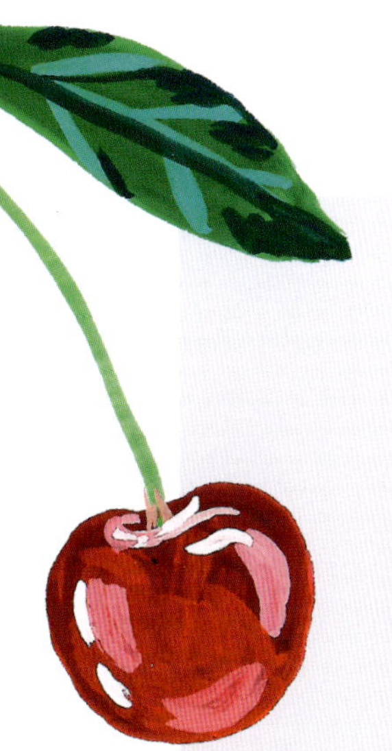

Yummy FRUITS AND VEGGIES

There is nothing better than fresh fruit, berries and veggies. The colors, shapes and textures are so vivid, and we can explore all these elements through painting projects from this chapter. Even though the section contains only a few lessons, I'm sure that you will learn new skills and have fun during the painting process.

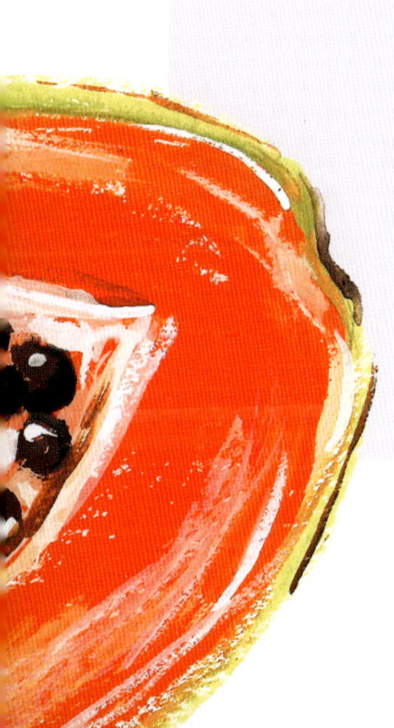

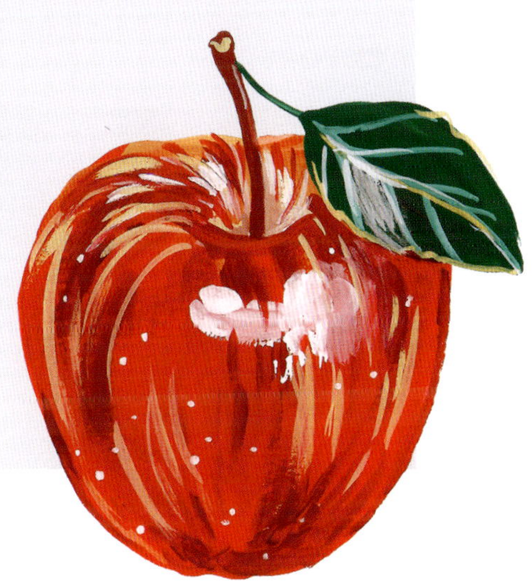

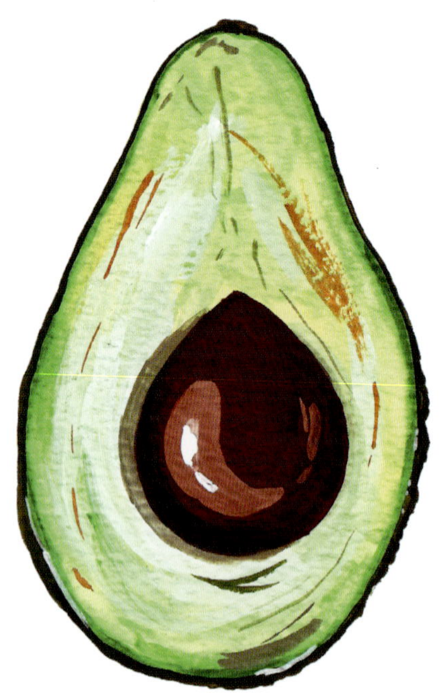

AVOCADO

Everyone loves avocado. It's yummy and healthy. But do you know how easy and fun it is to paint this wonderful fruit? In my opinion, a halved avocado is one of the more visually satisfying foods to paint with any medium, especially gouache. If you have an avocado at home, you can explore it by yourself: shape, colors, details, shadows and all its features. But first, let's paint it with the help of my example.

SUPPLIES

- White, craft or black paper
- Pencil and eraser
- Round brushes in different sizes
- Detail brush
- Flat brush (optional)

PROJECT COLORS

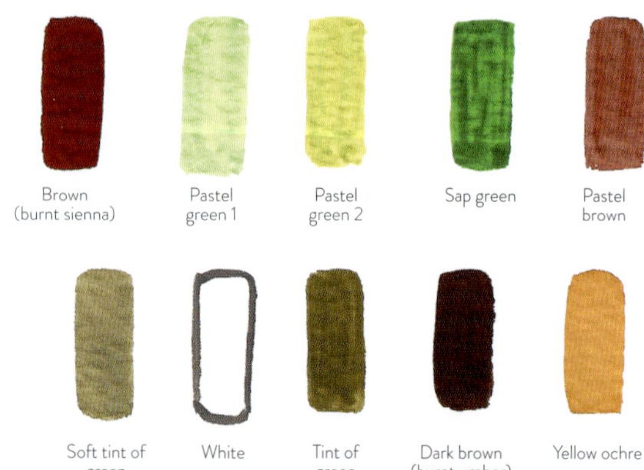

COLOR MIXING

- Pastel green 1 (yellow + sap green + white, proportion 1:1:5)
- Pastel green 2 (yellow + sap green + white, proportion 2:1:5)
- Pastel brown (burnt sienna + white, proportion, 1:5)
- Soft tint of green (burnt umber + sap green + white, proportion 1:2:1)
- Tint of green (burnt umber + sap green, proportion 1:2)

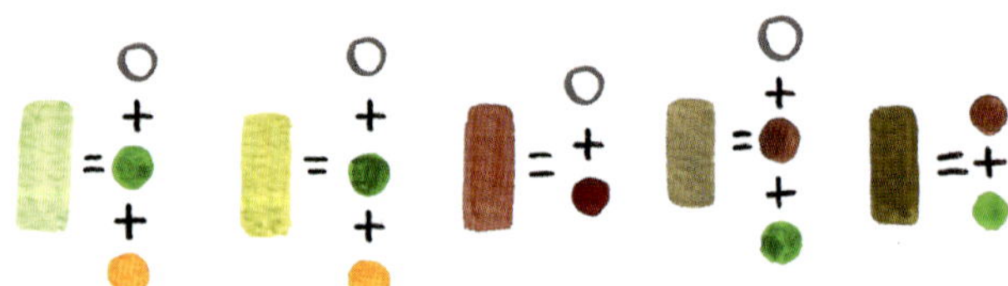

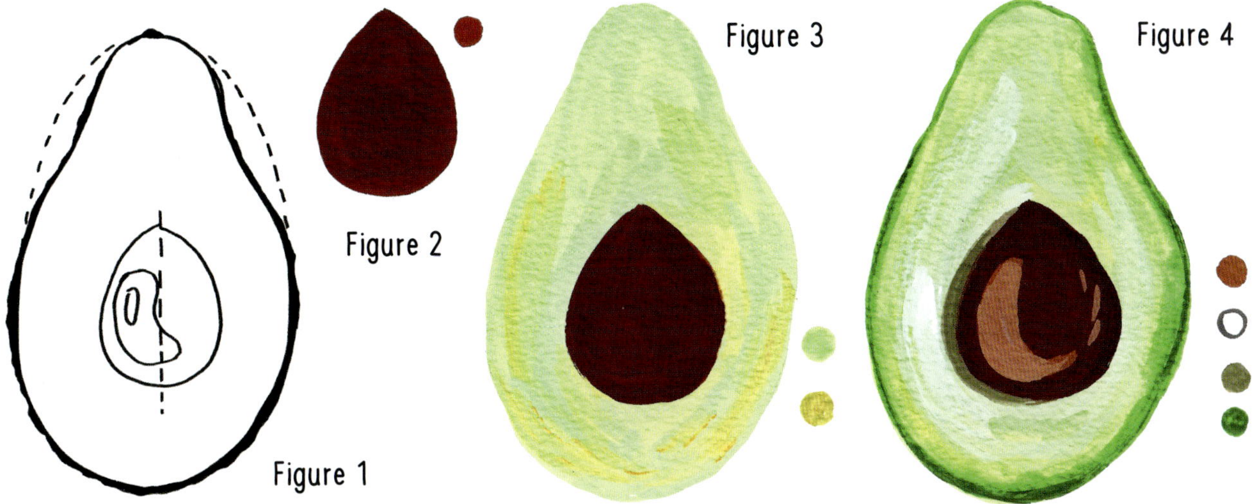

STEP 1

Let's get started with a sketch. Draw a light sketch with a pencil following Figure 1. Please note that the avocado body may be pear-shaped, egg-shaped or spherical, so start with the base shape and then get more specific.

Once the sketch is ready, you can begin painting (see Figure 2). Take a small round brush and paint the avocado seed with brown. Wait for the layer to dry and then jump to step 2.

STEP 2

In this step, we'll use the direct blending technique (page 11), which is just perfect for making natural-looking textures (see Figure 3). Take a medium round brush and paint the avocado body shape with pastel green 1 and pastel green 2 by using direct blending. Wait until the work is completely dry before moving on to the next step.

STEP 3

NOTE: During painting in steps 3 and 4, we'll use the layering technique (page 11).

Take a small brush and paint an outline using sap green (see Figure 4). To make the layer look softer, use the softening technique (page 12): Blur the painted line from inside with water.

Now, using pastel brown, add a layer to the avocado seed. Then, using a soft tint of green, add a shadow on the fruit body, from the left side of the stone. Let the paint dry completely.

The last touch in this stage is adding a lovely texture. For this purpose, use a dry-brush technique (page 12). With white gouache add a few brush strokes in the middle area of the avocado body.

STEP 4

It's time to add details. For this step, we will use a detail brush and a small round brush. First, paint the avocado skin with the tint of green. It can be any tint of green or even purple or brown. But I prefer to paint with this pretty dark green shade to create a nice and strong contrast.

Now add details to the avocado using the tint of green, dark brown, yellow ochre and white, as shown in Figure 5. It's especially important to add a highlight gloss to the seed with white gouache. It will make the painting look more realistic.

I recommend applying a dry-brush technique (page 12) for adding some of the details. It's optional but brings playful vibes to the painting. I hope you enjoyed this lesson and that my instructions inspire you to paint more pieces with avocado and other fruits and veggies.

As for the avocado painting, you can experiment with the shapes and finer details and play with the colors of the project. Also, you might want to try to add a background. Figure 6 shows a picture painted using this project's methods, but I've added a pastel background first and a shadow to finish the project.

TIP: For painting the background for this alternative project, I suggest using a flat brush and the dry-brush forming technique (page 12).

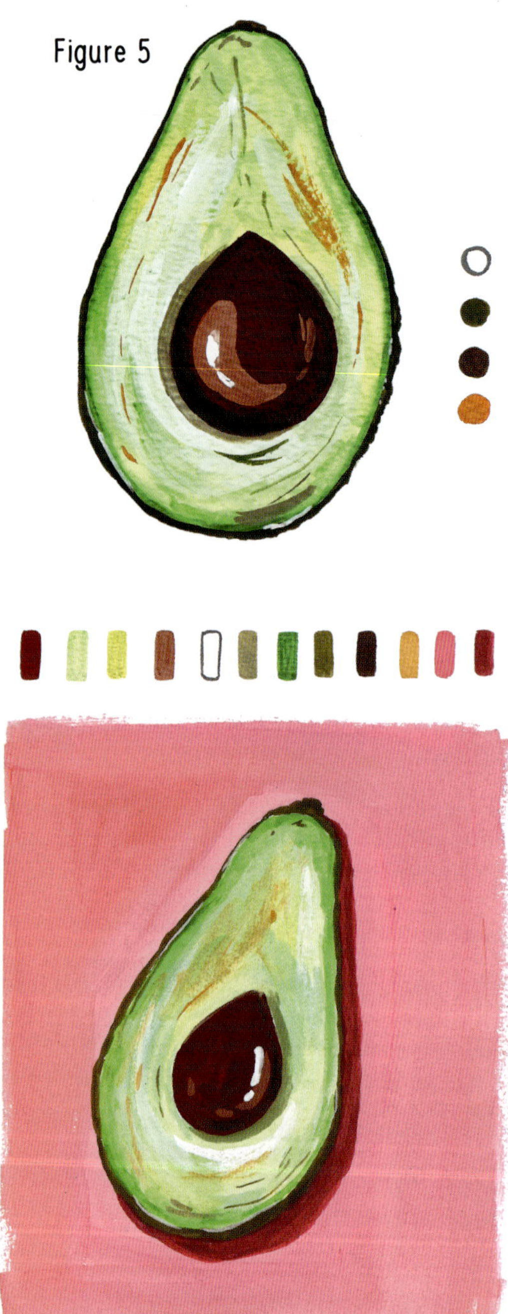

Figure 5

Figure 6

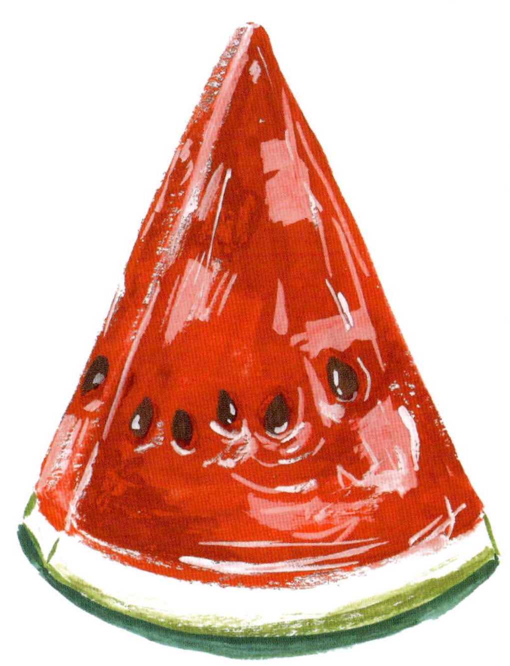

SLICE OF WATERMELON

This lesson is all about the dry brush and dry-brush forming techniques (page 12), which are so creative and show how awesome and versatile gouache is.

In painting a slice of watermelon, I will show how easy it is to implement these techniques in practice. Let's look at everything step by step and learn how to paint a juicy and colorful watermelon with gouache.

SUPPLIES

- White paper
- Pencil and eraser
- Round brushes in different sizes
- Detail brush

PROJECT COLORS

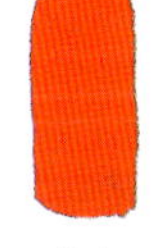

Red (scarlet red)

Pastel red

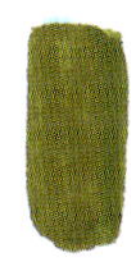

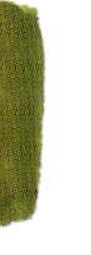

Tint of green

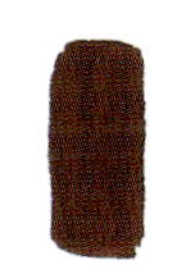

Brown (burnt sienna)

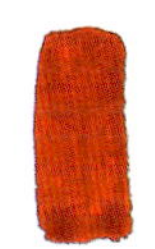

Crimson (crimson red)

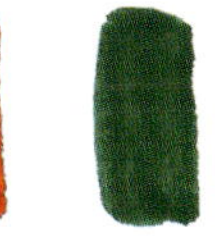

Viridian green

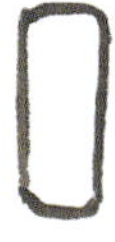

White

COLOR MIXING

- Pastel red (red + white, proportion 1:3)
- Tint of green (yellow ochre + sap green, proportion 1:2)

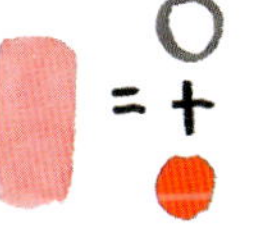

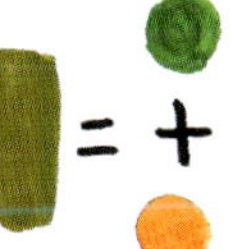

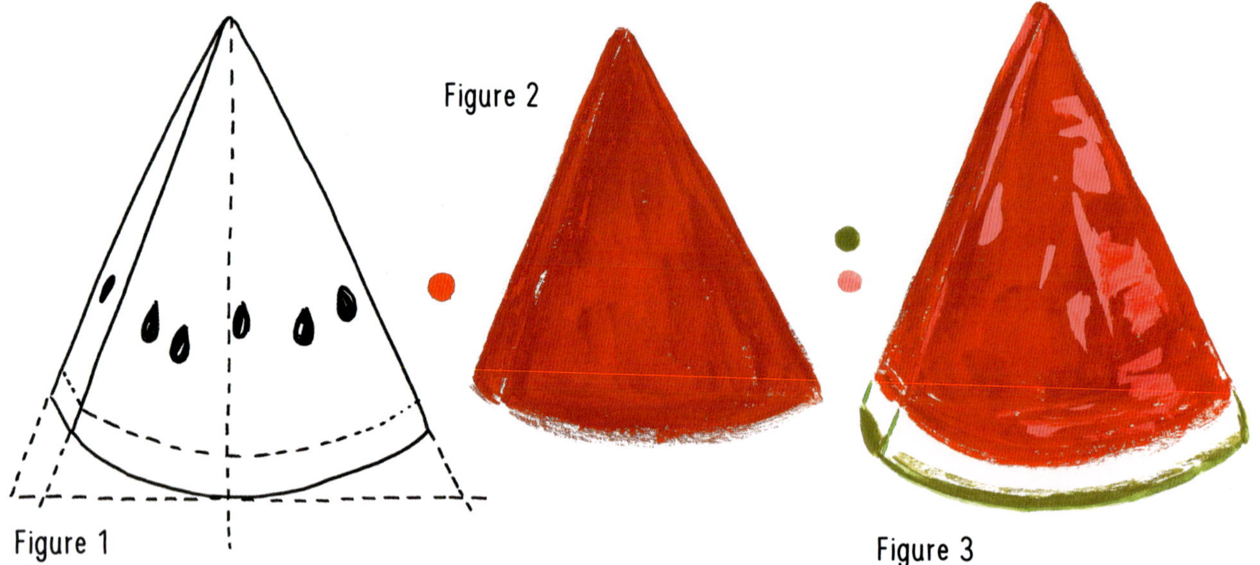

STEP 1

Let's start the project by making a sketch following the drawing outlines in Figure 1.

To draw any fruit, vegetable or berry you first have to understand the shape of it. If it's a complicated object, break it into simple shapes. Simplifying can help make it easy to draw the object and then to focus on other aspects of the object you paint. The slice of watermelon, for example, is simple and fits into a triangle. Once the sketch is ready, you can move on to painting.

NOTE: In this project, we will work with the layering technique (page 11).

With red, paint the shape of the watermelon by using the dry-brush forming technique (for more about the dry-brush forming technique, see page 12). Use a medium round brush for this purpose (see Figure 2). Pay particular attention to the textured edges at the bottom of the slice. Go on to the next step once the painting is dry.

STEP 2

Add another layer on top of the watermelon with pastel red, as shown in Figure 3. For this, apply the dry-brush technique (page 12). Do not overdo it with this layer; you don't want to drown out the red base.

Time to add the green part of the watermelon slice. Using the dry-brush technique, paint the bottom part of the watermelon in the tint of green. Try to make this part neat. I recommend using a small round brush for this step.

Let the painting dry.

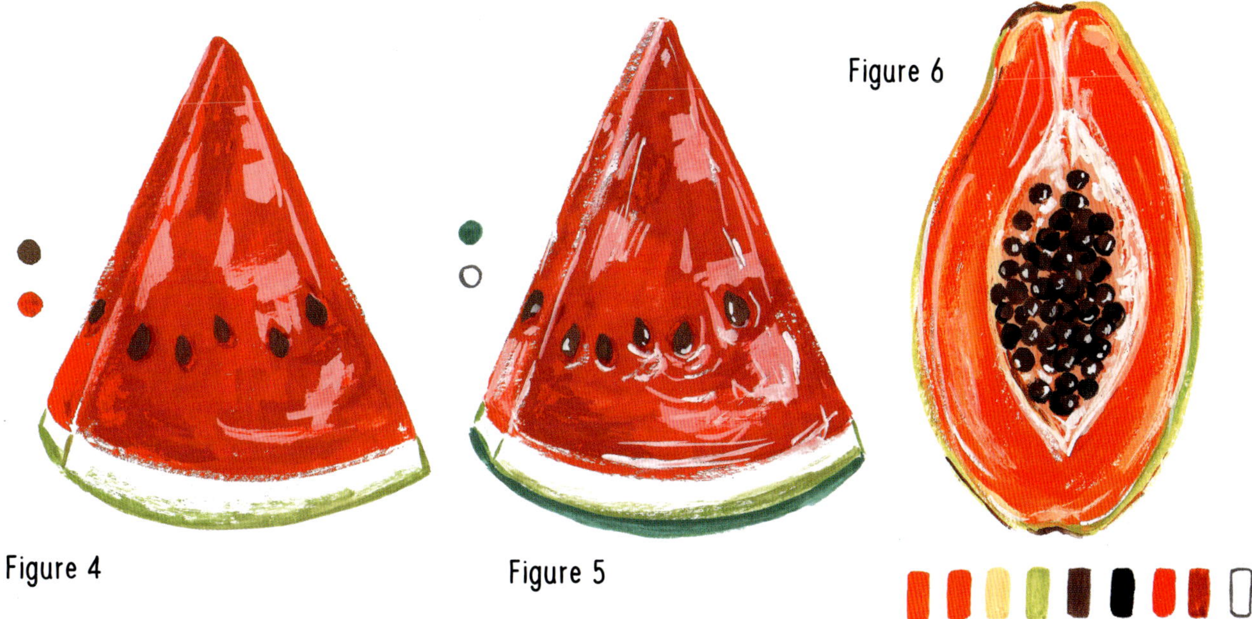

STEP 3

Now add a few seeds in brown to the slice (see Figure 4). Once the painting is dry, you can add a layer with crimson. It will give the object much more depth and realism. Make sure you also added a shadow for each seed with crimson. After the painted layer dries, go on to the last step.

STEP 4

Let's keep going and finish the piece (see Figure 5). Paint the arched line and the small side segment at the bottom of the watermelon with the viridian green. Use a small round brush.

Now take the detail brush and use white gouache to paint all the accents and details. Emphasize the line that divides the front and side of the slice. Also, don't forget to add shine to each seed. To emphasize and paint highlights, use the dry-brush technique. Feel free to play with different brush sizes at this stage and to paint various strokes to make the piece more interesting.

Don't stop after painting the watermelon project. Go ahead and paint more yummy and colorful fruits and vegetables. All you need to do is follow the principles of the lesson and not be afraid to experiment.

Figure 6 shows a vivid papaya painting. The papaya has a different shape than the watermelon, and the colors are different too. But it is painted using the same principles and steps of this lesson.

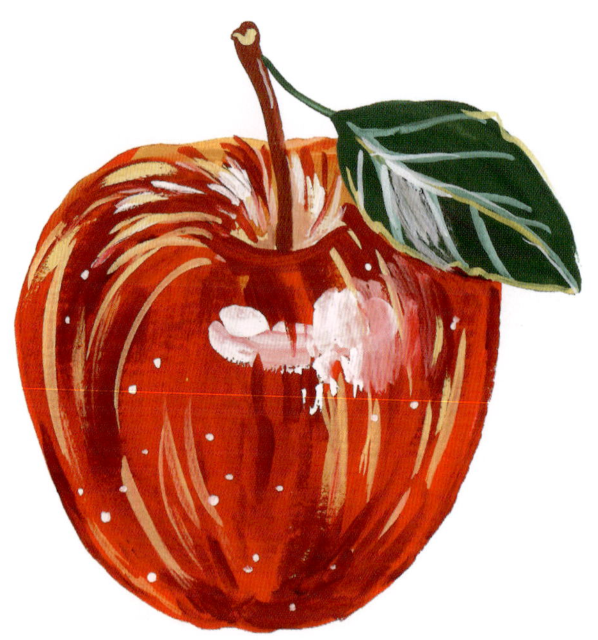

RIPE AUTUMN APPLE

In this project, I prepared another very beautiful and easy project for practicing gouache. We'll paint the ripe fall apple. The colors of this project are so rich and warm—they immediately take me to a cozy autumn atmosphere. I hope this project brings you all the happiness of apple picking in fall.

SUPPLIES

- White, craft or black paper
- Pencil and eraser
- Filbert brush (optional)
- Round brushes in different sizes
- Detail brush

PROJECT COLORS

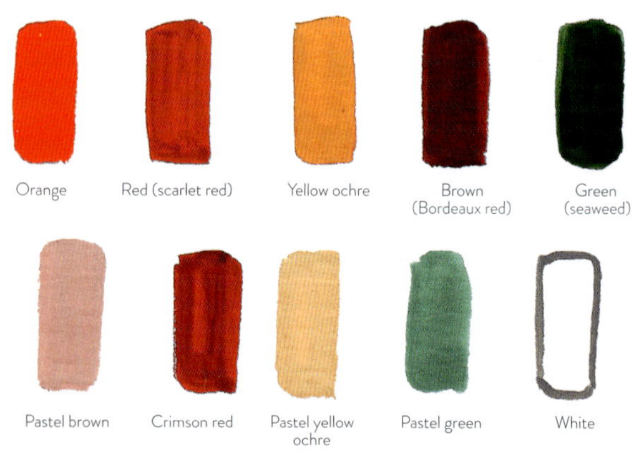

COLOR MIXING

- Pastel brown (white + burnt sienna, proportion 2:1)
- Pastel yellow ochre (white + yellow ochre, proportion 2:1)
- Pastel green (white + green, proportion 2:1)

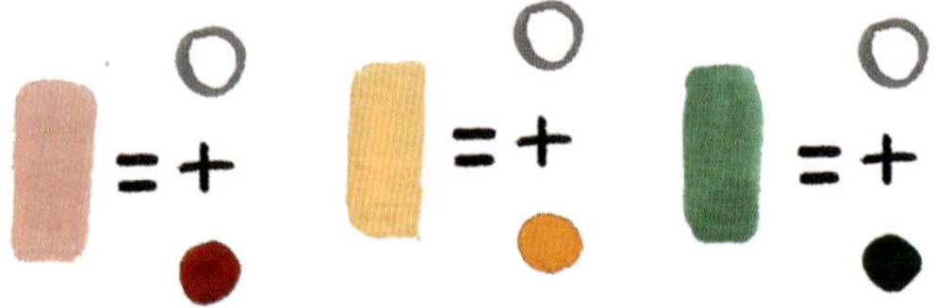

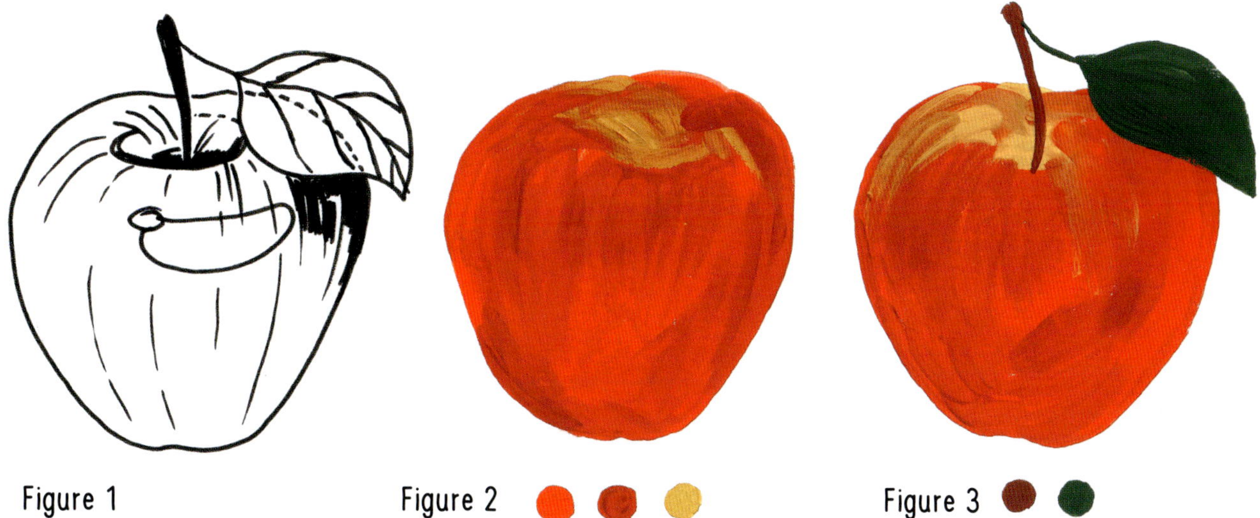

Figure 1

Figure 2

Figure 3

STEP 1

Draw a sketch of the apple with a pencil, as shown in Figure 1. The sketch doesn't need to be detailed; just mark the main lines. Once the sketch is ready, you can begin painting.

For painting the base layer of the apple, we'll use the direct blending technique (page 11). This technique is very creative, and this project is just perfect for practicing it.

Take a filbert or large round brush and start to fill the apple shape in the following colors at the same time: orange, red and yellow ochre (see Figure 2). Blend the paints directly inside the apple's outline for one continuous shape. However, don't mix these colors into one tint; blend only the transitions.

Allow the painted layer to dry completely.

TIP: I recommend you use a small round brush for working along the edge of the shape to get an accurate and neat painting at the end.

STEP 2

Take a small round brush and paint the stem of the apple in brown (see Figure 3). Try to make it thin and not too thick. Then paint the leaf in green. Use the round brushes in sizes convenient for you. For example, I use a medium round brush for painting leaves. And for painting the stem of the leaf I use the tip of the same brush.

Let the painting dry.

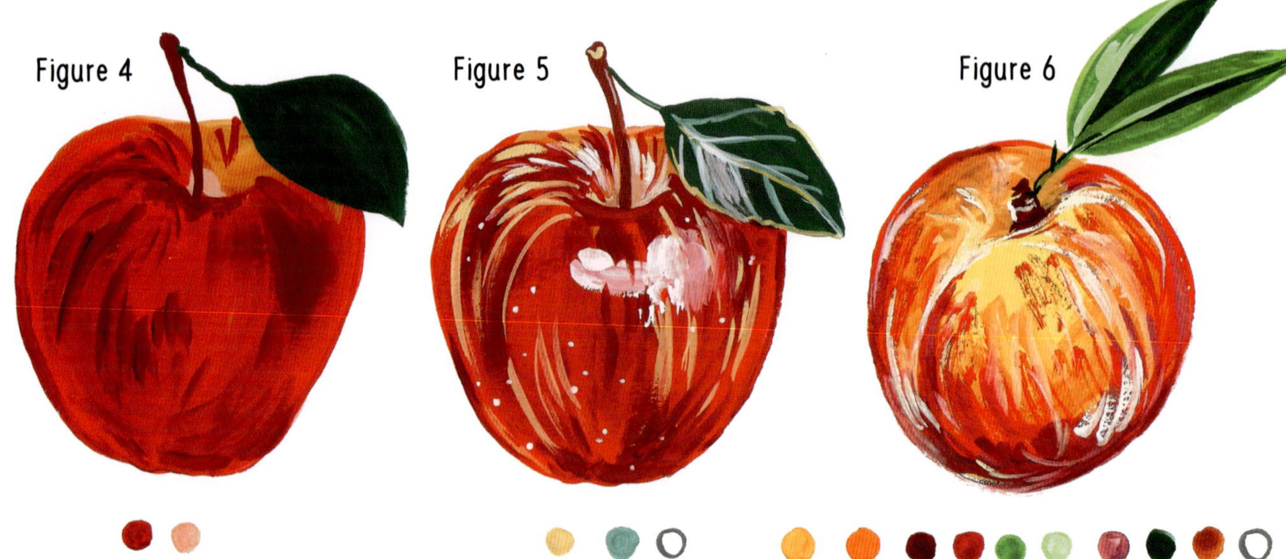

STEP 3

NOTE: During the next two steps, we'll use the layering technique (page 11).

With the help of the small round brush, accentuate the indentation for the stem with pastel brown, as shown in Figure 4. Once it's done, move to the next stage: adding texture with the dry-brush technique (page 12). Because the gouache paint is pretty thick, applying the dry-brush technique is easy. Use a large round or filbert brush for adding the texture in crimson red.

Don't cover the whole apple with this texture. Try to find the right balance and leave some areas free from it to show the beautiful base we completed in step 1. Let the layer dry.

STEP 4

After all this work, we finally can add the details. Prepare the following tints: pastel yellow ochre, pastel green and white. Arm yourself with the detail brush or the small round brush if it's easier for you to handle. Add the details first with pastel yellow ochre on the apple and the edges of the leaf and also paint the veins of the leaf by using pastel green.

Then use the white gouache and add the highlights and accents according to Figure 5. I also advise using the softening technique (page 12) to make the apple glossy.

And we're done!

Painting fruits and veggies with the methods in this lesson is so fun. Once you've done one, I'm sure you'll keep on creating these cute paintings by following the principles of the lesson. You can practice not only by painting apples, but also with other objects that have a similar texture on the skin. For example, it could be a peach, a coconut or a pomegranate. Find one example I painted in Figure 6.

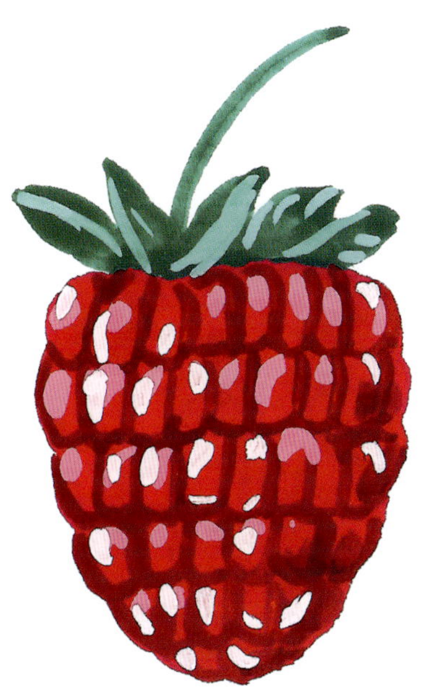

ADORABLE RASPBERRY

As you may guess from the title of this project, I will show you how to paint berries in a very cute cartoon style. I picked a raspberry, because it's not normally the easiest berry to paint. However, with gouache, all is possible, and even structured, complicated fruits, vegetables and berries are easy to illustrate. If you know what to do, of course. So follow my instructions, and let's paint the yummy raspberry.

SUPPLIES

- White, craft or black paper
- Pencil and eraser
- Round brushes in different sizes
- Detail brush

PROJECT COLORS

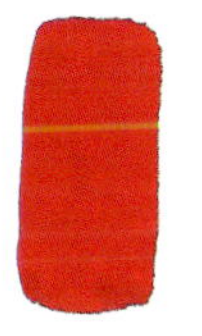

Red (primary red or crimson red)

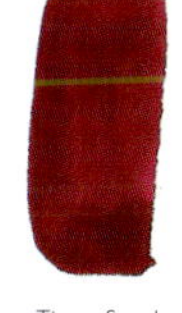

Tint of red

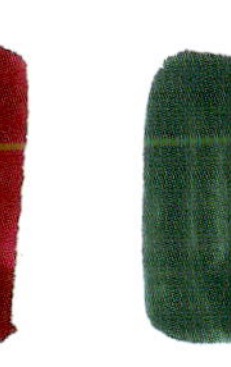

Green (viridian green)

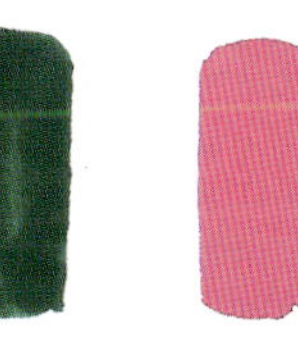

Pastel pink

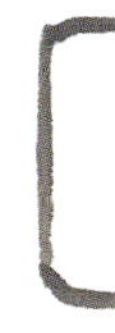

Pastel green

White

COLOR MIXING

- Tint of red (violet + red, proportion 1:3)
- Pastel pink (white + red, proportion 2:1)
- Pastel green (white + green, proportion 3:1)

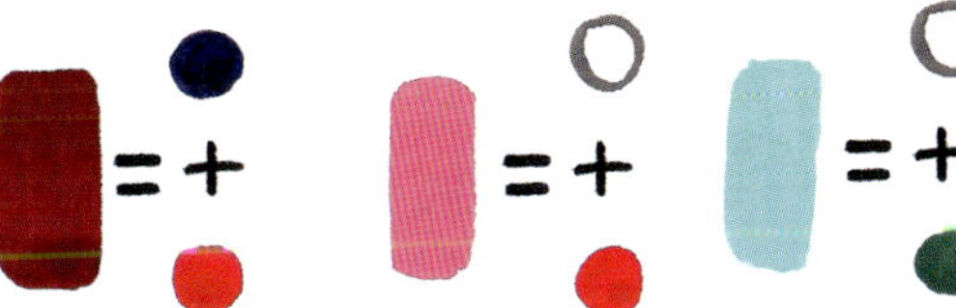

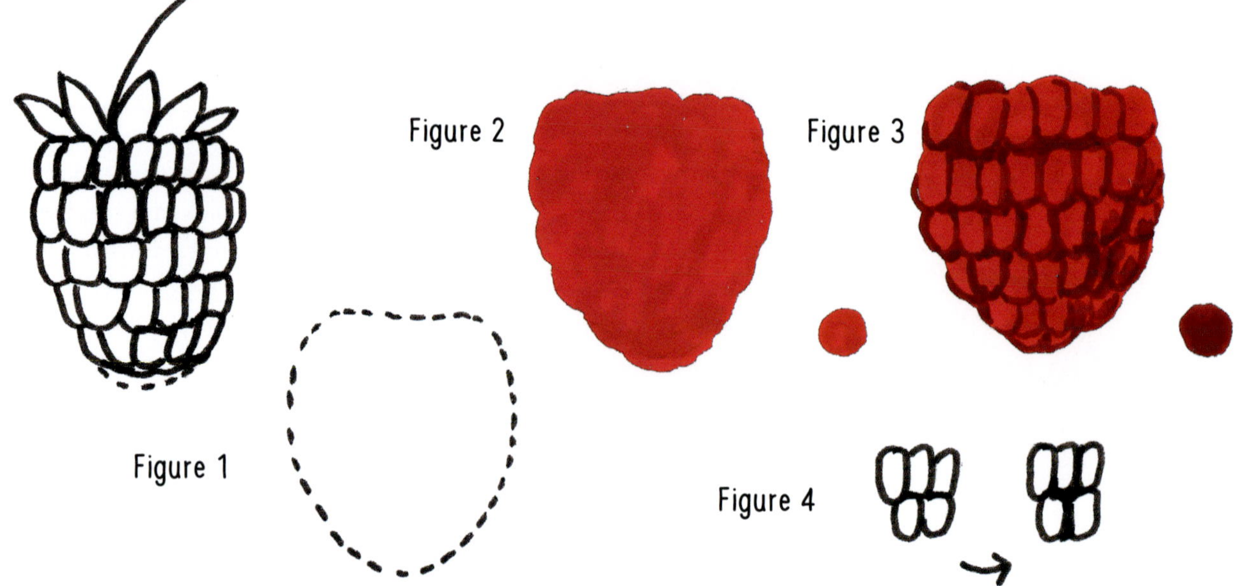

STEP 1

Start working on the project by making a sketch following the outlines in Figure 1. I advise you make a basic sketch that includes only the main lines of the berry and its stem. You don't have to draw the cells of the raspberry shown in Figure 1 at this stage; we'll figure them out later. Now let's turn to the main work.

NOTE: In this lesson we will be using only the layering technique (page 11).

With a small round brush, paint the base layer of the raspberry with red (see Figure 2). I recommend first painting the outline with gouache and then filling in the color inside the shape.

Let the layer dry.

STEP 2

Switch to the detail brush and, using the tint of red, paint the details that separate the cells of the raspberry (see Figure 3). Basically, we don't paint the cells, we just add shadows that compose the structure of the berry. Allow the layer to dry.

TIP: I advise first painting all the outlines of the raspberry cells and then filling in the areas between them with paint (see Figure 4).

STEP 3

Now it's time to add the green part of the raspberry. Arm yourself with a small round brush and paint the small leaves and stem of the berry (sepals and peduncle) in green. Once it's done, take the detail brush and add the shine in pastel pink, as shown in Figure 5. Allow the painting to dry completely.

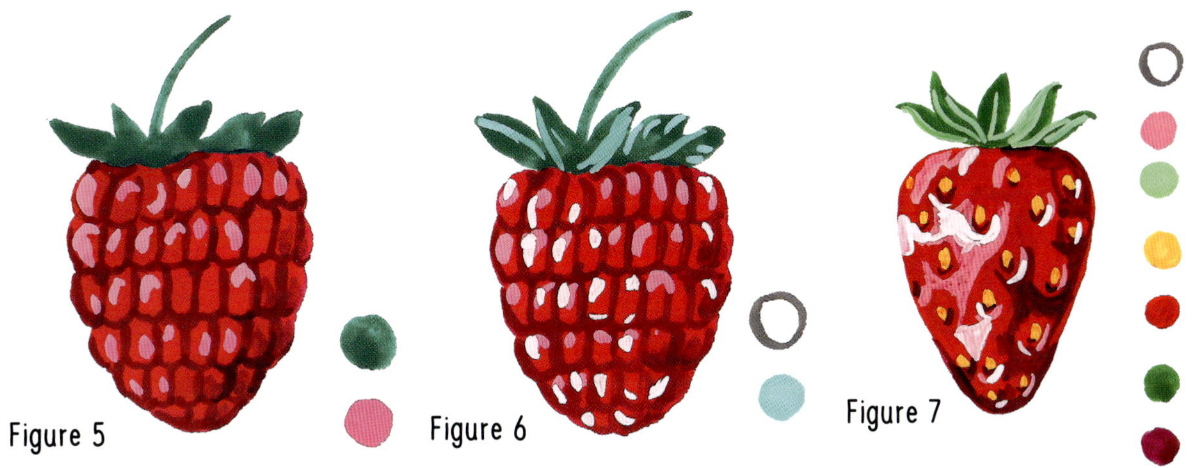

STEP 4

Finally, we can add the highlights and the little painting will turn into a cute illustration (see Figure 6).

Keep working with the detail brush and prepare pastel green and white. First paint the details on the green part with pastel green and then add the details with white gouache.

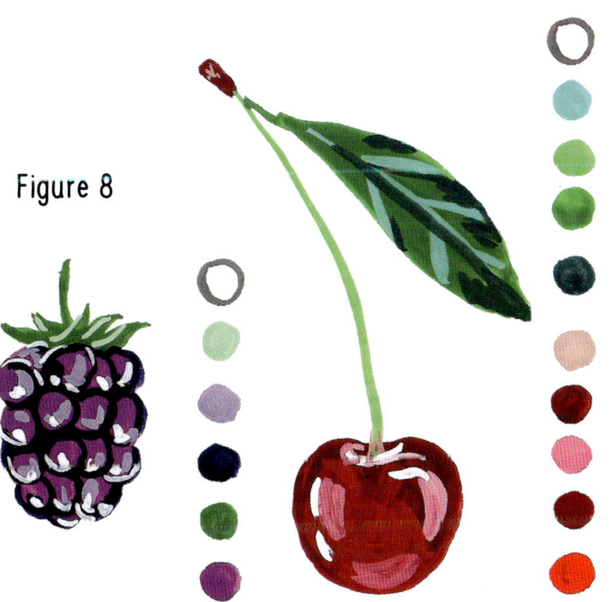

Note the highlights and accents are added randomly. It makes the illustration more realistic, even in a cartoon style.

As you can see, this project is really straightforward and the result is so cute. In addition, if you follow this lesson's principles, you can easily paint other berries, such as blackberries, cherries or strawberries (see examples in Figures 7, 8 and 9). All of these examples of berries have different shapes and colors and also have some specific features that it's important to note.

For the strawberry, you need to add the seeds in step 1. Also, instead of cells, it has shadows under the seeds from one side. Painting the blackberry is easy because it is very similar to the raspberry. Just make sure you choose the right colors and shape. And note that its cells are bigger and rounder when compared to the raspberry.

And finally, with simple fruits such as cherries or cranberries, you need to make sure to pay attention to the shape of the berry and its leaves. Also, instead of the cell's separation, paint the shadows and some specific details. I especially recommend that you use references for painting berries and add all the layers consistently and carefully. I hope you enjoyed the lesson and that you'll be painting more cute, little illustrations that are good enough to eat.

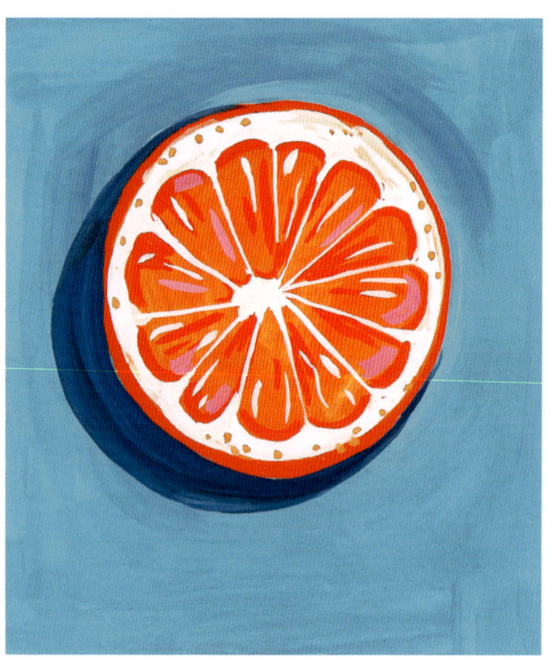

JUICY ORANGE

This project is all about colors and contrast in practice and how to achieve them with gouache. In this lesson, I'll show you how to paint a juicy slice of orange on a vivid blue background.

These color combinations are so bold, eye-catching and magnificent. And at the same time, the subject and composition of the painting should not be too complicated. All your attention is concentrated on the shapes, colors and feeling created by the piece. The project is broken into simple steps, so it will be easy for you to execute all stages and to understand the principles. I hope you are excited!

SUPPLIES

- White paper
- Pencil and eraser
- Compass or any round object
- Round brushes in different sizes
- Detail brush
- Masking tape
- Flat brush (optional)

PROJECT COLORS

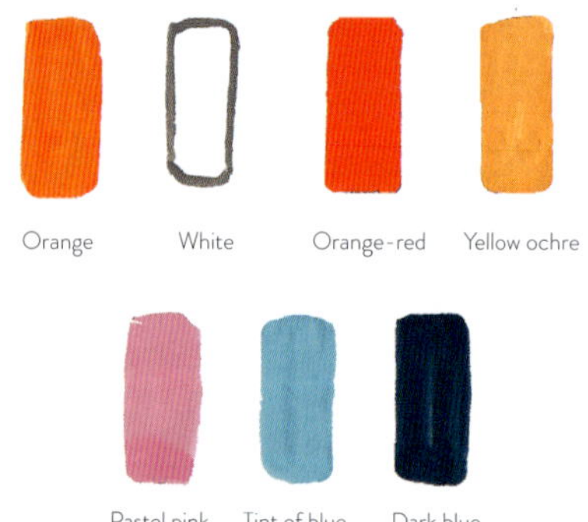

COLOR MIXING

- Orange-red (red + orange, proportion 1:3)
- Pastel pink (white + red, proportion 2:1)
- Tint of blue (white + cerulean blue, proportion 2:1)
- Dark blue (ultramarine blue + cerulean blue, proportion 1:3)

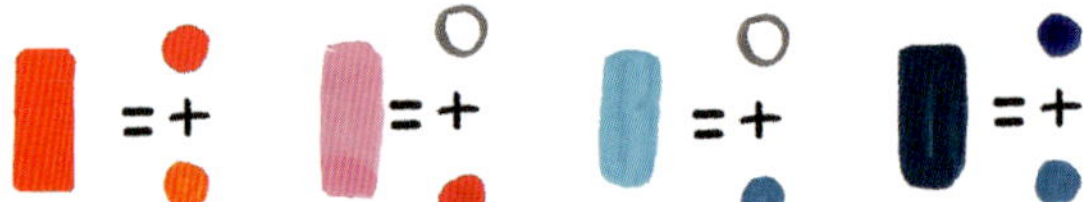

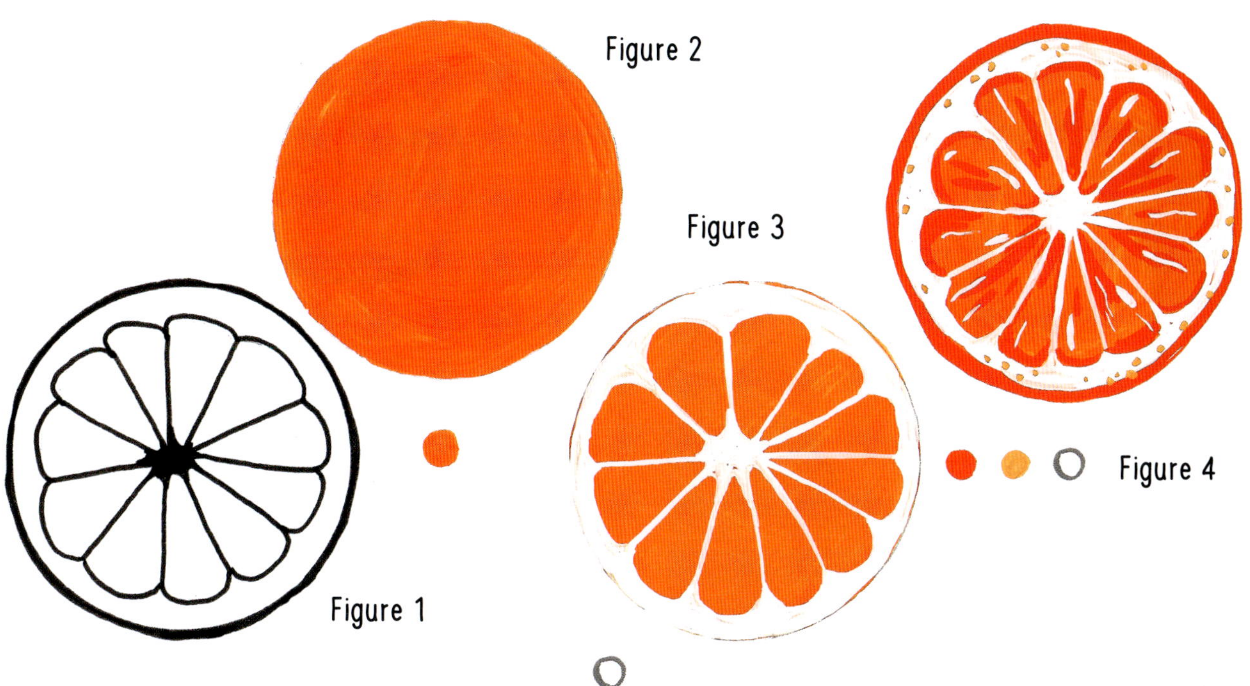

STEP 1

In Figure 1, you can find the outline of the project. However, a full sketch is not needed. Just draw the circle by using a compass or trace around a circular object with a pencil.

Now we can start painting the orange step by step.

NOTE: All steps in this project are done with the layering technique (page 11).

Fill the circle with orange by using a big round brush (see Figure 2). I also recommend using a small round brush for painting at the edges of the shape. Allow the painted layer to dry.

STEP 2

Prepare a small round brush and a detail brush. Now we need to paint the sections of the fruit as well as the center core and white rind (see Figure 3). First use the detail brush to start painting the center core in white, then add the walls of the sections. Try to make them thin and neat. Finally, add the rind in white with the small round brush. Let everything dry completely.

NOTE: If, after drying, the white layer still has some transparency, add one more layer in white on top to make it fully opaque. This especially makes sense for the center core and walls of the orange fruit.

STEP 3

Now it's time to add details. Prepare the next colors: orange-red and yellow ochre.

Take a small round brush and paint the rind outline and shadow accents on each section in orange-red (see Figure 4). The rind should not be perfect; make it look natural with little curving.

Now switch to the detail brush and paint small dots with the yellow ochre inside the sliced orange and highlights with white on the sections. Paint all those details randomly, without any order. This makes the painting look more realistic. Once again let the painting dry completely.

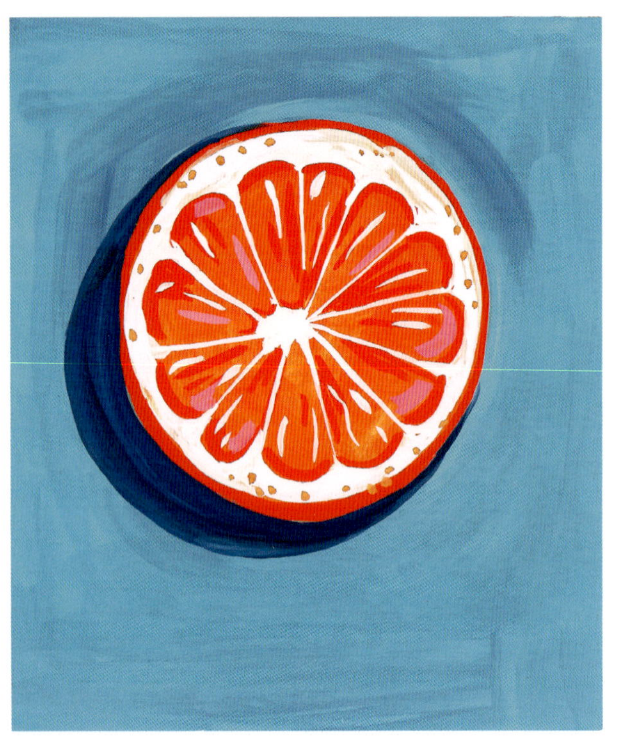

Figure 5

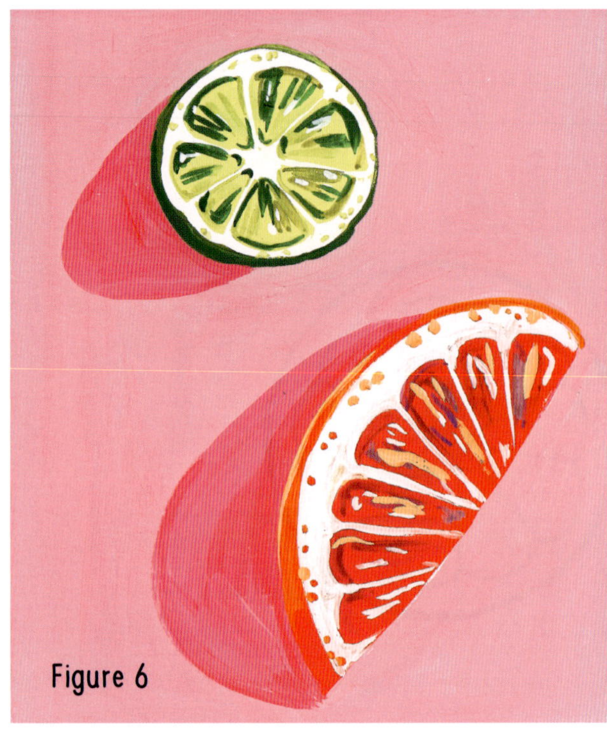

Figure 6

STEP 4

Take the detail brush and add accent details as shown in Figure 5 with pastel pink on the sections of the orange. We already have an orange fruit painting; nevertheless, this final stage will pop the colors and bring out that contrast I was talking about in the intro (see Figure 5). I definitely don't recommend skipping the background.

Define the background area with masking tape and carefully secure it to the paper. I advise you start with a small round brush and neatly paint the border area between the fruit and background with the tint of blue. Then, take a flat brush or large round brush and fill the rest of the background in the tint of blue.

As soon as the background dries, add the shadow from the orange fruit in dark blue. Use the round brush in a size handy for you or even a flat brush, which allows you to make a bold shadow.

Take off the masking tape and here is your painting!

I hope it was fun and easy for you. My recommendations for practicing this lesson are to try to paint any other citrus fruits, such as limes, lemons or grapefruit. Also, play with the color of the background. Keep it deep and bright and don't be afraid to experiment. In Figure 6, you'll see my experiment with slices of a blood orange and lime. Isn't it simply beautiful? If you want to explore this project more deeply, you can create such a composition by yourself. And in this case, you will be able to understand how the shadow works and to try different backgrounds. I'm looking forward to your beautiful and juicy projects.

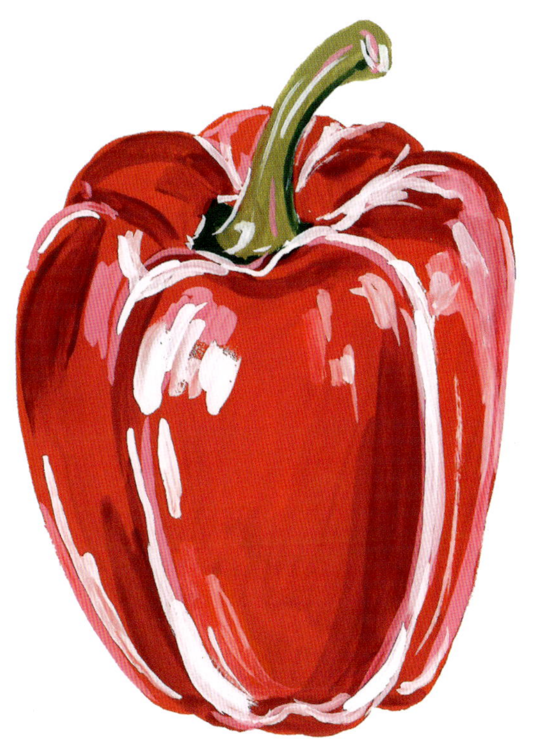

GLOSSY BELL PEPPER

Fruits and veggies are perfect objects to study painting with any art medium. First, because you can find some of them at home. Second, because you can play with the light and make a composition by yourself exactly how you want it. It gives you the freedom to explore the object. And last, it's so fun. The colors of fruits and veggies are so vivid and juicy that your final piece will always look bold and please the eye.

This project is dedicated to the glossy red bell pepper. However, I tried to make this lesson very universal so you can apply the principles of this lesson to any glossy, simple fruit or veggie. Sounds awesome, doesn't it? If you're ready, let's get started.

SUPPLIES

- White, craft or black paper
- Pencil and eraser
- Round brushes in different sizes
- Flat brush (optional)
- Detail brush

COLOR MIXING

- Pastel crimson (white + crimson red, proportion 2:1)

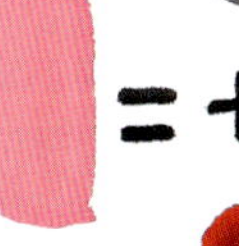

PROJECT COLORS

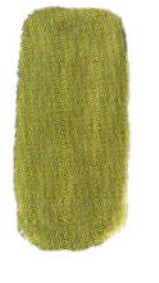
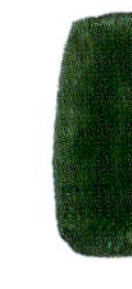
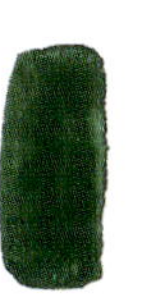
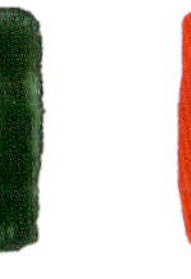
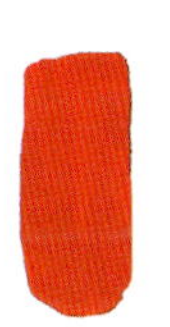
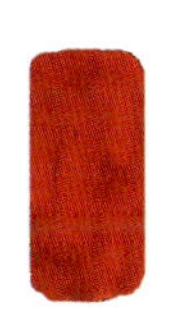
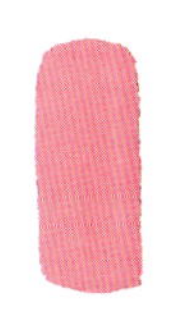
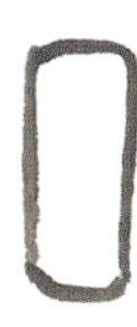
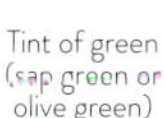

Tint of green (sap green or olive green)

Green

Red

Crimson red

Pastel crimson

White

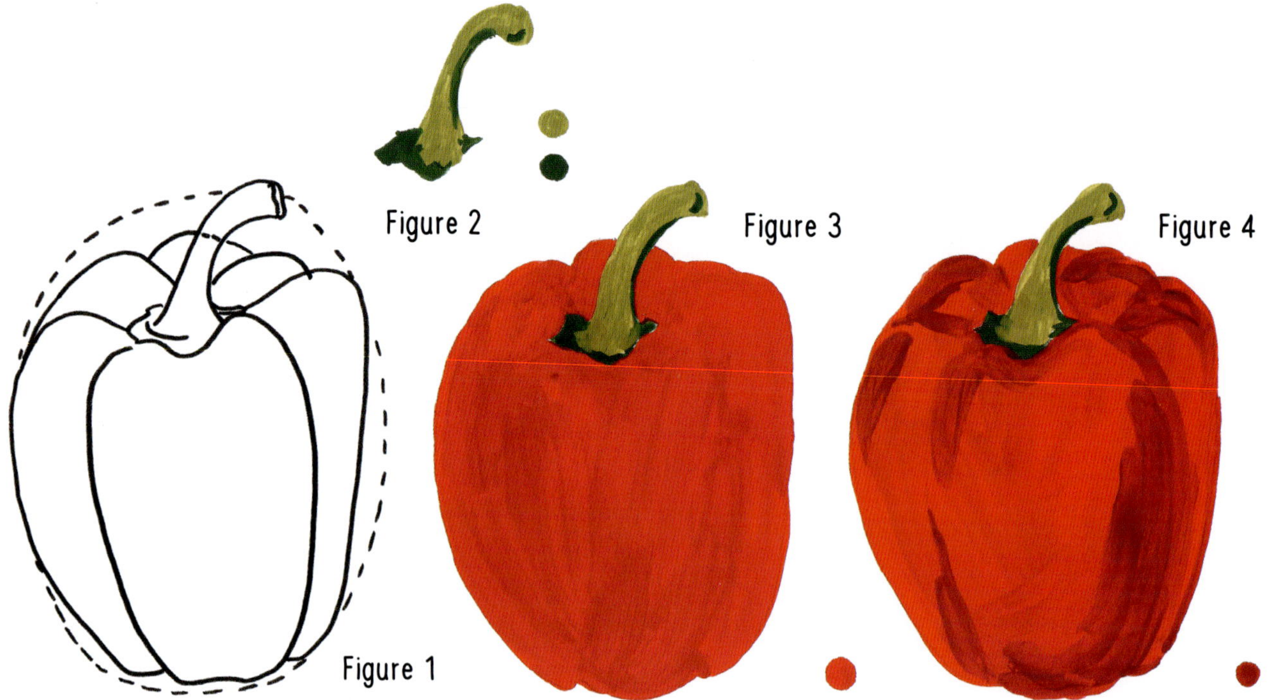

STEP 1

Make a preliminary pencil sketch following Figure 1. I advise you first draw the auxiliary oval shape and then move on to the final sketch.

When the sketch is ready, let's fill it with beautiful and rich colors. Start by painting the stem in the tint of green and green. First paint the areas in the tint of green, wait until it's dry, and then add next to it the shadow in green, as shown in Figure 2. Once the layer is dry, proceed to the next stage.

TIP: If you need to paint small areas in two colors, such as the stem of the pepper, you can wait until the nearby area dries or apply the direct blending technique (page 11), which gives a very smooth and natural color transition.

STEP 2

Prepare gouache in red and paint the base of the pepper with a medium round brush with a thin tip. Use the tip of the brush to accurately paint the edges (Figure 3). Or switch to the small round brush when painting close to the edges. Allow the freshly painted layer to dry, then go to step 3.

STEP 3

It's time to make the bell pepper more realistic and not so flat. For this, paint the layer with crimson red by using a medium round brush, as shown in Figure 4. If you have a flat brush, use it instead; it's even more suitable for painting such layers. Let the work dry completely. In this step we used the layering technique (page 11).

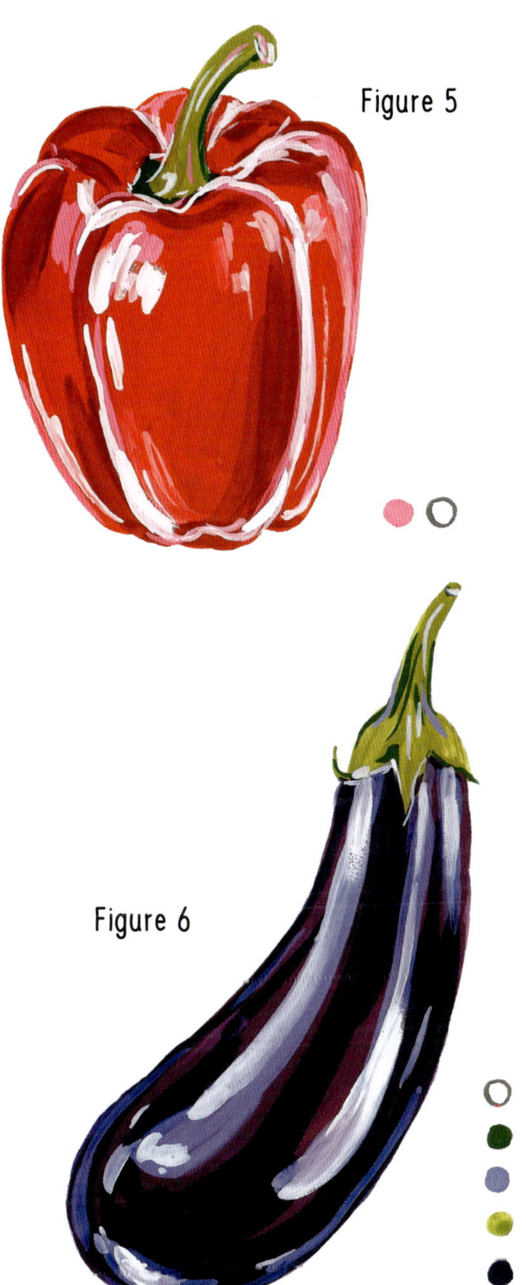

STEP 4

Now let's add some shine to the pepper. Use the small round brush and detail brush during this step (see Figure 5). Paint the highlights first in pastel crimson on the stem of the pepper and on the pepper itself and then add more accents in white gouache. This is the layering technique in action.

As I mentioned earlier, with the principles of this lesson you can paint other vegetables, as well as fruits and berries. Just choose a glossy and simple object for practicing. Always add the base layer, shadows and highlights. I used the example of the current project to paint the eggplant in Figure 6. It was so easy and fun to paint.

It's also great if you use the real object as a reference. Or take a photo of the object and refer to it. Anyway, practice and be consistent. If you master painting veggies and fruits, I am sure you will be able to paint any other more complicated pieces with gouache.

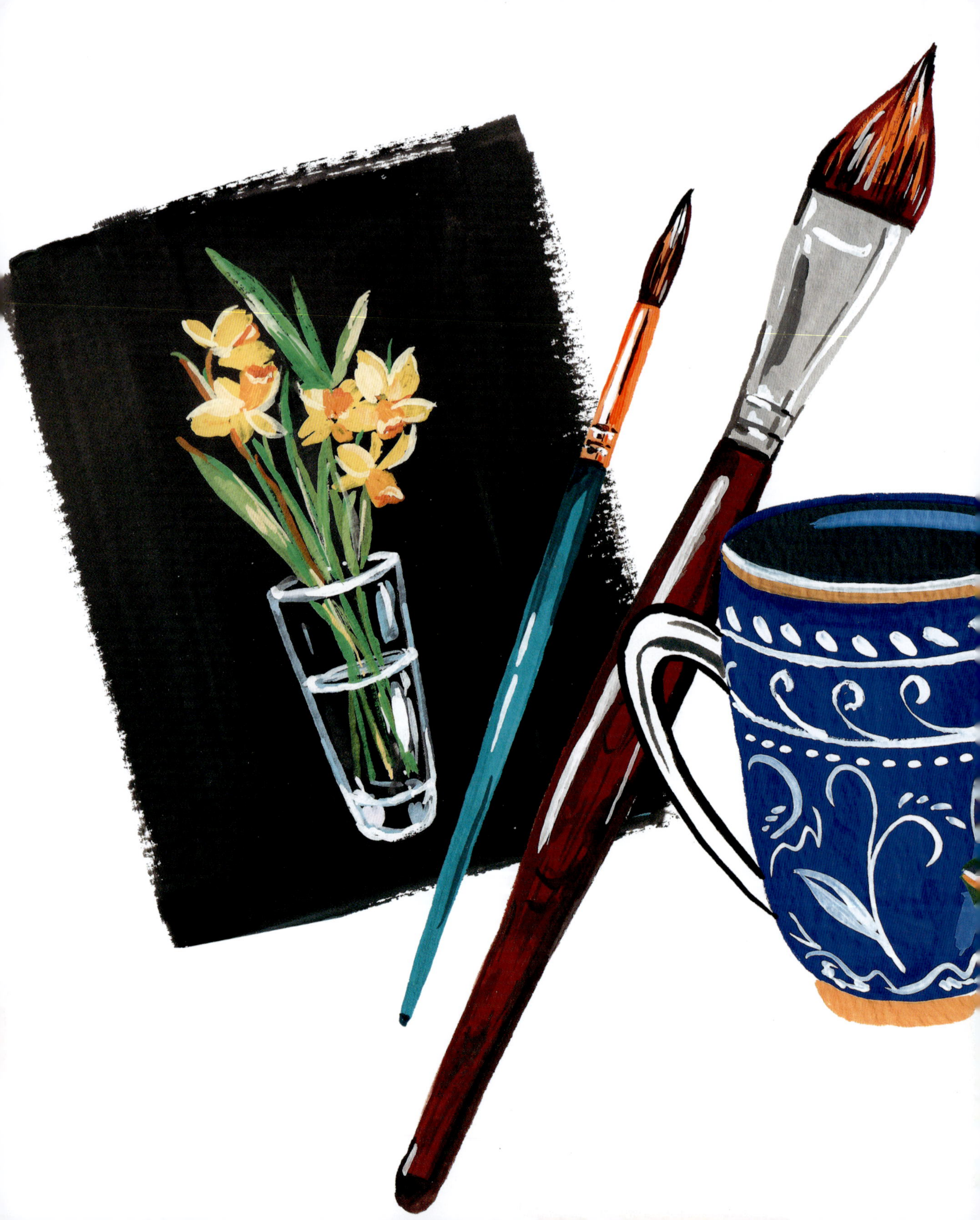

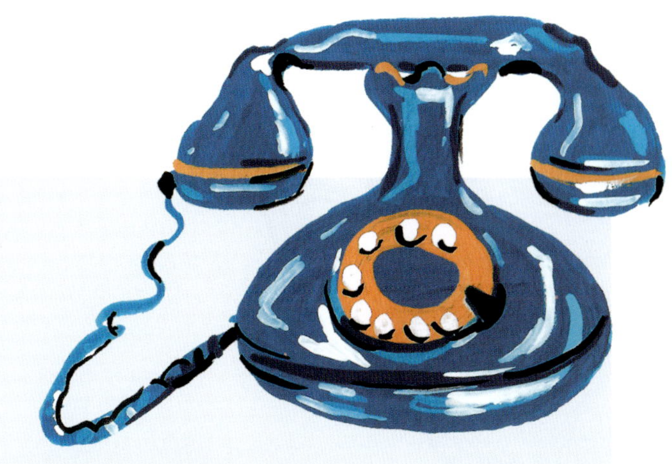

Super Cute SUNDRIES

I don't know about you, but I love the little things around us. All the decorations and little details in coffee shops or homes. Colors, texture, shapes—I always try to notice these. It's a good habit for boosting your art skills. And all those little things inspire me to take paper and do, at least, a quick sketch. Why not do this with gouache? I came up with some cute projects featuring items you may see or have. These lessons are not only great practice but also my way of showing that you can paint anything. Even your favorite coffee mug.

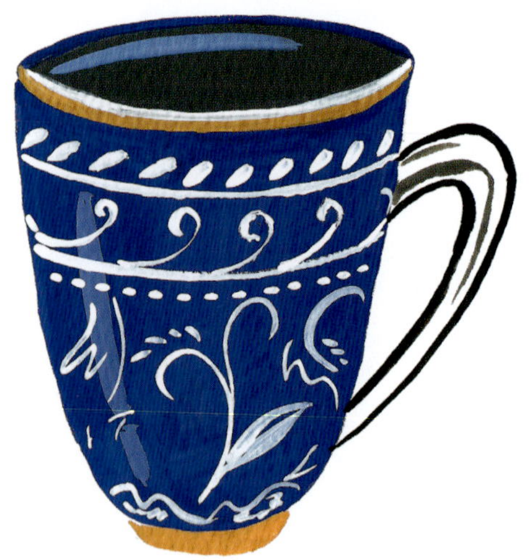

CHINESE-STYLE MUG

If you are looking for a meditative project, this one is just perfect. With gouache, you can paint any object, even a mug. Then just focus on painting some patterns or details. It can be such a relaxing and joyful process. But let's do it consistently, step by step.

SUPPLIES

- White or craft paper
- Pencil and eraser
- Round brushes in different sizes
- Detail brush

PROJECT COLORS

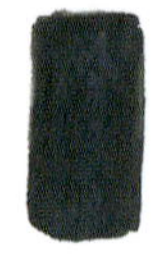
Tint of grey

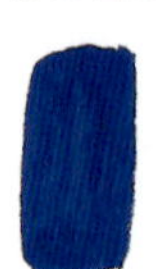
Ultramarine blue

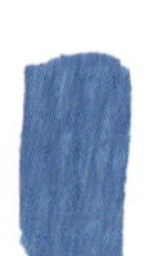
Pastel blue

Pastel ochre

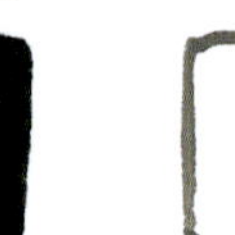
Black (noir)

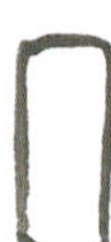
White

COLOR MIXING

- Tint of grey (black + ultramarine blue + white, proportion 1:2:1)
- Pastel blue (ultramarine blue + white, proportion 1:1)
- Pastel ochre (yellow ochre + white, proportion 2:1)

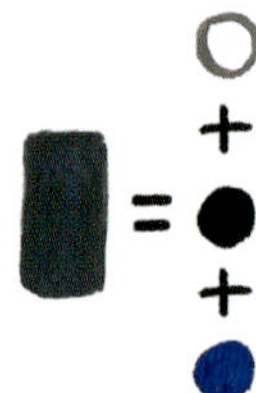

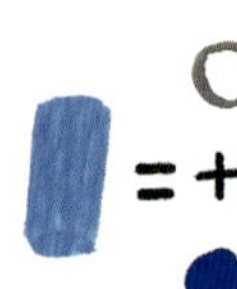

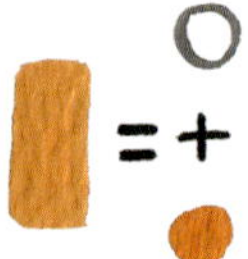

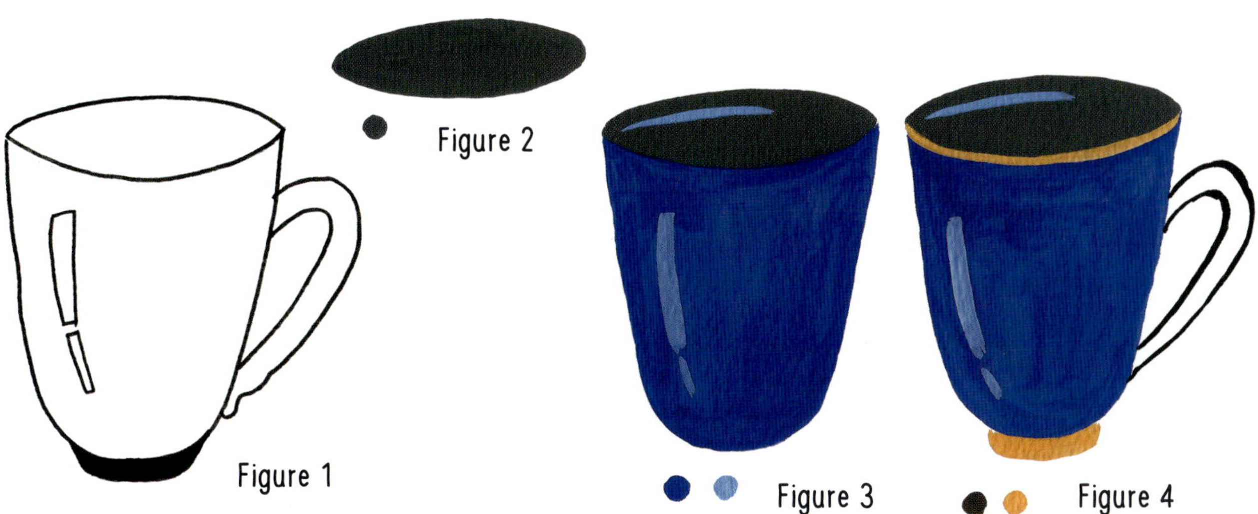

STEP 1

Let's start the project by sketching the drawing outlines in Figure 1. Do not draw details at this stage though; just baselines are enough. Once the sketch is ready, jump to the main work.

NOTE: In this project, we will apply only the layering technique (page 11). Before adding a new layer or details, make sure that the previously painted layer is dry.

Take a medium round brush and, with the tint of grey, fill the area inside the mug (see Figure 2).

Let the painted layer dry completely and go on to the next step.

STEP 2

Now use ultramarine blue to paint the shape of the mug. Keep working with the same brush.

Allow the layer to dry completely.

TIP: If, after drying, the layer looks transparent, paint another layer on top, with the same color. It will make it look more opaque.

Allow the layer to dry completely. Switch to the smaller round brush and, with pastel blue, paint the highlight areas, as shown in Figure 3.

STEP 3

Now, with the tip of the same brush, paint the golden details in pastel ochre and the handle of the mug with black (see Figure 4). After the painting is completely dry, move on to the final step.

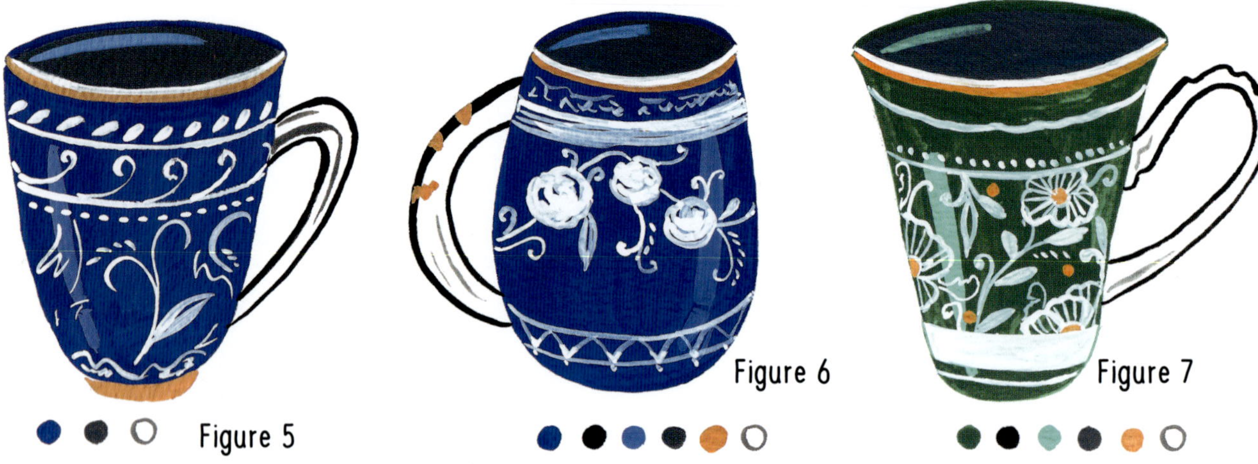

STEP 4

It's time to add details. Take a detail brush and add the outline of the mug with ultramarine blue. Also paint some touches in the tint of grey to the handle. Finally, we are ready for the "meditative" part of the project. Prepare white gouache and, using the detail brush, paint the pattern on the blue area of the mug. Of course, you can follow the example in Figure 5, but it's more interesting and fun to try your own version of the pattern. At this stage, you can unleash your creative abilities and paint whatever you want intuitively.

Figure 6 shows a mug, made using this lesson's techniques, but with the pattern and mug shape changed. Also, you can experiment with the colors. Pay attention to Figure 7, which is a great example of this experimentation. I advise you change the main color (blue in the project) and leave all the rest the same. Once again, it helps you to focus on painting the details of the pattern.

As for the decorative pattern on the mug, for inspiration you can use some references from the internet or find a good example in museums and exhibitions. It could even be some floral patterns, inspired by nature. Whatever you choose, don't forget to enjoy the process of painting. That is the most important thing.

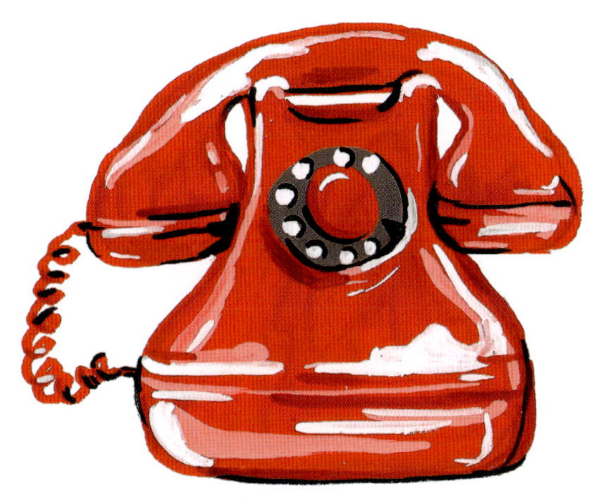

VINTAGE TELEPHONE

There are so many beautiful things that can inspire us—at home, in coffee shops or at museums. All these things can be awesome to portray on paper to explore their features and characteristics.

For this project, I've chosen exactly this kind of thing. This is a vintage telephone; you may see these phones in flea markets or at museums. I personally remember an old beige phone, but a pretty modern one, at my parents' home. The point is that these phones have different shapes and colors and are made from a glossy material that will be great to paint with gouache. I hope you're excited and ready to get started.

SUPPLIES

- White, craft or black paper
- Pencil and eraser
- Round brushes in different sizes
- Detail brush

PROJECT COLORS

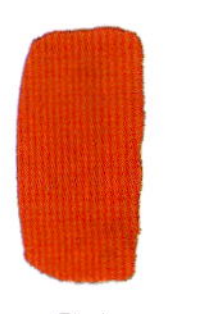
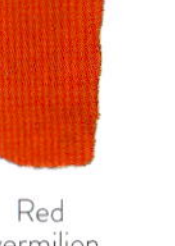
Red (vermilion red)

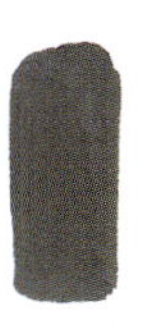
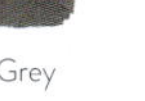
Grey

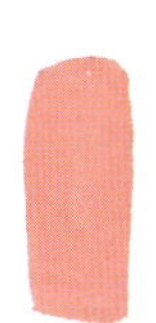
Pastel red

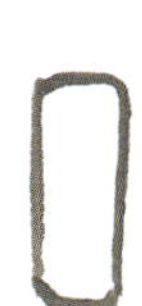
White

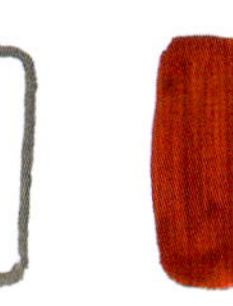
Crimson red

Black (noir)

COLOR MIXING

- Grey (black + white, proportion 1:3)
- Pastel red (red + white, proportion 1:2)

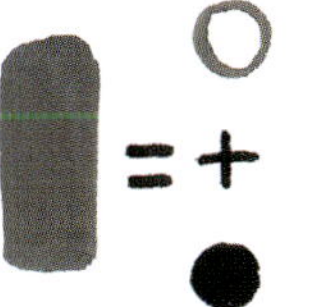

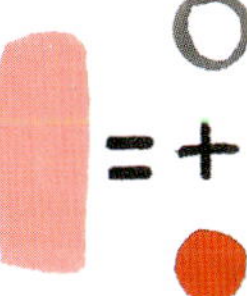

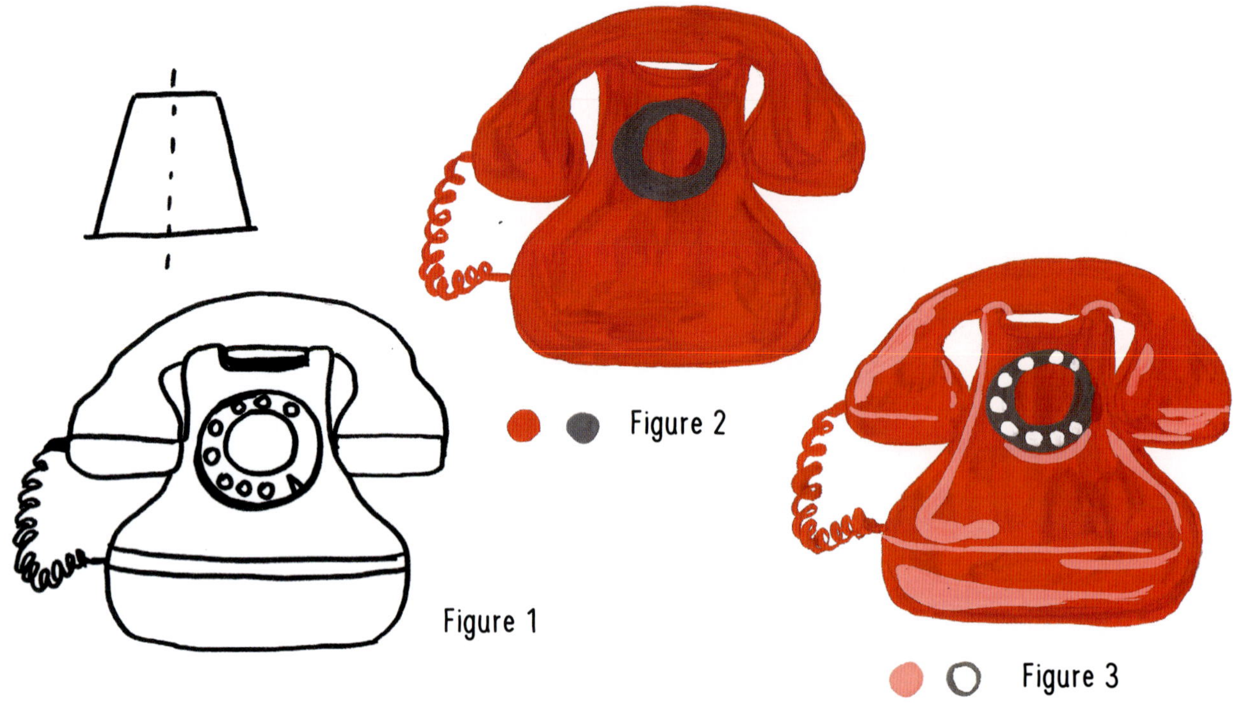

STEP 1

For this project it is especially important to draw a preliminary sketch. Take your pencil and sketch the outline of the phone following Figure 1. The sketch doesn't need to be very detailed. It is enough to show the baselines. The details will be added with gouache later.

TIP: I advise you first draw the trapezoid shape and then turn it into the final sketch.

With red paint, fill the shape of the phone, using a round medium brush (see Figure 2). Then take a detail brush and paint the spiral phone cord in the same color.

NOTE: In this project, we will be using only the layering technique (page 11).

Let everything you've painted dry. Switch to a small round brush and add the phone dial in grey. Once again, let the painting dry.

STEP 2

At this stage, we already have a recognizable object. But let's make it more realistic by adding more layers and making it 3D. As I mentioned earlier, the plastic material covering the telephone looks super glossy. We'll add the gloss by painting a layer in pastel red and then in white (in step 3).

Use the same small round brush and paint the layer with pastel red, as shown in Figure 3. Allow the painted layer to dry. Meanwhile, add the small circles on the phone's dial with white. For this purpose, use the detail brush or the tip of the small round brush. Let the work dry completely, then move on to the next step.

STEP 3

Through this step, use the detail brush and the small round brush, depending on the purpose and which one is more convenient at the moment. We will keep working on the depth of colors and the entire 3D look. For this, add shadows in crimson red and black. You can follow the example in Figure 4 or try to add the details yourself. Once it's all done, make sure that the painting dries and then add the highlights in white gouache.

Pay attention to how I've painted some highlighted areas. They are very smooth shaped, while others are very rough. This is the contrast of textures, making the painting look more interesting. But you can also use only the smooth effect if you choose.

NOTE: For making rough strokes, use a dry-brush technique (page 12).

The painting of our old telephone is now finished. Despite this lesson's simplicity, its principles work to create any phone or even some other objects. Figures 5 and 6 show an example of a phone following the lesson's methods. I've changed the colors based on the chosen phone model. Just look at this gloss and the contrasts—how simple and pretty! Experiment and play with details and textures. Let yourself enjoy the process and your creativity.

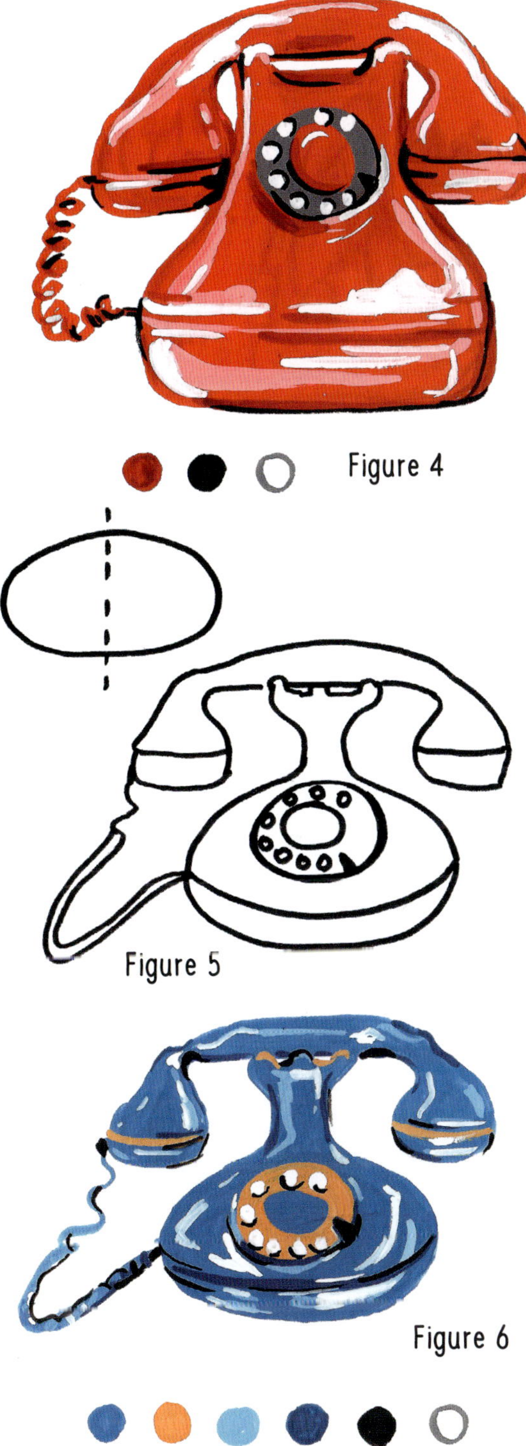

Figure 4

Figure 5

Figure 6

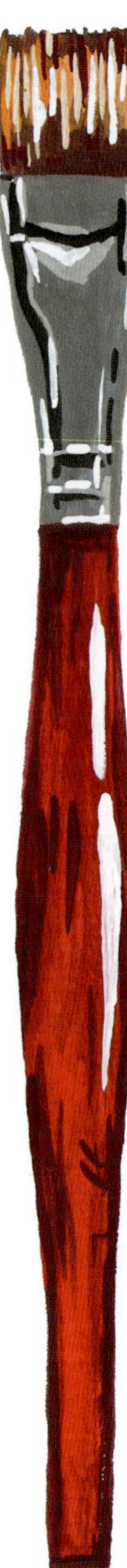

CLASSIC PAINTBRUSH

In this project, we'll paint something that you, I'm sure, have on your table if you're reading this book. It is so simple and pretty at the same time. And, of course, you can refer to the object at any time to get details and inspiration. Let's paint the paintbrush.

SUPPLIES

- White, craft or black paper
- Pencil and eraser
- Round brushes in different sizes
- Detail brush

PROJECT COLORS

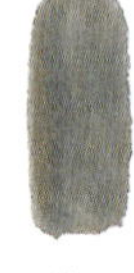

Grey

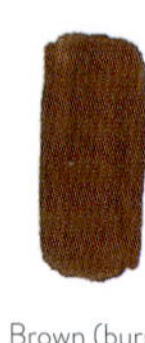

Brown (burnt umber)

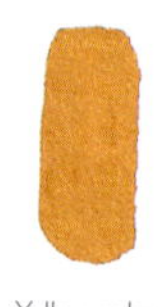

Yellow ochre

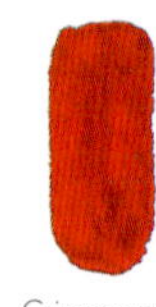

Crimson red

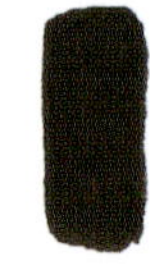

Dark grey

Tint of brown

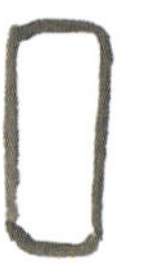

White

Pastel ochre

Light gre

COLOR MIXING

- Grey (black + white, proportion 1:2)
- Dark grey (black + white, proportion 3:1)
- Tint of brown (crimson red + burnt umber, proportion 1:2)
- Pastel ochre (yellow ochre + white, proportion 1:1)
- Light grey (black + white, proportion 1:6)

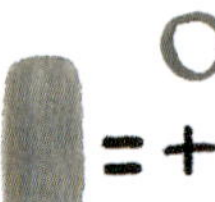
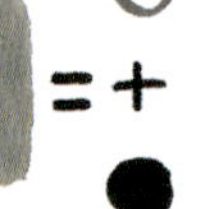
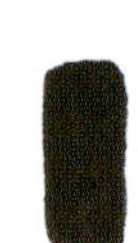
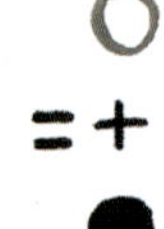
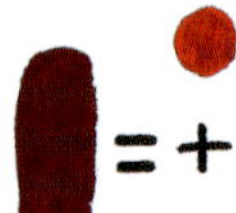
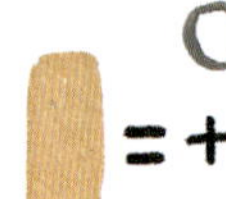
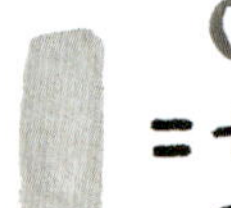

STEP 1

With a pencil, draw a sketch of the picture in Figure 1. Do not draw details at this stage though. Just baselines are enough.

TIP: I advise you start drawing with the vertical axis and then build the remaining lines of the sketch around it.

The ferrule of the brush is usually metallic. With grey paint, fill the shape by using the medium round brush (see Figure 2). Now paint the bristles of the brush in brown. Don't wait for the layer to dry. Add to the still wet layer some vertical stripes in yellow ochre (read more about blending on page 13). Make these details randomly to get a more realistic effect. Allow the painting to dry.

STEP 2

Let's keep working with the same brush, or change to a bigger round brush but with a thin tip. Paint the handle of the brush in crimson red (see Figure 3). Let the painted layer dry completely.

Now it's just the base of the handle, which we'll make more lifelike in the next steps. This part of the brush can be very different depending on the brand and type: matte or glossy, with some texture or without any pattern.

STEP 3

Take the small round brush and paint the details on the metallic ferrule in the dark grey color, as shown in Figure 4. As I mentioned earlier, the brush handle is different depending on the material from which it's manufactured. The one we're painting in this project has texture, so add the texture pattern in the tint of brown.

With the same color, don't forget to mark the darkest areas of the handle: the shadow from the metallic ferrule (in the upper part) and the tip of the handle at the end of it. Once all of this is done, add some details to the belly (hair) of the brush. For this, switch to the detail brush and paint the details in brown and the tint of brown, as shown in Figure 4. Allow the painted layer to dry completely.

NOTE: Through this step, we used the layering technique (page 11).

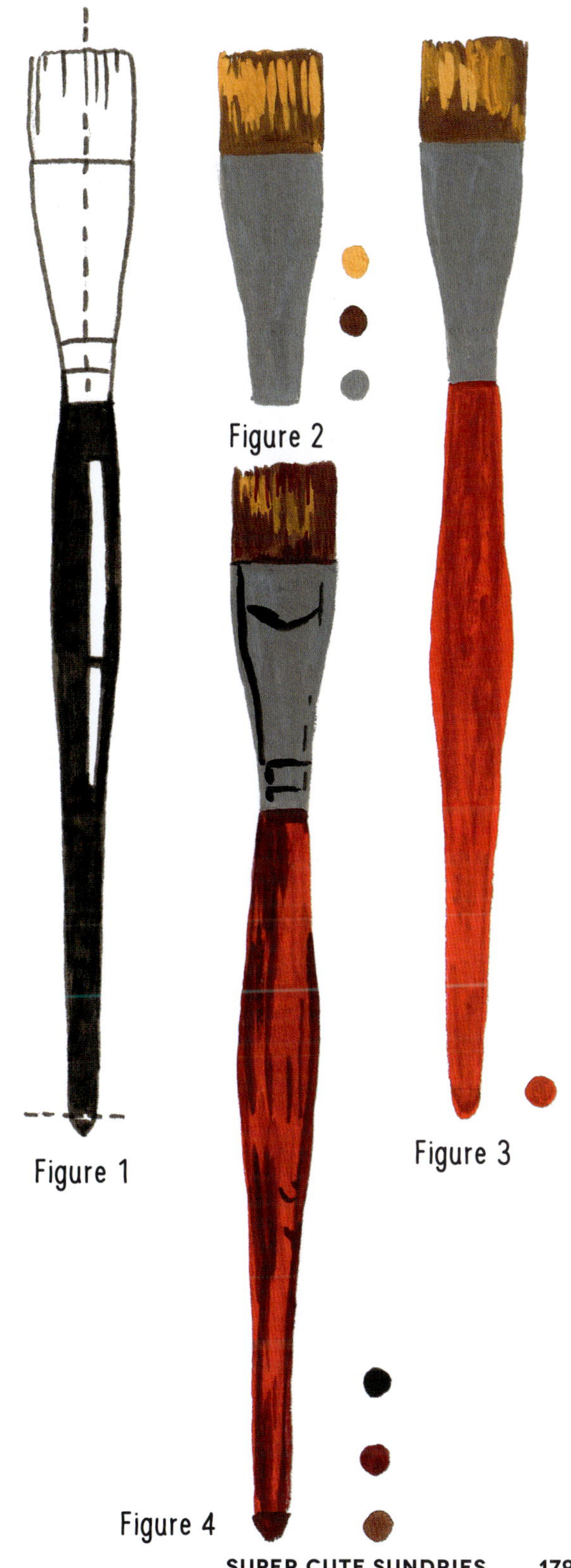

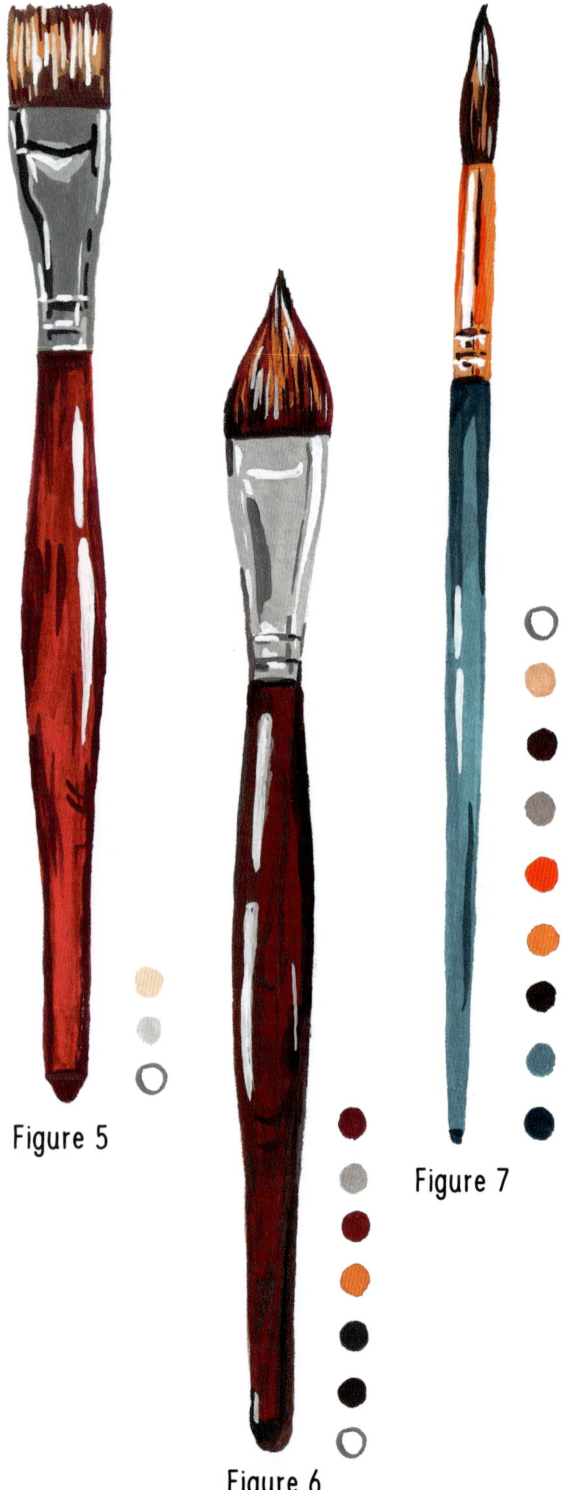
Figure 5

Figure 6

Figure 7

STEP 4

In this step, we'll use the layering technique (see Figure 5). It's time to add details and final touches. First of all, with the help of the detail brush, add the hairs on the brush belly in white and pastel ochre.

Once you're done with the brush belly, paint the details on the metallic ferrule in white and light grey. These are the reflections on the metallic surface, so they may vary depending on the surroundings and the light.

TIP: To better understand and explore where and how to add reflections on such surfaces, I recommend you take a few photos of your brush from different angles and take a look at all the details.

The final stage is to add highlights to the brush handle. If your materials have a matte surface, you don't need to paint these details. But for a glossy one, paint the highlight in white. In Figures 6 and 7, you can see some more examples based on the principles of this lesson. I love how the paintbrush looks painted on the paper. This is so impressive, isn't it?

Paint your version of the brush and use your own brushes as references, experiencing the colors and exploring the textures. There are no limits to your creativity.

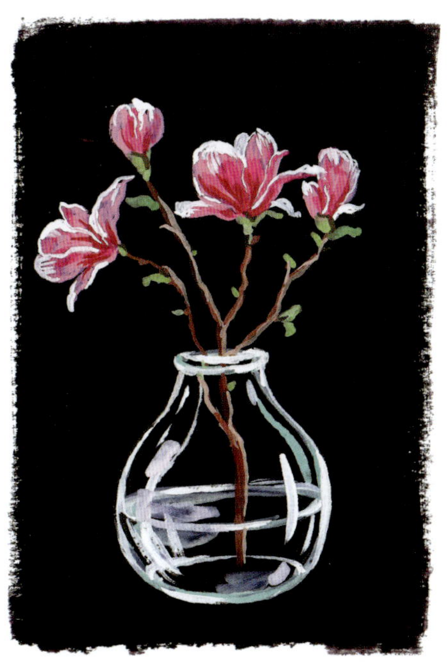

GLASS VASE WITH BLOOMS

This is a gorgeous project that anyone can create by following my instructions. On one hand, it's good evidence of how amazing the gouache medium is. And on the other hand, it demonstrates how easy it is to paint on a dark background and how impressive it can be. Just three simple steps and your masterpiece is done. You can re-create this project to paint any blooms and to make so many variations. I hope you'll enjoy it. Let's get started.

SUPPLIES

- White paper
- Masking tape
- Flat brush in medium size
- White pencil
- Round brushes in different sizes
- Detail brush
- Filbert brush

PROJECT COLORS

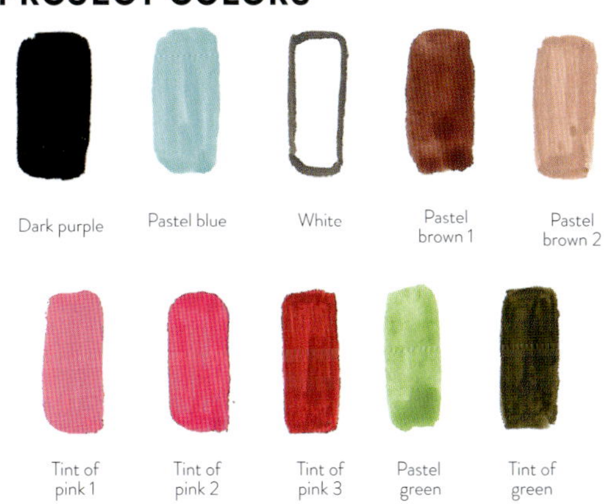

COLOR MIXING

- Dark purple (violet + black, proportion 2:1)
- Pastel blue (cerulean blue + yellow + white, proportion 2:1:5)
- Pastel brown 1 (burnt umber + burnt sienna + white, proportion 2:1:1)
- Pastel brown 2 (white + burnt sienna + burnt umber, proportion 3:1:1)
- Tint of pink 1 (rose + white, proportion 4:1)
- Tint of pink 2 (rose + white, proportion 8:1)
- Tint of pink 3 (burnt sienna + rose, proportion 1:2)
- Pastel green (green + yellow ochre + white, proportion 2:1:1)
- Tint of green (green + burnt sienna, proportion 1:1)

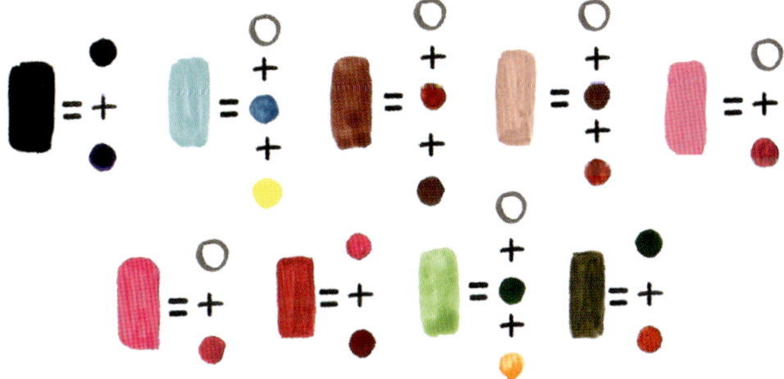

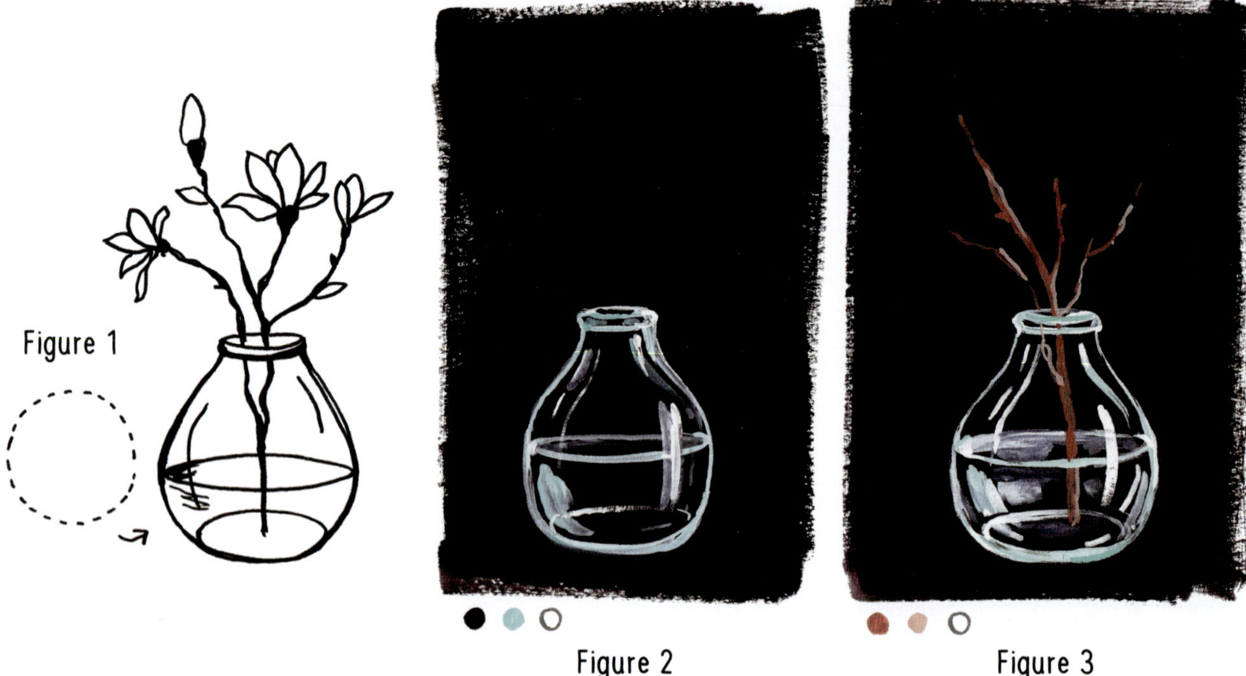

STEP 1

You don't have to make a pencil sketch for this project, but I've provided one (Figure 1) so you can get an idea of the composition. However, I recommend preparing for the painting by securing the paper with masking tape to the surface of your table or board.

Using the flat brush, paint the background in dark purple. You can make the edges of the background smooth or apply the dry-brush forming technique (page 12) for making rough edges.

NOTE: For painting the background, I've chosen a very dark tint of purple and not black. This makes the painting more interesting and gives depth to the colors.

Let the newly painted layer dry.

Now we will do some magic. For this, you need to make a very light sketch of the glass vase on the dark surface. I recommend using a chalk-white pencil and just lightly marking an outline of the vase by following Figure 1. Once the sketch is done, use a small round brush to paint the vase in pastel blue and then add the accents with white gouache (see Figure 2).

NOTE: During this and the following steps, we'll use the layering technique (page 11).

TIP: If something goes wrong and you make undesired lines with the white pencil or gouache paint, wait until the layer dries and then use the background color to paint the areas you don't need.

Allow the layer to dry.

STEP 2

Keep working with the small brush, or change to a detail brush if it's easier for you. Paint the branches of the magnolia in pastel brown 1 (Figure 3). Let the layer dry. Once the branch layer dries, add some details in pastel brown 2. Also paint details in white gouache. Pay attention to which parts of the branch are visible and which are not, and correct all this nuance with white gouache.

Allow the work to dry completely.

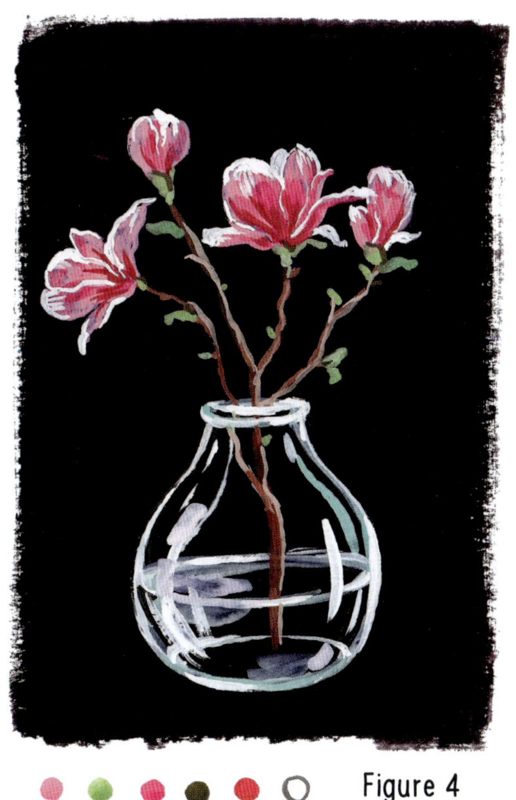

Figure 4

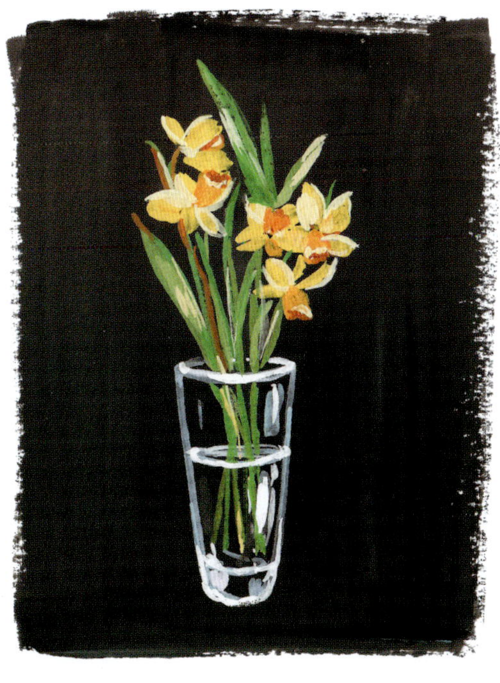

Figure 5

STEP 3

Let's start painting the magnolia flowers (see Figure 4). To form petals, I recommend using a filbert brush. First, paint petals in the tint of pink 1. Then, switch to the small round brush or even a detail brush and add details in the tint of pink 2, tint of pink 3 and white. Also paint some green details and small leaves in pastel green and the tint of green. Let the painting dry completely.

NOTE: For more on how to paint these flowers, see Branch of Magnolia, page 51.

As I mentioned earlier, by using the principles of this lesson, you can easily re-create the project and change it. Choose another color for the background. Paint flowers or maybe a foliage branch. Use your imagination. Also, why not play with the vase shape? There are so many options you can try.

Figure 5 shows the example of a spring vase with a bouquet of flowers, based on the lesson. Remember to keep the background in a dark shade, and as for the rest, experiment and have fun.

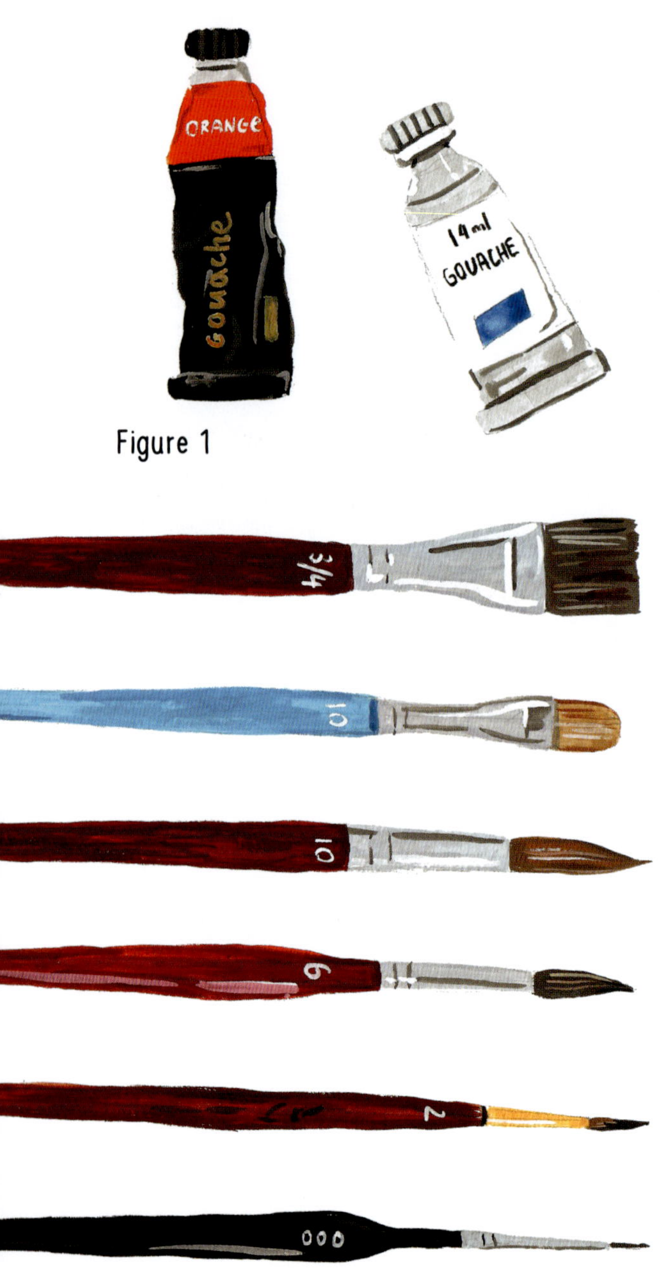

Figure 1

Figure 2

SUPPLIES

GOUACHE PAINTS

The first and the most important thing you need to get started with gouache is a basic set of paints, because in theory, you could paint with gouache even with your watercolor brushes and on watercolor paper, but you can't replace gouache with other paints. So purchase your gouache paints first before buying other supplies.

Usually, gouache paints come in tubes and have a creamy consistency (see Figure 1). And I personally recommend gouache in tubes. I have to say, however, that lately in art stores and online I have been seeing solid sets of gouache as well as gouache in jelly cups. So if you would like to experiment, you could try these types as well.

Now let's figure out exactly which paints to buy. You can purchase a set or a few tubes in your choice of colors. Always choose the professional grade of gouache—this should be notated on the box. Even if they are more expensive, you will never regret it.

If you decide to buy the set, it usually includes basic colors, and you can mix up the rest of the shades yourself. Buy an extra tube of white gouache, as white is the color most often used in gouache painting and for the mixing of pastels and other tints.

The second option is separate tubes of gouache paint. Once again, you will need a big tube of white gouache. And of course choose the primary colors: red, yellow and blue (see Color Mixing, page 9). For each of the primary colors, I recommend having two options: warm and cool tones. For example, for blue, I recommend buying Prussian blue and ultramarine blue.

It's also good to have the following colors: yellow ochre, brown (burnt umber), black, burnt sienna, crimson and purple.

NOTE: If you don't have a particular color, try to mix it by using the colors you already have. It will boost your color-mixing skills.

GOUACHE BRUSHES

Second on my priority list is the brushes for gouache. As I mentioned earlier, you can paint with your watercolor brushes or others you may have, but I highly recommend buying a few brushes more suitable for gouache. This will make your painting process much easier. The brushes for gouache should not be soft and they should not hold water. These brushes have to be medium-hard and flexible at the same time. Usually, they are shelved in the mixed-media section in the art stores.

So exactly which brushes will you need to paint the projects from the book?

Round and detail brushes. First of all, you will need a few round brushes in different sizes: a small (sizes 1–4), a medium (sizes 5–7) and a large (sizes 8 and up). One of each size will be enough, at least for practicing with this book.

Please note that this range of sizes is very approximate and is just intended to make the selection of brushes easier for you.

You will also need the detail brush, which in my opinion, is an essential brush for adding small details and accents. You can find this brush in the following brush types: mini round brushes, spotters and short liners. The watercolor detail brush is too soft for gouache, so try to find brushes with medium-hard or hard hairs.

Filbert and flat brushes. The next brushes I think you will use often and definitely will love are filbert and flat brushes. They are perfect for covering large areas of your paintings as well as for making many brush stroke types (see Brush Strokes, page 10). Any size you can afford would be great, but I recommend having large brushes: the filbert brush in size 10 and the flat one in size ¾ (see Figure 2).

Extra brushes. If you can afford to buy more brushes, then I advise you get a filbert brush in the medium size (size 4), a liner brush and a few more round brushes. But remember that you can start painting with gouache with just a few round brushes and then add more brushes according to your own artistic inclinations and sensibilities.

PAPER FOR GOUACHE

Finally, let's discuss the paper you can use for painting with gouache. I selected a few categories of paper that, in my opinion, work well. But before diving into this information, I have to say that unlike for watercolor, the paper is not the key for gouache. Nevertheless, it's important to have the right paper. So don't spend too much money and choose one or two options from the following list to start.

Watercolor paper is suitable for gouache painting. You can use either a smooth hot-pressed watercolor paper or the cold-pressed type, which has some texture. For gouache, I personally prefer the hot-pressed watercolor paper. As for the cold-pressed paper, especially for the first layer, don't use an absolutely creamy paint consistency; instead, add extra water to the wash in order to let the paint cover the textured surface of the paper.

Mixed-media paper is designed for painting with different art mediums in one piece, and it's perfect for gouache. I have been working with different brands of this type of paper and I haven't been disappointed with any of them. Usually, this paper is smooth and pretty thick, so the gouache lays down easily on it.

You may be surprised, but I find that paper for sketching is suitable for painting with gouache. The weight of this paper is usually around 150 gsm. This is not enough for painting with watercolor, but you can use it for painting with gouache, especially for separate objects without a background. At any rate, you can try it out and use it for practicing gouache or maybe for sketching some ideas.

Painting with gouache on black paper is an absolute pleasure. I highly recommend buying at least a few separate sheets and trying to paint on them. Even better, have an entire sketchbook or maybe a pad of some black paper. As for the weight of the paper, the thicker the paper the better, so it will not curl or buckle when you paint on it. In this book, I recommend black paper for some projects, so please check the supply list for any project before starting to work.

The last option on my list is a toned paper. There is a huge range of sketchbooks and pads with toned paper. I can also add craft paper to this category. And yes! You can paint on this type of paper with gouache. For some paintings, the toned background looks fantastic. For some projects in this book, I note on the supply list where craft/toned paper will work nicely. There's just one point you need to keep in mind: If you use a very thin craft paper, apply the minimum amount of water. It should be almost pure gouache paint.

ADDITIONAL MATERIALS

Now have a look at the additional materials, which are also essential for comfortable gouache painting.

Water containers. For a water container, you can use a jar, glass or cup. It's better to have a transparent container, which will let you see how clean the water is and when it's dirty enough to be changed. I advise using two or even three jars of water. Usually, I use one for diluting and mixing dark colors, the second for pastel and light tints and the third one just for rinsing brushes in between colors. Change the water in your jars whenever it becomes too dirty.

TIP: Don't use hot or warm water for painting, as it may ruin your brushes. It's best to fill the jars with room temperature water.

Paper towels. I advise having a few pieces of paper towel ready during the painting session. You will definitely need one for cleaning your brushes and also for absorbing extra water from them. I use a second paper towel piece for opening the tubes of gouache. To me personally, it's always hard to open up the small cap of the tube, so you may also need it. It's also good to have one more piece of paper towel, in case when opening the cap, any dry paint crumbles on the table. So to prevent a mess in my workspace, I cover the table with paper towel.

Pencil. Just as when painting with watercolor, for preliminary sketching for gouache, I use a mechanical or regular #2 pencil (also called an HB pencil). For gouache, you will also need an extra pencil for sketching on black paper or other dark backgrounds. This can be a white chalk pencil or soft white pencil.

Eraser. I personally love to use a kneadable art eraser, and I use it all the time for any sketching with a pencil. But you can use any eraser you have while working on the book projects.

Masking tape or washi tape. You will need it to secure sheets of paper to your work surface or to define the painting area if it's required in the project description. When your painting is done, you can just remove it without damaging the paper.

NOTE: Some types of paper and some tapes may not work together. So before painting the art piece and using masking tape, test the tape on paper. If after removing the tape, the paper is not damaged, go ahead with the project painting.

Palette. It can be a porcelain or plastic palette, or you can even use a white plate. I found the plastic palettes are the best for mixing gouache paint, and I usually use three simple plastic palettes at the same time.

Paper for testing. As for the paper for testing, you can use the reverse side of a sheet of used or damaged paper. This scrap paper is very good to have on your table for testing colors or for making quick sketches.

Hair dryer. Because gouache dries very quickly, using the hair dryer is not a requirement. However, sometimes if I apply too much paint and I am in a hurry, I use the hair dryer to speed up drying for wet painted layers.

TIPS & ADVICE

GOUACHE TRICKS

I have shared my tricks and tips with you throughout the entire book. But I have also picked up some tricks that are more specific to gouache, and I thought that it would be great if you can read them in one page.

Repaint areas. Because gouache gives an opaque layer, you can repaint your layers one or two times and without worrying that your painting looks overpainted like it might with watercolor. So you can, for example, repaint and cover your mistakes.

Please note that you can repaint when the previous layer is completely dry. Also, don't use too much water for the covering layer. Water may blur your previous layer and instead of covering it, you will get a mix of the previous and new layers. Don't overlayer gouache too many times; only if it is necessary and makes sense.

Add a bit of white to the color to get a matte finish. Some colors of gouache may not have the specific gouache matte finish. So if you want your painting to look more matte after drying, add a small amount of white to it.

Unlike watercolors, you can paint with gouache on dark or saturated layers. Use this ability of gouache to paint some light or white objects on a saturated background. For example, a white jellyfish will look awesome on a deep blue ocean background.

Gouache is all about contrast. Plan how to use this feature of gouache in advance, and always analyze if your new layer makes sense and if it contrasts with the previous layer. For example, if adding details to a flower petal, pick the color that will be in contrast to the base layer. For dark petals, choose light or pastel details. And for light-colored petals, dark details work well.

INSPIRATION

Let's now talk about inspiration. What is it? Where does it come from? And most important, how do you sustain inspiration through days, weeks, months and years to be transformed into artwork?

Inspiration, in my opinion, is a feeling inside you that helps or pushes you to create something beautiful and unique. It's like a start button for your creative process, and you can't start creating without it. I am sure there is no perfect recipe for how to get inspired. However, I would be happy to share with you some methods that really work for me and that I have been practicing for years.

The first way is participating in any activity not related to your creative process that gives you a feeling of happiness. It can be watching a movie, walking around, dancing, listening to music, cooking, shopping. . . . Anything you really like to do can help you get into a flow of inspiration and naturally feel that you want to create something beautiful and share it with the world. Don't skip this moment, and even if you don't have time to follow through at that moment, capture your ideas on paper with some notes or a quick sketch.

The second method is a mood board. I have been using this method since I was a graphic designer. It always works and gives quick results. A mood board is a visual representation of images you like and are inspired by. Essentially, it contains anything you feel you need to keep for current or future inspiration.

Your mood board can be arranged around:

- Mood and atmosphere
- Colors or color combinations
- Works by other artists
- A mix of all these categories

You can practice mood boarding all the time and use your "library" at any moment. Or you can create a specific mood board for the project you are currently working on. Usually, I create a mixed mood board before starting work on a painting or project. Once I feel I am ready, I jump to the sketching stage. I close the mood board and move on to the next step.

And the last thing on my list is daily sketchbook practicing. It's the method, in my opinion, everyone has to at least try. And it's just a wonderful way to keep yourself in a creative flow. In the next section, I will explain what it is and how to practice in a sketchbook.

GOUACHE SKETCHBOOK PRACTICE

As I mentioned earlier, sketchbook practice is one of the ways to get and keep yourself inspired.

I recommend you paint in a sketchbook every day. No matter how long and which mediums you use, just keep up practicing. For gouache, you can use a separate sketchbook or you can mix different mediums in one sketchbook. I have both: mixed-media sketchbooks and a separate one for gouache only. Now let's figure out what you can paint in your sketchbook.

First of all, in a sketchbook, you can capture something that inspires you and that you would like to remember or use later. For example, if you notice a beautiful composition on the street with potted flowers, a door and a cat, just quickly paint it in your sketchbook when you get back home, and then if needed you can paint it in more detail later. Usually, these quick sketches look very lifelike and unique and can be real masterpieces.

Second, if you want to try to paint some ideas you have in mind or you want to experiment with colors, shapes and compositions, use a sketchbook. Where else if not in a sketchbook? If you capture your idea on a sheet of paper, there's a good chance you'll lose this piece of paper. A sketchbook always works as an archive, and you can go back to it any time.

Another very important advantage of using a sketchbook for the realization of your ideas and experiments is that you don't need to focus on technique or details. Focus on the main points and don't spend too much time on it. Then you can use these ideas and experimentations from the sketchbook later to create beautiful paintings in much more detail.

Finally, use a sketchbook for quick warm-up painting sessions. This could be a quick painting of a little object or you could paint part of a big painting every day. Paint anything that doesn't take too much of your time, and you will see that it also works as art therapy. You can also be challenging yourself each day with painting something from one theme. For example, choose herbs, and every day paint a branch of an herb. Soon you will have a page in your sketchbook with herb illustrations. Or you could focus on sea creatures . . . or anything you come up with.

You may have your own ways to fill the pages of the sketchbook. That's okay because we all are different. But I hope my methods and approach will be helpful as well.

ACKNOWLEDGMENTS

The biggest thanks goes to my husband, Ignat, who keeps supporting and believing in me. Thank you for keeping me going despite whatever is happening around me, and for all your love, warm hugs, care and positive vibes.

To my family and all my friends. It means so much when you have support from your loved ones.

To my lovely editor, Lauren, and the entire Page Street Publishing team. You bring all this hard work to life and make dreams come true.

Thank you to my followers and social media friends. You support me and give me so much energy and love. I can't imagine my life without all of you. Thanks for all your interest, questions, activity and kind words.

ABOUT THE AUTHOR

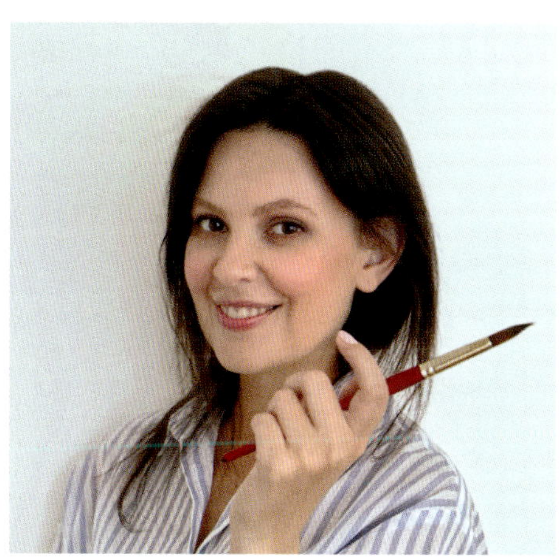

ANNA KOLIADYCH was born in Ukraine. She received a technical education, and having independently studied the basics of design, she worked for international graphic design companies for more than five years. She then emigrated to Malta, where she met her husband. With the support of her family, she left the design industry and began to study watercolor and gouache painting on her own. In 2017, she moved to London with her husband and began working as a freelance illustrator, successfully completing a large number of diverse projects, including illustrating two children's books and a cookbook. In 2018, Anna began to lead workshops in London, teaching beginners the art of watercolor. Since then, teaching has become an integral part of her life.

In 2018, she founded the online art school DearAnnArt, where she is successfully teaching watercolor painting. In 2019, she wrote her first book, *15-Minute Watercolor Masterpieces*. Also that year she started working on developing study materials to introduce gouache to other artists.

At present, Anna lives in Tallinn, Estonia. She continues teaching workshops in London and also shares her knowledge online with people from all over the world.

INDEX

R

S

T

V

W